D1570155

Capitalism from Within

Capitalism from Within

Economy, Society, and the State in a Japanese Fishery

David L. Howell

UNIVERSITY OF CALIFORNIA PRESS
Berkeley · Los Angeles · London

The costs of publishing this book have been
defrayed in part by the 1994 Hiromi Arisawa
Memorial Award from the Books on Japan
Fund with respect to *Encounters with Aging:
Mythologies of Menopause in Japan and
North America*, published by the University
of California Press. The Fund is financed by
The Japan Foundation from generous dona-
tions contributed by Japanese individuals
and companies.

Grateful acknowledgement is given for permission to
reprint material that previously appeared in an article entitled "Proto-Industrial Origins of Japanese
Capitalism," *Journal of Asian Studies* 51:2 (1992):
269–86. © Association for Asian Studies.

University of California Press
Berkeley and Los Angeles, California

University of California Press, Ltd.
London, England

Library of Congress Cataloging-in-Publication Data

Howell, David Luke.
    Capitalism from within : economy, society, and the
state in a Japanese fishery / David L. Howell.
        p.   cm.
    Includes bibliographical references and index.
    ISBN 0-520-08629-5 (alk. paper)
    Fish trade—Japan—History—19th century.
2. Fisheries—Economic aspects—Japan—History—
19th century. 3. Fishers—Japan—History—19th
century. 4. Capitalism—Japan—History—19th
century. I. Title.
HD9466.J32H69 1995
338.3'727'0952—dc20   94-11838

Printed in the United States of America
9   8   7   6   5   4   3   2   1

The paper used in this publication meets the mini-
mum requirements of American National Standard
for Information Sciences—Permanence of Paper for
Printed Library Materials, ANSI Z39.48–1984. ⊚

For Kōko

Contents

Tables, Figures, and Maps

Tables

Figures

Maps

Preface

The search for the roots of Japan's modern economic growth and industrialization has long occupied Western scholarship on the Tokugawa era (1603–1868). However various their methodologies and approaches, studies of peasant society and economy, demography, commercialization, urbanization, religion, and ideology reflect this concern, at least implicitly. It is a tribute to the efforts of a generation of scholars that we are now ready to proceed to a new level of analysis—that is, instead of merely asking *if* modern Japan's roots lay in the Tokugawa period, we can now look at *how* the nineteenth-century transformation of the Japanese economy actually took place.

In the chapters that follow I shall illustrate the indigenous origins of capitalism in nineteenth-century Japan with a case study of the fishing and fertilizer-processing industry of the northernmost island, Hokkaido. Let me introduce the study with a brief listing of what I consider to be its five principal objectives.

First, my concern here is to identify the origins and trace the development of capitalism as a mode of production. Rather than frame my discussion in terms of aggregate growth or some other quantitative measure of economic development, I focus on *qualitative* changes in the basic structure of social and economic relations, particularly the organization of production.

Second, I have employed the concept of proto-industrialization (rural manufacturing for long-distance trade) to clarify the relationship between state institutions and social and economic structural change. The proto-industrialization model helps us to see how a feudal institutional environment can give rise to capitalist production and how, in turn, nascent capitalist production can pressure state institutions to adapt to economic change.

Third, because the Hokkaido fishery was not directly affected by Japan's opening to the West in the 1850s, the nineteenth century can be treated as a single, coherent unit, in which the critical connections between Tokugawa proto-industrialization and Meiji (1868–1912) capitalism are revealed. The continuities of demand, labor, and technology in the fishery make it possible to highlight social and economic structural changes and the role of state institutions with much greater clarity than in analyses of industries, such as textiles, transformed by the impact of Western technology and the world market.

Fourth, in examining the Hokkaido fishery I bring into focus social groups like fishers and the Ainu people that heretofore have been excluded from Western narratives of Japanese history. The physical mobility of fishers and the interregional economic and social integration engendered by their activities further undermine the surprisingly resilient stereotype of a Japanese peasantry tied to the land. The presence of the Ainu in the fishery raises questions concerning the nature of the Tokugawa polity and of Japanese ethnicity.

Finally, this study challenges well-established notions of center and periphery in Japanese history. By discarding the assumption that the geographical center of Japan was similarly the source of all important social and economic developments, I am able to locate critical changes in social and economic relations in ostensibly "backward" areas. In particular, I explicitly reject the prevailing image of Hokkaido as an untamed frontier, neither politically nor economically a part of Japan before 1868.

I pause here to offer a word of thanks to the many people and institutions who have given me guidance and assistance over the course of researching and writing this study. Marius B. Jansen and Sheldon Garon have been unfailing in their support for this project and indeed all of my professional endeavors. Martin Collcutt, Gilbert Rozman, Saitō Osamu, and Anne Walthall read the dissertation on which this book is based and offered numerous suggestions for improvement. I owe special thanks to Gary Allinson for his thoughtful reading of two versions of the manuscript and for his encouragement during the difficult transition from dissertation to book. Ralph Meyer helped me with computer graphics and Kōko Fujita Howell made the drawings of nets that adorn Chapter 3. My father encouraged my initial interest in things Japanese and taught me to respect serious scholarship and clear writing; my parents' financial and moral support saw me through my study of the Japanese language.

A number of people gave me invaluable advice and assistance while I was doing archival research in Japan. Professor Nagai Hideo smoothed the way for me to do research in Sapporo and generously shared his extensive knowledge of Hokkaido history with me. Professor Nagai and Professor Tanaka Akira both graciously allowed me to sit in on their seminars on modern Japanese history at Hokkaidō University. Kasahara Akiko, Yamamoto Kazushige, and the other members of the Department of Japanese History at Hokudai expended much time and effort on my behalf as I puzzled my way through the labyrinth of Japanese academic bureaucracy. The staffs of the Hokkaidō University Library, Hokkaidō Prefectural Library, Hokkaidō Prefectural Archives, Hakodate Municipal Library, Aomori Prefectural Library, and Iwate Prefectural Library were uniformly generous with their time and knowledge.

I was welcomed into the community of scholars working on Hokkaido history in Sapporo. I want to express my thanks to all the members of the Kindai Nihon to Hokkaidō Kenkyūkai and to Seki Hideshi, Hasegawa Shinzō, and Katada Seishi in particular. Special thanks go also to Tajima Yoshiya of Kanagawa University, who shared with me his extensive knowledge of the contract-fishery system.

Perhaps my greatest debt in Japan is to the former curator of Hokkaidō University Library's Resource Collection for Northern Studies (Hoppō Shiryōshitsu), Akizuki Toshiyuki. For more than thirty years until his recent retirement Mr. Akizuki worked to build the world's finest collection of research materials on Hokkaido and northeast Asia. His encyclopedic knowledge of the history, geography, and cultures of the northern Pacific region—and his readiness to share it with me—helped me spot the red herrings before they colored my whole work. His capable assistant, Yoshida Chima, helped me locate sources, introduced me to other scholars, and generally made me feel at home in the archives.

If it were not for the generous financial support of a number of institutions I would not have been able to undertake the research and writing of this study. A dissertation research fellowship from the Japan Foundation allowed me to go to Hokkaido in the first place, and a subsequent year as a Whiting fellow made it possible for me to concentrate on writing once I had emerged from the archives. A grant from the University Research Institute of the University of Texas at Austin supported me while I reworked the dissertation into a book.

Preface writers as a rule save the most important acknowledgement for last; I am no exception. My wife, Kōko Fujita Howell, has endured every bump in the rocky road of academic life with grace and good humor. With love and gratitude, I dedicate this work to her.

A Note on Dates

I have used the lunar calendar to express dates through 1872 and the Gregorian calendar for those after 1 January 1873. Dates under the lunar calendar are expressed as year/month/day; thus, 1782/11/6 is the sixth day of the eleventh month of 1782.

A Note on Weights and Measures

I have converted weights and measures to the metric system throughout. Herring meal is the thing most often weighed and measured here. One *koku* of herring meal equals 0.75 metric tons or about 1,654 pounds. A metric ton is about 2,205 pounds. A handy source for metric equivalents of other units is Watanabe Shigeru, ed., *Hokkaidō rekishi jiten* (Sapporo: Hokkaidō shuppan kikaku sentā, 1982).

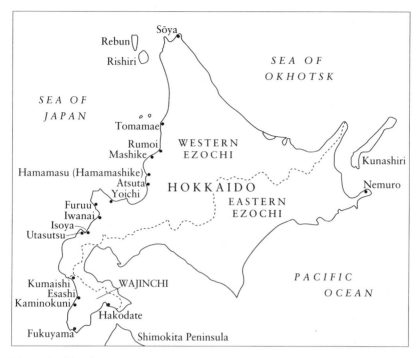

Map 1. Hokkaido

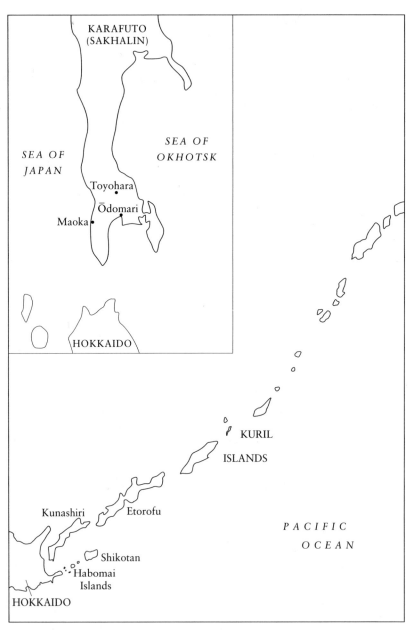

Map 2. Karafuto and the Kuril Islands

CHAPTER ONE

Commercialization, Proto-Industrialization, and Capitalism

In the summer of 1861, Thomas Wright Blakiston, a British merchant, naturalist, and spy, visited Hakodate, a port on Japan's northernmost island of Hokkaido. His first and lasting impression of the place was that it stank:

> On my arrival at Hakodate, I was at once made aware of the principal occupation of the inhabitants, and the consequent trade of the place, by the all-pervading stench of dried fish and seaweed; in the streets, in the houses, on the mountain side, everywhere the same scent haunted me of fish, shell-fish, and sea-weed, fresh, drying, and dried. Even like the eternal cocoa-nut oil in Ceylon, the food, the water, and everything one touched, seemed to be scented in the same manner.[1]

What Blakiston smelled was the livelihood of the people. Hakodate was one of several important shipping centers for the Hokkaido fishery. Prosperity in Hokkaido had the foul odor of herring that had been boiled, pressed, and dried into a mealy state for use as fertilizer. In 1861 the fishery—centering on herring, but including also salmon, trout, kelp (*konbu*), cod, cuttlefish, and many other varieties of marine life—was the mainstay of the island economy, just as it had been for more than a century and would continue to be for decades to come.

Hokkaido's commercial herring fishery originated in the early eighteenth century as merchants, based mostly in central Honshu, responded to a growing demand for herring meal (*nishin shimekasu*) for fertilizer and dried herring (*migaki nishin*) for food among cultivators in the Kinai

1

plain and elsewhere. During the Tokugawa period (1603–1868) production took two basic forms: the family fishery, in which a multitude of independent petty fishers worked with household members and perhaps a few hired hands; and the contract fishery, in which merchants specially licensed by the Matsumae domain (or the bakufu) enjoyed a variety of economic and administrative powers, including the right to supervise large-scale fishing operations using native Ainu and some Wajin (non-Ainu Japanese) labor. The family fishery was Matsumae's answer to a peasantry of smallholders, while the contract fishery was an integral part of the domain institutional structure, inasmuch as it evolved out of the official trade between the native people and the daimyo and his leading retainers.

After the Meiji Restoration of 1868 the contract-fishery operators (*basho ukeoinin*) lost their privileges, and the entire fishery was opened to exploitation by anyone who cared to participate, although production remained divided between the family and entrepreneurial fisheries. The period from about 1870 to 1900 saw a rapid expansion of the fishery, fed in no small part by strong demand for herring by-products in Honshu. Indeed, by the latter part of the nineteenth century Hokkaido was by far Japan's most important source of commercial fertilizer. However, over-fishing—the result of intensive production with increasingly efficient technology—depleted the stocks so that catches declined steadily throughout the first half of the twentieth century. The last herring run, and therefore the demise of the inshore fishery that is the subject of this study, came in 1958, though boats operating in deep water offshore continue to haul small catches to this day.

Commercialization, Capitalism, and Rural Society

In his discussion of economic change and social relations in nineteenth-century Japan, William Kelly argues that "it was not the commercializing of exchange, but the capitalist reorganization of production that was the thrust of change in the 19th-century rural economy."[2] Kelly is reacting to the preoccupation of many Western historians of Japan with the relationship between expanding commercial networks and peasant society. Much of the literature portrays the social and economic history of Japan in linear terms, beginning at some point in the past "before" widespread participation in market relations and ending at a later point "after" full commercialization had been attained. Changes in rural social relations, such as the growth of landlordism and tenancy, are seen as by-products of commercial expansion—important to be sure, but still secondary to issues of income and living standards. Most of the debate has thus concentrated on the relative costs and benefits of the peasant's journey from a largely self-sufficient, but materially poor, member of an insular community to a free agent, independent of the community but dependent, for better or worse, on commercial relations.

This concern with commercialization is of course important for works that deal exclusively with the Tokugawa era, but studies of the countryside in the Meiji period share this preoccupation with the effects of involvement in markets. This reflects a failure by many historians to distinguish between a quantitative expansion of economic activity and a qualitative change in the organization of production. In effect, scholars have debated whether capitalism is good or bad for peasants without really addressing the basic issue of how the development of capitalism altered rural society, either directly in the form of capitalist agricultural production or indirectly in the form of the changing relationship between agriculture and a growing industrial sector. Many of the difficulties scholars have in interpreting the continuities and disruptions of nineteenth-century Japanese history can be traced ultimately to this confusion.[3]

One problem is periodization. Despite numerous recent attempts to bridge the gap between the Tokugawa and Meiji eras and to write studies of modern Japanese institutions with an awareness of their Tokugawa roots, Japanese historiography remains compartmentalized into the early modern (i.e., Tokugawa) and modern (i.e., post-Meiji Restoration) periods.[4] Since the origins of Japanese capitalism lay in the Tokugawa period, but the transformation was not complete until well into the Meiji era, studies that deal with one or the other necessarily tell only half the story. Indeed, Kelly, who so perceptively identifies the problem, ends his own study during the early 1870s.

Periodization is not, however, the only problem. The ultimate culprit is confusion over the essential characteristics of capitalism. Maurice Dobb has discerned three prevalent definitions of capitalism: a Weberian spirit of enterprise; the investment of money to gain profit; and, in Marx's sense, as a particular mode of production.[5] Capitalism as an entrepreneurial ethic or spirit suggests that people in precapitalist societies are basically satisfied with fulfilling their subsistence needs. Accordingly, the desire to amass wealth is seen as a uniquely bourgeois cultural phenomenon and as such indicative of capitalism. James C. Scott and other substantivist social scientists argue that precapitalist societies are characterized by distinctive value systems that place subsistence above other material goals.[6] While substantivists would probably not define capitalism as an entrepreneurial spirit, they do link the two concepts, with the result that the impulse to amass wealth somehow appears inimical to the culture of subsistence peasants. It ought to be possible, however, to recognize that production and exchange in precapitalist societies follow their own sets of rules without seeing the desire for material gain as unnatural; viewing capitalism as nothing more than an entrepreneurial spirit clouds the issue.

Another school sees capitalism as the organization of production for distant markets, motivated by a hunger for profit. In a small village or town barter and informal exchange of services can meet those needs that people cannot satisfy for themselves. But trade over distances is impersonal and therefore implies a sort of tension, as participants may see exchange as a zero-sum game in which they have to maximize their advantage at the expense of others. This view, therefore, tends to equate all commerce characterized by the acquisitive use of money with capitalism. The problem, of course, is that people have been using their money acquisitively throughout history. Tokugawa merchants, who certainly made profitable use of their spirit of enterprise, would have to be considered every bit as capitalist as twentieth-century industrialists. But, as we shall see, they were not.

Much more simple and precise is Marx's definition of capitalism. According to Marx, the key to capitalism—or any other mode of production, for that matter—is the organization of production. Under capitalism labor power becomes a commodity, bought and sold on the market just like any other, and for many people the sale of that labor power is their only source of livelihood. In contrast to feudalism, capitalism is characterized not by the coercive power of landowners over peasants but by the sale of labor power on the basis of a wage contract.[7]

The critical difference between commercialization and capitalism lies in the impact capitalism has on social relations. While commercialization refers to the widespread commodification of agricultural produce and other goods, under capitalism the last great commodity—people's labor power—is bought and sold on a large scale, and, for the first time, the organization of production becomes characterized by that buying and selling. It is important to add that the presence of isolated instances of capitalist production does not mean that society has undergone a fundamental transformation to capitalism; only when capitalist relations of production predominate can society as a whole be characterized as capitalist.

Whether capitalist relations of production predominate is as much a question of politics as of economics. In Japan, the transformation to capitalism was very much evolutionary, not revolutionary, the political upheaval of the Restoration period notwithstanding. Capitalist production had already begun to emerge in early-nineteenth-century Japan, and the Tokugawa state had already begun to formulate a response—albeit an inadequate one—before it fell in 1868. The succeeding Meiji regime completed its accommodation to capitalism over the remainder of the nineteenth century, with the result that scattered instances of capitalist productive relations gave way to a capitalist mode of production. I will devote much of this study to an examination of the dialectical interaction between economic and political forces in the development of the Hokkaido fishery as an illustration of the types of changes that were occurring throughout Japan.

Scholars critical of the Marxist interpretation of Japanese history have, in an effort to discredit conflict-driven analyses of social relations within the peasantry, endeavored to demonstrate that the standard of living of ordinary people improved during the nineteenth century. Their scholarship is an understandable reaction to the grim picture of unmitigated misery painted by Marxist and Marxist-informed Japanese historians. As Susan Hanley and Kozo Yamamura, the leading proponents of what might be called the growth school, write:

> In summarizing the Japanese [i.e., Marxist] view, it is important to stress at the outset that most Japanese scholars make two crucial analytical assumptions: The first is that "the question of distribution" (who gets how much at whose cost) is much more important than "the question of growth" (how or whether total output grew). The other often implicit, but consistently made, assumption is that commercial transactions leave one party worse off and the other better off. Most of the Japanese literature on commerce is difficult to understand without an awareness of this "zero-sum" view of commercial transactions.[8]

Hanley and Yamamura have gone in the other direction, stressing the "question of growth" to the exclusion of the "question of distribution." To their credit, they have convincingly demonstrated that the Japanese economy was growing in the early nineteenth century and that the material standard of living of ordinary Japanese was higher than had been previously thought. Indeed, their work has changed the tenor of scholarship on the Tokugawa economy: whereas in 1965 Kazushi Ohkawa and Henry Rosovsky dismissed all evidence of economic development before Meiji as nothing more than "isolated islands of modernity" typical of "backward countries" like Japan, now the economic historian Eric

Jones counts Tokugawa Japan—along with early modern western Europe and Song China—as one of only three readily demonstrable cases in world history of what he calls "intensive" economic growth before industrialization.[9]

Saying that the late Tokugawa economy was growing is one thing; assessing the significance of that growth is another question entirely. Hanley and Yamamura see cultivators as rational actors in control of their economic lives; for them the very fact of growth says much about Japan's successes after 1868.[10] For others, such as Thomas C. Smith, Tokugawa economic development fostered attitudes toward work and time management that prepared the Japanese peasantry for the discipline of the factory.[11] Hayami Akira takes a similar approach when he argues that an "industrious revolution," predicated upon heavy investments of labor (rather than capital) in production, occurred in late Tokugawa Japan.[12] In Hayami's view, the commercialization of the agricultural economy gave peasants greater independence, but at the same time forced them to work longer and harder to raise the productivity of their landholdings.

Together with recent contributions in cultural and intellectual history, these perspectives have finally put to rest the tired image of Tokugawa Japan as a backward and stagnant society. Building upon this foundation, this book seeks to approach questions that persist concerning *structural* changes linking the Tokugawa peasant economy to Meiji industrialization. One way to find such structural changes is to take another look at "the question of distribution"—who got how much at whose cost— because noting the phenomenal growth in total output during the late nineteenth century says nothing directly about qualitative changes in the lives of the people involved in production. After all, even though capitalism does involve the expropriation of the surplus value of labor by the owners of the means of production, it does not necessarily follow that (especially in the long run) wage laborers end up worse off materially than before they turned to wage labor. It does, however, mean that workers are more vulnerable to exploitation because they depend on markets—for labor and commodities—to such a degree that they cannot maintain themselves without participating in those markets. Life under capitalism is not necessarily better and not necessarily worse, but it is necessarily different.

The degree of difference—dependence—is clearly higher when we speak of capitalism rather than simple commercialization. A cultivator producing indigo or cocoons may be a profit-maximizing entrepreneur with plenty of land and resources, or he may be a tenant whose only chance of supporting his family is to switch from growing an insufficient amount of food to planting a risky but potentially lucrative cash crop.[13] In either case the cultivator is dependent to some degree on outside economic forces; the wage laborer (whatever his wages) is absolutely dependent in the sense that he *must* find a market for his labor.

How life became different under capitalism for the people in the Hokkaido fishery is the subject of this study. My analysis would be easy if I could describe the transformation of a community of completely self-sufficient fisher families into a disparate group of completely dependent fishery laborers. But the process was not nearly that simple. For one thing, no one in the fishery was ever completely self-sufficient. Ecological factors, such as bad climate, militated against self-sufficient food production, but they were hardly insurmountable. Instead, merchants fostered relations of dependency between fishers and themselves by supplying fishing families with cash, food, and gear before each herring season and claiming first lien on their catch after it. Very few fishers, large or small, could afford to operate without credit; likewise few merchants could afford not to supply credit to fishers.

Talking about the new relations of dependency that accompanied Japan's transformation to capitalism is difficult without an understanding of the old ones that preceded them. In a precapitalist economy people are bound by what we might call community-based, or endogenous, dependency. The peasant relies on the community for all sorts of social and economic support. Economic support ranges from help with irrigation, planting, and harvesting to assistance in dealing with tax collectors and moneylenders. Socially, the peasant is a member of a community of other peasants, with whom he or she interacts and intermarries, trades goods and services, and joins in a wide variety of other religious and cultural activities. Endogenous dependency may not always be quantifiable, but it is very real, even for ostensibly self-sufficient subsistence cultivators. A chilling reminder of this fact is that one of the worst punishments the community can inflict is ostracism—an imposed "self-sufficiency" that most people would find intolerable.

The second form to consider is market-based, or exogenous, dependency, in which the individual is cut off from the community if not physically or socially at least economically. Unable to rely on community ties to provide his or her livelihood, the peasant is forced to turn elsewhere. Contractual bonds to employers and landlords, expressed in cash, supplant customary ones to real or fictive kin, expressed in social obligations. Exogenous dependency does offer a sort of freedom—there are no village elders to hold the ambitious young person back, and the potential rewards for the especially diligent or able are great—but freedom is hard to eat: when the material support of wage labor is withdrawn (for whatever reason) the worker is left in the lurch.

The movement from endogenous dependency to exogenous dependency—which in any case represent the two extremes of a spectrum—is almost always an incremental one, as in the case of peasants who gradually get involved in commercial relations outside the community, but eventually there comes a point at which outside forces dictate the individual's ability to earn a livelihood. Smith has traced this process in agricultural villages.[14] In the Hokkaido fishery, the point of no return was reached when someone left household-based production in fishing or agriculture for wage labor in an entrepreneurial fishery.

It is tempting here to forgo judgment about which type of dependency is worse. There seems to be little choice, after all, between a romantic vision of precapitalist society, on the one hand, and a celebration of relentless market rationality, on the other. One is nurturing yet constraining; the other liberating yet risky. Moreover, it is a false choice, inasmuch as the people involved did not consciously opt for one sort of dependency over the other (at least not in those terms). In any case, once the locus of dependency had moved from the community to the marketplace, there was no turning back. Still, in a study of this nature, concerned as it ultimately is with the quality of people's lives, disavowing explicit normative judgments seems cowardly, even dishonest.

There is no question that for most of the people involved in the Hokkaido fishery the exogenous dependency of capitalism was worse than the community-based dependency—warts and all—that preceded it. How it was worse will become evident over the course of the following chapters, so I will make just one or two points here. The endogenous dependency that prevailed in precapitalist villages throughout Japan, while hardly static, was nevertheless in place for many generations. As a result, a kind of moral economy had evolved to regulate human interaction. The social equilibrium thereby engendered could not, however, survive the emergence of capitalism because it could not compensate for the exploitative mechanism inherent in capitalist relations of production. The capitalists themselves, whatever their rhetoric, were not about to help; after all, the dynamism of early capitalism lay in its freedom from communal bonds: capitalists were capitalists because they invested in production, not paternalism. Eventually a new balance was reached—through labor unionization and state welfare policies, for example—that took the edge off of capitalist social relations and spread the material benefits more evenly, leaving many people better off than they had been before capitalism. But this balance occurred only after decades of conflict, adjustment, and hardship. Disputes like the Chichibu rebellion of 1884, the Hibiya riots of 1905, and the rice riots of 1918 can be seen as diverse manifestations of this process of adjustment.[15] In Hokkaido, unfortunately, the fishery collapsed before a stable capitalist equilibrium was ever reached.

Proto-Industrial Origins of Japanese Capitalism

The nexus between commercialization and capitalism is proto-industrialization. Proto-industrialization has been defined as a transitional phase on the way to modern, factory industrialization, characterized by "the development of rural regions in which a large part of the population lived entirely or to a considerable extent from industrial mass production for inter-regional and international markets."[16] The concept represents an effort to find the roots of the industrial revolution in the gradual evolution of industries in the European countryside. While historians of proto-industrialization in Europe have yet to reach a consensus on the exact relationship between proto-industry and capitalism,[17] it is clear that "proto-industrialization preceded factory industrialization where it occurred, and paved the way for it."[18] Proto-industrial development did not, however, lead inevitably to full factory industrialization, as a proto-industrial region could stagnate or even "deindustrialize."[19]

The proto-industrialization model includes an important demographic element.[20] Proto-industrial regions in Europe typically saw an increase in population as people married earlier and had more children once the value of household labor was no longer constrained by the size of a family's landholdings—that is, people could support larger families on less land because of the opportunities for nonagricultural employment. Ironically, the economic growth engendered by proto-industrialization was often accompanied by a *decline* in living standards because incomes, while much higher than in an agricultural economy, did not keep pace with the growth in household size.[21] For this reason we cannot assume that economic growth necessarily translated into better lives for people in the countryside.

The Hokkaido fishery is an attractive case study of proto-industrialization for a number of reasons. First, Hokkaido, better than any other region in Japan, fits the proto-industrialization paradigm of rural indus-

try for distant trade. No domestic trade was more distant than that between Hokkaido and central Honshu, and no people more dependent on
industrial production than those of Hokkaido, who lived under climatic
conditions too harsh to support much agriculture before the mid-Meiji
period. Because of their reliance on manufacturing and trade, Hokkaido
fishers were already intimately involved in commercial relations with
Honshu merchant houses in the mid-eighteenth century, yet the social relations of their fishing communities changed immensely over the following two hundred years. The change cannot be explained in terms of increasing involvement in markets but must rather be seen as a result of the
development of new economic, legal, and political institutions after the
mid-nineteenth century.

Second, unlike silk and cotton textile manufacturing or other important early industries, fertilizer production in Hokkaido was not affected
by Japan's opening to trade with the West after 1854.[22] Technology and
labor were native, and demand and supply remained domestic until the
fishery's collapse after World War II. The fishery therefore provides an opportunity to trace indigenous Japanese developments and thus strengthens
the case for proto-industrialization as a model of economic development
not bound to the European experience. This analysis speaks to Frank
Perlin's call for a conceptualization of proto-industrialization as a tool to
analyze historical change rather than simply as a euphemism to describe
the phenomenon of rural manufacturing for long-distance trade.[23] In
contrast to the Hokkaido fishery, small-scale production by peasants in
the textile industry was supplanted by modern industrial manufacturing.
Peasant textile producers who found themselves unable to compete with
new factories for the most part left textiles and turned to production of
other commodities and/or supplied their children to meet the labor requirements of new capitalist enterprises, including but by no means limited to the textile industry. By the same token, the young women working
in the new factories were only incidentally the daughters of peasant
weavers.[24] Thus, even though peasant textile production was replaced by
capitalist enterprise, it does not follow that peasant textile producers became proletarian textile workers. This is the illusion of unilinear development, which arises because it is so easy to assume that movement from
one way of organizing production to another entails a similar, concurrent
movement by the people whose livelihoods are affected in the process.

Finally, the peculiarly proto-industrial features of the fishery in the
early nineteenth century contributed most directly to the emergence of
capitalism in Hokkaido: fertilizer production for distant markets gave

rise to an economy only partially subordinated to the institutions of the Matsumae domain. Capitalism emerged through a dialectical process of change in the organization of production within the fishery and domain-level institutional response. The Hokkaido fishery stands out in the history of the Japanese economy because the fundamental transformation to capitalism was complete *before* the establishment of a regime dedicated to Western-style economic development. But the fishery, for all its precocity, was not an isolated capitalist sprout. Rather, the development of the fishery during the late Tokugawa period was part of a broader process of proto-industrial development that affected social and economic relations throughout Japan.

The fishery was by no means the only, or even the best-known, example of proto-industrial development in nineteenth-century Japan. The textile industry stands out in particular, but others included papermaking, sake and soy-sauce brewing, iron and other metalworking, and the processing of agricultural and marine products, such as tea, indigo, sugar, wax, vegetable oil, whale by-products, and a variety of fertilizers.[25] The historical significance of these industries is obscured by the course of Japanese development after the opening to the West in the 1850s. Factory industrialization did not occur as the result of natural evolution so much as through a deliberate policy of modernization implemented by a state anxious to emulate the more advanced West. Given the dramatic transformation of the Meiji years, it is natural enough to ascribe the origins of Japanese industrialization to the policies of the Meiji state. But overlooking the existing base of proto-industrial development restricts our understanding of Japan's rapid and successful transformation.

Application of the proto-industrial model to nineteenth-century Japan is not, however, without its pitfalls. Saitō Osamu, who has made the most extensive study of the problem to date, concludes that the differences between Europe and Japan were such as to make the model basically inapplicable in the Japanese case, the widespread incidence of rural industry notwithstanding.[26] Saitō sees three critical differences between the two cases.[27] First, in Japan there was never a clear-cut distinction between agricultural and industrial regions. While some regions did rely heavily on rural industry, and others on grain production, their differences were not great enough, in his view, to spark a fundamental transformation of the peasant economy. They were insufficient because the inseparability of agriculture and industry in the peasant household, as reflected in the sexual division of labor, inhibited regional specialization. Second, even in those regions with rural industry, Japan did not conform to the demographic model of European proto-industrialization, which predicts a drop in age at first marriage, leading to higher fertility and a decline in living standards. If anything, people in proto-industrial regions in Japan tended to marry *later* than those in agricultural ones, with the result that they benefited from the economic growth engendered by manufacturing. Saitō sees this difference as a function of the fact that proto-industrial development generally followed agricultural expansion, so that population densities were already high before the onset of proto-industrialization.[28] Hence, third, Japanese proto-industrial regions did not develop higher population densities than agricultural ones and thus did not generate a large pool of dispossessed peasants vulnerable to proletarianization.[29]

While Saitō's misgivings about the applicability of a European model of proto-industrialization to Japan are certainly compelling, they should not obscure the fact that rural industry was an important and widespread phenomenon in nineteenth-century Japan; Saitō himself says as much.[30] In fact, many of his objections can be accommodated by examining the political constraints placed upon the late Tokugawa economy, for the role of the state was critical in determining the degree and significance of rural industrialization in any given area. Before turning to a discussion of this problem, however, we must first locate proto-industrialization relative to commercialization and capitalism.

Proto-industrialization was distinct from the expansion of commercial agriculture. Whereas the growth of commercial agriculture changed the way things were bought and sold but not the way they were produced, proto-industrialization facilitated the penetration of capital into the realm of production, thus—potentially, at least—leading to the emergence of capitalism. To be sure, commercialization affected the peasant economy in important ways: Smith has shown how the expansion of the money economy after the middle of the Tokugawa period weakened hereditary bonds of dependency and led to a restratification of society on the basis of wealth, as village elites came to function as landlords, merchants, and moneylenders.[31] Nevertheless, insofar as household rather than wage labor remained primary, the growth of commercial agriculture did not immediately affect the social relations of agricultural production. While rural industry could and sometimes did emerge in regions with highly commercialized agriculture—and often involved the processing of agricultural products—there was no necessary connection between the two; indeed, industrialization frequently proceeded more rapidly in regions without much commercial agriculture.[32]

But if proto-industry was qualitatively different from commercial agriculture, so too was it distinct from modern industry. Proto-industrialization instead occupied a sort of middle ground between the two. Peasants working in or near their homes provided the labor for rural industry, and most no doubt maintained a strong identity as tillers of the soil. Although such peasants were assuredly not an industrial proletariat, their participation in proto-industrial production did affect the household economy in profound ways.

Ultimately more important than the identity of the producers or the location of production, however, is the organization and purpose of production. As Jürgen Schlumbohm writes, "There exists . . . a basic distinction between the two forms of commodity production: either its goals are in principle limited to satisfying the needs of the producers, or its goals consist in the essentially unlimited maximization of profit." [33] Peasant production is geared to the producer's subsistence, in the broadest sense of the word—that is, the market does no more for the peasant than to facilitate the exchange of commodities he cannot produce for himself. While the use of cash in exchange is certainly significant, it does not affect the fundamental nature of the transaction. In other words, the peasant uses money to obtain goods and is thus distinct from the capitalist entrepreneur, who uses money to make more money. With proto-industrialization, the economy goes beyond "mere" commercialization, as capital moves from the realm of circulation (the buying and selling of goods) into the realm of production (investment in tools, raw materials, and labor) for the first time, thereby opening the door to the possibility of capitalism and sustained economic growth.

Proto-Industrialization and the Economic Geography of Nineteenth-Century Japan

The failure to distinguish between commercial agriculture and rural industry has resulted in an unfortunate rendering of the economic geography of nineteenth-century Japan. Economic historians commonly classify regions as "advanced" or "backward" based on the extent of commercial agriculture and the development of local markets. According to this view, central Honshu—particularly Osaka and the surrounding Kinai plain—is the archetypical advanced region, and the northeastern and southwestern peripheries of the country the most backward.[34] While this dichotomy works well when talking about things like markets and technology, it unfortunately diverts attention from those "backward" areas where critical changes in the organization of production—the key to the development of capitalism—were occurring.

Rural districts in the Kinai, where commercial agriculture developed early and effectively, did see some proto-industrialization, but the impetus for industrial development was weak because villagers could easily participate in commercial agriculture to meet urban demand for foodstuffs.[35] Conversely, proto-industry thrived in many ostensibly backward regions. For example, the northern Kantō plain and Shinano were centers of silk-thread production, Tosa was a leading producer of paper, Nanbu had a large ironworking industry, and Hokkaido, of course, was a center of commercial fertilizer production. These regions lagged in agricultural development and lacked extensive internal demand for industrial commodities but were well-suited to proto-industry. Indeed, since in some cases even subsistence agriculture was impractical because of poor soil or climate, people had little choice but to turn to proto-industrial endeavors and long-distance trade with the Kinai and similar areas. The influx of industrial products from peripheral areas in turn spurred growth in commercial agricultural regions and thus furthered the development of the economy as a whole.

The development of the Hokkaido fishery, located as it was on the physical and political periphery of Japan, illustrates this point perfectly. The stereotypical image of Hokkaido is that of a wild and remote frontier, colonized only after 1868 by agricultural pioneers who went north under the auspices of the Meiji government's Development Agency (Kaitakushi). In fact, however, the growth of the herring fishery during the Tokugawa and Meiji periods placed Hokkaido firmly within the proto-industrial economy of greater Japan. The fishery developed as an element of two overlapping regional economies: a labor economy that encompassed all of Hokkaido (and included its Ainu and Wajin residents alike), northernmost Honshu, and the Japan Sea coast as far west as the Hokuriku area; and a marketing economy that extended the length of the Japan Sea coast and beyond, into the Inland Sea region to Osaka and Ōmi (Shiga). These regional economies matured nearly a hundred years *before* the birth of the Meiji regime and its colonial policies; indeed, their ultimate origins lay in medieval trade and communications networks that themselves antedated the emergence of commercial herring fishing by centuries.

These regional labor and marketing economies continued to sustain the fishery even after Hokkaido acquired its juridical status as a colony of Japan in 1869. After the Meiji Restoration the fishery developed rapidly, and stretches of coast once only sparsely inhabited saw an influx of both seasonal and permanent migrants from Honshu and southern Hokkaido. The large-scale movement of people both to and within Hokkaido was possible only because the island was a frontier. However, the frontier conditions that people encountered when they populated the coast of Hokkaido were less important in the long run than the economic relations that had brought them north in the first place and sustained them once they had arrived. Even as the geographical boundaries of the herring fishery spread, it remained firmly a part of the same regional economies that had given rise to it in the first place. This was true even after 1905, when the fishery expanded into Karafuto (southern Sakhalin), which had never been Japanese territory before.

Far from being a unique by-product of its peripheral location, the geographical expansion of the Hokkaido fishery conformed to a pattern seen in fisheries throughout the country. People have, of course, been fishing in the seas surrounding Japan since prehistoric times, but it was not until the Tokugawa period that marketing networks developed sufficiently to sustain a significant number of full-time fishers. Village communities devoted more-or-less exclusively to fishing were typically founded not by local peasants but rather by migrant fishers, who often established coastal bases at the behest of domain authorities.[36] Migrants from Kii (Wakayama) and Settsu (Osaka) were particularly active in developing fisheries in Kyushu and the Kantō region, but they were not alone, as Arne Kalland has shown in his study of Fukuoka abalone divers (*ama*).[37]

Migrant fishers filled space that was economically and socially empty, even if physically occupied. It was common for fishing and farming communities within a single village to remain culturally, socially, and on occasion even spatially distinct, with the fishers' houses physically oriented toward the sea, and those of the farmers oriented toward their fields.[38] Although peasants in adjacent farming communities might eventually participate as equals in fisheries established by newcomers, they were more likely to be mobilized as wage laborers on a seasonal basis. Such was the case in the sardine fishery of present-day Chiba prefecture, where fishers originally from Kii engaged in proto-industrial fertilizer production and hired local peasants as unskilled labor.[39]

In sum, rather than looking at Japanese economic history in terms of a dichotomy between "advanced" and "backward" areas, it is better to see the regions as complementing one another. Given the importance of long-distance trade—both in industrial products and tax rice—"backward" areas were hardly isolated from market forces, even if commercial agriculture was slow to develop.[40] Indeed, "backward" regions turned to proto-industrial production for distant markets in more developed areas—instead of developing commercial agriculture and local markets for industrial commodities of their own—in response to developments that had already occurred elsewhere.[41] This was certainly the case in Hokkaido, where fertilizer production became viable only after commercial agriculture in central Honshu had developed enough to create a demand for herring meal.

Moreover, dividing Japan into just two or three regions does not do justice to the complexity of development at a lower level of geographical abstraction.[42] This point is especially important if considered in conjunction with Smith's observations about the movement of industry from urban to rural areas during the latter part of the Tokugawa period.[43] Shinbo Hiroshi and Hasegawa Akira discuss urban deindustrialization in the Kinai soy-sauce brewing and cotton textile industries, and I have elsewhere looked at intraregional specialization in the southern Kantō plain.[44] By looking at economic differentiation as a phenomenon that occurred within broad regions more than between them we can at least circumvent the questions raised by Saitō's observation that Japan lacked regional specialization on a scale comparable to that of Europe. Perhaps there need not be much specialization—whether within regions or among households— to get the proto-industrial engine of economic growth and institutional tension started.

Situating the Frontier in Hokkaido

Remote, cold, and inhabited by the aboriginal Ainu people, Hokkaido has always straddled a physical, political, and intellectual boundary, its status as Japanese territory both conditional and suspect. The specter of Russian claims to the island—potential, not real, and in any case predicated upon expansionist ambitions rather than actual economic engagement—have long accentuated this condition. This image of Hokkaido is a political as well as an intellectual construct: throughout the modern period policies of "development" (*kaitaku, takushoku, kaihatsu*) have reinforced the island's frontier identity. Intellectually, these policies have relegated Hokkaido not merely to the edge of the map but to an inset, utterly detached from the social and economic history of the rest of Japan.

To be sure, Hokkaido in many respects deserves its reputation as an untamed wilderness. The British consul at Hakodate in 1859 aptly described Hokkaido as "a nutshell," with "innumerable fishing villages" along the coast but not "a city, town, or village of importance five miles" inland.[45] Even after a quarter century of colonization under the official auspices of the Meiji government, an English visitor, A. H. Savage Landor, considered his horseback ride around the circumference of the island so trying that he wrote a self-congratulatory travelogue to commemorate the feat.[46] (Of course, sensible travelers went by steamship.) To this day, Hokkaido's sparse population and wide-open spaces (at least by Japanese standards) endow it in the popular imagination with qualities of youth and natural vigor but not a sense of history.

The frontier is a product of history. Any discussion of Hokkaido's history that starts with the assumption that it is and always has been Japan's northern frontier necessarily, even if inadvertently, distorts the process by which the island and its people were absorbed into the Japanese polity. The prevailing image of Hokkaido as a frontier was, in effect, superimposed upon the island by the Meiji state and its colonial policies. For discussions of agricultural immigration this superimposed imagery has an element of authenticity, but for our purposes it is misleading. A look below the surface of Hokkaido's uncertain sovereign status before the Meiji era illuminates the continuities that underlay the superficial disruptions of the nineteenth century and, consequently, places the economic processes that are the focus of this study into better perspective.

Reducing Hokkaido's history to its frontier nature, moreover, risks trivializing the impact of capitalist development on its residents, Wajin and Ainu alike. Wajin wage laborers in Hokkaido—whether in the fishing, mining, lumber, or other industries—had a tough and untamed image, not unlike that of Hokkaido itself. It is all too easy to ascribe the dehumanizing aspect of work in Hokkaido to the isolation and primitive conditions of the physical environment and, consequently, to overlook the exploitative nature of wage labor in a burgeoning capitalist economy. But the fact is that poor, tenant farmers from northeastern Honshu did not seek work in the fishery or other Hokkaido industries in response to a romantic call of the wild or out of a desire to further the expansion of the Meiji state; they went because they needed to make a living, and Hokkaido was the most reasonable place for them to seek that living. It was the *work*, not the place, that stripped them of an element of their humanity.

Likewise, the decline of Ainu culture and society was as much a byproduct of centuries of economic dependency as a consequence of the Meiji state's aggressive policy of assimilation through deculturation. One important reason that the Meiji state's deculturation policies, which sought to eliminate the Ainu language, religion, and other manifestations of the native culture, were so devastatingly effective was that the Ainu economy had long since been disabled beyond hope of recovery. Trade originating in the medieval period and the proto-industrial production that eventually evolved out of it made the Ainu dependent for their subsistence upon the Matsumae domain and its agents, the contract-fishery operators. By the end of the Tokugawa period labor in the commercial fishery was at least as important to the Ainu economy as traditional hunting and gathering activities. The Ainu people's tragic history, in other words, began long before the Meiji state imposed its will upon them in the context of its program of colonial development.

The frontier is less a place than a relationship. Invoking the frontier as an explanatory device is unsatisfactory because it skirts the question of how Hokkaido came to be a frontier in the first place.[47] The emergence of Hokkaido as Japan's northern frontier was a product of hundreds of years of cultural, economic, and military intercourse. Before the Tokugawa era Hokkaido was not a frontier in part because it is difficult to posit the sort of dyadic relationship between a center and a periphery that the concept of the frontier demands. People in northeastern Honshu and Hokkaido, whether Wajin or Ainu—and it is problematic even to apply ethnic labels like these before the fifteenth century—did not consistently recognize the imperial court in Kyoto, or its proxies, the Kamakura and Ashikaga bakufu, as sources of authority and legitimacy. Nor did they perceive themselves to be on a frontier—and for good reason: throughout much of the medieval period the port of Tosaminato on the Tsugaru peninsula in northernmost Honshu (now a sleepy fishing village) was a lively center of trade linking the Japan Sea region with northeastern Asia. The Andō, who controlled Tosaminato, called themselves the "shoguns" of "Hinomoto," a country they distinguished from Japan, and on at least one occasion dispatched emissaries to the Korean court.[48] For the people living there, northern Honshu and Hokkaido was a political, economic, and diplomatic center in its own right. It appears peripheral only in hindsight.[49]

Hokkaido became a political frontier only as a consequence of the establishment of a coherent centralized regime in the late sixteenth and early seventeenth centuries. Tokugawa Japan defined itself in relation to other East Asian countries in such a way as to allow the Matsumae domain to act as an intermediary between Japan and the Ainu people.[50] Hokkaido served as a buffer between Japan and areas to the north and east, and Matsumae was the custodian of that buffer.[51] Absorbing Hokkaido fully into the Japanese polity was not a goal of the state; indeed Matsumae's legitimacy hinged on most of Hokkaido's remaining formally distinct from, yet bound securely and subordinately to, the Tokugawa state.

By the beginning of the nineteenth century Hokkaido's ambiguous sovereign status had become untenable in the face of mounting Western pressure to establish commercial and diplomatic ties. Urban intellectuals at this time "discovered" Europe and in the process "discovered" the Ezochi, which for them was a vaguely defined and decidedly uncivilized wasteland that included Hokkaido, the Kurils, Sakhalin, and other areas to the north. Later historians, concerned primarily with policymakers' perceptions of the Russian threat, have tended to accept the intellectuals' misconstrual of the social and economic realities of Hokkaido at face value.[52]

After 1868 the Meiji state treated Hokkaido as a colony and implemented policies of development to ensure that the Western powers would respect its claims to the island. Its juridical status as a colony notwithstanding, Hokkaido's situation was quite different from that of Korea, Taiwan, the South Pacific islands, and other territories acquired as a result of Japan's foray into modern imperialism. Rather, it was analogous to that of Okinawa, which, before its annexation by Japan in 1879, had been formally independent yet subordinated to Japan through the Satsuma domain. Both Hokkaido and Okinawa had been incorporated into the Tokugawa state's version of the East Asian world order without being considered fully part of Japan.

In sum, Hokkaido's peripheral location raises intriguing questions concerning ethnicity and the nature of sovereignty in the Tokugawa state; regional development and economic expansion in both the Tokugawa and Meiji periods; and the formation of social and economic structures in areas unencumbered, as it were, by centuries of local custom and administrative precedent. In every case, however, the answers to these questions must be formulated in relation to conditions in Japan as a whole and not simply as a response to life on a generic frontier.

Continuity and Disjunction

One reason cited earlier for distinguishing between commercialization and capitalism was for the light it would shed on the continuities and disjunctions of nineteenth-century Japanese history. Let us turn now to a brief examination of this problem as it relates to the material in the following chapters. Before beginning, however, I should note that until now historians have addressed this question largely in terms of the causes and meanings of the Meiji Restoration. Those who argue for continuity see the Restoration as essentially a political event, albeit one with profound long-term social consequences, while those who stress disjunction look instead to the reorientation of intellectual discourse and the chiliastic nature of much of the peasant protest of the late Tokugawa–early Meiji period for evidence of widespread change in the popular consciousness.[53]

The Meiji Restoration does not represent a sharp break in the social or economic history of the Hokkaido fishery. If, as Harry Harootunian argues, "there existed a revolutionary situation among the Japanese peasantry" at the end of the Tokugawa period, fishers in Hokkaido were well away from the vanguard.[54] They did rise in protest several times during the middle decades of the nineteenth century, but they were more interested in debt renegotiation than world renewal. Even the Boshin War ended in Hokkaido on a consensual note as the commander of the imperial forces presented Enomoto Takeaki and his Tokugawa loyalists with his congratulations and five barrels of sake after their surrender at Hakodate in July 1869.[55] The new regime eventually did implement a series of legal and institutional reforms that fundamentally altered the way fishers produced herring by-products and reproduced their own communities, but most of them were already in the works during the immediate pre-Restoration years. Some of the changes, like the Tenpō famine, which encouraged thousands of Tōhoku peasants to migrate north, and the development of new nets in the 1850s, which increased both productivity and demand for wage labor, had at least as big an impact as later legal reforms yet were only indirectly related to government policy. For fishers the first order of business was always the catch; new political and ideological structures had to be adapted to that fact.

Continuity would be the metaphor of choice in describing the experience of the Hokkaido fishers if it were not for the fact that continuity somehow implies a consensus about that continuity on the part of the people involved. In Hokkaido, the actual business of catching, processing, and marketing the fish changed relatively little over the course of more than two hundred years. However, conflict—implicit always and explicit sometimes—characterized social relations within the fishery right down until the 1930s. At first this conflict was between merchants trying to attain economic dominance and family fishers striving to maintain their mode of production and with it their way of life. Such conflict did not occur in isolation but rather developed within the context of the Tokugawa social order. Neither the merchants who operated the contract fisheries nor the family fishers could act as free agents: aside from purely economic constraints, they had to deal with social and legal limitations imposed by the state. The state in effect determined both the substance of and the ground rules for the struggle between the entrepreneurial and family fisheries. Accordingly, when the nature of the state changed after 1868, the conflict within the fishery changed with it.

The contract-fishery operators were privileged merchants whose ostensible role was to act as agents for the Matsumae domain in its trade relationship with the Ainu. Their fishing operations emerged out of the Ainu trade and remained formally subsidiary to it even after the fishery became much more important economically. Although many of these merchants aggressively used their capital to "yoke labour to the creation of surplus-value in production,"[56] ultimately they proved to be half-hearted capitalists in the sense that they retreated from direct control over production to reliance on the protection of the domain (which guaranteed them an advantageous position in their dealings with family fishers) whenever that appeared to be more profitable. Sure enough, although a number of them remained prominent in the fishery after the Meiji government stripped them of their special privileges, the influence of the contractors as a group declined greatly.

The family fishers of Hokkaido were officially part of the peasant (*hyakushō*) class, the backbone as well as the beast of burden of the Tokugawa social order. Although they enjoyed considerably more officially sanctioned freedom of movement than peasants in Honshu domains, the family fishers were subject to domain authority in their comings and goings and economic activity; and domain authority in Hokkaido, as elsewhere, generally worked against the interests of the peasantry. The Matsumae domain had to balance its dependence on the privileged merchants, who brought economic stability to Hokkaido, against its political responsibilities to the small fishers who made up the great majority of permanent Wajin residents in the domain. In many individual instances it took the side of the family fishers, but its overall policy was to limit the economic options open to them by, first, restricting the movement of all commodities between Hokkaido and Honshu and, second, delegating tax-collection powers to the merchants running the contract fisheries. The net effect was to ensure the dependence of family fishers on contract-fishery operators and other merchants. As events in the Meiji period would prove, family fishers were destined to be dependent on merchants anyway, but during the Tokugawa period the Matsumae domain, not the fishers, largely decided which merchants would be the object of the fishers' dependency. This arrangement, of course, limited the bargaining power of the fishers and resulted in constant, even if not explicit, tension between the fishers and merchants. Ultimately the outcome of this conflict determined whether the entrepreneurial fishery or the family fishery would emerge as the dominant economic and social force in Hokkaido.

Eventually the entrepreneurial fishery prevailed, and the conflict turned instead to a struggle over participation in it. This outcome was partly the result of the increasing difficulty family fishers had maintaining their livelihoods in the face of declining catches and partly the result of their accommodation to entrepreneurial goals. As Japan turned to a capitalist mode of production, the family fishers realized that their continued independence hinged upon their ability to establish themselves as petty capitalists.

The Meiji government paved the way for the transition from a commercial to a capitalist fishery by instituting a series of legal reforms between the time it assumed power and the end of the nineteenth century. The reforms did not actively discriminate against family fishers so much as they made the fishery an attractive investment for up-and-coming capitalist entrepreneurs. These capitalists, who, true to their name, could marshal considerable wealth in their pursuit of profit, proved to be formidable competitors for the limited resources of the herring fishery. Some family fishers did nevertheless successfully establish themselves as petty capitalists; others continued to do things the old way, relying mostly on household labor; and still others—those who could neither move up nor stay put—left fishing entirely or became part of the seasonal labor force.

One group of family fishers, accepting the social and economic realities of modern Japan, migrated to Karafuto (southern Sakhalin) after the Russo-Japanese War of 1904–5 in an attempt to maintain their independence by assuring themselves a secure place as petty capitalists. After a long battle with entrenched operators, some of them made the transition, but by that time catches had declined to unprofitably low levels, and Japan was headed toward a costly war.

The Karafuto fishers' experience reveals how preindustrial formulations of the relationship between ruler and ruled can be reworked to fit new, capitalist realities. Their appeals for benevolence, articulated in the language of self-sacrifice for the good of the realm, drew from the lexicon of the Tokugawa peasant-protest canon. Yet their movement recognized—indeed, embraced—the fundamental changes that had occurred in the Japanese economy, and in the relationship between the state and the individual, during the decades since the Meiji Restoration. In short, a moral economy that had evolved over the course of Japan's indigenous proto-industrial and capitalist development lent credibility to the fishers' market rationality.

Disjunction cloaks itself in the mantle of continuity, thereby rendering a dichotomy between the two untenable. Rather than a single, sharp turning point or a fundamental reordering of the popular consciousness, we see a long and continuous series of small disjunctions, adjustments and readjustments to the changing economic, political, and ecological environment of the fishery, punctuated only occasionally by outbursts of overt conflict, such as the destruction of contract-fishery operators' nets in 1855 or the riot by family fishers in Ōdomari, Karafuto, in 1909. Although the Meiji Restoration brought a decisive end to the institutional barriers to capitalist development, the actual transformation came slowly and in small stages.

CHAPTER TWO

Not Quite Capitalism

*The Rise and Fall of the
Contract-Fishery System*

A giant octopus appeared off the Japan Sea coast of Hokkaido at Yoichi in the ninth month of 1828. Its twelve-foot head and sixty-foot tentacles "filled the sky with a shining, blue light." Local fishers adhered to a belief system that could handle the physical and spiritual damage inflicted by bears, foxes, and whales, but through some oversight they had failed to provide for monster octopuses. After consulting at the local shrine, they prudently decided to stay out of the water until the rogue cephalopod left of its own accord, which it did a couple of days later.[1]

Hayashi Chōzaemon, who operated the Yoichi fishery, could hardly have been pleased to see two days' salmon catch escape, but, after all, it was his own son, Heikichi, who had first discovered the octopus. At any rate, he and his workers could afford the luxury of their beliefs because it was already well into autumn, long past the spring herring runs that provided up to eighty percent of their annual income. Six months earlier they might have tried to think of some way to accommodate the beast without losing any fish.

Chōzaemon was the contractor (*ukeoinin*) of the Upper and Lower Yoichi fisheries (*basho*). He was a merchant, not a fisherman, at heart, though his business included fishing operations as well as the generally more lucrative processing and marketing of marine products. He also lent money to small fishers as a profitable sideline. He secured his rights as contractor by paying an annual fee (*unjōkin*) to the Matsumae domain in exchange for a monopoly over trade with local Ainu residents. "Trade," by 1828, was broadly interpreted to include supervision of fishing operations by the native people. In addition, as an increasing number of small fishers from the Wajinchi (southern Hokkaido)[2] and Tōhoku came seasonally to fish, Chōzaemon and contractors like him assumed broad powers over Wajin as well, including local political authority delegated by the domain and monopsonistic rights to fish landed within their fisheries.

The purpose of this chapter is to examine the relationship between merchant capital and the state in the emergence and growth of the Hokkaido herring fishery between about 1672 and 1868. It will serve as an introduction to Chapter 3, which covers social and economic developments within the fishery during the same period. The two discussions are separated to highlight the dual nature of the basic problem at hand—that is, that the transformation to capitalism manifested itself both at the level of state policy and institutions and at the level of economic and social relations among individuals. The contract-fishery system will figure prominently in both discussions, for it was the nexus between state and economy in Hokkaido.

The contract-fishery system was the cornerstone of the Matsumae economy. It put production of a large proportion of the domain's most important commodity under the control of a handful of merchants. And because that commodity was so important economically, the system shaped the development of Hokkaido society as well. The Matsumae domain, working within the constraints of the bakuhan system, developed institutions like contracting to ensure that trade between Hokkaido and the rest of Japan was conducted on its own terms. Although it was not the only domain to rely heavily on nonagricultural pursuits, Matsumae was unique in that it never even bothered to maintain the fiction that rice cultivation was the mainstay of its economy and society.[3] So while rice, not herring, made the rest of the Tokugawa world go around, the populace of Hokkaido—Wajin and Ainu alike—depended throughout the period on trade with Honshu for their livelihood and on fishing, especially herring fishing, to fuel that trade.

The contract-fishery system as Hayashi Chōzaemon knew it was the product of two centuries of institutional evolution. The Matsumae domain began as an intermediary in trade between the Ezochi (Hokkaido beyond the Wajinchi) and the rest of Japan. Fishing emerged in the late seventeenth century as an outgrowth of that trade, and the institutions governing commercial fishing reflected those origins. In lieu of fiefs high-ranking retainers received rights to operate trading posts (*akinaiba*) scattered along the coast of Hokkaido north of the Wajinchi. The samurai sent boats laden with ironware, sake, rice, tobacco, clothing, and other household items to exchange for exotic products like bear gallbladders, falcon feathers, and sea-mammal pelts, as well as fish, which they then sold for cash. Between the late seventeenth and mid-eighteenth centuries merchants gradually took over management of the trading posts in exchange for a set, annual fee. Eventually, instead of simply trading for whatever the Ainu offered, the merchants began to supervise herring, salmon, and other fishing operations themselves, so that by the time Hayashi Chōzaemon took over the Yoichi fishery in 1811 there was no question that fishing, not simple trade, was the basis of the contracting institution.

Chōzaemon and his three dozen peers, along with a group of shipping agents and fertilizer brokers, were responsible for whatever economic well-being the Matsumae domain enjoyed. Only through the merchants' organization and contacts with commercial houses in Ōmi and Osaka was it possible to market the herring-meal fertilizer that was the domain's major revenue earner. Indeed, the emergence of the contracting system in the eighteenth century saved Matsumae from financial and political ruin. The domain appreciated the merchants' position and responded accordingly by creating institutions designed to ensure the contractors' continued domination of fishing.[4]

The dependence was mutual. Men like Hayashi Chōzaemon were privileged merchants. Their prosperity derived from the protection of the Matsumae domain. At the same time, although they probably neither intended nor even realized it, they represented a new way of organizing production. Their privileged position allowed them to create fishing empires that operated on a far greater scale than anything the fishers of Matsumae could match. The contractors were not, however, capitalists. Indeed, given a choice between being privileged merchants or capitalist entrepreneurs—and many were, in effect, given such a choice—most would have chosen privilege. But almost despite themselves they paved the way for the development of capitalist fishing in the Meiji period.

Small fishers had to live with the fact of the contractors' privileged position. In many ways this was easy enough to do, as the contractors invested heavily in the buildings, boat landings, warehouses, and shrines and temples that made it possible for small operators to fish herring in the Ezochi in the first place. But small fishers also had ample cause to dislike or at least to mistrust the merchants. For one thing, the contractors did not provide their civil services for free: they could claim up to about half a fisher's catch in the form of access fees, interest on loans, and commissions for transporting and marketing the fish. Moreover, the contractors did not hesitate to use their privilege and power to their own advantage when their interests and those of the small fishers clashed. Indeed, by the end of the Tokugawa period most contractors had made such free use of their privilege and power that their operations could not remain afloat without the income from fees, interest, and commissions levied on small fishers.

So long as there was some kind of equilibrium of domination and dependence—and there usually was—the contractors and fishers put up with each other. During the last decade of the Tokugawa period, however, the merchants' stranglehold on access to markets and their early monopolization of new and efficient fishing technology caused unrest among their clients and led to a series of disputes with small fishers. Yet during the same decade, after the bakufu assumed direct control over Hokkaido, fishers in Matsumae conducted a campaign to have the daimyo reinstated, in part to protect the contract-fishery system and with it their own livelihoods.

The institutions created by the Matsumae domain weakened during the final decades of the Tokugawa period and fell apart quickly after the Meiji Restoration. The new regime's colonial administrative organ, the Development Agency (Kaitakushi), abolished the contract-fishery system in 1869 and rescinded the contractors' special economic privileges and political authority in stages through 1876.[5] The new government, over the course of the late nineteenth century, introduced new ideas of fishing rights and land tenure that changed the economic structure of the herring fishery and with it the social relations of herring-fishing communities. Unrestricted migration to productive fisheries, heightened demand for herring meal, and improvements in the technology of herring fishing led to production far greater than under the contract-fishery system.

The Origins and Nature of the Matsumae Domain

Two characteristics of the Matsumae domain had a decisive influence on the formation of Hokkaido society and institutions, including, of course, the herring fishery. The first was the presence of a sizable indigenous ethnic group, the Ainu. The second was the lack of agriculture, particularly rice cultivation, on an economically significant scale. The two are more closely related than they might appear, for the ready availability of opportunities to trade with the Ainu gave domain leaders little incentive to promote farming. The domain's reliance on the Ainu trade and its consequent lack of an agricultural base meant that its institutions were founded upon a set of mutual dependencies: the Ainu's dependence on Japanese commodities; its own dependence on the Ainu trade and the merchants who managed that trade; and the merchants' dependence on the domain for protection and privileges. The domain manipulated these dependencies to its own advantage by keeping the Wajin and Ainu populations separate and by reserving to itself the right to regulate trade and other contact between the two peoples. Matsumae institutions were thus not only highly conducive to commercialization, they were predicated upon it. Moreover, insofar as the Ezochi was left largely to the Ainu and the merchants sent to exploit them, the domain's position did not change even after trade was supplanted by fishing with Ainu labor.

The same institutions that were so well suited to commercialization, however, proved vulnerable in the face of the beginnings of capitalist development. Unlike the contract-fishery system, which worked to the mutual advantage of the domain and the contractors, the capitalist fishery developed outside Matsumae's network of dependencies. Rather, it emerged out of the household fishery and used Wajin instead of Ainu labor. As a result, large-scale fishing operations ceased to be the functional equivalent of the Ainu trade; and without the Ainu trade the domain had no legitimate reason to exist. Let us begin, then, with an examination of the institutional structure of the Ainu trade.

Bands of "armed merchants," as Kaiho Mineo calls them, began making incursions into Hokkaido from northern Honshu in the twelfth century, if not earlier.[6] By the mid-fifteenth century about a dozen strongmen, most notably Takeda Nobuhiro (1431–94), progenitor of the Kakizaki (later Matsumae) house, had established forts (*tate*) in the Oshima peninsula in southern Hokkaido. Although they maintained ties to the warlords fighting for hegemony in Honshu, they differed from other Sengoku-period military men in that control over trade, not land, was their principal goal. Between 1457 and 1672 Wajin intruders fought against the Ainu and among themselves; Ainu natives fought against the Wajin and among *themselves*; and all the while Wajin fishers and merchants established footholds in places like Nobuhiro's base of Kaminokuni and the port of Usukeshi (later Hakodate).[7]

The Matsumae domain became a part of the bakuhan state even before the Wajin-Ainu struggle had reached a decisive conclusion. The head of the Kakizaki house, renamed Matsumae Yoshihiro, received documents from the national hegemons Toyotomi Hideyoshi (1593) and Tokugawa Ieyasu (1604) affirming his right to trade with the Ainu.[8] The documents gave the Matsumae neither specific territorial rights nor a fictive rice income, although in practice the head of the Matsumae house was usually accorded treatment equivalent to an outside (*tozama*) daimyo with a 10,000-koku income. Moreover, the Matsumae did not have formal authority over the Ainu. Ieyasu's letter, which provided the model for those issued at each shogunal succession, granted the Matsumae house the power to regulate all Wajin human and commercial traffic between Hokkaido and Honshu, and it prohibited mistreatment of the Ainu, but a proviso specifically stated that the Ainu were free to come and go as they pleased.

The Ainu retained their formal freedom of movement until the failure of a war against Matsumae in 1672; the document issued in 1682, on the accession of the fifth shogun, Tsunayoshi, guaranteed them mobility only within the Ezochi.[9] Ainu boats in fact traded in ports in Tsugaru and the Shimokita peninsula through at least the 1640s, and the Ainu leaders of Shakushain's War (1669–72) clearly expected to secure steady supplies of necessary commodities from Tōhoku domains had their struggle for independence from Matsumae been successful; evidence suggests that Tsugaru, at least, would have been happy to accommodate them. Even after 1672 Ainu in southern Hokkaido apparently maintained sporadic contact with the isolated Tōhoku Ainu communities that survived in the Tsugaru and Shimokita peninsulas, and Ainu fishing boats, such as the one that landed near the Shimokita village of Shimofuro in 1833, occasionally drifted across the Tsugaru Strait. (In that instance the two Ainu fishers aboard were returned safely home after Nanbu domain officials first interrogated, then wined and dined, them.) These examples and the bakufu's formal guarantees of freedom notwithstanding, however, the Matsumae domain was generally successful in restricting Ainu access to markets outside of the Ezochi even before 1672.[10]

Shakushain's War, put down in 1672 by the Matsumae domain with the help (at bakufu orders) of Tsugaru, was the final attempt by the Ainu to preserve their political independence and regain control over the terms of their economic relations with the Wajin.[11] Shakushain, the chieftain of the Hidaka Ainu of eastern Hokkaido, led the struggle after the domain imposed a drastic reduction in the size of rice bales used for exchange, a move that made all Japanese commodities much more expensive for the Ainu. Shakushain's ultimate goal, however, was not simply to rectify the terms of trade but rather to eliminate the Wajin from Hokkaido entirely and thereby reestablish the Ainu's right to trade freely in Honshu.[12]

Although a bakufu official reportedly countered Shakushain's vow to eliminate the Wajin from Hokkaido with a threat to "kill all the Ainu"

(*Ezo nokorazu metsubō*),[13] it would be a mistake to ascribe Shakushain's War primarily to ethnic hatred. Economic interest, rather than ethnic identity, motivated the actors in the conflict. This interest can be seen most readily in the presence of Ainu troops and spies in the Matsumae and Tsugaru forces, on the one hand, and in the participation of at least four Wajin on behalf of the Ainu, on the other hand. Indeed, one of the Wajin, Shōdayū of Dewa province, was Shakushain's son-in-law.[14] More significantly, the Ainu rebellion failed in large part because Shakushain was unable to forge a viable alliance among the five major Hokkaido Ainu groups, whose relations had long been characterized by competition and conflict. Indeed, in 1668, just a year before Ainu forces launched attacks upon Wajin gold miners and falconers in the Ezochi, Shakushain had arranged the murder of a rival leader, Onibishi, thus breaking a truce between the two groups that a leading Matsumae retainer, Shimonokuni Hirosue, had mediated in 1655. According to Kaiho, competition for access to fish and animal pelts to trade with the domain had caused the dispute between the two chieftains.[15] Onibishi's supporters immediately approached the domain for weapons, provisions, and other assistance in their planned war of retribution. The domain did not provide support, and, thanks to apparently unfounded rumors that an emissary from Onibishi's group had been poisoned by domain officials, many of the slain chieftain's supporters eventually rallied around Shakushain's banner.[16] In any event, the incident reveals that the Ainu were anything but a monolithic group.

The Matsumae domain, fearful of losing its territory, chose to try to bring the war to a quick conclusion rather than pursue total victory. Nevertheless, it took nearly three years for the domain forces to win a compromise settlement, in which the Ainu retained formal autonomy throughout most of Hokkaido and won important concessions on the rice-bale issue that was the immediate cause of the conflict. Still, it was enough of a victory that by the time the smoke cleared the Ainu had been driven out of the Oshima peninsula and into subjugation and Hokkaido was clearly divided into an area for the Wajin (the Wajinchi) and another for the Ainu (the Ezochi).

Kaiho has argued that the area of exclusive Wajin residence, the Wajinchi,[17] originally represented a Wajin sphere of influence, not unlike those held by a number of major Ainu chieftains. Shakushain's War resulted in both the defeat of politically powerful Ainu leaders and an expansion of the Wajin sphere, but the Matsumae victory was not nearly so complete as to permit the complete absorption of all of Hokkaido into the domain. The domain instead ensured its monopoly over the Ainu-Wajin trade by formally segregating the two groups: Ainu could live and travel only within the Ezochi, and Wajin could enter the Ezochi only with domain permission and then only for limited periods. After the Ainu defeat in 1672 the Wajinchi was expanded to encompass most of the Oshima peninsula rather than the small district in the Matsumae peninsula that the Matsumae had controlled since 1550. As Kaiho has noted, the enlarged Wajinchi still comprised only about four percent of the area of Hokkaido, but, at 3,374 square kilometers (about the size of Rhode Island), it was larger than six modern prefectures and, of course, the overwhelming majority of early-modern domains. The effectiveness of the segregation policy can be seen, on the one hand, in the decline of the Ainu population of the Wajinchi from 152 in 1717 to 97 in 1761 and 12 in 1788, and, on the other hand, in the growth in the year-round Wajin population from 15,530 in 1716 to 26,564 in 1787.[18] The separation of the Wajin and Ainu populations not only facilitated the domain's enforcement of its bakufu-sanctioned monopoly on contact between the two peoples but also assured domain control over the development of the fishery when it eventually emerged. Indeed, it worked so well that Emori Susumu has suggested that the creation of the Wajinchi was the product of deliberate domain policy, rather than an ad hoc response to the incomplete military victory of 1672.[19]

The domain's segregation policy worked because the Ainu needed to trade. After their defeat by the Wajin, Ainu groups in southern and central Hokkaido could not simply retreat to the self-sufficiency of their ancestors. Centuries of contact with the Wajin had made the native people dependent on Japanese commodities, particularly ironware. Ainu leaders therefore had little choice but to continue their trade relationship with the Wajin. Moreover, because the war had resulted in the elimination of Ainu chieftains capable of commanding broad, regional loyalty, the native people succumbed to their exploitation without significant physical resistance, aside from a bloody uprising of mistreated fishery workers in northeastern Hokkaido in 1789.[20]

The Matsumae domain organized the Ainu trade through the creation of some sixty trading posts (*akinaiba*) along the Ezochi coast, each corresponding roughly to the area under the influence of a local Ainu leader.[21] Under the system important retainers or the daimyo himself held exclusive rights to trade with local Ainu; a corollary, imposed after the failure of Shakushain's War, was that the Ainu had to trade with the retainer who held the nearest post. The system was functionally equivalent to enfeoffment in other domains, although, as Kaiho has noted, it was predicated on exchange (however disadvantageous to the Ainu) rather than outright expropriation, and the retainers had no rights in the land per se.[22]

The retainers were permitted an annual trading mission to the posts under their control. Trade took a corrupted form of the Ainu *umsa* ceremony, in which an exchange of "gifts" accompanied a ritual submission to Wajin "protection" by the Ainu. The samurai derived monetary income by marketing the tribute received in this manner in Honshu. The institution did not, however, survive long in its original form. Sometime in the early eighteenth century ranking samurai began turning operation of their trading posts over to merchants in exchange for an annual fee. Both sides benefited, as the retainers were assured of a stable income and the merchants could utilize their connections in Ōmi and Osaka to run the posts at a profit. This sort of arrangement became more or less universal by the middle of the eighteenth century, when it became known as the contracting system (*basho ukeoisei*).

The position of merchants in the domain would have been strong even had the Ainu trade been their only area of influence. It was doubly so, then, because of their role in the economy of a domain almost devoid of agricultural production. The Matsumae domain, born of trade, never made a serious attempt to overcome the considerable (but perhaps not insurmountable) difficulties associated with creating an economy based on agriculture in Hokkaido's harsh, northern climate. Rice was in fact beyond the capabilities of the time, but hardier grains like barley and millet were grown and taxed and could have formed the basis of an agricultural economy. In northern Tōhoku, where the climate was not much more favorable for farming than in southern Hokkaido, virtually all Ainu had been assimilated, expelled, or exterminated before the Edo period, with the result that medieval trade networks disintegrated and the Tsugaru and Nanbu domains were left to develop institutions predicated upon the centrality of rice cultivation, however impractical that might be.[23]

The inability of the Matsumae domain to produce enough food to feed its population meant, of course, that the residents of the Wajinchi had to rely on trade with Honshu to acquire necessary commodities. Matsumae thus proved to be an especially congenial environment for merchant capital to dominate the domain and its population. Powerful merchant houses emerged in the three authorized ports of Fukuyama, Esashi, and Hakodate. The most influential merchants originated in the province of Ōmi and particularly the villages of Satsuma, Yanagawa, and Hachiman on the shores of Lake Biwa. The domain recognized their power by allowing them to form a special organization, the Ryōhamagumi, which received preferential treatment in transactions involving the domain. The Ryōhama merchants acted as shipping and marketing agents for samurai involved in the Ainu trade and dealt in marine products from the Wajinchi, buying either from small fishers or from the domain's stock of tax fish. They guided commodities entering and leaving Hokkaido through the customs houses (*okinokuchi bansho*) in the three authorized ports and either operated or were closely allied to the shipping agencies that carried merchandise down the Japan Sea coast and around to Osaka. Many of them eventually became involved in the contract fishery system.[24]

Let us pause here to consider the Matsumae domain's position within the Tokugawa polity and how the unusual circumstances of its origins affect our understanding of the nature of that polity. First, the "state" here refers both narrowly to the Matsumae domain and more broadly to the bakuhan system as whole. The imprecise use of such a key term merely reflects the ambivalent nature of the Tokugawa polity. In principle, the 260 or so domains retained autonomous authority over their own lands and people, while the bakufu exercised power over matters of national concern. In fact, the functional autonomy of the domains varied greatly depending on their size, location, and the historical relationship of their lords to the Tokugawa shogun; and in any case the domains widely emulated bakufu policies even when they were not, strictly speaking, required to do so.[25] In short, the domains articulated policies only within broad outlines established by the bakufu. Matsumae was no exception to this rule, its unique location, climate, and ethnic makeup notwithstanding. The contract-fishery system, like all of Matsumae's institutional responses to its unusual situation, was predicated upon the domain's participation as an integral part of the bakuhan system. Any reference to the policies of the Matsumae "state" must therefore carry with it at least an awareness of the sanctioning power of the bakufu.

Our discussion here is further complicated by the confusing administrative history of the island of Hokkaido. For most of the Tokugawa period Hokkaido was under the administration of the Matsumae domain, and the institutions of the commercial herring fishery all developed under its auspices. In that sense, the "state" with which fishers, contractors, and other participants in the fishing economy were most immediately concerned was the Matsumae domain. However, the bakufu twice assumed direct administration over large parts of Hokkaido, first between 1799 and 1821 and again from 1854 until the collapse of the Tokugawa regime in 1868; during the latter period, moreover, it assigned parcels of territory to six northeastern Honshu domains. Finally, both Matsumae and the bakufu distinguished between the Wajinchi, seen as the "home" territory of the domain, and the Ezochi, which was ostensibly the autonomous realm of the Ainu, even if under the effective political control of Matsumae and the economic domination of the contract-fishery operators. Any ambiguities regarding Hokkaido's sovereignty concerned the Ezochi alone.

Asao Naohiro has argued that the three institutional pillars of the Tokugawa order were the policy of national "seclusion" (*sakoku*), the use of putative rice yields (*kokudaka*) to organize economic and political institutions, and the separation of the samurai and peasantry (*heinō bunri*).[26] The case of Matsumae reveals how surprisingly supple Tokugawa political institutions were in practice. The domain, as Kaiho has pointed out, seemingly met none of Asao's criteria for participation in the bakuhan system: its relations with the Ainu undermined the principle of "seclusion"; its failure to conduct land surveys and extremely low agricultural productivity left it without even a nominal assessed yield; and, consequently, there was no agricultural peasantry from which to separate the samurai.[27] Yet Matsumae was an integral part of the Tokugawa state. This apparent paradox can be resolved through a closer examination of each of these defining features of the early modern polity.

As the revisionist scholarship of Ronald Toby, Arano Yasunori, and others has demonstrated, the notion of national "seclusion" seriously misrepresents the Tokugawa bakufu's foreign policy.[28] Arano instead writes of the bakufu's prohibition on foreign travel (*kaikin*) in the context of a bifurcated international order of "civilized" and "barbarian" countries modeled after the traditional Sinocentric world view (*ka-i chitsujo*). Seen in this way, the bakufu's ordering of foreign contacts conformed to practice elsewhere in East Asia.[29] The prohibition of foreign travel did not isolate Japan but rather ensured that foreign relations would be conducted according to terms set by the bakufu. Inasmuch as the bakufu delegated responsibility for maintaining contacts with Korea, Ryukyu, and the Ainu to the Tsushima, Satsuma, and Matsumae domains as part of their respective feudal obligations, the fact that Matsumae was not "secluded" merely reflects its role as the bakufu's proxy.[30]

A major purpose of the *kokudaka* system was to make explicit the relative status of the daimyo and hence to order their feudal obligations to the shogun.[31] Agricultural productivity was, at least in the early seventeenth century, a reasonable indicator of a domain's wealth and hence its ability to support the military potential that formed the core of its obligations to the bakufu. But there was never a necessary correlation between a domain's actual productivity—its "real" *kokudaka*—and its relative standing in the institutional hierarchy of the bakuhan state, as reflected by its official *kokudaka*. In that respect, Matsumae's lack of agricultural production was not important so long as its obligations to the bakufu were clear. Although it did in fact take more than a century for the bakufu finally to determine the value of Matsumae's contribution to the functioning of the Tokugawa state, its core obligation—maintenance of trade relations with the Ainu—remained unchanged throughout the early modern period.[32]

Kitajima Masamoto, following Sasaki Junnosuke, distinguishes between the separation of the samurai and peasantry (*heinō bunri*) as an organic process—that is, as a by-product of the social division of labor in late-sixteenth-century central Honshu—and *heinō bunri* as an institution of the Tokugawa state, imposed in areas where a clear distinction between warriors and cultivators had not yet emerged.[33] In Matsumae the separation of the samurai from the merchants—the functional equivalent of *heinō bunri*—was clearly an artificial imposition, and an incomplete one at that, considering the fact that the daimyo and his retainers traded with the Ainu.[34] The fact remains, however, that the same social distinctions between samurai and nonsamurai were observed in Matsumae as elsewhere. In this critical respect Matsumae was no exception to the rule. After all, the point of the process was to identify the samurai as a distinct and privileged class.

In sum, Matsumae was hardly a "typical" domain, yet it conformed, in function if not form, to the major institutional patterns of the Tokugawa state. Matsumae's participation in the bakuhan system ensured that in responding to its unique circumstances its point of reference would always be the institutions of the broader state. In other words, for our purposes, social and economic relations within the herring fishery developed securely within the context of Tokugawa feudalism. This observation by no means denies the importance of the Hokkaido environment for the development of proto-industrial and capitalist production. Rather, it simply reveals that the Tokugawa polity was organized around a set of universal principles, which could be adapted even to such an unlikely location as Hokkaido.

The Contract-Fishery System

In 1691 the Matsumae domain declared that "no one shall discharge a firearm within earshot of the sea" during the second through fifth months. It might startle the herring; startled herring do not spawn, and only spawning herring come close enough to shore to be caught. Bonfires scare herring, too, so the domain banned them as well. The domain also prohibited night fishing as dangerous and the loose casting of nets and float cutting as likely to cause contention among fishers. Such were the provisions of Matsumae's herring-fishing ordinances (*nishinryō okite*), which were enforced by a number of herring magistrates (*nishin bansho bugyō*), who traveled around the Wajinchi each spring.[35] One might expect that a domain that took fishing seriously enough to make it a crime to frighten herring would formalize the central institution of its fishery in law, but it did not. Never formally created, only abolished, contracting was an institutional anomaly that emerged piecemeal over the course of the early eighteenth century as the daimyo and his retainers found it more convenient and more profitable to turn management of their trading posts over to merchants than to run them themselves.

    Without a formal basis in domain law, the exact nature of the contracting institution necessarily remained ambivalent. Under the earliest contracts the merchants' only responsibility, other than paying the annual fee, was to "obey the laws of the land." However, by the nineteenth century the contractors had assumed an official function as agents of the state. Their contracts reflected this new responsibility with stipulations that they provide food to the Ainu; maintain roads, station houses, and facilities for government officials traveling in the Ezochi; rescue shipwreck survivors; keep an eye out for strange ships; and, perhaps most importantly, collect a levy of ten to twenty percent of the catch of independent fishers operating at their fisheries.[36] Contracts could run anywhere from three to twenty years, but renewable, seven-year leases were most common. The fee was negotiated on the basis of the productivity of the fishery. According to the figures in Table 1, the typical western Ezochi fishery in 1854 commanded a fee of about one ryō for every 7,500 kilograms of marine products processed. There was, however, a great deal of variation, in part because the profitability of a fishery depended on a number of factors other than productivity, such as its proximity to markets and the number of independent fishers who utilized the fishing grounds and therefore relied on the credit of the local contractor.

    The fisheries spread with the influence of the Matsumae domain, appearing first in the southwest and extending north and east as far as Karafuto (southern Sakhalin) and Etorofu (in the Kurils) by the early nineteenth century. In 1786, there were thirty-eight contract fisheries in the eastern Ezochi and twenty-eight in the west, but the number fluctuated slightly as old ones were combined or became defunct and new ones were created.[37] Reflecting their greater productivity, the total fee for the

TABLE 1

FEES AT CONTRACT FISHERIES
IN THE WESTERN EZOCHI, 1854

Fishery	Fee (ryō)	Productivity (metric tons)
Okushiri	32	—
Kudō	60.5	40
Futoro	50	342
Setanai	65	709
Shimakomaki	200	3,517
Suttsu	100	2,519
Utasutsu	210	1,324
Isoya	220.5	1,400
Iwanai	515	5,637
Furuu	197	4,376
Shakotan	219	2,897
Bikuni	215	2,822
Furubira	389.5	2,744
Yoichi	556	3,797
Oshoro	327	3,12
Takashima	350	2,411
Otarunai	547	1,805
Ishikari	1,039	3,610
Atsuta	340	3,604
Hamamashike	267	1,003
Mashike	1,350	11,447
Rurumoppe	1,045	2,815
Tomamae	(included with Rurumoppe)	
Teshio	527	267
Sōya	600	2,018
Rishiri	350	2,276
Rebunshiri	(included with Sōya)	424
Shari	(included with Teshio)	750
Total	9,771.5	68,616
Average	349	2,541

source: Calculated from Shirayama, *Matsumae Ezochi basho ukeoi seido no kenkyū*, p. 107 (contracting fee for Yoichi fishery); fig. 3, following p. 264 (all other figures).

western fisheries was 3,932 ryō as compared with only 1,578 ryō for the east. By 1854, the figure for the western Ezochi fisheries had risen to 9,772 ryō, while those in the east commanded 8,608 ryō and those in Karafuto, 1,560 ryō. The rapid development of fishing in the Ezochi is evident from the jump in average fee per fishery from 71 ryō in 1786 to almost 407 ryō in 1854.[38]

The herring-meal fertilizer (*nishin shimekasu*) that kept the contract fisheries in business and the Matsumae domain prosperous was apparently known in Tōhoku from an early date but did not become a major commodity until cultivators of cotton and other commercial crops in Ōmi began using it sometime around the Kyōhō period (1716–36). It spread through the Kinai region over the course of the eighteenth century and by the Meiji Restoration was found all over Japan. The introduction of herring meal relieved farmers of their dependence on dried sardines, which had grown prohibitively expensive as rapidly expanding demand outstripped limited supplies.[39] Although herring meal had to be transported over far greater distances to market than did dried sardines, after the Meiji Restoration it was almost always cheaper, the result of a combination of abundant supply and low production costs. By the beginning of the twentieth century herring meal and other herring fertilizers (such as dried herring and processed milt) dominated the commercial fertilizer market, outselling dried sardines by about fourteen to one.[40]

Herring and other marine products were shipped either to Japan Sea ports like Tsuruga and Obama for transshipment to the Kinai plain via Lake Biwa or, much more commonly, to Hyōgo and Osaka via Shimonoseki. The Kinai region remained the main destination for shipments throughout the Tokugawa years, receiving about forty-four percent of the total in 1857, with another fourteen percent going to ports in nearby Kaga, Noto, Etchū, and Wakasa provinces on the Japan Sea coast. Herring meal was not common in the Kantō region until the mid-Meiji period, but that seems to have been the result of poor marketing as much as anything else.[41] The vessels used to carry merchandise to and from Hokkaido were *kitamaebune*, large boats with capacities ranging from 500 to 1,000 koku (1,515 to 3,030 cubic meters). About 2,300 of the 2,500 boats sailing in 1857 were registered in Hokuriku provinces; another 120 were based in Matsumae and the rest in Tōhoku and Pacific coast ports. The boats were operated by independent shippers, agents of the contractors, or by merchants involved in the herring trade but not in contracting.[42]

Most contractors spent little or no time at their fisheries. A few, such as Takadaya Kahei in Etorofu, kidnapped by the Russians during the Golovnin Incident (in which the crew of a Russian surveying ship was held in Matsumae for two years), or Yamadaya Bun'emon, who discovered a scientific way to grow kelp, took great interest in their operations; others never even set foot on Hokkaido, much less their own fisheries. Indeed, some did not even really exist: when three Ōmi merchants combined their capital to run the Sōya fishery, they put it in the name of a fictive merchant, Ōmiya Sōbei, whose name can be rendered "all the Ōmi merchants."[43]

Life at the contract fisheries centered on the store (*unjōya*) and adjacent buildings. The manager (*shihainin*) handled everyday business with the assistance of a bookkeeper (*chōba*) and an interpreter (*tsūji*). The rank-and-file of Wajin laborers consisted of overseers (*bannin*) and ordinary workers (*kasegikata*), who participated in fishing, herring-meal processing, odd jobs, and supervision of Ainu labor.

The operators of the contract fisheries used Ainu labor whenever possible because it was cheap and available locally. It gradually became less available because of a steady decline in the Ainu population, which probably began in the seventeenth century or even earlier—largely as a result of smallpox and measles epidemics brought by Wajin—and continued unabated throughout the Tokugawa era. Between 1807, the first date for which even remotely reliable figures are available, and 1854, the Ainu population fell by more than twenty percent, from almost 24,000 to under 19,000.[44] As the number of Ainu in the western Ezochi fell, fishing contractors sometimes turned to their colleagues in the east for "loans" of native workers, but for the most part they augmented their labor force with workers from Tōhoku and the Wajinchi.[45]

Those Ainu who survived the epidemics found that the intruders had preempted the most desirable lands in southern Hokkaido and introduced a pattern of wage work in contract fisheries that conflicted with traditional hunting and gathering routines.[46] They were thus confronted with an impossible choice: retreat to mountainous areas with insufficient resources or work in the spring and summer fisheries for poor wages and face the winter with inadequate food supplies. If they chose to work for the Wajin they were subjected to brutal working conditions under cruel and insensitive employers. Wajin workers and supervisors took advantage of the vulnerability of the Ainu to subject them to systematic and even institutionalized abuse. For example, the same contractors who put pregnant Ainu women to work carrying heavy loads insisted that because the fate of the native people was "in nature's hands, beyond anyone's control," they could not be held responsible for the Ainu's welfare.[47] Far from protecting the native people, contractors and their agents, particularly interpreters, used their power to cheat them in trade, appropriate their women as concubines, and terrorize them into working harder. The Ainu's position at the contract fisheries was so weak that resistance was difficult, and when it did occur was generally limited to individual acts of flight.[48] The only significant instance of organized physical resistance occurred in 1789, when Ainu workers at Kunashiri, in the southern Kurils, and Menashi, in northeastern Hokkaido, rose and killed seventy-one Wajin employees of the local contractor.[49] In addition to inflicting widespread physical and sexual abuse upon the local Ainu, Wajin workers at Kunashiri and Menashi engaged in extensive psychological terrorism: they drowned dogs before groups of Ainu, threatened to poison uncooperative workers, and, in one particularly disturbing instance, even placed an Ainu woman and her infant child in a large pot with the apparent intention of boiling them alive. Although some workers treated the Ainu well (the rebels made a point of sparing two who had been particularly kind), it is clear that the mistreatment was too extensive and too systematic to dismiss as the excesses of a few sadistic supervisors. The rebellion was quickly put down with the assistance of Ainu chieftains from neighboring districts—including even the father of one of the uprising's organizers—who relied too heavily on Matsumae's sponsorship for their leadership positions to allow the rebellion to succeed. This action alone testifies all too eloquently to the collapse of Ainu society.

The development of the contracting institution was greatly affected by the bakufu's intercession into the administration of the Ezochi, first between 1799 and 1821 and later from 1854 until the downfall of the Tokugawa regime in 1868.[50] The bakufu assumed responsibility for the Ezochi when it became apparent that the Matsumae domain was neither able nor particularly eager to deal with the threat posed by Russia. Moreover, the Ainu uprising of 1789 had occurred in the far northeast—just the area that seemed most vulnerable to foreign incursion—giving rise to the fear that Japanese claims to the Ezochi and Kurils would be jeopardized if the Ainu fled north to the protection and assimilating influence of the Russians.[51] In 1799 the bakufu took control of the eastern Ezochi and promptly abolished the contract fisheries in favor of a program of direct administration (*jikisabaki*). Under the policy, the Nanbu and Tsugaru domains deployed garrisons to Hokkaido to cope with military exigencies, while bakufu officials administered fishing and the Ainu trade, supervised road and station-house construction projects, implemented Ainu welfare programs, established Buddhist temples, and introduced iron coins to the region. The bakufu also opened trade offices in Hakodate and Edo and sent agents to major ports to buy or hire boats to transport Hokkaido products to Honshu. Officials even entertained plans for agricultural development and colonization, though they met with little success.[52]

In 1802 the bakufu made its takeover of the eastern Ezochi nominally permanent and switched administration from a five-member board of commissioners (the Ezochi *torishimari goyō gakari*) to two magistrates (Ezo or Hakodate *bugyō*) who reported directly to the senior council (*rōjū*) in Edo. John Stephan sees the period between 1799 and 1807 as one of positive achievement, as concerned and able officials, particularly Habuto Masayasu, overcame fiscal problems and a lack of enthusiasm in Edo to forge an aggressive and even profitable program of development throughout the eastern Ezochi. Direct administration was extended to the western Ezochi in the spring of 1807, but Habuto and his colleagues lost their opportunity to prove themselves there when they were forced to take responsibility for Russian raids on Rishiri island and Karafuto that summer.[53]

After 1807 bakufu concern turned almost wholly to defense. Consequently, the contract fisheries were never disturbed in the west, and the institution was reinstated in the east in 1813 with a new set of contractors. After the amicable resolution of the Golovnin Incident in 1813, Russo-Japanese relations remained good—that is, there were none—until the opening of the first treaty ports in 1854, with the result that support for direct administration waned, despite the fact that the policy was generating annual profits of about 20,000 ryō for the bakufu. The decision to return the Ezochi to the Matsumae domain in 1821 apparently came after vigorous lobbying by Matsumae, which, languishing in a far less lucrative territory at Yanagawa in Tōhoku, had been forced to fire most of its low-ranking samurai.[54]

The legacy of the bakufu's direct-administration policy was that the operation of fisheries throughout the Ezochi became literally a matter of national security. This change did not have much lasting impact on the actual business of harvesting and processing marine products, but because it affirmed the public nature of the contract fisheries and thereby strengthened the position of the merchants operating them, it blurred the line separating the private economic interests of contracting merchants and the security concerns of the bakufu. It hardly mattered in 1821, as few fishers were in a position to challenge the preeminence of the contractors anyway, but it created problems in the last decade or so of the

Tokugawa period, when independent fishers from the Wajinchi, including some with substantial operations, began settling permanently in the
vicinity of fisheries on the west coast.

The second period of bakufu control came after the opening of Hakodate as a treaty port in 1854. The following year, the entire island save
the Matsumae peninsula (including Fukuyama and Esashi) came under
two, later three, magistrates based in Hakodate. Defense was again the
bakufu's primary concern, but the promotion of agriculture and industry
was an important corollary. For example, the magistrates sponsored several moderately successful experimental farming communities near Hakodate and in the Ishikari plain and even proposed sending Hakodate prostitutes into the interior to deflower virgin territory for the state. The
bakufu also encouraged—even coerced—Ainu to adopt Japanese ways.[55]
At the end of 1859, financial problems forced the bakufu to divide most
of the Ezochi among six Tōhoku domains (Nanbu, Tsugaru, Akita,
Shōnai, Aizu, and Sendai). While some did little other than their assigned
coastal-defense duties, others, particularly Shōnai, took an active interest in improving conditions for local fishers.[56]

The second period of bakufu control had a tremendous impact on the
contract-fishery system, even though the institution itself was protected
by the bakufu.[57] First, it destroyed the insularity of the contractors' relationship with Matsumae by subverting the domain's control over the
flow of goods in and out of Hokkaido. For example, beginning in 1858
the bakufu attempted to control the marketing of Ezochi products by establishing trade offices (*sanbutsu kaisho*) in Osaka, Edo, Hyōgo, Hakodate, Sakai, and Tsuruga; a sales office (*urisabaki dokoro*) in Kyoto; and
supply agencies (*goyōtashi*) in Shimonoseki, Niigata, and Fukuyama. In
1861 it even tried to get Edo and Osaka capital behind a scheme to cor-
ner the fishery credit market. Although the plan was not successful, it did
affect the way herring meal and other marine products were marketed.[58]

Second, the bakufu takeover destroyed the insularity of the contractors' relationship with independent fishers. Soon after assuming control
of the Ezochi the bakufu began gradually to eliminate restrictions on
travel to the area, which in effect made it possible for fishers to move
there permanently. Many did so eagerly. In Utasutsu and Isoya, for example, the number of permanent residents rose from 792 in 1858 to
1,558 by 1866.[59] In some areas, like Utasutsu and Isoya, the contractors
were able to maintain a measure of authority over resident fishers, but
elsewhere administrative power passed into the hands of officials of
Tōhoku domains. For example, the Shōnai domain encouraged peasants

from its home territory to migrate to Hokkaido, where it was hoped they would take up farming rather than fishing. The domain also enticed fishers to the relatively undeveloped Rumoi district with promises of loans and other material aid. This assistance policy deprived the local contractor, Suhara Kakubei, of a potential source of income.[60] Shōnai's policy at the Hamamashike fishery, further south, was to replace the previous contractor, Date Rin'emon, with a merchant formerly based in Sakata, Nakagawaya Yūsuke. Yūsuke had neither the experience nor the resources to run a contract fishery, so he ended up being little more than a conduit for loans of domain funds and rice to independent fishers. Moreover, soon after taking over the fishery in 1865, the new contractor found himself embroiled in a struggle with a number of independent fishers over control of the apparatus to market herring products. Yūsuke's predecessor had fought off a similar challenge easily, but the newcomer could not, in part because the bakufu and Shōnai were torn between their desire to foster economic development and their need to maintain firm control, through the contracting system, over fishers.[61]

Hokkaido remained outside the control of the Matsumae domain until the Meiji Restoration. Considering that much of the Boshin War was fought in and around Hakodate harbor, the coup d'etat and subsequent fighting of 1868 and 1869 had remarkably little immediate impact on life in Hokkaido. A blockade imposed by the Imperial forces of course hurt business, but the battles themselves were fought between groups of outsiders who just happened to be in Hokkaido. The real change did not come until later.

Immediately after the Restoration Hokkaido was divided among a mishmash of domains, government agencies, private colonization groups, and even temples. Within three years, however, the entire island was put under the new Development Agency. In 1869 the agency tried to abolish the contracting system on the grounds that it hindered the growth of population and productivity in the former Ezochi. That was certainly true enough, but it did not alter the fact that the Development Agency had neither the manpower nor the financial resources to administer the island without the help of merchants, especially contractors. The merchants themselves banded together and presented a document to the government asking that their privileges not be revoked. Within months the government and contractors reached a compromise agreement in which the contracting system was formally abolished but the former contractors were nevertheless allowed to retain many of their privileges. But rather than being private merchants, most of them were installed as local officials of the Development Agency. Now called "fishery operators" (*gyobamochi*) instead of contractors, they retained use of their fishing grounds and some economic privileges, although they lost whatever rights to other fishers' produce they had retained under the bakufu and domains. Perhaps the most important privilege they lost was the exclusive right to employ Ainu labor. After the Restoration the native people were designated "former aborigines" (*kyūdojin*) and made Japanese citizens and therefore eligible to work and travel without restriction. The merchants continued in their new function until 1876, when the Meiji land-tax law was applied to Hokkaido.[62]

Merchant Capital and Feudal Institutions

The contract fisheries were not capitalist enterprises, superficial characteristics like their large scale, extensive ties to Honshu commercial houses, and the entrepreneurial energy of their operators notwithstanding. From its origins the contract-fishery system was an institutional appendage of the Matsumae domain, maintained to regularize economic relations between the domain and the Ainu people. The presence of Ainu labor at the contract fisheries in this context was hardly an accident. It was these two factors—the institutional dependence of the contract fisheries upon the state and their use of Ainu labor—that preclude treating them as capitalist enterprises.

A key element of capitalism as I characterized it in the opening chapter is the use of wage labor in production. Since wage labor under capitalism is a commodity sold by the individual worker to earn his or her living, it follows that that labor must be free because only free labor can enter into a wage contract. Ainu labor was not free, and therefore production based upon it cannot be called capitalist. Rather, Ainu labor in the fishery was a product of the feudal institutions of the Matsumae domain. The Ainu were not formally bound to their Wajin employers, either as slaves or indentured servants, or even through the long-term credit relations that tied Wajin fishers to their creditors. Moreover, they enjoyed formal freedom of movement within the Ezochi and, ostensibly at least, could elect to work at the fisheries at their own discretion. Nevertheless, Ainu labor was not free. First, after 1672, the Ainu could not leave the Ezochi to seek employment or indeed for any other reason. Moreover, their formal freedom of movement within the Ezochi was constrained by their inability to enter into economic relations with whomever they chose. Because labor at the fisheries was formally a manifestation of the trade relationship between the Matsumae house and the Ainu, and because the Ainu trade was the economic support of the Matsumae house and its retainer band, the native people could only trade with (or work for) the holder of the nearest trading post or his agent (i.e., the contractor). This arrangement worked in part because the contractors respected one another's rights to Ainu labor—we have already seen how surplus labor was sometimes "lent" to other fisheries—and in part because the Ainu themselves maintained strong ties to particular localities and therefore were not eager to move about.

A second and more immediate constraint on Ainu freedom was the native people's dependency on Japanese commodities like ironware, lacquer ware, weapons, rice, sake, and tobacco—a dependency so strong that their communities simply could not function without them. The only way to obtain such commodities was by working for Wajin fishing contractors, but that work merely further undermined Ainu independence because labor in the various fisheries—herring in the spring, trout in the summer, and salmon in the fall—precluded participation in hunting and gathering activities. Sadly, even Ainu who had avoided direct contact with the Wajin often found it necessary to turn to wage labor because the contractors' resource-depleting salmon-fishing operations undercut the basis of the traditional Ainu economy, which was centered on rivers used by spawning salmon.[63]

Compounding the tragedy of economic dependence was the significance assumed by certain Japanese commodities in Ainu culture. An important measure of social standing among the Ainu was the possession of "treasures" (*ikor*), which not only served a critical function as indemnities in conflict-resolution but also benefited their possessor in his relations with the gods (*kamui*). These treasures—lacquer ware and especially swords—were almost invariably of Japanese origin. Matsumae and its agents actively manipulated the Ainu's need for these goods by, for instance, distributing swords to leaders who provided labor for the contract fisheries or otherwise cooperated with the Wajin authorities. (The swords, incidentally, were considered too precious actually to be used as weapons; and, at any rate, they were usually of such low quality that they would not have been very useful in battle.) Thus, even Ainu with no immediate economic need for dealings with the Wajin were often drawn by cultural imperatives.[64]

In this manner contact with Wajin destroyed the traditional Ainu economy. The damage was so severe that, for example, during the rice shortage caused by the Tenpō famine in Honshu, the domain instructed contractors to see to it that local Ainu stored sufficient supplies of edible roots and fish to get through an expected two-year suspension of grain shipments to the Ezochi. As hunters and gatherers, the Ainu ought to have been better equipped than anyone to handle the crisis, but their need for rice and other goods had led them to sell even the fish and game they caught for themselves in their free time from the Wajin fisheries.[65] The effect of wage labor on Ainu culture was not, however, limited to times of economic crisis. Thomas Wright Blakiston, who traveled around the Ezochi in the 1860s, commented on the pitiful state of the native people at the contract fisheries:

> Few things strike a traveller in Yezo more than the subdued nature of the Ainu; careless and good natured as they are, they appear to have lost all idea of independence, and to have assigned themselves almost as slaves to the more civilized Japanese. Throughout the leased fishing basho [i.e., the contract fisheries] they are used as menials about the stations. They act as fishermen only under the direction of masters. . . . The inordinate love of ardent spirits, militates greatly against their social elevation; and unfortunately this propensity is by no means discouraged by the Japanese, who thereby profit in their transactions with them.[66]

It is not simply a question of the Ainu being unfree because they had no realistic alternative to wage labor—if that were the case they would be no different from a modern industrial proletariat. Here the critical factor is not the *fact* of dependency so much as the *causes* of that dependency. The native people's lack of freedom was a function of the institutional structure of the Matsumae domain. Their participation in the fishery as wage laborers was an integral part of the contracting system as it had evolved by the beginning of the eighteenth century, yet they could not participate in the fishery on the same terms as Wajin. Similarly, their dependence on Japanese commodities was more than just a matter of dietary preferences; as a manifestation of the Matsumae house's "trade" with the native people, it too was a necessary element of the domain political economy.

The Ainu were in a kind of political and cultural limbo, barred by their ethnicity from full inclusion within the structure of the bakuhan state yet tied to the Wajin because their culture had lost its ability to survive independently. The Matsumae domain could not function unless the Ainu were defined as outsiders; thus, ironically, the Ainu's alien ethnicity became institutionalized within the feudalism of the domain and, by extension, the bakuhan state. Its institutionalization within the bakuhan state is revealed by the use of Ainu labor, under conditions very similar to those prevailing at the contract fisheries, by the Ōno domain of Echizen, which was awarded territory in Karafuto by the bakufu at the close of the Tokugawa period.[67] The Ainu's dependency was thus qualitatively different from that of Wajin workers, whose increasing presence in the fishery reflected the erosion of the feudal social order of northern Honshu and the concomitant emergence of a new mode of production.

The contract fisheries, then, were not capitalist enterprises because their existence depended upon their privileged position within the domain, as symbolized by their monopoly over Ainu labor. But even if production at the contract fisheries was not "really" capitalist, there is no question that it established the model for capitalist production later emulated by entrepreneurs independent of the feudal regime. It was the contractors, after all, who developed the Ezochi fishing grounds, brought their organizational and financial resources to the development of markets for Hokkaido marine products, and first used wage labor on a large scale in the fishery.

The contractors did not take the final step to capitalist production because, quite simply, it did not seem worth their while. It was much easier to rely on the privileges accorded to them by the Matsumae domain to profit from low-risk, high-yield ventures like dealing in the wholesale fertilizer market, supply lending, and—lowest risk and highest yield of all—collecting taxes and access fees from small fishers operating in areas under their control. The contractors showed their conservatism especially clearly in the closing years of the Tokugawa period, when many retreated from direct involvement in production in the face of challenges from independent entrepreneurs from the Wajinchi. Tabata Hiroshi has made a detailed study of the account books of Nishikawa Den'emon, the Ōmi-based contractor of Oshoro and Takashima, two fisheries in the vicinity of present-day Otaru. He finds that fishing had become a relatively minor part of Nishikawa's operations by the end of the Tokugawa period and that the contractor maintained tenuous direct ties to production simply to retain access to the twenty-percent fee levied on all independent fishers' catches. Nishikawa also reaped huge profits from supply lending and from shipping cargo between his fisheries and ports in the Wajinchi and Honshu.[68] Similarly, at Hamamashike, the contractor Nakagawaya Yūsuke limited his fishing operations to three sites and concentrated instead on his role as supply merchant and shipper.[69] This seems to have been the general pattern at most contract fisheries, except those in the far north and east, which were under the authority of the three largest contractors, Fujino Kihei, Date Rin'emon, and Suhara Kakubei, and were for the most part closed to significant development by independent fishers.[70]

However, the place of the contract-fishery system as a precursor to capitalist production is clear from a look at the transition from Ainu to Wajin
labor. The Ainu entered into communal labor agreements with the contractors who employed them, in which the head of an Ainu community
offered to supply the labor of the people under him in exchange for a seasonal wage, expressed in cash but in fact paid in kind (if at all). When
contractors recruited Wajin workers to supervise or, eventually, to replace the Ainu, they drew up wage contracts very similar in form, though
not in substance, to those used with the Ainu: they paid a percentage of
the seasonal wage in advance and the remainder upon the expiration of the
contract, less wages docked for sick days or other nonperformance and
debts incurred for food and miscellaneous commodities purchased at the
fishery store (*unjōya*).

Free Wajin labor did not replace unfree Ainu labor suddenly. Rather,
the transition came about gradually, partly in response to a decrease in
the Ainu population and a simultaneous increase in Wajin immigration
from Honshu, and partly because even at its peak the Ainu population
was not sufficient to meet the rapidly increasing labor needs of the fishery, much of which came from independent fishers who did not have access to Ainu labor in the first place. Thus, the influx of Wajin labor did
not result in the immediate dislocation of the Ainu labor force. Rather,
Ainu laborers worked in the fishery until its collapse in the 1950s. However, under the Meiji regime the Ainu's ethnicity lost its former institutional meaning; they too became free labor, eligible to find work on the
open market under conditions similar to those faced by Wajin workers.[71]

The contract-fishery system represented a transitional stage, not yet
capitalist but necessary to the later development of truly capitalist production. In that sense the contractors played a critical role in the process
of transformation—one typical of merchant capitalists in a declining feudal economy—by acting as a solvent of the old forms of production. At
the same time, paradoxically, the institution impeded the emergence of
capitalism, insofar as it drew financial and human resources away from
the more vibrant independent fishery.[72]

The history of the contract-fishery system illustrates the difficulties of
positing a teleological connection between proto-industrialization and
capitalism. Gary Leupp makes a useful distinction between two major
forms of proto-industry, putting-out and manufactures. He likens putting-
out to commercial agriculture and manufactures to capitalism.[73] Leupp's
characterization highlights important differences in the outward forms

of production; considered together with the political dimension, it helps to explain the emergence of capitalism in the Hokkaido fishery and other industries in nineteenth-century Japan.

Putting-out, in which merchants provided raw materials, credit, and sometimes tools to peasants who then engaged in handicraft production at home, was the most common form of proto-industrial production in both Europe and Japan. Its functional equivalent in Hokkaido was the supply-lending institution, in which merchants provided advances of cash, daily necessities, and gear to small fishers in return for exclusive marketing rights to the fishers' herring, plus interest and commissions. Insofar as the individual fisher had control over his productive activities and usually owned his means of production, the arrangement was not capitalist: the fisher sold fertilizer—not labor power—to the merchant. The same could be said of other putting-out arrangements, making them akin to commercial agriculture (which often entailed credit relationships between cultivators and merchants).

The strength of the putting-out arrangement lay in its relative freedom from the institutions of the feudal polity. Unlike the contract-fishery system, supply lending emerged in response to the exigencies of the fishing economy and never became an integral part of the domain political or administrative structure. As we shall see in the following chapter, this element of leeway made it possible in Hokkaido for some supply merchants and their clients to circumvent the domain and bakufu and take advantage of developments in the use of labor, technology, and capital to bring about a capitalist transformation from within the fishery.

Production at the contract fisheries corresponded to manufactures, in which an entrepreneur brought peasant workers together at a single location, provided them with tools and raw materials, and oversaw their labor.[74] The contract fisheries, like other examples of manufactures, were *superficially* capitalist enterprises in the sense that the workers sold their labor power rather than some other commodity to their employer. But they were *only* superficially capitalist because their existence was predicated upon their ties to the feudal authorities. Beneath the veneer of apparently capitalist production one finds merchants whose control over both the means of production and their workers' labor was linked so closely to the protection of the domain that once that protection was removed—as indeed it was after 1868—their operations ceased to be viable. The contract-fishery operators were "capitalists" who needed feudalism to survive.

CHAPTER THREE

The Capitalist
Transformation

Everyone in the Wajinchi fished. For three or four days at a time, several
times each spring, local residents—whether they were fishers, farmers,
merchants, or even samurai—abandoned all other work and heeded the
call of "*Kuki!*"—Herring run! They were beckoned by the huge shoals of
herring that traveled from the Sea of Okhotsk down the west coast of
Hokkaido to spawn. In late March or early April the first shoals approached the shore, their arrival heralded by flocks of sea gulls and gams
of whales. During a large run the sea turned white and sticky from milt;
the beach was littered with eggs, milt, and the bodies of fish washed up
onto shore; and the water was so crowded with herring that a pole could
almost stand unsupported. Anyone not too old, too young, or too sick
joined in the business of hauling fish with nets, baskets, or bare hands:
"Leaving only the aged and infirm at home, everyone—elder and councilor, vassal and lady, manservant and handmaiden—heads for the beach,
rolls up his sleeves, and joins in the catch, with no distinction left between
lord and townsman."[1]

During the herring season itinerant merchants from Honshu crowded
the streets of Fukuyama, Esashi, and Hakodate. In Esashi enterprising
townspeople rented their houses to the traveling salesmen and moved
into makeshift huts on the beach for several weeks.[2] Some offered more
than their houses:

> [The women of Fukuyama] are all as beautiful and fair as the courtesans of
> Kyoto—Edo women could never compare. Whether they have husbands or
> not, but especially if they do not, they readily sell themselves to anyone. This is
> quite routine and is not considered at all shameful. . . .

Esashi . . . is as lively a port as Matsumae [Fukuyama] or Hakodate. In the huts on the seashore countless *gannoji* (prostitutes) play the shamisen and sing Matsuzaka *bushi*.[3]

This picture of retainers, townspeople, and fishers jostling for herring in the waters of Esashi harbor and for the pleasures of the floating world in the back alleys of Kagenomachi is actually an excellent characterization of social relations in the Matsumae domain. Seasoned fishers may have had the upper hand in the physical struggle to haul the most herring during a run, but that probably did not perturb the merchants and samurai in the fracas because they were fishing mostly for drinking money anyway—they got their cut where it really counted, at the marketplace and customs house.

The preceding chapter recounted the rise and fall of the paradoxical contract-fishery system, an institution that inhibited the development of capitalism even as it laid the foundation for it. Now the discussion turns to the structures built upon that foundation. We shall see how entrepreneurs were able to take advantage of a confluence of developments in labor, technology, and capital allocation—all fed by vibrant demand for fertilizer—to forge new social and economic relations of production in the fishery during the final decades of the Tokugawa period. This description will in turn lead the discussion back to the questions of distribution ("who got how much at whose cost") and growth ("how or whether total output grew") raised in the first chapter.[4] It is clear that total output grew considerably, but that means little unless we know who benefited from increased production and how they contrived to do so. Accordingly, the discussion that follows will focus mostly on distribution.

The distribution of wealth in the fishery was governed by the distribution of labor, technology, and capital. For most of the Tokugawa period the three were allocated in such a way as to ensure the primacy of the contract-fishery operators. During the last thirty years of the period, however, the balance shifted, resulting in a sort of domino effect of social and economic change. First, the decline of the Ainu labor force at the contract fisheries of the Ezochi and the subsequent emergence of a seasonal proletariat of fishery workers from Tōhoku facilitated the emergence of large, entrepreneurial fishery operations, particularly among independent fishers from the Wajinchi who would not have had access to Ainu labor anyway. Changes in the use of labor had significant implications for the class structure of the fishery, particularly in creating a clear distinction between family fishers and Wajin wage laborers.

Second, the development of the pound trap, a large and expensive but very efficient type of net, in the middle of the nineteenth century gave those fishers with access to sufficient capital and labor a highly productive way to use them. The cost of technological change was the social conflict that accompanied the pound trap's introduction into Ezochi fisheries and its subsequent spread into the Wajinchi in the 1850s and 1860s.

Finally, the development of better technology in turn created a demand for even more labor, some of which came from the ranks of once-independent fishers who had lost their access to credit. The economic power wielded by suppliers of capital was as great in its way as the political power of the state: merchants acting in concert could seriously disrupt the entire domain economy by withholding credit, while individual creditors could and did literally control the lives of their fisher clients. Although merchants exploited small fishers through their ability to provide credit, fishers were sometimes able to transform the dependency relations caused by chronic debt into a kind of insurance against bad years. But this use of dependency became increasingly difficult once a market for the labor of skilled Wajin fishers developed in response to the emergence of the pound-trap fishery, as creditors now had an incentive to foreclose on insolvent clients and thereby reduce them to wage labor.

Because demand for herring by-products was always strong, patterns of distribution ultimately determined the extent of growth in the fishery. Growth—higher catches—came only when fishers made effective use of labor, technology, and capital, the distribution of which were determined by the power relations within the domain. Indeed, there would have been virtually no growth at all—that is, no commercial fishery—were it not for the active efforts of the Matsumae domain to create a surplus available for expropriation, for without the contracting institution there would not have been enough capital and labor to sustain the fishery even with strong demand. Growth in total output was desirable when it fostered higher revenues for the domain and prosperity for the populace, but undesirable when it threatened the domain's political and social foundations. Even when the impetus for growth came from within the fishery, such as in technological improvements like the pound trap, the state tried to intervene to prevent that growth from upsetting existing patterns of distribution. In the case of the pound trap, the Matsumae domain prohibited growth (that is, it banned the trap) because growth would undermine the social order of the Wajinchi, the economic order of the Ezochi, and the ideological order of the domain. Later, as we shall see, the Meiji government encouraged growth in production, with socially devastating consequences for many small fishers. Total output in the fishery is therefore no guide to understanding the social or economic position of small fishers in society; only when we know "who got how much at whose cost" does the question of growth in each group's absolute share take on any meaning.

The state did not, however, simply dictate patterns of distribution and hence the extent of growth in the fishery. On the contrary, if one purpose of Chapter 2 was to highlight the state's ability to shape social relations in the fishery, this chapter seeks to demonstrate how the evolution of social relations within the fishery brought pressure on the political and institutional structures of the state. The state fostered the growth of a commercial fishery but inhibited the emergence of a capitalist mode of production; the development of capitalist relations of production within the fishery despite the institutional barriers forced the state to reevaluate those institutions and eventually come to an accommodation with the emergent capitalism. Moreover, as we shall see in Chapters 4 and 5, once the state made its accommodation, social relations underwent further adjustment to catch up to the capitalist institutions created by the state.

Before proceeding to a discussion of the initial transformation to capitalist production in the Hokkaido fishery, I should like to make it clear that the process outlined below did not represent a sudden or complete decimation of the household production of small fishers. Rather, what we shall see is a shift, relatively subtle at first, in the focus of development from household to entrepreneurial production. In a process analogous to the early history of factory industrialization at the national level, where competing proto-industrial production not only persisted but even thrived well into the Meiji era,[5] the small-scale production of gill-netters survived and indeed grew considerably during the latter half of the nineteenth century. However, as a result of the economic and political changes described here and in the chapters that follow, the capitalist production of entrepreneurial fishers dominated, and, conversely, household producers found themselves in an increasingly precarious position.

Labor

The principal characteristic of wage labor in the herring fishery was that it was not needed most of the year. The fishing itself was done in a few spurts over the course of a dozen weeks; even allowing time for setting up and closing down, fishers' demand for hired labor lasted no more than five months at a time. The work force reflected the nature of the work: most hired laborers ostensibly did something else for a living—farming in the case of Wajin, hunting and gathering in the case of Ainu—even if wage labor in the herring fishery was their principal source of income.

The impetus for the growth of wage labor came from within the fish-

ery. Contractors began turning to Wajin wage labor as the number of
Ainu available to work declined; and once the larger independent fishers
began exploiting the wealth of the Ezochi fisheries, many of them found
that they could no longer rely on networks of friends and relations to
provide them with enough labor, particularly after the emergence of the
pound-trap fishery in the 1850s.

Because demand for wage labor grew particularly rapidly after the introduction of the pound trap, it is tempting to credit technological innovation with a pivotal role in bringing about capitalism in the fishery. In
fact, however, the introduction of new technology in the 1840s and
1850s was a response to the growing availability of wage labor from
northeastern Honshu, which was experiencing significant social and economic dislocation. Although part of that dislocation can be attributed to
economic crises accompanying natural occurrences like the Tenpō famine,
the root of the problem lay in the political and economic institutions of
the Tōhoku domains.

For the first hundred years or more of the Tokugawa period, fishers in
the Wajinchi remained small and only moderately mobile—and had little
use for hired hands. The factors that would later attract large numbers of
new residents to Hokkaido and Wajin to the Ezochi—the contract-fishery system, a market for processed herring and the transportation networks to get it there, improved gear, and famines in Honshu—came together only over the course of the late eighteenth and early nineteenth
centuries. With competition for marine resources minimal, technology
primitive, and marketing opportunities limited, fishers had little incentive to venture far from their bases in southern Hokkaido. But even if the
scale of early Tokugawa fishing and trade was much smaller than during
the nineteenth century, the dependence of local residents on the herring
catch was the same. A 1739 visitor to Matsumae, Sakakura Genjirō, reported that "the peasants [*hyakushō*] cultivate no fields, but fish herring
in place of agriculture. . . . Matsumae has not seen a poor catch in decades . . . and in the span of about twenty days the people earn enough to
support themselves for a year."[6] The residents of Fukuyama were "prosperous" in 1758,[7] while the lives of the townspeople and fishers in and
around Esashi were "simple . . . [but] not lacking in housing or furnish-
ings" in 1784.[8]

The dependence of Wajinchi residents on fishing meant, however, that
hard times were just a poor catch away, though a bad year was more
likely to entail deep debt than outright starvation. During the last quarter of the eighteenth century southern Hokkaido was hit by the first of a

series of extended periods of poor fishing. The herring stopped running in the Fukuyama area in 1776, and by 1783 catches were bad throughout the Wajinchi. They remained poor until the first decade of the nineteenth century. "People will starve to death this year," predicted gloomy residents of Esashi in 1784,[9] but there is no evidence that conditions were ever nearly that desperate. Indeed, the domain's low population, combined with the ready availability of an abundance of marine life other than herring, put Wajinchi residents in a much better position during this period than their neighbors to the south, stricken by the Tenmei famine. Furukawa Koshōken, who toured Hokkaido with bakufu inspectors in 1788, saw "no poor houses" in Esashi or elsewhere in Matsumae and concluded that the availability of goods in Esashi was "no different" from that in the Kinai region.[10]

People did not starve when the fishing was bad because the market mediated between their production and consumption. For peasant cultivators a failed crop might precipitate an immediate subsistence crisis, but a bad catch in the fishery usually led to higher prices so that fishers got a higher return per unit for whatever fish they did harvest. Moreover, readily available credit enabled fishers to ride out bad years, although at the cost of long-term dependency. At any rate, Koshōken reported that despite cuts of about half, fishers' incomes were still at a level "unheard of anywhere else on the coasts of Japan."[11]

When they were not occupied by the herring fishery, small fishers participated in a variety of other, secondary economic activities. After the herring stopped running in the fifth month, fishers in the Wajinchi harvested kelp for about a month. Then, if they had access to the rivers the fish spawned in, they turned to trout and salmon throughout the summer and autumn. Many also took cuttlefish and various types of shellfish in the winter. The income from these secondary fisheries helped to alleviate some of the problems caused by fluctuations in the herring catches. Fishers in Matsumae also cultivated vegetables and some grain for domestic consumption.

Production in the herring fishery fit into an annual work routine. In the Wajinchi, preparations for the herring season began before the lunar new year, when fishers contracted for loans of cash and supplies and hired workers. The physical preparations included making necessary repairs to boats and gear, clearing snow away from the area where the fish were dried and processed, and cutting and hauling lumber for fuel. Lumber was a significant requirement everywhere but particularly at contract fisheries where a large volume of fish was processed. In some areas the

deforestation caused by herring fishing led to serious erosion and posed a
major ecological hazard until the decline of the fishery reduced the demand for wood.[12] In the Wajinchi repairs and other work continued
throughout the winter, but at the contract fisheries most preparations,
particularly cutting and hauling wood, were done by small crews of workers in the weeks immediately preceding the arrival of the first herring
shoals. In addition, independent fishers wintering at contract fisheries
supplied firewood to the contractors as part of their tax obligation.[13]

Fishers made spiritual preparations for the fishing as well. Temples in
Matsumae offered prayers for a bountiful catch, while shrines held per-
formances of Shintō music and dance and read roasted azuki beans to
predict the size of the catch.[14] In addition, fishers observed a number of
taboos. Some involved prohibitions of certain words (deer, whale, trout,
sardine, snake, fox, and bear) thought to cause bad luck. Others sought
to avoid the pollution that was associated with giving birth and menstru-
ation. The people of Matsumae believed that any contact with pregnant
women or new mothers (including eating food cooked on the same fire as
their food) would have a deleterious effect on the entire catch. Such
women were therefore isolated from others and anyone who did have
contact with them was barred from fishing for seven days—which could
mean economic disaster if the herring happened to run during that period. However, fishers did not fear pollution associated with death and
indeed even considered it good luck to recover the body of a drowned
sailor, provided the procedure was handled correctly. Like most customs
in Hokkaido fishing communities, these practices are said to have originated in the Tōhoku and Hokuriku regions.[15]

Because independent fishers in the Wajinchi could not use Ainu labor,
they had to turn to northern Honshu to supplement household and other
labor recruited close to home. Whether they considered it desirable or
merely inevitable, officials of the Matsumae domain made provisions for
labor mobility between Honshu and Hokkaido and for the absorption of
newcomers into the permanent domain population. So long as the increased population did not strain the domain's administrative apparatus
the growth brought economic benefits to the domain in the form of
higher tax revenues. Similarly, the domain's policy of allowing independent fishers from the Wajinchi into the Ezochi ensured the profitability of
the contract fisheries. In any case, profitable or not, the domain probably
had little choice but to allow independent fishers access to labor and to
herring outside the Wajinchi because the domain needed to maintain a
viable base in southern Hokkaido. But the domain, through these poli-

cies, sowed the seeds of its own downfall because the growth of the fishery ultimately weakened the distinction between Wajinchi and Ezochi and undermined the domain's role as intermediary between the two entities and the peoples inhabiting them.

Matsumae's policy toward labor reflected both its need for a stable fishery and its desire to maintain a monopoly over access to Hokkaido. The domain therefore regulated, but did not prohibit, the movement of Wajin between Honshu and Hokkaido and between the Wajinchi and Ezochi. It also set strict general guidelines concerning the movement and use of labor while giving fishers considerable leeway on specific matters. Actual labor conditions were not as a rule within the provenance of official concern, although the domain, enjoined by the bakufu to prevent mistreatment of the Ainu, did urge contract-fishery operators to protect native workers. But whether through a lack of personnel to enforce the law or, more likely, a lack of genuine concern by officials, the domain's injunctions on Ainu labor generally went ignored.

Wajinchi villages were populated mostly by migrants from northern Tōhoku and the Japan Sea coast. Their earliest settlements probably emerged gradually through the fifteenth century, though most villages were not settled until much later. According to Suzue Eiichi, early Wajin military leaders apparently exerted little economic or political control over the communities, but rather left them to develop on their own. This neglect set the tone for administration under the Matsumae regime.[16] The modicum of political stability afforded by the establishment of Matsumae hegemony at the beginning of the seventeenth century encouraged something of a wave of migration to the Wajinchi, though its scale was necessarily limited by the undeveloped state of the fishery. Not until the mid-eighteenth century, when the contract-fishery system emerged, and especially the nineteenth century, when famine in Honshu pushed and further development of the fishery pulled newcomers to Hokkaido, did Wajinchi villages grow appreciably.[17] Whatever the period, most new villages were founded when fishers from extant Wajinchi villages or Honshu first occupied land near desirable fisheries on a seasonal basis and later relocated permanently. Many new villages were thus initially associated with a "mother" village elsewhere in the Wajinchi, but such ties soon became tenuous as newcomers moved in.[18]

The ready availability of new land for settlement gave the Wajin population a degree of fluidity not found in Honshu. This fluidity, combined with the domain leaders' proclivity for trade and the villagers' for fishing, left the domain poorly positioned and poorly motivated to exercise tight control over the productive activities of the people. This lack of control contrasts with the control exercised in other Tokugawa domains, whose financial well-being was directly related to their ability effectively to expropriate the surplus agricultural production of their peasants. In practical terms, Matsumae had no need for most of the usual trappings of Tokugawa village administration, including cadastral surveys and land-yield assessments.

The domain did levy taxes, but on individuals, not villages—another departure from the usual practice in other regions. At first primary taxes were payable in herring at a flat rate, but in 1719 they were commuted to cash and calculated on the basis of ownership of boats and fishing gear. Since the administrative village in Tokugawa Japan was a corporate unit to organize tax collection, and not necessarily a single, natural economic entity, by this standard it would appear that the Matsumae domain had no need for formal villages at all. Indeed, the dearth of village-level documents strongly suggests that local administrative structure in Matsumae was weak. The domain did, however, follow the practice of compiling registers of religious affiliation (*shūmon aratamechō*), and it is evident that headmen and other officials were appointed in larger villages beginning sometime in the eighteenth century.

The pool of potential fishery workers in the Wajinchi expanded throughout the Tokugawa years as the population rose from about 20,000 at the beginning of the eighteenth century to just over 31,000 a century later; by 1839 it had reached nearly 42,000, and in 1850 it was almost 60,000.[19] Many of the new arrivals were refugees from the Tenpō famine, which ravaged northern Honshu between 1832 and 1838.[20] Ironically, Matsumae's lack of agriculture helped it through the scarcity because its trade networks assured it sufficient income to secure food from areas not badly affected by the famine. For example, when grain shipments from Echigo, Sakata, and Tsugaru ceased, merchants used their connections to arrange imports of rice from Kyushu. Many people were of course unable to afford expensive southern rice, but it was usually possible for them to survive on hardy roots like daikon and bracken (*warabi*), as well as the abundant fish, shellfish, and seaweed available in nearby waters. For the desperate, the domain and leading merchants distributed *oshime*, a gruel of rice and kelp, at relief centers in Fukuyama and Hakodate.

The relatively good conditions in Matsumae naturally attracted afflicted people from Honshu. Matsumae officially refused to admit such refugees, but sympathetic boat pilots carried starving peasants across the Tsugaru Strait and released them at small inlets before coming into port at Hakodate. Some of these people received small amounts of grain and cash from domain officials before being put on boats headed back; many others managed to stay in Matsumae, where they eagerly sought work to earn their sustenance. They saw little point in returning to Tōhoku after the famine, especially when there was ready employment for good wages in the fishery.

The domain never actively encouraged migration to Matsumae, whether motivated by famine, work, family, or a predilection for bracing weather; it hardly could, given the bakufu's official disdain toward unnecessary movement by peasants. However, that does not mean that the domain was fundamentally hostile toward outsiders. In fact, it was easy, if hardly pleasant, for merchants, fishery workers, religious travelers, and even tourists to enter the domain so long as their papers were in order and they were willing to submit to a cumbersome and humiliating bureaucratic procedure before being admitted.

Upon arrival in Matsumae all transients (*tabibito*) went through a series of interrogations regarding their origins, occupation, and reasons for coming to the domain. The questioning process was harsh, and the officials involved—like immigration officers everywhere—made every effort to appear stern and forbidding. Hirao Rosen, a painter and nativist scholar from Hirosaki who visited Matsumae in 1855, saw the system in action. After arriving in Matsumae he first found a room at a transients' inn (*tabibito yado*), then returned to the boat that had brought him to have his luggage inspected. The following day, he recalled,

> I was accompanied by the innkeeper, one Takedaya Jintarō, to the customs office for inspection. Upon reaching the office we found perhaps seventy people, all recent arrivals, already waiting. . . . After a while the customs officials came in. They called each of us in turn and, without exception, made us strip off all our clothes and raise our arms so they could check us for wounds or scars. We were then asked about our reasons for leaving home and our business in Matsumae. We were eventually led to the town office, where we were again put through the same questioning and a reading of the domain laws before finally being released.[21]

Rosen's complaint—"They certainly take their laws seriously around here!"—notwithstanding, only two of the seventy in his group were actually denied admittance because they lacked guarantors or were otherwise deemed unacceptable.[22] Transients who sustained the inspection were allowed to remain in Matsumae upon payment of an entry tax, which was slightly more than one ryō in 1865, or around one-sixth of a typical fishery worker's seasonal wage.[23] They were then entrusted to the care of their

guarantors, who were either relatives or local innkeepers. When leaving
Hokkaido transients were required to pay an exit duty and obtain an exit
visa (*dekitte*). Every year, around the tenth month, officials rounded up
and registered any illegal aliens they could find in the domain.[24]

The domain allowed transients with ties—real or fictive—to common-
ers registered in the domain to undergo a naturalization process called
"entering the peasantry" (*hyakushōiri*).[25] Recipients of permanent resi-
dency, particularly in Fukuyama, were more likely to be involved in commerce than directly employed in the fishery. Fishery workers typically
came to Hokkaido only for the fishing season unless they were permanent employees of a contractor or other entrepreneurial fisher, in which
case they often wintered in the Ezochi.

The Matsumae domain had established procedures for workers traveling within the Wajinchi and to and from the Ezochi. All persons entering
the Ezochi had to pass through either the barrier established at Sekinai,
just outside of Kumaishi village on the west coast, or the one at Kameda,
near Hakodate on the east coast. The only people who normally went
into the Ezochi were domain or bakufu officials, merchants, or fishers.
All required a pass or some other credential; fishers had to pay an additional fee of 0.25 to 0.875 ryō for their boats, depending on capacity.
Nonresidents were also required to pay a tax equivalent to the entry tax
if they wintered in the Ezochi. Moreover, those wintering in the Ezochi,
whether Matsumae residents or not, were required to supply firewood
(or mats in the case of women) to the local domain post. In all cases,
women had to pay only half the taxes and fees levied on men.[26]

The domain tried to keep track of fishery workers traveling within the
Wajinchi as well. For example, when Fukumatsu, a resident of Hekirichi
village, near Hakodate, went to work in Tomari, on the west coast of the
Wajinchi, in 1841, he received a pass from his village headman. The pass
was endorsed by a domain official when Fukumatsu crossed a mountain
pass on his way to work and twice more by village and town officials in
Tomari and Esashi when he was ready to return home. The pass was one
of several issued to residents of various Wajinchi communities and kept
by Sasanami Kyūemon of Kaminokuni, who may have received the documents in his capacity as a village official or who may have been the fishers' employer.[27]

Prices for herring by-products rose as harvests fell off during the 1780s.
This price increase encouraged fishers to venture into the Ezochi to get to
the fish if the fish would not come to them. The domain responded by allowing fishing forays (*oinishin*) as far as Ishikari after 1793; previously

fishing was officially limited to the Wajinchi-Ezochi border at Sekinai, just west of Kumaishi village (though fishers frequently went farther up the coast in violation of domain orders). For many marginal operators, however, the cost of traveling up the coast to good fishing grounds offset much of the potential profit. Those who could went anyway, but contract-fishery operators, supply merchants, fertilizer brokers, and shippers were ultimately the ones who benefited most from the rising prices.[28] The fishing improved in the Wajinchi in the beginning of the nineteenth century, so the next spurt of activity in the Ezochi by independent fishers did not come until the 1830s and 1840s, when the Tenpō famine and the development of the pound trap gave fishers an incentive to venture away from home. Again, the domain cooperated by lifting restrictions on seasonal fishing at the productive fisheries beyond Mashike in 1840.[29]

Until the second bakufu takeover of Hokkaido in 1855 independent fishers were not officially allowed to settle permanently in the Ezochi. The domain tried various measures to prevent migration, such as prohibiting travel beyond Cape Kamui at the tip of the Shakotan peninsula by Wajin women,[30] but enforcement was difficult. Many people first went to the Ezochi to spend one winter, as permitted by the domain, but ended up remaining permanently. Table 2 shows that by 1859 there were small Wajin communities at every contract fishery in the western Ezochi; all had substantial numbers of women, which suggests that the fishers transplanted their household production to new fisheries in the north. The 1869 population register for Isoya reveals that 114 of 159 resident households had been fishing (if not actually living) in the area before 1853, including a number who had first been to Isoya in the early 1830s.[31] Table 3 shows a gradual climb in the number of independent fishers at Yoichi between 1828 and 1854.

Many of the new permanent residents of the Ezochi stayed simply because they could not afford the expense of traveling to and from home bases in the Wajinchi every year, a situation that left them vulnerable to exploitation by contractors. Perhaps that accounts for the advice given to Akita domain officials that they overlook the fact that a large number of fishers at the Mashike fishery did not have valid travel documents because they had wintered (and summered) in the Ezochi for several consecutive years.[32]

Of course, not all of the fishers who migrated to the Ezochi in the final years of the Tokugawa period were indigent. According to the 1871 population register, of 188 households (1,051 persons) in Isoya village, the majority—129 households (757 persons)—were headed by independent

TABLE 2

POPULATION OF WESTERN EZOCHI
FISHERIES, 1859

Fishery	Households	Male	Female	Total
Kudō	3	3	7	10
Futoro	18	38	33	71
Setanai	17	27	33	60
Sutsuki/Shimamaki	9	27	7	34
Suttsu	15	37	26	63
Utasutsu	20	42	19	61
Isoya	5	11	6	17
Iwanai	22	37	29	56
Furuu	16	33	40	73
Shakotan	17	40	34	74
Bikuni	9	18	5	23
Furubira	54	118	122	240
Yoichi	79	258	232	490
Oshoro	33	68	66	134
Takashima	19	47	32	79
Otarunai	26	58	43	103
Ishikari	167	356	396	752
Atsuta	11	27	24	51
Hamamashike	59	105	90	195
Mashike	39	55	60	155 (sic)
Rurumoppe	66	113	112	223 (sic)
Tomamae	25	86	64	150
Teshio	40	110	104	214
Sōya	123	233	250	483
Monbetsu	250	473	486	959
Shari	177	356	369	725
Rishiri/Rebun	19	33	33	66
Karafuto	373	1,304	1,447	2,651

SOURCE: Satō Eiemon, "Kaei rokunen, Bunsei gonen Ezochi ninbetsuchō" [1860], "Sho-kakitodome," Hokkaidō shi hensan shiryō 198, RCNS.

TABLE 3

INDEPENDENT FISHERS

AT YOICHI, 1828–1854

Year	Fishers	Boats	Average Boats/Fisher
1828	24	55	2.3
1830	26	39	1.5
1832	35	57	1.6
1834	43	43	1.0
1835	46	73	1.6
1836	59	80	1.4
1837	63	95	1.5
1838	62	100	1.6
1840	52	154	2.9
1842	40	128	3.2
1854	63	—	—

SOURCE: Hayashi-ke monjo, YCS, 1: 126–28, 301–2, 346–48, 382–84, 426–28, 439–40, 499–501, 651–54, 729–31, 839–41.

producers (including 8 with one pound trap each), while just 43 households (97 persons) were headed by hired laborers.[33]

Fishers recruited labor during the Tokugawa period in several different ways. The Wajin labor force at the contract fisheries included overseers (*bannin*) and ordinary workers (*kasegikata*). At Yoichi the overseers were always from Matsumae while other workers came from Tōhoku; at Isoya and Utasutsu, however, the principal distinction between the two was that overseers were hired on annual contracts while the others (called *yatoi*) worked on six-month contracts.[34] According to Tajima Yoshiya, most new employees of all categories at Isoya and Utasutsu were hired either through introductions from current workers or through employment agents.[35] The agents could be the keepers of transients' inns, who were licensed to act as guarantors for new arrivals,[36] or they could be merchants in Tōhoku villages with a business connection to the contractor. No doubt many potential laborers simply crossed the Tsugaru Strait in the hopes of being picked up by an agent at one of the domain's customs houses. Alternatively, when Nakagawaya Yūsuke took over management of the Hamamashike fishery in 1865, one employee of the previous contractor sought out Yūsuke's business agent in Fukuyama to secure

continued employment at the fishery. Other former employees simply
traveled directly to Hamamashike to seek work.[37] In contrast to the usual
practice after the Restoration, there is no evidence that contractors or
their agents traveled directly to Tōhoku to recruit labor.

At Isoya and Utasutsu in 1859, the average pay for forty-eight overseers was 8.75 ryō per annum, while the twenty ordinary workers earned
an average seasonal wage of 5.75 ryō. Wages for overseers who had been
associated with the fishery for several years were generally much higher,
and managers and other employees in supervisory positions earned as
much as 25 ryō per year. In addition, workers received bonuses based on
productivity that often exceeded their base wage, so that a group of
seven workers whose base pay was 6 to 8 ryō actually grossed between
9.5 and 25 ryō each. These wages seem quite good,[38] but the workers
never saw a large portion of their earnings because, whatever their
wages, they necessarily got involved in credit relations with the contractor. Credit for workers operated in much the same way as supply lending
(shikomi) to independent fishers. After the price of foodstuffs and other
commodities purchased on credit from the contractor's store was deducted, there was often very little left over to support the worker and his
family for the remainder of the year. The seven workers mentioned above
ended up with net earnings ranging from 10 ryō to minus 12.75 ryō.[39]

The labor-recruitment practices of independent fishers probably varied considerably with the size of their operations. From the 1869 population register for Isoya it is apparent that some small fishers did not use
hired labor at all, or at least not on a full-time basis. In those cases the
fisher and his family no doubt worked together to catch and process the
fish. Other households included dependents (yakkai), who could be either single persons (usually but not always men) or entire families. Presumably, these dependents contributed to production in the fishery
whether they were kin of the household head or not.[40] Although it is impossible to tell for sure whether the relations between household head
and dependent were informal and long-term or contractual and short-
term, the 1871 register drops the term "dependent" in favor of "laborer"
(temadori), suggesting a contractual relationship.[41] Similarly, a register
for Atsuta in 1868 lists "hired workers" (yatoi) in addition to other
household members, again strongly implying a contractual association.[42]

At Hamamashike, fishers with substantial operations employed labor
in a clearly contractual relationship. Table 4 was compiled from travel
documents for thirteen fishing teams that came to Hamamashike for the
1866 herring season. Hanbei of Karatsunai ward, Fukuyama (no. 2 in

TABLE 4

INDEPENDENT FISHERS AT
HAMAMASHIKE, 1866

No.	Home[a]	Boats	Employees	Employees' Home
1.	Fukuyama	2	3[b]	Fukuyama, Matsumae
2.	Fukuyama	6	11	Tanabu, Ikokuma, Nanbu
3.	Esashi	1	2	Minmaya, Tsugaru
4.	Fukuyama	3[c]	6	Nakanome, Tsugaru
5.	Hakodate	3	5[b]	Aomori, Kanita, Nanbu
6.	Esashi	6[c]	12	Akaishi, Tsugaru
7.	Fukuyama	6	12	Ōdomari, Tsugaru
8.	Esashi	12	24	Ōdomari, Tsugaru
9.	Esashi	7	14	Akaishi, Tsugaru
10.	Fukuyama	4	7	Aomori, Tsugaru
11.	Fukuyama	4	7	Aomori, Tsugaru
12.	Fukuyama	8	16	Fujishima, Tsugaru
13.	Esashi	6	12	Yamori, Akita

SOURCE: "Oboe" [1865/12–1866/1], "Hamamashike yōyōgaki tojikomi," Satō-ke monjo.
[a] Hakodate, Fukuyama, and Esashi include the towns and their environs.
[b] Worked with crew personally (*jikinori sendō*).
[c] Borrowed boats.

the table), is a typical example. Ten of Hanbei's eleven workers were from Tanabu village and the other from Ikokuma village, both in the Shimokita peninsula at the northern tip of Honshu. The crew's travel documents reveal that they all came in one large boat, then broke into five two-man teams, each consisting of a pilot (*yatoi sendō*) and an ordinary worker in a skiff.[43] The crews listed in Table 4 share a number of characteristics. First, while the proprietors were all from Matsumae, only 3 of 131 workers were. (They had accompanied their employer from Fukushima village, near Fukuyama.) Second, each proprietor's workers overwhelmingly came from a single village, which certainly implies that they were hired as a team. It is probably safe to assume, if difficult to demonstrate, that the proprietors had some sort of connection with the Tōhoku village that supplied the laborers, either directly or through an agent of the type that supplied workers to contractors. Third, with the exception of two relatively small operators identified as "working pilots" (*jikinori sendō*), the proprietors apparently did not join their crews in working the nets, which suggests that they may have been pound-trap operators. Although the travel documents do not touch on this question, at least three of the thirteen appear to have been among a group of pound-trap fishers who borrowed 100 ryō each from Nakagawaya Yūsuke that year; Hanbei, mentioned above, is listed separately as the headman (*hama nanushi*) of the independent fishers' settlement.[44]

A number of factors contributed to the growth of Wajin wage labor during the final decades of the Tokugawa period. The first was the decline of the Ainu population, which forced contractors to look elsewhere to augment their work forces. The second was the spread of independent fishers from the Wajinchi into the Ezochi during the late eighteenth and early nineteenth centuries. This was a critical element in the overall expansion of the fishery, and it naturally entailed an increased demand for labor. The third factor had nothing directly to do with the fishery but rather was the result of events and policies in Tōhoku domains that made it attractive for peasants to seek opportunities in Hokkaido. Some of these events were natural disasters like the Tenpō famine and the earthquake that devastated the village of Shiokoshi in southern Akita at the beginning of the nineteenth century (and was perhaps the reason that Shiokoshi, alone among villages in the vicinity, supplied large numbers of people—contractors like Hayashi Chōzaemon and Satō Eiemon as well as workers—to the fishery).[45] But in the long run domain policies were more important because their effect was systematic and prolonged.

A good example comes from the Shimokita peninsula, which was a major source of fishery workers. Shimokita was perhaps the poorest part of Nanbu, a domain renowned for its poverty and high incidence of peasant protest. It was so poor, in fact, that the Meiji government chose to exile the samurai of the Aizu domain there after their defeat in the Boshin War.[46] Although the peninsula's inhospitable climate and lack of arable land contributed to the chronic economic depression of the region, the flow of workers from Shimokita to Hokkaido was, as Hasegawa Toshiyuki notes, principally a result of the Nanbu domain's forestry and fishery policies.[47] Between the late seventeenth and mid-eighteenth centuries the domain enclosed the area's valuable wooded land and leased rights to harvest lumber to a small group of merchants. In the Kanbun period (1661–72), the domain reserved rights to thirteen of the peninsula's Japanese cypress (*hinoki*) forests for itself; by the Kyōhō period (1716–35) that number had risen to thirty-eight. In the following decades it appropriated progressively more land, so that by 1760 all 208 of the peninsula's forests were closed to local residents.[48] Without access to local forests, peasants had to look for other ways to earn a living, and many of them took up fishing, either locally or for wages in the Ezochi.[49] Fishing at home did not, however, remain an option for long because at about the same time that the domain cut Shimokita peasants off from forestry, it made it difficult for them to make a living from the sea as well. The domain required Shimokita fishers to harvest marine products like abalone and sea cucumber (*tawaramono*) suitable for the lucrative China trade but imposed a domain monopsony that ensured that the prices fishers received were too low to make fishing worthwhile. Without a suitable base in agriculture and unable to make a living from local forestry or fishing, Shimokita peasants were forced to look north for other opportunities.[50]

Many migrants from places like Shimokita no doubt found prosperity in Matsumae, but others sank to the bottom of the Wajin labor hierarchy. Their ties to home severed, they wandered from job to job in Hokkaido. Sannojō, from Shōzukawa village in Shimokita, was such a man. In the spring of 1830, when he was forty-one years old (by Japanese reckoning), Sannojō secured employment on a boat owned by an eastern Ezochi contractor. Between then and the summer of 1837 he held at least four other jobs, including two stints at Ezochi herring fisheries working under independent fishers from Matsumae. His life of itinerant labor was interrupted when he was caught after he and two other drifters broke into a storehouse owned by one of his former employers, a village official in a community near Hakodate. An associate of the former employer noted that Sannojō had been a good and honest worker and suggested that he had been driven to crime because both his pockets and his belly were empty at the time. The case is especially poignant because Sannojō had embarked upon his life of crime immediately after being released from employment at a herring fishery.[51] It is possible that he was broke because debts to his employer exceeded the balance of wages due him.

The relationship between Tōhoku domain policies and the growth of wage labor in the Hokkaido fishery is indicative of the intimate, transdomainal connections between political and economic structures in Tokugawa Japan. When Nanbu enclosed its forests and tried to coerce production of marine products for the China trade, it did so because it needed to generate revenue to finance its feudal obligations to the bakufu. Hasegawa therefore characterizes changes in domain policy toward the productive activities of Shimokita peasants as being the result of the extension of bakuhan state authority into the countryside after the establishment of the Tokugawa regime. Clearly, the capitalist transformation of the fishery is best understood in the context of regional and national politics and institutions.[52]

Figure 1. Gill net

Technology

There are a lot of ways to catch a herring, but fishers in Hokkaido relied mostly on two, the gill net and the pound trap. The gill net (*sashiami*) (Figure 1), which tradition holds was introduced into Hokkaido around 1672 by an Echigo merchant,[53] was the choice of virtually all fishers until the middle of the nineteenth century and most family fishers throughout the life of the fishery. Its principal advantage was its relatively small size, which made it easy to obtain, readily portable, and practical for fishing teams of as few as two or three men in one boat. The pound trap (*tateami*) (Figure 2) was introduced into the eastern Ezochi in the first decade of the nineteenth century from Nanbu (where its origins are unknown) but did not appear on the west coast of Hokkaido until the early 1840s. Once it appeared, however, it quickly supplanted several other large nets that had been used in the Ezochi sporadically since the end of the eighteenth century.[54] Pound traps came in various shapes and sizes, but all were big and expensive: even the smallest required fifteen to twenty fishers in three boats to operate. One late-Meiji writer estimated that a good pound-trap fishery was roughly equivalent to a substantial agricultural holding of about 250 koku of rice.[55] Unlike gill nets, pound traps were anchored in place near shore, so fishers could not easily go after the fish if the fish did not come to them during a run; but if the fish did come, a pound trap could land more fish in a single haul than many small fishers harvested in an entire season. In other words, the pound-trap fishery was capital intensive, but the economies of scale made the expenditure more than worthwhile provided the fish ran.

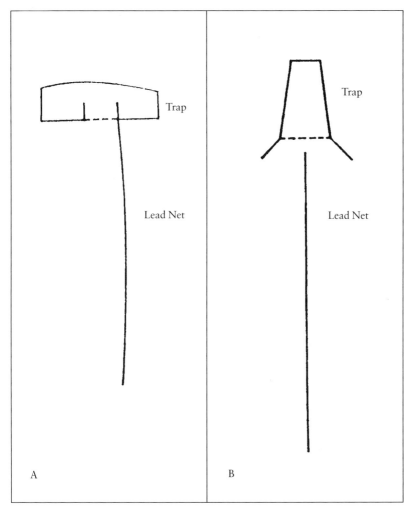

Figure 2. Pound traps. A: square trap (*kakuami*). B: free-running trap (*ikinariami*).

Gill nets and pound traps were not incompatible, technologically or economically. Even in a crowded fishing ground the highly mobile gill-netters could work between pound traps or, if necessary, out to sea beyond the stationary gear;[56] and since there were plenty of fish for everyone in a sizable run, a bigger catch for gill-netters should not have meant a smaller share for pound-trap fishers, or vice versa. Pound-trap operators, despite their tremendous advantage in production costs and productivity, should not have represented much of an economic threat to gill-netters either, in part because the market for herring meal and other herring by-products was large enough to absorb increased output without necessarily resulting in lower prices. (To be sure, prices for herring meal often fluctuated violently but not always in strict correlation with supply.)[57] Moreover, since pound-trap fishers and gill-netters processed their catches in the same way, large operators did not have an inherent competitive advantage of the sort enjoyed by mass producers against handicraft artisans, though their preferential access to credit certainly made their operations relatively more profitable. However, since gill-netters dealt with a much smaller volume of fish, they could usually process a higher proportion of their catch into dried herring (*migaki nishin*), a foodstuff worth more than herring meal, before the fish spoiled.

Given the compatibility of the technologies, innovation in the fishery ought to have been welcomed by everyone except the herring, but it was not. Quite the contrary: small fishers in the Wajinchi reacted violently when contractors in the Ezochi tried to introduce various types of large nets intermittently between the end of the eighteenth century and the middle of the nineteenth century. Small fishers felt pound traps were responsible for poor catches in the Wajinchi and thus represented a significant threat to their way of life. They were wrong about the nets being the immediate cause of bad fishing in the 1850s, but they were right about the threat to their way of life. The pound trap contributed to the emergence of new production relations in the fishery, and overfishing with pound traps eventually devastated the herring stock and with it the fishery. As it was, however, small fishers' opposition to the new nets continued only until they received monetary compensation for their perceived loss.

It would be tempting to attribute the violent reaction of small fishers to a misunderstanding of the ecology of the herring fishery if it were not for the fact that gill-netters and pound-trap operators fought every time a new fishery was opened, most notably in Nemuro in the 1890s and Karafuto after 1905 (for which see Chapters 4 and 6, respectively). Moreover, in contrast to the first disputes, later conflicts were initiated by pound-trap fishers who claimed that gill-netting jeopardized their operations. Clearly, the problems between small gill-net fishers and pound-trap operators were based on more than a disagreement over the most effective fishing method. Rather, technological innovation exacerbated conflict between the household production of small fishers and the increasingly industrial production of entrepreneurs.

Small fishers fought the introduction of new nets into the fishery every chance they got. The first such chance was in 1790, in the midst of an extended period of bad catches throughout the Wajinchi. A reported 2,300 fishers gathered near Fukuyama to protest the "self-serving business practices"—including fishing with large dragnets—of the Suhara and

Murayama houses, two of the domain's most influential contractors. According to the report of a Nanbu domain official, Matsumae authorities gave into demands for a ban on large nets in the herring fishery but refused to acquiesce to a further demand that the agents of Suhara and Murayama be expelled from Hokkaido, on the simple grounds that the domain itself owed the merchants too much money.[58] Within just three years, however, the domain permitted use of dragnets and seines but with a proviso limiting them to remote fisheries and use for species other than herring. The stipulation proved unenforceable,[59] but the issue lost its urgency after catches in the Wajinchi picked up at the beginning of the nineteenth century.

Large nets became increasingly common during the first half of the nineteenth century, particularly in fisheries in the far north and east of the island, where only the occasional government official or Russian explorer disturbed the privacy of the contractors and their agents. Persistent lobbying by contractors led in 1844 to a lift of the ban on pound traps wherever gill-netting was not feasible, but because the contractors were the self-appointed arbiters of feasibility, the action was tantamount to permitting pound-trap use throughout the Ezochi, not only by contractors but by a growing number of Wajinchi-based independents as well. Thus in 1846 eleven independent fishers in Yoichi added their large nets to the nine already operated by the contractor; and in 1855 there were thirty-two pound traps in use at Hamamashike, of which only six belonged to the contractor.[60] Small fishers did not organize protests against pound-trap use at that time, but soon catches in the Wajinchi began to fall, leading the domain to reissue its ban on large nets on the eve of the 1854 herring season. Users of pound traps largely ignored the order and so incurred the wrath of gill-netters.

The net-cutting incident (*amikiri sōdō*) was the small fishers' way of encouraging pound-trap operators to comply with domain orders. In the spring of 1855 several hundred fishers from eight Wajinchi villages west of Esashi sailed up the west coast of Hokkaido as far as Furubira on the Shakotan peninsula, stopping at every fishery to cut pound traps and otherwise wreak havoc, sometimes with the support of gill-netters who lived in the Ezochi. The protest was curtailed only when the leaders were tricked into going ashore and into the arms of officials sent to intercept them. The net cutters—who were not punished for their acts—had the last laugh, however, as a tremendous shoal of herring reached the Shakotan peninsula just after the pound traps had been rendered useless.[61]

The incident left the pound-trap operators in an awkward position since there was no doubt they had been using their nets in violation of domain law. Rather than take their lumps quietly, however, the contractors from the southwestern Ezochi submitted a series of petitions asking for a relaxation of the domain policy. They were joined by independent pound-trap fishers, who took their case to the bakufu's newly established Hakodate magistracy in late 1855. Gill-netters countered with two mass meetings in the autumn and winter of 1855–56. In every case the domain remained firm in its prohibition of pound traps.[62]

The process of trading petitions and protest meetings might have gone on indefinitely had the bakufu not taken over the entire Ezochi and most of the Wajinchi at the end of 1855. The Hakodate magistrates announced that fishers were free to use large nets until they made a final disposition of the problem. It turned out the herring catch in the Wajinchi in 1856 was indifferent but hardly disastrous, which led the magistrates to the conclusion that far from a need to ban pound traps, their prohibition would prove detrimental to the development of the fishery. That decision was made tentative, however, pending the results of the fishery over the following three to five years. To defuse gill-netter opposition the officials announced a levy of three ryō per annum on all pound traps in the eleventh month of 1856, of which two-thirds was earmarked for loans of rice and other foodstuffs to fishers in the eight villages responsible for the net-cutting incident. Herring catches remained good for the next three seasons, so in 1860 the magistrates gave permanent sanction to pound-trap fishing in areas under bakufu and Tōhoku-domain administration but kept the three-ryō use tax intact.[63] The ban on pound traps issued by the Matsumae domain remained in effect in the area still under its authority (the district between Esashi and Fukuyama), but even there the domain granted permission to use the nets in a few locations after 1865.[64]

Pound-trap use spread steadily after 1860, even in villages involved in the net-cutting incident, in part as a result of active efforts by the Hakodate magistrates. Kumaishi, on the Wajinchi-Ezochi border, was the largest village to participate in the protest. The poor herring catches that had precipitated the incident in 1855 were also causing a loss of population in the area. One of the magistrates, Muragaki Noritada, decided that the best way to check the decline of the village population would be to develop a pound-trap fishery, but local fishers were leery about using a technology they still considered harmful to gill-netting. Muragaki therefore hired a group of workers to set up a pound trap at Ōta, the nearest contract fishery, to demonstrate the efficacy of the new net. Muragaki's "red net"—so called because the trap and the workers' clothing were dyed red—brought in a respectable 225 tons of fish without any adverse effect to the gill-net fishery; that was enough to persuade several well-to-do fishers to overlook whatever intravillage tensions might occur and cash in. After the 1860 season one villager applied for and received a loan of 300 ryō and some rice from the magistrates' office to set up a pound trap in Kumaishi. He was joined the following year by two others, and by 1869 there were twenty-one pound traps employing 315 workers in the village (as compared with 358 gill-netters). There were close to another thirty traps distributed throughout the area between Esashi and Kumaishi.[65]

The western Wajinchi was by no means the only area to see a rapid expansion of the pound-trap fishery. The traps were more prevalent the farther one went from the Wajinchi,[66] but even at Isoya, south of the Shakotan peninsula, there were twenty-four pound traps in use by 1868, all but four of which belonged to independent fishers (none of whom, however, had more than one).[67] Further north, at Atsuta, at least five and perhaps as many as eight independent fishers operated pound traps in 1868.[68] Firmly established by the fall of the Tokugawa bakufu, the pound-trap fishery continued to expand during the Meiji period, though it never supplanted the gill-net fishery so ideally suited to household production.

The conflict surrounding the introduction of pound traps into the herring fishery raises questions about the political and social significance of the new technology. One such question concerns the relationship between the state and the fishery. The domain's relationship with small fishers had a moral element absent from its contractual ties with contract-fishery operators.[69] While merchants simply bought commercial privileges for a set period of time, small fishers had a significant stake in the political and economic well-being of the domain. That the fishers understood their role is reflected in the lines of a song dating to about the time of the net cuttings:

> Give up the pound trap and throughout the island
> We'll see bountiful catches.
> It's thanks to the herring in the Wajinchi
> That many boats come from far and wide and our lord
> Receives his due.
> This year the catch will indeed be fine![70]

Domain officials had to weigh the economic benefits of the pound-trap fishery against the political costs of violating their moral obligation to protect the interests of small fishers.

Ultimately the domain chose to oppose technological innovation for two reasons. First, it stood to realize limited economic gains from the pound-trap fishery because the fees paid by contractors were only indirectly correlated to actual catches. From the domain's point of view higher productivity was desirable but hardly compelling enough to risk political instability when faced with determined opposition from small fishers. The domain therefore made frequent concessions to the contractors but inevitably backed down when Wajinchi fishers protested. Second, and perhaps more importantly, the rapid expansion of the poundtrap fishery undermined the ideological justification for the domain's existence. The Matsumae house, under its mandate from the bakufu, was charged with the supervision of trade between the Ezochi and the rest of Japan. The contract-fishery system was ostensibly an outlet for that trade, and so long as Ainu labor was used in relatively small-scale fisheries, the domain could rationalize its role as intermediary. The poundtrap fishery, however, was worked mostly by Wajin who crossed over in large numbers from northern Honshu every year. Moreover, many of the new pound-trap operators were not contractors at all but independent fishers from the Wajinchi whose activities had nothing to do with the Ainu trade. (Indeed, trade and other contact between independent fishers and the native people were explicitly prohibited.)[71] In other words, heightened economic activity in the Ezochi meant an erosion of the barriers separating the Wajinchi and Ezochi and that in turn threatened the domain's legitimacy. And legitimacy was a practical concern for a domain that faced an imminent loss of its territory.

The bakufu had no such ideological stake in maintaining the distinction between the Ainu and Wajin spheres. On the contrary, it had a compelling need to do just the opposite. Only by asserting the Japanese nature of the Ainu and the full economic and social integration of Hokkaido into the bakuhan state could the bakufu establish the legitimacy of its territorial claims in Hokkaido, Sakhalin, and the Kurils in the face of a threat from Russia. The bakufu dealt with the ethnic problem by trying after 1855 forcibly to assimilate the Ainu,[72] and with the social and economic problem in part by encouraging fishing with pound traps. Although the bakufu did levy a tax on pound-trap use as a way to compensate gill-netters for their losses, it clearly considered the welfare of individual small fishers to be secondary to its goal of expanding the fishery as a whole.

A major consequence of the rise of the pound-trap fishery was the emergence of large, independent fishers as an intermediate stratum between the contractors and ordinary gill-netters. Possession of the new technology put large independents in a position to challenge the monopoly on political and economic authority enjoyed by contractors at their fisheries.[73] For example, in 1858 a group of fourteen independent operators at the Yoichi fishery submitted a document to the bakufu post there concerning the use of pound traps at the fishery. Twelve years earlier they had received permission from the Matsumae domain to use large nets on a limited scale, but now they wanted to have most of the restrictions lifted. In exchange, the pound-trap operators promised to make payments to resident gill-net fishers in the event of a large pound-trap catch and to supply loans of gill nets to fishers who lost their gear during inclement weather. Moreover, they pledged to refrain from activity that interfered with the livelihoods of local Wajin and Ainu and to move their families from the Wajinchi to Yoichi as soon as possible. The agreement was accompanied by a document signed by five representatives of resident Wajin fishers acquiescing to the expansion of the pound-trap fishery.[74]

Tajima Yoshiya sees the agreement as an attempt by the pound-trap fishers to gain a voice in the operation of the contract fishery commensurate with their economic power.[75] But the price of that new voice was a responsibility for the welfare of gill-netters not borne by the contractor himself. Hayashi Chōzaemon, in a document presented to the bakufu in 1856, promised only that he would continue to make waterfront land available for small fishers and aid them in other ways so that everyone could "go about his business in peace."[76] No doubt the welfare provisions were added to the independent fishers' agreement in deference to the net slashers from the Wajinchi, but the only thing the eight villages involved in the net-cutting incident got out of it was a share of the use tax paid by pound-trap fishers everywhere. Indeed, there was an important difference between the three-ryō pound-trap tax and the provisions of the Yoichi agreement: while the use tax represented compensation for the decline of the Wajinchi fishery, the Yoichi agreement called for a distribution of dividends to resident fishers regardless of the state of the gill-net fishery. Formally, independent pound-trap operators and gill-netters were social equals, so there should have been no reason for the pound-trap fishers either to assume responsibility for foul weather or to distribute a portion of their income to gill-netters who may themselves have enjoyed a large catch. Clearly, then, the pound-trap fishers' rights and responsibilities stemmed solely from their possession of a highly productive, new technology.

Hayashi Chōzaemon did not like the intrusion of the fourteen new pound-trap fishers onto his turf, but he seems to have resigned himself to their presence without much of a struggle.[77] In other instances contractors tried to make entrepreneurial fishers assume part of the financial burden of maintaining a contract fishery. For example, in 1866 the contractor of the Isoya and Utasutsu fisheries, Satō Eiemon, wrote to his colleague at Hamamashike, Nakagawaya Yūsuke, suggesting that he raise the use tax for pound traps at Hamamashike from three to six ryō and use the additional revenue to cover a substantial increase in the contracting fee (*unjōkin*) assessed by the Shōnai domain. Eiemon justified the action by citing a similar move at the nearby Mashike fishery.[78] Since payment of the fee was the principal source of the contractors' legitimacy, Eiemon's proposal was tantamount to franchising the contracting institution out among all local pound-trap fishers.

In conclusion, the emergence of the pound-trap fishery had a twofold effect on the development of social relations in the Hokkaido fishery. First, it made it easier for independent fishers with substantial operations to challenge the monopoly on economic power held by the merchants who ran the contract fisheries. As we shall see in detail below, independent pound-trap fishers fought successfully to secure the right to market their own produce, which undermined the contractors' local political authority. This move had a liberating effect on all fishers because it reduced even if it did not eliminate their dependence on the contractors. As a result, both population and general economic activity increased greatly in what were now becoming permanent fishing villages on the coast of Hokkaido. For example, in 1848—just a few years after the introduction of pound traps—Iwanai had a population of 1,940 and all the comforts of home: a school (*terakoya*), a brothel, and three shops selling foodstuffs, sake, and dry goods.[79] Earlier all such enterprise (with the possible exception of prostitution) would have been managed by the contractor's store (*unjōya*).

If the first effect of the development of the pound trap was to undermine the political structure of the fishery, the second was to encourage socioeconomic stratification. Rather than dealing with a single merchant, small fishers in the Ezochi now faced the collective power of a group of pound-trap operators—some of whom held offices in Wajinchi villages—who acted not out of responsibility to the domain but rather in their own economic interests.[80] However, the pound-trap fishery did not perforce result in the economic differentiation of herring fishers into a small group with control over its means of production and a larger group without because growth in the pound-trap fishery did not necessarily entail the exploitation of gill-net fishers. But it did facilitate differentiation later in the century because it provided an outlet for the labor of proletarianized gill-netters and tenant farmers from northern Honshu. Ironically, the ascendancy of independent pound-trap fishers was short-lived because in the Meiji period the fishery came to be dominated by men who had made their fortunes in commerce and turned to fishing as a speculative investment.

Capital

Setting up as a herring fisher was a simple matter. All one needed was a small boat, a few sets of gill nets and other gear, access to land for processing the catch, and the labor of two or three able-bodied workers. The biggest problem was securing enough cash, foodstuffs, and other necessities to support oneself until the end of the season and the income that that brought. Fishers in Hokkaido could outfit themselves with their own funds, seek credit from merchants in the Wajinchi, or borrow from contractors in the Ezochi. Self-financing was obviously the most attractive option, but it was available only to that small minority of fishers with large sums of money. Therefore almost all fishers relied on credit from merchants or contractors. Receiving funding from Wajinchi merchants was preferable to borrowing from contractors because it permitted the fisher to retain more options in choosing a fishing site. The clients of Wajinchi merchants could remain at home or "chase herring" (*oinishin*) up the coast as they saw fit; even if they became indigent, they retained more flexibility than fishers left to the mercy of a single contractor. "Flexibility," however, could mean little more than a choice between surrendering a child to indentured servitude or flight.[81]

Supply merchants (*shikomi oyakata*) in the Wajinchi provided loans to fishers before each season and in return claimed substantial interest and fees as well as first lien on the catch, which they bought below the prevailing market price. It was a lucrative livelihood. Hezutsu Tōsaku, a visitor to Matsumae in the 1780s, described the merchants in this way:

> Whatever the fishers catch immediately goes over to merchants, who buy and sell among themselves to set a market price. . . . The merchants receive twenty percent interest from fishers, who put up their houses, storehouses, land, and other things to get loans, but after taking another twenty percent of the return on sales, they end up with profits of nearly fifty percent. In this way merchants from outside make themselves rich in just a short while.[82]

Supply merchants generally ran businesses related to some aspect of the herring fishery, such as fertilizer brokering or shipping, or were themselves large fishery operators. Contractors holding fisheries in the Ezochi supplied small fishers active in areas under their control; for many of them this part of their business was considerably more profitable than fishing itself.[83] When the fishing was good the relationship between a supply merchant and his client worked to their mutual advantage. Even after surrendering up to half of his catch in taxes, interest, and fees, a fisher would still have enough to live on for the rest of the year. But it only took one bad season for the system to catch small operators in a vicious circle of chronic debt—and bad seasons were common in the volatile herring fishery. Consequently, very few fishers were ever free of debt. Credit relations of this sort were by no means unique to Hokkaido but instead were common to fisheries throughout Japan and elsewhere.[84]

The Kishida house of Esashi was a major supplier of funds to fishers in the western part of the Wajinchi. The family moved from Noto to Matsumae in the late seventeenth century and by the 1750s was the most prominent merchant house in Esashi. The Kishida house served as official purveyor (*goyōtashi*) to the domain and participated in a number of commercial and financial ventures, including a revolving-credit association (*mujinkō*), but its main business was shipping.[85] Shipping and supplying credit to fishers went hand in hand because shippers involved in the Japan Sea trade usually purchased their cargoes rather than carry freight for a set rate.[86] Getting first lien on their clients' catches therefore assured the family of a steady supply of merchandise to market in Honshu.

An examination of promissory notes received by the Kishida house between 1790 and 1870 reveals much about the nature of credit relations in the Wajinchi.[87] The house had a varied clientele, ranging from petty producers to small merchants who themselves lent funds to fishers in outlying villages. The loans reflected this variety, with the smallest under the 3 to 5 ryō it cost to hire one worker for a season and the largest over 200 ryō.

Borrowing from a supply merchant was expensive. The fisher paid the cost of the loan, which included interest plus commissions taken by the supply merchant upon delivery of commodities and receipt of the herring catch. Interest was usually set at twenty percent per annum, which was above both the twelve-percent rate sanctioned by the bakufu and the ten to fifteen percent that Ronald Toby estimates was typical elsewhere for retail loans, though still within the normal range of practice. The promissory notes in the Kishida collection did not usually stipulate the price to be paid for the catch, but when they did it was five percent below the (presumably local) market rate. Prices charged by all supply merchants for commodities were similarly several percent above normal market rates.[88]

Fishers risked long-term debt or loss of their means of production every time they took out a loan. It was inevitable that they would sometimes find themselves unable to settle their accounts at the end of the season because they had to make heavy outlays of cash for foodstuffs, gear, and advances to workers months before they had any clue as to the outcome of the catch. And of course buying dear and selling cheap—on top of interest and taxes—did not make things any easier for small operators. In about two-thirds of the loan documents included in the Kishida sample fishers offered some sort of collateral, such as labor services, land, buildings, boats, or gear, to offset the risk of the loan. Generally, fishers offered labor services and real estate as collateral for small loans and boats and gear for larger ones. This arrangement no doubt reflects the level of resources held by borrowers. The smallest fishers—who took out the smallest loans—often did not own the gear to offer as security in the first place; and all fishers were reluctant to risk waterfront land as collateral (it is mentioned in only four cases in the sample) because it was the one essential item in the fishery that did not depreciate in value. However, Kishida apparently did not hesitate to claim land from defaulting clients and then rent it back or sell it to third parties for up to 430 ryō. Clearly, however, Kishida's evaluation of the credit-worthiness of individual clients was in the end the most significant factor in determining the amount of collateral. For example, in 1830, a fisher had to offer fifty sets of nets, his house and land, and a medium-sized boat to secure a loan of ten ryō and six bales of rice; in 1845, however, another fisher had to put up only fifty sets of nets as collateral for a 100-ryō loan.

Although supply merchants had the option of confiscating all or part of the security put up by defaulting debtors, they usually added the shortfall to the next season's debt rather than foreclose. Thus twenty-six of the sixty-six loans listed in Table 5 are renegotiations of old debts. For example, one Ryūjirō of Tazawa village, finding himself unable to repay a six-ryō loan taken out in 1829, was allowed to renegotiate a new debt of nine and one-third ryō the following year, but only after he surrendered a small boat that he had bought for one ryō.[89] After a number of years clients sometimes accumulated debts far beyond their ability to repay, as in the case of one Riemon, who was nearly 1,816 ryō in debt to Kishida in 1847. The merchant forgave all but 715 ryō of the debt, of which Riemon paid 50 ryō down and promised to return 35 ryō per year for nineteen years, apparently without interest. Riemon missed several subsequent payments, however, so Kishida agreed to yet another renegotiation in the apparently vain hope of getting his money back.[90]

Credit relations at the contract fisheries worked in much the same way

TABLE 5

LOANS OWED TO THE KISHIDA HOUSE, 1789–1868

Amount (ryō)[a]	Number[b]
0–10	10 (2)
10–19	11 (2)
20–99	23 (6)
100–199	11 (8)
200 and up	11 (8)
Total	66 (26)

SOURCE: "Kishida San'emon monjo: Ryōke shikomi," ECS, 2: 1070–1233.
[a]All debts have been converted to approximate gold equivalents:
  Gold-copper conversion: 1 ryō = 6 kan 800 mon
  Gold-silver conversion: 1 ryō = 60 monme
Original denominations of loans:
  Gold: 41 (62%)
  Copper: 14 (21%)
  Mixed: 9 (14%)
  Silver: 2 (3%)
[b]Renegotiated loans in parentheses.

as in the Wajinchi, except that contractors could levy an access fee from all independent fishers on top of other interest and commissions assessed in connection with the provisioning of supplies. The access fee, which was ten percent at a few relatively unproductive fisheries below the Shakotan peninsula and twenty percent elsewhere, symbolized the political authority of the contractors. The combination of this political authority with the monopoly on local economic activity enjoyed by the contractors ensured that the bonds of dependency tying fisher to creditor were even stronger than in the Wajinchi. Accordingly, independent fishers in the Ezochi tended to be either entrepreneurs with substantial operations (often including pound traps) who could afford the high overhead costs of fishing away from home or marginal family fishers who, lured to the Ezochi by the prospect of better catches than at home, could not afford to leave. Contractors cut off many of the marginal fishers, so that in the 1850s hundreds of fisher families found themselves stranded in the Ezochi without the wherewithal to return home or even to fish because they owned no boats or gear of their own. These people were forced to turn to wage labor to support themselves; contractors even used them as a potential pool of workers to justify pound-trap fishing.[91]

While the smallest fishers at the contract fisheries had limited opportunities to resist the contractors, larger independents sometimes fought back. An example of the breakdown of the authority of contractors, which involved extending credit and controlling the marketing of independent fishers' catches, comes from the Hamamashike fishery during the period it was under the Shōnai domain. The problem started during preparations for the 1861 fishing season, when the contractor, Date Rin'emon, acting through two wholesalers in Fukuyama, suddenly cut off credit to independent fishers in Hamamashike.[92] Rin'emon, who was one of the largest merchants in the domain, apparently took this action out of concern that the increasingly close ties between independent fishers and shippers operating at his fishery were jeopardizing an important source of profits.[93] Although fishers at most contract fisheries had nominal control over the disposition of their catches, those at Hamamashike and fisheries to the north had to sell all their produce to the contractor, regardless of the source of their capital. This requirement forced them to seek credit from the contractor or his agents. The contractor's tight control over capital severely constrained the operations of large independent fishers.

The dispute at Hamamashike was precipitated by an attempt by independent fishers to capitalize on a provision in their credit agreement with Rin'emon that permitted their Wajin employees to sell small amounts of fish (which represented a wage bonus tied to productivity) directly to shippers. Independent fishers and shippers took advantage of this loophole to trade in herring meal and other commodities. His monopsonistic rights thus threatened, Rin'emon apparently decided to teach the independent fishers a lesson.

The independent fishers resisted as well as they could. They managed to scrape together enough funds to take small crews to Hamamashike in 1861, but they knew they would not be able to last long without credit. They also knew that no one would give them credit unless they had control over the disposition of their catch. Accordingly, a group of fishers petitioned the Shōnai domain's local intendant for permission to sell the first seventy-five tons of fish they produced (less the twenty percent access fee and other levies) at their own discretion; anything above seventy-five tons they would sell to the contractor. Unfortunately, the independent fishers' petition drive failed because all requests to the domain had to go through an intermediate authority—Date Rin'emon.

In his own defense, the contractor admitted to lending money to the Fukuyama wholesalers but denied having any control over the merchants' lending activities. He could not assume responsibility for supplying the fishers, he said, because he made it a policy not to have financial dealings with petty producers, other than to make occasional small advances of commodities during the fishing season. Finally, he pointed out that the fishers should have known about his monopsony before they set up their operations in Hamamashike. In short, if they did not like the way he did business, that was just too bad.

In 1865 Date Rin'emon forfeited his contracting rights after a dispute with Shōnai officials over the contracting fee. The independent fishers at Hamamashike soon began pressuring Shōnai officials and Rin'emon's successor, Nakagawaya Yūsuke, for rights to market their own produce, even though Yūsuke was prepared to provide them with funds and supplies. The Shōnai authorities, eager to encourage independent fishers to come to Hamamashike, decided to end the contractor's monopsony. They did, however, allow Yūsuke to appropriate five percent of each independent fisher's catch as compensation for his loss of business.[94]

Yūsuke's business advisor and fellow contractor, Satō Eiemon, lobbied vigorously to have the change rescinded. Like Rin'emon, he argued that a free market at Hamamashike went against all precedent. He added that since he and Yūsuke had already placed supply orders with Kinai merchants on behalf of the independent fishers, they stood to lose a considerable amount of money if the fishers did not borrow from them.[95] Eiemon gave up only after he learned that the Hamamashike intendant of the Shōnai domain had already ordered Yūsuke to accept the change.[96]

The independent fishers at Hamamashike won more than just control over their credit relations when they received the right to market their own produce. Their victory eliminated a barrier to capitalist production in the fishery because it made it difficult for the contractor to use credit as a means to restrict the size of the operations of local independent fishers. Thanks to the growing activity of independent shippers in the western Ezochi, fishers had a ready market for their goods.[97] The same shippers were also a source of credit to supplement or even supplant the supply loans of the contractor. Free access to markets and hence credit made it easier for fishers to acquire the technology and labor necessary to move to capitalist production.

The conflict at Hamamashike also demonstrates that the credit relations between a contractor or supply merchant and a fisher were part of a network that connected the fishery in Hokkaido with merchant houses in Ōmi, Osaka, and many points along the Japan Sea shipping routes and even deep into the interior. For example, a study of Fukaura in Tsugaru has shown that behind a lively trade in herring meal, rice, sake, and cloth in the port itself was an elaborate network of local merchants that oversaw distribution to the surrounding countryside.[98]

The relationship between a supply merchant and his client was always asymmetrical, with the merchant clearly dominant. Yet changes in the structure of the fishery profoundly affected the way that relationship operated in practice. During the period of the commercial fishery, supply merchants in the Wajinchi and their clients were mutually dependent. Fishers needed credit to pursue their living, and merchants needed fish and fish by-products to pursue theirs. The organization of the fishery before the emergence of capitalist production left few alternatives to long-term credit relations. Merchants who traded but did not produce had to assure themselves of access to their clients' catches by extending credit. Acts of magnanimity like renegotiating or even forgiving part of a debt (much of which represented back interest anyway) no doubt lent the supply merchant an air of benevolent paternalism that veiled his fundamental vulnerability.

The credit relations practiced by Wajinchi supply merchants survived until the emergence of the pound-trap fishery because, until the use of Wajin wage labor became widespread, there was no way systematically to proletarianize insolvent fishers. After the emergence of capitalist production in the fishery, however, creditors were themselves increasingly involved in production and therefore did not depend so heavily on petty producers for commodities to market. Entrepreneurial fisher-creditors could take their relations with small fishers a step beyond the credit dependency of merchant capital to the wage dependency of capitalist relations of production. In other words, it was in the interest of Wajinchi-based merchants to see their clients maintain control over their productive activities only so long as domination occurred at the point of exchange not of production. Creditors who themselves maintained significant fishery operations were under no such constraint: they could freely transfer the locus of domination from exchange (credit) to production (wage labor) by forcing defaulting clients to work for wages at their fisheries. The shift was particularly smooth in the fishery because employment for wages was itself treated as a credit transaction in which workers borrowed their wages several months in advance and repaid the debt in "kind"—that is, through labor at the creditor's fishery. The only thing that stopped a supply merchant like Kishida San'emon from demanding the services of more defaulting fishers was his own inability to use the labor.

The impact on petty fishers of this reallocation of credit is clear. During the commercial phase of the fishery small producers benefited from the fact that creditors had no strong motivation to foreclose on them; they sacrificed control over the disposition of their produce—but not control over production itself—in exchange for the security that they would not be forced under after a bad season or two. When work for wages emerged as an alternative to petty production, small fishers' independence was threatened. They apparently recognized the threat: resident fishers forced pound-trap operators in Yoichi to provide them with gill nets after storms as a way to preserve their independence and guard against their own proletarianization. Participation in credit relations (borrowing gear after a storm) insured them against becoming part of the pool of potential labor for the pound-trap fishery.

Changes in the distribution of credit were exacerbated by political developments at the end of the Tokugawa period, as seen in the effect of the second bakufu takeover of Hokkaido on residents of the Wajinchi. The bakufu assumed direct administration of villages in the vicinity of Hakodate and west of Esashi, while the rest of the Wajinchi was left to the Matsumae domain. Residents of towns and villages still under Matsumae control were hurt by the bakufu's announcement that it would allow direct shipments (*jikiho*) of commodities from some bakufu-controlled areas of the Wajinchi and Ezochi to markets in Honshu, thus bypassing the Matsumae customs offices in Fukuyama, Esashi, and Hakodate. Although the reform made for faster and cheaper marketing and thus promoted the overall economic development of Hokkaido, it deprived wholesalers and innkeepers of valuable business, especially in Fukuyama, which did not have a good enough harbor to sustain shipping without official protection. Fishers in the Matsumae territories were hurt indirectly because bad times for Fukuyama merchants meant more expensive credit for them. Their response was to appeal twice to the bakufu and other outside authorities to return the Matsumae house to power.

The first appeal came in the summer of 1855, shortly after the bakufu annexed most of the island. Encouraged by the recent success of Shōnai peasants in preventing the transfer of their daimyo, nearly one hundred representatives of Wajinchi villages went to Sendai in several groups to ask that domain to lend its good offices to the restoration of the Matsumae house.[99] When the Sendai daimyo and his retinue went to Edo that autumn the petitioners followed him to the capital. There, Hisasue Zen'emon, the headman of Kaminokuni village, is said to have attempted a direct appeal (*jikiso*) to a senior councilor.[100] Although the movement was not successful in securing the reinstatement of the Matsumae domain, it did achieve the next best thing, maintenance of the customs offices in the three principal ports.

The second round of appeals was similar in intent to the first but was, if anything, even more spirited. Beginning at the end of 1859 and continuing into the following summer, groups of Matsumae villagers organized large demonstrations in Fukuyama, while others traveled to Edo and each of the six Tōhoku domains that had received parcels of territory in the Ezochi, again asking that the Matsumae house be restored or, at the very least, that the integrity of the contract fisheries and customs houses be protected. According to perhaps apocryphal reports, petitioners made five separate attempts at direct appeal to high bakufu officials, including the shogunal regent Ii Naosuke himself, despite the efforts of Matsumae officials in Edo to prevent them. In any case, they again failed in their principal goal but did get assurances that the contract fisheries and customs offices would not be touched by the Tōhoku domains.[101]

Suzuki Takahiro suspects that the domain and leading merchants orchestrated both protest movements and that the ordinary villagers involved "were nothing more than the puppets of privileged capital."[102] Moriya Yoshimi agrees that Matsumae officials and merchants may have been involved, though he rejects Suzuki's conclusion that the villagers were simply tricked into following along.[103] The behavior of fishers in and around Fukuyama certainly suggests that they were not mere dupes.

In the eleventh month of 1859 a group of contractors presented a petition asking that the Ezochi be left intact on the grounds that otherwise it would be difficult for them to guarantee supply loans for the following year (presumably because of their uncertainty regarding the future of contracting). The merchants stood to gain nothing directly from the fishers through this action, though they of course realized that suspending credit to small fishers was tantamount to destroying the economy of the territory left to the Matsumae domain. Perhaps they were trying to goad the bakufu into action; instead they aroused the ire of the people of Fukuyama. The next month, just as leading wholesalers (*ton'ya*) announced that they too would suspend credit to small fishers, a group of Fukuyama townspeople demanded that Fujino Kihei, a leading contractor, supply rations for the eight thousand expected participants in a demonstration to restore the domain. The townspeople also asked contractors to comply with a "general strike"—a suspension of all commercial transactions, monetary exchange, production at the contract fisheries, and travel outside Hokkaido—until the crisis was resolved. Hayashi Chōzaemon and others were warned that a large crowd of people would present itself at their homes if compliance was not forthcoming. The contractors reluctantly agreed to curtail their activities, though the economy did not shut down completely. The situation was not defused until early the following year, when word was received that the bakufu would not close the contract fisheries and, more importantly, Matsumae officials persuaded merchants to provide loans to small fishers.[104]

Clearly, if the contractors had been trying to manipulate ordinary fishers, their plan backfired seriously. Still, the confrontation between fishers and contractors in Fukuyama does not explain the behavior of the village officials and other leading citizens who ventured to Tōhoku and Edo in support of the domain. Suzuki and Moriya treat events in Fukuyama and Honshu as two facets of the same episode, but it is better to distinguish between small fishers, who relied on credit every winter to finance their operations, and larger fishers and village officials, who both borrowed from contractors and leading merchants and lent to smaller fishers. Ordinary villagers originally saw restoration of the Matsumae domain as the key to stability and steady credit but did not allow themselves to be bullied by the contractors. However, village officials had more to lose through the transfer of the Matsumae house and the dismemberment of the Ezochi. Not only was their political authority in jeopardy, but their economic power over other villagers would be endangered if fishers entered into economic relationships with shippers and other merchants not connected to either Fukuyama or contracting capital. In that sense, it appears that petitioners like Hisasue Zen'emon were not acting as mere proxies of the contractors; rather, their interests and the contractors' happened to coincide.

For small fishers, the protest movements served two purposes. First, most immediately, they were an attempt to forestall the reallocation of credit to the emerging capitalist fishery. Independent pound-trap fishers building capitalist fishing operations in the Ezochi stood to benefit from the bakufu's policy of allowing direct trade between the Ezochi and Honshu. Conversely, small fishers saw that ensuring a steady flow of credit into the Wajinchi was their best chance to maintain their own fishing operations, free from the control of entrepreneurs up the coast; the Matsumae domain, with its vested interest in the economic vitality of the Wajinchi, was their ally in this endeavor.

Second, the village officials who led the petition movement were concerned to preserve their own position as intermediate providers of capital. They did not want to compete with shippers or other new sources of credit. They stood to lose whether small fishers succumbed to proletarianization at the hands of capitalist fishers in the Ezochi or somehow managed to secure credit from shippers or others not linked to the Matsumae domain.

In sum, credit was the lifeblood of the commercial fishery. Creditors fulfilled a vital function in the local economy, and it would be unfair to dismiss them as a group as predatory usurers. Indeed, Toby argues that the growth of local credit markets in the early nineteenth century, facilitated by an evolution from simple money lending to genuine banking, contributed importantly to proto-industrialization by making it easier for entrepreneurs to gain access to capital to invest in production.[105] Although it is impossible to say whether true banking had emerged in the Hokkaido fishery by the end of the Tokugawa era, there is no question that without the credit networks that linked small fishers to supply lenders and contractors, and in turn tied Hokkaido merchants to fertilizer wholesalers in Ōmi and Osaka (not to mention the credit relations that helped get herring meal from wholesalers to consumers), the fishery would not have been a viable enterprise.

The transformation of credit relations in the Hokkaido fishery, seen in a positive light, served as a catalyst of growth. After the emergence of the pound-trap fishery, credit became less a means of sustaining long-term patron-client relations between supply merchants and small fishers and more a positive force behind the growth of entrepreneurial activity. The fishing economy grew as large, independent fishers invested in pound traps, which were far more productive, and hence more capital-efficient, than the gill nets favored by household fishers. By denying small, inefficient producers access to funds, creditors reduced the wasteful duplication of resources and effort that necessarily accompanied the household production of gill-netters and instead helped to consolidate production into increasingly large and efficient units.

This positive assessment, however, should be qualified. Unlike the situation in agricultural districts such as the one studied by Toby, the use of credit in the Hokkaido fishery was universal and therefore not necessarily either an act of desperation or a sign of entrepreneurial vigor. If, despite their chronic indebtedness, small fishers could claim a "right" to continued credit, the realignment of credit relations represented a serious breach of trust. Conversely, seeing each annual renegotiation as a discrete expression of the creditor's benevolence makes the denial of credit after the emergence of the pound trap a neutral act. The small fishers who protested when merchants threatened to withhold credit acted as if they perceived a "right" to continued credit. Or, to rephrase in the idiom of Tokugawa society, the fishers seemed to feel that the supply lenders had an "obligation" to provide credit. In any event, clearly the reorientation of the credit market after the emergence of the pound-trap fishery

was particularly disruptive because it made continued production difficult for small fishers who might otherwise have been able to continue to
fish independently.

Indigenous Capitalism and the Meiji Restoration

Capitalism had emerged in the Hokkaido fishery by the end of the Tokugawa period—but just barely. A fisher surveying the social and economic
structure of his world in 1867 might not have foreseen the fundamental
changes that it would eventually undergo. To be sure, he would have recognized differences from a generation or two before: the Matsumae domain had been reduced to a token stretch of coast in southern Hokkaido,
supplanted elsewhere by the bakufu and its proxies; the number of people
coming from Honshu to work in the fishery had increased tremendously,
with more arriving all the time; and a new technology had transformed
the face of production at many fishing grounds. Moreover, sporadic, but
often intense, conflict—net cuttings, mass meetings, foreclosed debts—in-
dicated that all was not well in the fishery. Still, if a revolution was in the
works, it was an inchoate one. After all, most resident Wajin fishers still
lived in the Wajinchi and worked on small gill-netting teams. Contractors remained dominant at the Ezochi fisheries, even if their economic
power and political authority were waning. "Proletarianization" was not
yet a word in anyone's vocabulary.

But however scattered and disjointed they may have appeared at the
time, the changes were indeed coming together to alter the structure of
economy and society in Hokkaido. These profound developments were
not more readily apparent to the people involved because state institutions had yet to be transformed in a basic way. The groundwork had
been laid however. After assuming administration of most of the island in
1855, the bakufu and Tōhoku domains implemented a number of policies—some new, others based on measures previously instituted by the
Matsumae domain—that encouraged the emergence of capitalist production. They permitted use of the pound trap as well as the direct marketing of produce to shippers venturing into the Ezochi; they allowed
fishers to migrate beyond the Wajinchi and fish with a measure of freedom from the control of contractors. In short, they weakened the two
critical supports of the feudal polity in Hokkaido: the contract-fishery
system and the insularity of the Ezochi. These policies alone were not
enough to alter the basic structure of the fishery, but they did anticipate
the more thorough institutional reforms of the Meiji period, which then
assured the supremacy of capitalist production.

This view of the origins of capitalism in Hokkaido raises vexing questions concerning the role of economic change in bringing about the Meiji Restoration. It seems more than simply fortuitous that a state dedicated to rapid economic development came along just as a critical realignment of the economy was occurring. However, the reactionary demeanor of many key activists makes the Restoration an unlikely bourgeois revolution, complete or otherwise.[106] In Hokkaido, at least, the quiescence of the population during the Restoration years likewise precludes positing a direct, causal relationship between the economic transformation of the fishery and the political transformation of the state. Yet the fact remains that the new regime oversaw a revolutionary transfiguration of Japanese society.

Any interpretation of the material bases of the Meiji Restoration is ultimately tied to one's assessment of the Tokugawa economy's ability to adapt to structural change. The bakuhan system was surprisingly supple after all: the evolution of the contract-fishery system is proof of that. Moreover, as Edward Pratt's analysis of several silk and cotton textile regions and Luke Roberts's study of mercantilism in the Tosa domain reveal, political authorities throughout Japan had reconciled themselves to commercial expansion by the middle of the eighteenth century. Instead of trying to restrict or even prohibit commerce, a number of domains implemented policies designed to harness markets and exchange to serve political ends.[107]

But an accommodation to commercial expansion is not the same as an accommodation to capitalism because commercialization is compatible with feudal institutions in a way that capitalist development is not. The rent-seeking conservatism of the contract-fishery operators once again exemplifies this difference, as does the behavior of merchants and officials studied by Pratt and Roberts. Pratt sees the rural elite, the *gōnō*, as "a transitional class," a product of the proto-industrialization of the late Tokugawa period whose functions in agriculture and industry were later assumed by landlords and true capitalists, respectively.[108] Similarly, Roberts's mercantilists in Tosa formulated an ideology of the domain's "national" prosperity (*kokueki*) that represented a significant advance over an older subsumption of the domain's interests within those of its daimyo. National-prosperity thought was progressive in its historical context, but it was an ideology predicated on the preservation of the existing feudal political structure.[109] In short, the sorts of economic and social change seen in Hokkaido and elsewhere throughout the country in the early nineteenth century emerged "naturally" out of the Tokugawa feudal structure but could not be completely contained within it. Change thus contributed importantly not only to the downfall of the bakuhan system but to the formation of the new order that succeeded it as well.

Tokugawa feudalism died giving birth to Meiji capitalism. Seen in this light, the Meiji regime's policy of rapid industrialization was more than just an astute ad hoc strategy to avoid Western domination; it was the next logical stage of economic development. In that sense, it *almost* did not matter what the self-avowed Imperial loyalists thought they were try-ing to achieve with their Restoration. Any attempt to preserve the basic economic and social structure of the Tokugawa state in a new guise— say, through the creation of a new bakufu led by Satsuma and Chōshū— was bound to fail because structural change had already rendered the old order obsolete. This was the case in areas of indigenous industrial devel-opment like Hokkaido, in regions linked through sericulture and other industries to the world market after the opening of the ports in the 1850s, and indeed throughout the country. The Meiji Restoration was as much the effect as the cause of change.

The capitalist transformation of the Hokkaido fishery was not the product of a single, tumultuous event. This is not really so surprising, es-pecially when we consider the role of proto-industrialization in Japan's structural transformation. The mere existence of rural manufacturing did not of itself cause capitalism; it did, however, open a window of op-portunity for the emergence of capitalism. Whether capitalist production actually arose or not hinged on the place of merchant capital in the feu-dal structure of a given location. In Hokkaido, merchant capital, as rep-resented by the contract-fishery operators, laid the groundwork for large-scale production but resisted taking the final step to capitalism. Once the series of changes set into motion by the influx of labor and adoption of new technology began, the contractors lost the initiative, and independent capitalist entrepreneurs appeared and eventually came to dominate the fishery.

Proto-industrialization did not lead inevitably to capitalism, however, so similar circumstances could culminate in very different results. A good example comes from the sardine fishery of Shingū, a community in north-ern Kyushu examined by Arne Kalland.[110] Like their counterparts in Hok-kaido, sardine fishers in Shingū processed their catches into commercial fertilizer. They shared Hokkaido fishers' need for credit and access to marketing networks, with the result that during the late Tokugawa period the fishery was dominated by merchants who ran large-scale fishing oper-ations with the financial and political backing of the Fukuoka domain.

As was the case with the contract-fishery operators, the merchants of

Shingū were conservative, eschewing the risks—and potential rewards—of capitalist production in favor of the relative security of money lending and commerce. After the Meiji Restoration, the merchants lost the support of the local authorities; when sardine catches began to fall during the following decades, many left fishing altogether. In contrast to the situation in Hokkaido, however, they were not replaced by a new class of capitalist entrepreneurs. Instead, the fishery reverted to small-scale, household-centered production, mostly for the large, urban market at nearby Fukuoka.

Whereas proto-industrialization in Hokkaido had led to capitalist development, Shingū deindustrialized. The depletion of the sardine stock, the proximity of a large, urban market for small fishers' catches, and a relatively egalitarian local culture (as reflected in inheritance patterns that discouraged the accumulation of wealth) all worked against the transformation of the Shingū fishery along the same lines as the Hokkaido fishery.

Still, the basic pattern of development seen in Shingū was identical to that in Hokkaido: the expansion of the commercial economy in the seventeenth and eighteenth centuries supported the rise of a vibrant proto-industrial complex of commodity production for distant markets, dominated by merchant capitalists who used their ties to the local feudal authorities to good advantage. As in Hokkaido, this pattern of proto-industrialization linked to feudal political institutions became unworkable by the mid-nineteenth century and collapsed once its political supports were removed. The only difference—albeit an extremely important one—was that a new, dynamic capitalist mode of production did not appear to take its place. But the fact that capitalism did not emerge in Shingū in the late nineteenth century does not undercut the significance of earlier developments. The potential for capitalist development was there even if an actual transformation did not take place.

In conclusion, if proto-industrialization was not the direct cause of capitalism in Japan, it was a symptom of stress in the structure of the feudal polity. This correlation is perhaps about as much as we can ask of the concept of proto-industrialization as an explanatory tool. After all, the push for structural transformation was not a foregone conclusion; the rent-seeking tendency of feudalism was much more the "natural" state of affairs.[111]

This view of the role of proto-industrialization in the emergence of capitalism not only contributes to our understanding of Japanese economic history but refines the proto-industrialization model as a theoretical construct as well. The emergence of capitalism from a proto-industrial base within the Hokkaido fishery, before the transformation of the Japanese economy as a whole, supports Jürgen Schlumbohm's character-ization of proto-industrialization as a process in which the structural transformation from feudalism to capitalism is played out in microcosm within a region.[112] In contrast, Schlumbohm's collaborators, Peter Kriedte and Hans Medick (as well as Franklin Mendels), see proto-industrializa-tion as an intermediate stage between feudalism and capitalism,[113] but the Hokkaido evidence, when seen in the light of cases like Shingū, does not support the teleology suggested by their model. Although the precon-ditions for Hokkaido's development as a proto-industrial region lay in the structure of Japanese feudalism and, moreover, capitalism could not have emerged in the fishery had it not undergone a proto-industrial stage first, there was nothing inevitable about the course of development in the industry.

Proto-industrialization in the Hokkaido fishery did not represent a distinct stage of historical development but rather consisted of a series of interrelated developments—in demand, labor, technology, capital, and state institutions—the net effect of which was to undermine feudalism and replace it with something new—capitalism. Until that theoretical magic moment when capitalism was born in Japan, the fishery was still very much part of the Tokugawa feudal economy, even as it served to undermine the social and economic foundations of that economy.

CHAPTER FOUR

The Institutions of a Capitalist Fishery

Todojima, Tanbakke, Chiyoshibetsu. These were the battlefields of the Ofuyu Incident, a bitter time of name-calling and rock-throwing that pitted the fishers of Hamamasu against those of Mashike in 1896.[1] The incident occurred on 21 May, when fishers from Hamamasu came upon a small fleet from Mashike as it was setting up pound traps in the waters near Todojima, a group of islets several hundred meters off Cape Ofuyu, at the border of Hamamasu and Mashike districts. According to one version of the story, the fishers from Hamamasu politely asked the poachers from Mashike to leave and the poachers readily complied, with not an angry word exchanged—the group from Hamamasu even helped short-handed crews bring in their gear. In another account, a flotilla of boats from Hamamasu descended upon innocent fishers from Mashike with a barrage of rocks—brought specially for the purpose—and, once their unfortunate victims had been rendered completely helpless, ripped out their nets and sent them paddling for the safety of home.

The incident itself was merely the high point of a long-standing dispute between the Hamamasu and Mashike fishing associations (*gyogyō kumiai*). Pound-trap operators from Hamamasu, who had been using Todojima and nearby grounds for fishing expeditions (*oinishin*) since the late 1880s, resented the competition when fishers from the neighboring district moved into the area. The violence—if indeed there was any violence—occurred even as leaders of the two associations negotiated over the fishing rights to the waters off Cape Ofuyu. Eventually officials from the outside were brought in as mediators, and in April 1898 the two groups agreed to make Todojima a common fishing ground (*iriai gyoba*),

93

available on a first-come-first-served basis to fishers from both districts. The Ofuyu Incident was not much of an incident, but it is the best known of a number of similar disputes over fishing rights between residents of adjoining districts. In fact, before the Ofuyu Incident the Hamamasu fishing association had already been involved in a dispute with its southern neighbor, Atsuta, in 1887–88, and the Mashike association had fought over fishing rights with its neighbor to the north, Rumoi, in 1891.[2] Under the Matsumae domain, villages and contract fisheries had occasionally been involved in border disputes, but only after the establishment of private rights to the sea during the Meiji period were such conflicts carried offshore. In the Tokugawa period fishers would not have fought over the right to fish at Todojima or Tanbakke—or anywhere for that matter—because access to the sea (if not the land adjacent to it) in Hokkaido, as in most Japanese fisheries, had been open to all.[3]

This chapter examines how a series of reforms undertaken by the Meiji state affirmed the primacy of the capitalist fishery. As we saw in the preceding chapter, social relations in the fishery had already begun to change well before the Restoration and no doubt would have continued to do so even had the political structure of the state not undergone such drastic alteration. But it is also true that the political changes of the Meiji period accelerated the pace of structural transformation in the fishing economy. Indeed, the state's policies—designed more than anything to increase the population of Hokkaido and raise the output of the fishery—worked so well that social relations had to play catch-up and change more rapidly than they might have otherwise.

There is no reason to believe that officials of the Development Agency (Kaitakushi) or other organs of the Meiji government thought in terms of establishing the capitalist mode of production in the fishery. The fishery was very much on the periphery of their plans, despite the fact that it was the island's most important industry throughout the nineteenth century and that Hokkaido had the largest fishery in Japan at the time. Rather, they sought to promote the development (*kaitaku*) of Hokkaido, which meant encouraging colonization (that is, agricultural immigration) and promoting industry (that is, mining and forestry).[4]

The state treated the fishery mostly as a convenient source of much-needed tax revenue, essential to support mass agricultural immigration and industrial development but not itself a central focus of policy. This approach struck Thomas Blakiston as irrational: "It seems evident . . . that attempts to plant purely agricultural settlements in Yezo before the coast becomes thickly inhabited by a permanent fishing population, is simply going against the ordinary desires of human nature."[5] The Development Agency imposed taxes that were onerous everywhere but especially heavy in southern Hokkaido, where the prospects for future development were dim. Marine-product taxes, which ranged from ten to twenty percent, were payable in kind at Hakodate. Fishers had to transport fertilizer for tax payments to government warehouses at considerable personal expense before the authorities would certify the rest of their catch for sale. To add insult to injury, the agency levied an export tax on all produce leaving Hokkaido. Taxes on marine products accounted for more than nine-tenths of all national taxes paid in Hokkaido in 1875, even though protests by fishers in Fukuyama and Esashi two years earlier had resulted in significant reductions.[6]

Given the state's concern for rapid economic development, it is natural that it favored the interests of entrepreneurial fishers, whose large-scale operations were clearly better suited to the state's goals than the household production of gill-netters. While it is true that the growth of the fishery during the latter part of the nineteenth century brought short-term material benefits to gill-netters as well as to pound-trap operators, the long-range effect was to open the door to the proletarianization of small fishers. This proletarianization occurred because the creation of a rational structure of land tenure and fishing rights, while essential for sustained economic growth, made it easy for people with a background in commerce but not in fishing to become pound-trap operators. Had there been no geographical or ecological limits to the fishery's expansion this might have worked out well for everyone, but in fact the major fishing grounds were fully occupied before the end of the nineteenth century. The control of fishing rights in productive areas then became a zero-sum game, with someone—often a gill-netter—being squeezed out every time a new merchant decided to try his luck at herring fishing.

The new regime's first significant reform was to eliminate the formal distinction between Ainu and non-Ainu Japanese. The Ainu became "former aborigines" (*kyūdojin*), free to come and go as they wished—and free to work for wages just like Wajin. The Meiji state's fundamental policy toward the Ainu people was to deny the validity of their ethnicity and to remake them in the image of the Japanese. This policy continued and expanded upon an assimilation program pursued by the bakufu since 1855. In practical terms, the state pressured the Ainu to adopt Japanese names, clothing, and hairstyles, learn the Japanese language, and, when feasible, take up farming. This policy culminated in the 1899 enactment of the despised Law for the Protection of Former Hokkaido

Aborigines (*Hokkaidō kyūdojin hogohō*), which remains on the books in revised form to this day.[7]

The Meiji state's policies toward the Ainu had undeniably tragic results: the Ainu language is for all practical purposes dead, the culture is moribund, and the thirty thousand or so people who identify today as Ainu are subjected to considerable discrimination.[8] In the narrow context of the herring fishery, however, the new regime's denial of the Ainu's ethnicity was, if anything, a positive development. Permitting the Ainu to work under the same conditions as Wajin undermined the systematic abuse that had characterized ethnic relations in the contract fisheries.[9] Of course, the Ainu's proletarianization was a "positive" development only because the ability of Ainu society to function independently had been so thoroughly compromised during centuries of contact with the Japanese that a return to self-sufficiency was out of the question. In light of the damage that had already been done, any policy that put an end to the unspeakable treatment of Ainu labor was necessarily a step forward.

The Meiji state's policy of treating the Ainu legally as ordinary Japanese subjects eliminated the contract fisheries' raison d'etre. By removing the last vestige of the fiction that trade with the Ainu was the purpose of the contracting institution, the new regime in effect opened the coasts of Hokkaido to anyone who could afford to fish. Not surprisingly, giving the coast back to the Ainu was never a consideration. But in any case, as we have already seen, the traditional Hokkaido Ainu ecosystem was centered on river systems, not the sea; very few Hokkaido Ainu had lived on the coast before they were drawn there by work in the contract fisheries.[10]

Still, an enlightened administration might have provided the Ainu with assistance in establishing themselves as independent fishers or at least given them preferential access to waterfront land. The failure of the new regime to do either was a source of dissatisfaction to many Ainu. However, Meiji officials were more concerned to make the Ainu into farmers than to keep them in the fishery. Some Ainu, such as those in the kelp fishery of northeastern Hokkaido, managed nevertheless to establish independent or communal fishing operations, while many others worked for wages in the herring fishery.[11] But, in any event, the Ainu's ethnicity lost the political significance it had had during the Tokugawa period.

Between 1869 and 1876, the state abolished the contracting system itself and revoked the privileges enjoyed by the contractors. This process was completed with the application of the land-tax reform to Hokkaido, which recognized private rights to waterfront land (*kaisan kanba*), essential for processing the herring catch into fertilizer, throughout the island. Although fishers in the western Wajinchi had recognized private ownership of waterfront land since the late seventeenth century, elsewhere land either had been communal (as in the southern Wajinchi) or had come under the authority of the local contractor (as in the Ezochi).

Allowing individuals exclusive rights to waterfront land was the initial step in a process that ultimately made fishing rights a commodity. The second step in that direction was the government's creation, between 1884 and 1886, of fishing associations empowered to regulate the entry of fishers from the outside into local grounds. Conflicts like the Ofuyu Incident resulted when the new associations tried to formalize their rights to rich fisheries. Finally, in 1901, the authorities applied the national fishery law to Hokkaido. This law permitted fishers to mortgage their fishing rights and gave legal sanction to the already well-established practice of selling and leasing rights to fish and to utilize both a fixed area of the sea and the adjoining waterfront land.[12]

Property Rights and Fishing Rights

The contract-fishery system was the most obvious impediment to the Meiji government's plans for the development of the Hokkaido economy. Although it had weakened considerably during the second period of bakufu administration (1855–68), the institution still stood as a barrier to the growth of the fishery in the former Ezochi.[13] The Development Agency tried to abolish contracting in the ninth month of 1869, declaring that it was "unbecoming their status" (*meibun ni oite yoroshikarazu*) for merchants to exercise authority over the land and people.[14] However, it ran into such strong protests from the contractors—whose support was crucial if the new regime was to establish a secure basis of authority in Hokkaido—that it partially rescinded the order just a month later. In the end only a few east-coast contractors lost their fisheries outright.

In declaring their opposition to the Development Agency's policy, the contractors warned that the whole economy of the island would collapse if their position were undermined. But in fact the abolition of contracting did not disrupt the economic lifeline of the fishery, which was the flow of credit from Honshu fertilizer brokers to small fishers via the contractors. And because the contractors had never been conscientious guardians of Ainu welfare, that cause was not jeopardized either. Indeed, the decline of the native population under the contracting system had been so acute that the new government felt compelled to forbid pregnant Ainu women to work and to require the registration of all workers over the age of eighty (if any!).[15]

The compromise policy eventually adopted by the Development

Agency was to designate most contractors "fishery operators" (*gyoba-mochi*) and allow them to retain many of the privileges they had enjoyed under the Matsumae domain. However, actual application of the reform varied considerably in response to local conditions.[16] Most contractors received appointments as Development Agency officials and continued to fish and supply goods to small fishers as they had before. However, because they had to recruit workers on the open labor market and could no longer collect a twenty-percent tax from independent operators, many former contractors found that business was not nearly as profitable as it had once been.

In addition, the government attempted to implement direct administration (*kansabaki*) over thirteen fisheries on the west coast after the 1869 season, in much the way the bakufu had run eastern Ezochi fisheries at the beginning of the century. But because it could find no compelling need for direct intervention into the day-to-day affairs of the fishing industry, the colonial administration almost immediately abandoned direct control everywhere except Ishikari and Hamamasu (as Hamamashike was known after 1869), and even there the policy was applied only through the 1870 fishing season.[17]

Although most former contractors did not lose their residual privileges until September 1876, the contract-fishery system was essentially dead after 1869. As the government had hoped, its demise led to a phenomenal growth in output at fisheries throughout the island. Herring catches rose from about 208,000 tons in 1871 to a peak of over 969,000 tons in 1897.[18] Much of this increase resulted as ordinary fishers responded to the liberalization of access to waterfront land at prime fishing grounds, which occurred once the former contractors had been stripped of most of their privileges.

A corollary to the dismantling of the contract-fishery system was the revision of land-tenure laws. In 1872 the Development Agency followed the lead of the central government in granting full rights of alienation to all land, including plots used by permanent residents of Hokkaido for processing marine products; seasonal residents, conversely, were granted free use of land, although legal title remained with the state and use rights were not transferable. All waterfront land was declared exempt from taxation from 1872 through 1877, and fishers who developed new tracts of shoreline received a two-year exemption from all levies on produce in addition. Finally, in November 1877, as part of the application of the land-tax reform to Hokkaido, the state recognized all waterfront land as private property, though owners risked the loss of any land not used in actual production in the fishery.

The government's policies toward waterfront land tenure in Hokkaido reflected its desire to rationalize landholding—and the taxation of land—throughout the nation. This program culminated in the implementation of the land-tax reform (*chiso kaisei*) in Hokkaido (where, because it created, not reformed, a land tax, it was called the *chiso sōtei*) in 1876, three years after it had been carried out in the rest of Japan.[19] While waterfront land in Honshu was treated as a peripheral category of property, it was the first concern of government authorities in Hokkaido. Teams of officials surveyed the entire coastline of the island, marking out plots of waterfront land wherever fishing was practiced. Each site was assigned a value that became the basis for taxation at the rate of one percent per annum.[20]

This marked the first significant step toward the creation of a uniform structure of fishing rights in Hokkaido. The next step came when the state recognized rights of exclusive access to the sea. As noted above, this was a radical departure from customary practice in most parts of Japan.[21] In 1875, the central government declared null all fishing rights that had existed up to that time. In its place it installed a system whereby the state retained legal title but allowed fishers to lease access rights. However, this policy met with such fierce resistance throughout the country that the following year the government was forced to reverse itself and recognize all customary fishing rights, though the state did assert ultimate authority over the sea. In Hokkaido this recognition of customary rights should have meant open access to all comers, but in fact pound-trap fishers successfully asserted exclusive rights to the sea fronting their waterfront landholdings.[22]

The next major policy shift came in 1886, when the national government mandated the creation of local fishing associations. Because the government's goal was not to restructure fishing rights per se but rather to minimize disputes among fishers, actual application of the law varied widely around the country. In Hokkaido the first associations dated back to 1884, but most were not created until after 1886. They were established to prevent overfishing, regulate the use of fishing methods, and standardize product-inspection procedures. Most importantly, each association retained control over access to the sea fronting the coastline under its jurisdiction, which it could distribute to members as it saw fit.[23] To put it another way, however, the groups could deny access to local fishing grounds to outsiders, which severely restricted the mobility of gill-netters in particular.

Although the fishing associations ostensibly represented the interests of all resident fishers, in fact they were dominated by pound-trap operators and tended to concern themselves mostly with issues of importance for large-scale fishing operations. The Hamamasu fishing association, for example, was organized so that its governing board included fourteen members to represent the district's thirty-eight pound-trap operators but only nine to represent the fifty-two gill-netters. Moreover, pound-trap fishers who also owned gill nets were allowed to vote twice in board elections.[24]

In 1901 the central government enacted a unified national fishery law that delineated several categories of fishing rights.[25] Under the 1901 law the right to fish was treated as a commodity that individuals could sell, lease, or otherwise transfer as they saw fit. In Hokkaido most fishing rights initially went to actual users (eighty-five percent of the 41,901 persons receiving fishing rights between 1901 and 1946 lived where they fished), but as time went on they changed hands with increasing frequency. Thus in 1924, forty-nine percent (2,191 of 4,477) of set-net (mostly pound-trap and seine) operators leased fishing rights; by 1946 tenants of this sort comprised 2,395 of 3,418 operators, or seventy percent of the total.[26]

To appreciate the impact of institutional change on social relations in the fishery it is necessary first to look briefly at land tenure, fishing rights, and social structure during the Tokugawa period. Until the development of the pound trap it had been unnecessary as well as impractical for fishers to define the right to fish in terms of access to the sea. However, because herring fishing is pointless without land to process the catch into fertilizer, fishers did recognize various rights of exclusive access to waterfront land. During the Tokugawa period those rights varied by locale. At Ezochi fisheries, the contractor, acting as the daimyo's agent, assigned areas of beach to independent fishers. For example, when Nakagawaya Yūsuke took over the Hamamashike fishery in 1865, one of the first things he did was to conduct a survey of land used by local fishers.[27] In most parts of the Wajinchi, however, villagers held waterfront land in common with the other members of the community. In the event of a herring run, village elders made an ad hoc allocation of land, reserving one area of beach for local residents and another for outsiders; as soon as the run ended all land reverted to the village. Only along the Japan Sea coast between Kaminokuni and Kumaishi did fishers have clearly established property rights in land, traceable as far back as the late seventeenth century.[28]

This diversity of attitudes toward land tenure was rooted in the circumstances surrounding the development of the herring fishery in each region. Contract fishers leased trading rights from the domain and acted as the daimyo's representatives in administrative affairs, but they did not claim legal title to the territory under their control—but then, neither did the domain. In the comparatively late-developing western Wajinchi, according to Suzue Eiichi, private rights to waterfront land were recognized as fishers returned to the same fishing grounds year after year before establishing permanent settlements. Individuals established claims to land as personal property on the basis of actual use, with the result that fishers from a variety of localities and status groups, including even samurai, owned waterfront land. Their rights were confirmed by the compilation of land registers, such as those for Kaminokuni in 1747 and Esashi in 1748.[29] In contrast, notions of exclusive rights to land were weak in the Fukuyama area, in part because the initial settlement of villages there antedated the herring fishery and in part because herring runs in the area were so erratic that the local fishery was not sufficient for much more than supplemental income.[30]

Some scholars have posited a connection between waterfront land tenure and class structure in Matsumae. Ishikawa Hiroshi and others have concluded from the high incidence of transfers of land from fishers to merchants that as early as the eighteenth century many small fishers had forfeited both the right to fish and the right to participate fully in village affairs.[31] The weakness of this approach is that it assumes a functional equivalence between waterfront land and agricultural land as the principal means of production and hence as the primary criterion for membership in the village community—that is, it assumes that just as only landholders were full-fledged peasants (*honbyakushō*) in farming communities, only fishers with their own waterfront land were eligible to participate in the allocation of village resources, including access to the sea and the fish in it. According to this view, a differentiation of the fishing population (*gyominsō bunkai*) occurred as merchants accumulated waterfront land from fishers unable to repay their debts, in a process analogous to the differentiation of the Honshu peasantry into landlords and tenants (*nōminsō bunkai*). Of course, access to waterfront land was important to fishers but not more so than possession of the nets, boats, and other fishing gear that made it possible to harvest herring in the first place. Moreover, because fishers often had to leave home in search of good catches, even those who did possess land in their own villages frequently found themselves too far away from home to make much use of it. For that reason the Matsumae domain never assessed levies on waterfront land but after 1719 structured taxation around boat ownership. Anyone fishing with his own gear was subject to domain taxes, whether he processed the catch on his own land or not.[32]

This relative unimportance of landholding was a distinctive feature of social relations in Matsumae. In most places the possession of agricultural land symbolized a covenant between the peasant proprietor and feudal authority, but in Matsumae landholding carried with it no such significance. Rather, any fisher who owned his means of production— that is, nets and boats—was eligible to participate in a special relationship with the daimyo and therefore be included as a full member of the domain community. This is an important point because economic relations within the fishery were articulated only within the context of the political structure of the state. Because the possession of land said little about a fisher's ability to produce and nothing about his right to produce, we cannot read a critical transformation of social relations into the movement of land from fishers to merchants during the Tokugawa period. Seen another way, the entry of merchant capital into the village economy via the accumulation of waterfront land did not itself lead to the dispossession and subsequent proletarianization of an entire class of villagers. Dispossession and proletarianization were instead the result of changes in the use of labor, technology, and capital—and changes in state structure. Proletarianization occurred only when small fishers lost the ability to maintain independent production. And independent production—as it was defined under the Matsumae regime—was not critically impaired by the loss of waterfront land.

Insofar as proletarianization was a political construct as well as an economic condition, once the political structure of the state changed, the social significance of land tenure and other economic institutions changed as well. Thus, after 1876 land tenure became an element in a broader structure of fishing rights, and the ability to produce did in fact hinge upon the possession of waterfront land. This change had an especially constraining effect because the spread of the pound-trap fishery both restricted the physical mobility of fishers and put a premium on the best land, which was needed to meet the heavy requirements of pound-trap operations for processing space. Proletarianization eventually occurred because the Meiji state had neither an ideological nor an economic need for broadly based independent production in the fishery; consequently, it had no reason not to register and tax waterfront land, even at the cost of lost mobility and economic dependency for those small fishers who failed to secure rights to land at productive fishing grounds.

The power of political institutions to shape social relations in the fishery is particularly evident in the way the land-tax reform was implemented in southern Hokkaido. As we have already seen, fishers in and around

Fukuyama saw no point in assuming exclusive rights to waterfront land because catches in the area were too erratic for any one fishery to be a steady source of income. Rather than monopolize all the fish from the occasional herring run at their own village, fishers preferred to guarantee themselves some sort of catch any time fish ran in the general vicinity. It appears to have been an excellent way of assuring a modicum of economic security for all local fishers.

This system of communal landownership was working just fine when a group of Development Agency bureaucrats, surveying sticks and deed registers in hand, arrived on the scene in November 1876. Their work up to that point had been going very smoothly, as they had been in Esashi, where fishers were delighted to have the state give its blessings to land-holding customs that had prevailed in the area for two hundred years or more. This previous experience may help to account for the disconcerted tone of the surveyors' request for assistance after they encountered difficulties in Haraguchi and Eramachi, villages just outside Fukuyama. "Contrary to our expectations, not a single person has laid claim to any land. . . . Since the welfare of the people is at issue, we have been unable to make a determination on our own."[33] While waiting for guidance from their superiors, the officials tried to persuade the villagers to submit to land surveys, explaining that it was necessary to "rectify the heinous custom [*akushū*] of communal ownership of fisheries," so that the use of the land would be "left to the free will of each individual [*meimei no jiyū ni makasesōrō*]."[34]

The fishers were not biting however. Representatives of Eramachi petitioned the authorities for recognition of customary practices, saying that while they understood the reasoning behind the officials' repeated exhortations (*setsuyu*) to accept private ownership, they still preferred to hold the land communally. The assurances of officials to the contrary notwithstanding, the villagers were convinced that without communal landholding they would not be able to fish wherever they wanted (*katte ni gyogyō tsukamatsurikanesōrō*).[35]

Development Agency authorities in Fukuyama, having decided to worry about Haraguchi and Eramachi some other time, ordered the surveying team to continue on to neighboring communities, where they met no opposition. The surveyors were surprised a few days later when ten fishers from Haraguchi—who perhaps succumbed to fears about the consequences of not cooperating with officials—caught up with them to apologize for having resisted the government's will. After receiving the villagers' assurances that everything would proceed smoothly this time, the officials returned to Haraguchi and conducted the survey, assigning land on the basis of net holdings. As promised, the residents were cooperative; the surveyors' biggest problem was deciding how to assign a value to land that had never been bought or sold before. That left only Eramachi, whose residents remained adamant in their refusal to submit to land registration. In the end it took a month of stern lectures from exasperated bureaucrats before the people of the village finally gave in.[36]

The bureaucrats who decided that the residents of Eramachi, Haraguchi, and other southern Hokkaido villages should have their own land seem to have been genuinely puzzled by the fishers' stubborn resistance to reform. After all, they reasoned, since the fishers did most of their important fishing in Esashi or even further west, they ought to have realized that the land-tax reform would bring them the benefits of private property without really impairing their ability to fish.[37] At any rate, the officials were really more concerned with taxation than with the fishing economy. Indeed, the land-tax reform ostensibly had nothing whatsoever to do with the right to fish; it was only because fishers needed land close to their fishing operations that fishing rights were an issue at all.

The residents of Eramachi may have opposed private landownership in part because they realized that individual plots would be too small to be of much use, yet they would be taxed (albeit only a few sen per year) all the same. The distribution of waterfront land left the average fisher in Eramachi with a holding of slightly over 100 square meters (in contrast, the average plot in Kumausu village, near Otaru, was 1,033 square meters). That gave the hypothetical typical fisher about seven square meters of land for each of the fourteen sets of gill nets he worked; in fact, holders of six of the eighty-two plots in the village had less than three and one-third square meters (one tsubo) per set of nets, and no villager had so much as half the government's prescribed standard holding of 66.2 square meters (twenty tsubo) per set.[38]

The officials' actions effectively deprived the village community of its ability to regulate the economic activities of its members. Once waterfront landholdings came within the sphere of individual economic interests, small fishers became much more vulnerable to immiserating influences from the outside because their economic base was only as secure as their individual resources: the community was no longer there to offer help in an institutionalized way. As herring catches in southern Hokkaido fell, fishers were forced to venture ever farther afield to fish. Those who could not afford to travel or move someplace with a more productive fishery had little choice but to try to live off of whatever the waters near home provided. Under the traditional system of communal landholding such fishers were free to fish and process their catches whenever there was a herring run anywhere in the general vicinity of their home villages. Their livelihoods were thus partially underwritten by the community, which guaranteed them fishing rights throughout southern Hokkaido. But after the land-tax reform the community was no longer able to assure its members access to the resources of the sea; fishers who could not afford to fish elsewhere were forced to limit their production to the waters immediately off their own landholdings. Unable to expand their operations beyond the capacity of their land to hold the fish, otherwise solvent fishers were forced into relations of dependency as a way to supplement the income from their personal fishing operations.

This development further demonstrates that proletarianization was a political construct. Proletarianization occurred when fishers who had lost their means of production turned to wage labor to earn a living. Waterfront land—along with boats, nets, and other gear—had of course always been necessary in herring-meal production, but until the application of the land-tax reform, land had had no political significance in southern Hokkaido as a means of production because access to it was open to all members of the community. After the reform, however, landownership became necessary for independent production. The economic distinctions among producers engendered by having or not having land took on a political significance that had not been there before: fishers were differentiated into those who retained control over their production and those who did not.

This was a political construct because little in the actual process of production changed. Fishing operations in southern Hokkaido villages remained for the most part small and centered on the household,[39] but now some fishers had to look to others to provide them with land (or credit to acquire land) when they had not before. Thus we have an excellent illustration of social relations evolving in response to political change. This is not to say, however, that the connection between the land-tax reform and the proletarianization of southern Hokkaido fishers was direct and immediate. After all, the possession of waterfront land was just one of many factors affecting a fisher's ability to maintain control over his productive activities. Proletarianization occurred only in conjunction with social and economic changes within the fishery. But that conjunction of events does not alter the fact that the intervention of the state into the institutions governing waterfront land tenure left fishers in the south vulnerable to other immiserating forces.

The social effects of the land-tax reform were similar in agricultural districts outside of Hokkaido. Official sanctions notwithstanding, Tokugawa peasants had exercised de facto alienation rights over land for generations before the enactment of the new law in 1873. Thus the reform seemed to serve more to affirm the results of an earlier process of change than to legislate a new set of social relations. Farmers were freed to pursue prosperity at their own risk, and many indeed prospered, at least until the Matsukata deflation took its toll during the 1880s.[40] At the same time, however, it is important not to underestimate the effect of formal institutional change. With the land-tax reform, the village community ceased to serve as a legal intermediary between cultivators and the outside world. Peasants became free agents in their dealings with other cultivators, merchants, and the state, a position that was as imperiling as it was liberating. Those cultivators whose rights to land were recognized at least had an opportunity to make the most of their position in the new order. However, those whose rights were *not* recognized were dispossessed, not only of their land but of their position as members of a community as well. The village community ceased to exist as a politically meaningful entity and instead became, formally, an amalgamation of competing economic interests. Of course, the village continued to function as a social unit, and this role no doubt mitigated the worst immediate effects of institutional change. But, at the same time, the land-tax reform, by stripping away the formal supports for the endogenous dependency of village social relations, made tenancy a harsher institution after the Meiji Restoration.

Production

"Due to the growth of the local population and expanding scale of the fishery, herring runs have become somewhat shorter in duration and fishers have been forced to move their nets to deeper waters," noted Katsura Gengo in 1894, "but there can be absolutely no doubt that with further improvements in fishing techniques, catches will continue to rise."[41] Katsura was referring to the fishing grounds on the southern coast of the Shakotan peninsula, but the problems he saw there occurred at one time or another everywhere herring were harvested (for example, see Figure 3, which graphs Hokkaido herring production from 1871 to 1958). He did not seem particularly disturbed by what he saw, and in his complacent confidence that technology would eventually triumph over ecology, Katsura subscribed to a misconception—a self-deception—shared by fishers throughout the world. Thus the ecological history of the Hokkaido fishery conforms to a general pattern identified by Arthur McEvoy:

> Usually, after a few pioneers demonstrate a fishery's profitability, capital and labor rush into it, and the harvest increases exponentially for a time. At some point, unable to bear the strain of exploitation indefinitely without sacrificing its ability to replenish itself, the resource begins to yield less and less to economic effort. As depletion erodes its productivity, a fishing industry may even improve its technical ability to find and catch fish, thereby sustaining profits for a time but drawing ever more effort into the harvest and ever more life out of the stock of fish. Ultimately, harvesting so depletes the resource as to cripple it.[42]

Hokkaido fishers big and small participated willingly, if not willfully, in the destruction of the herring stock and, ultimately, the economy that it supported. This is an important point because in a study like this, concerned as it is with the social and political aspects of the transformation of the fishery, it is tempting to portray small fishers as the passive victims of capitalist development. In fact, to the extent that the rise and fall of the herring fishery was an ecological event as well as an economic one, they were complicitous in their fate. Again, the economics of ecological destruction were the same in the Hokkaido fishery as elsewhere:

> Everyone has an incentive to keep fishing so long as there is any money to be made in the effort, whereas no one has an individual incentive to refrain from fishing so as to conserve the stock. Every harvester knows that if he or she leaves a fish in the water someone else will get it, and the profit, instead. This is what economists call "the fisherman's problem": In a competitive economy, no market mechanism ordinarily exists to reward individual forbearance in the use of shared resources.[43]

Complicitous though they may have been, gill-netters were affected more immediately and more severely by the depletion of the herring stock than most pound-trap fishers. Gill-net fishers generally turned to wage labor in the pound-trap fishery only when the herring population in their home villages had dropped to the point where independent production was no longer possible. In an ironic way, then, the depletion of the herring stock worked out well for pound-trap fishers, especially since yields fell first in the older fishing grounds in the south, where the gill-net fishery was concentrated, and only later in the newer pound-trap fisheries of the north. Moreover, since the entrepreneurs in the Hokkaido fishery did not usually have deep roots in the industry, it was relatively easy for them simply to leave once they had destroyed the resource.[44]

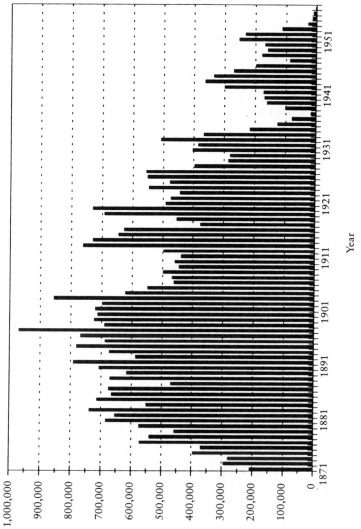

Figure 3. Hokkaido Herring Production, 1871–1958
SOURCE: Imada Mitsuo, *Nishin bunka shi* pp. 256–57.

One is thus faced with the admittedly cynical conclusion that for many capitalist fishers the destruction of the resource was in their best long-term interest. So, too, for the state: short-term economic growth, even at the cost of the resource's sustainability, seemed worthwhile to a regime consciously emulating the industrial power of the United States and Western Europe. The only real losers were the household fishers remaining in the fishery; they had nowhere to go and thus faced considerable dislocation.

Nonetheless, the point here is not so much to apportion blame for the decimation of the herring stock but rather to highlight the fact that the socioeconomic, political, and ecological histories of the fishery are intimately connected. The goal of this section, then, is to provide an overview of production in the fishery as a way to link the discussion of political and institutional change offered in this chapter with the analysis of social and economic conditions presented in the following one.

The economic imperatives of fishing fueled the process of ecological damage, which in turn affected the social and political dynamics of the fishery. But because the economics of fishing cannot be divorced from social and institutional factors, what we see in fact is a synchronous process of social, economic, political, and ecological change, each element affecting and being affected by the others. We have already seen, for example, how the political concerns of the Matsumae domain and the bakufu determined the economic structure of the Tokugawa fishery and how, in turn, ecological changes (falling catches in the south combined with better technology and hence increased productivity in the north) put pressure on the institutional framework of the state. After the Meiji Restoration, the continued decline of the herring stock in southern Hokkaido coincided with the abolition of contract fishing and the opening of the northwest coast to exploitation by a broad spectrum of fishers. Opening the northwest coast led to several decades of rapid economic growth, but when those fishing grounds inevitably came under ecological pressure and fishers sought to relocate to northeastern Hokkaido or Karafuto, legal and institutional barriers blocked their way.

The phenomenal expansion of production in the fishery in the years after the Meiji Restoration is attributable to a number of factors. First, the dismantling of the contract-fishery system opened productive fisheries in most parts of Hokkaido to any fisher who could afford to participate. This development contributed to a steady increase in the fishing population, which meant of course that the fishery was exploited much more intensively than it had been in the past. Second, fishing also became

TABLE 6

NUMBER OF POUND TRAPS BY PROVINCE, 1888–1893

Province	1888	1893	Increase (%)
Oshima	281	445	58.4
Shiribeshi	1,452	1,708	17.6
Ishikari	143	228	59.4
Teshio	402	800	99.0
Kitami	306	761	148.7
Iburi	31	33	6.5
Hidaka	—	2	—
Tokachi	—	5	—
Kushiro	3	23	666.7
Nemuro	113	224	98.2
Chishima	17	41	141.2
Total	2,748	4,270	55.4

SOURCE: *Hokkaidō gyogyō shi*, p. 322.

more efficient after 1885, when pound-trap fishers began switching from the conventional free-running trap (*ikinariami*) to the larger and more efficient square trap (*kakuami*), an innovation that raised the productivity of a typical pound-trap fishery by half (but labor requirements by only a third). Third, and perhaps most importantly, the development of the fishery came during a period when the agricultural economy of Honshu was expanding, which ensured that demand for herring meal and other marine products would remain strong enough to absorb the increased output.

The rapid, if erratic, growth of the total output of the fishery after about 1871 gives the industry an aura of prosperity, particularly if one looks only at aggregate production data. But it is important to emphasize that there is no necessary correlation between total output and the living standards of individual fishers, particularly since increases in production were the result largely of an influx of new fishers and gear. Tables 6 and 7, for example, show how fishers stepped up their exploitation of the fishery's resources in the years immediately following the low prices and scarce credit of the Matsukata deflation.[45] During the five years from 1888 to 1893 the number of pound traps in use rose from 2,748 to 4,270, while gill-net use increased from 165,735 to 256,938 sets, a growth of about fifty-five percent for each type of gear. This trend continued, so

TABLE 7

NUMBER OF GILL-NET SETS BY PROVINCE, 1888–1893

Province	1888	1893	Change (%)
Oshima	86,697	95,931	10.7
Shiribeshi	61,544	104,546	69.9
Ishikari	2,679	5,258	96.3
Teshio	11,066	30,398	174.7
Kitami	2,961	20,065	577.6
Iburi	788	731	(7.2)
Hidaka	—	—	—
Tokachi	—	—	—
Kushiro	—	9	—
Nemuro	—	—	—
Chishima	—	—	—
Total	165,735	256,938	55.0

SOURCE: *Hokkaidō gyogyō shi*, p. 325.

that by 1897 fishers operated a total of 6,157 pound traps and 314,282 sets of gill nets, for a cumulative increase over 1888 of about 124 percent and 90 percent, respectively. Although some of this increase came when individual fishers expanded the scale of their operations, much of it was due to growth in the fishing population. Thus, while about 18,000 fisher households had employed 98,000 workers in 1888, 45,000 households were using 135,000 workers by 1907.[46] Moreover, as Tables 8 and 9 reveal, the greatest increase in fishery workers during this period of rapid expansion at the end of the nineteenth century came on the northwest coast of Hokkaido, where the pound-trap fishery was concentrated.

The imperatives of the "fisherman's problem" were such that even when fishers realized that they were collectively jeopardizing the sustainability of the resource, they were at a loss to take effective action. In Yoichi, for example, gill-netters perceived by the mid-1890s that the stock was being harvested too intensely. They responded by prohibiting the entry of newcomers into the district but did nothing to curtail their own increasingly reckless fishing practices. Thus, instead of waiting, as they had in the past, for the herring to spawn before lowering their gill nets, they now lowered about half their gear before the fish had had a chance to reproduce. The eyes of their nets, moreover, were smaller than

TABLE 8

HERRING FISHERY WORKERS BY PROVINCE, 1887

Province	Workers	% of Total
Oshima	8,976	15.2
Shiribeshi	30,893	52.3
Ishikari	2,801	4.7
Teshio	7,617	13.0
Kitami	4,513	7.6
Iburi	240	0.4
Hidaka	—	0.0
Tokachi	—	0.0
Kushiro	1,531	2.6
Nemuro	2,323	3.9
Chishima	154	0.3
Total	59,048[a]	100.0

SOURCE: Hokusui kyōkai, *Hokkaidō gyogyō shikō*, pp. 104–5.
[a]Source gives total as 59,348.

in the past, with the result that they were catching more immature fish. Fear of the immediate hardship forbearance would bring, combined with an awareness that the pound traps with which they competed indiscriminately swallowed all fish—big and small, lascivious and chaste—prevented them from taking action to conserve the resource.[47]

Sometimes steps were taken to decrease the pressure on the herring stock, but the main effect was usually to exacerbate conflicts among fishers competing for dwindling shares of a diminishing resource. For example, when, in 1894, the Rumoi fishing association passed a resolution urging the prefectural government to disallow new gill nets in the area under its jurisdiction, "several hundred" angry fishers staged a protest. In 1897 the government did set a quota of 8,500 sets for the district, but that simply encouraged supply merchants to foreclose on debtors with gill-net fishing licenses, which they then lent back to their former owners for several yen per set per season. Foreclosure created even more hardship than overfishing had, so in 1903 the prefectural authorities rescinded all restrictions on gill-net use. Production in the local fishery boomed in the years immediately following: gill-net use in Rumoi increased from about 15,200 to 32,500 sets in the four seasons from 1904 to 1907. The local

TABLE 9

FISHERY WORKERS BY PROVINCE, 1902

Province	(A) Herring Fishery	% of Total in Herring Fishery	(B) All Fisheries	A/B (%)
Oshima	10,594	9.4	35,566	29.8
Shiribeshi	37,436	33.4	43,294	86.5
Ishikari	7,512	6.8	8,359	89.9
Teshio	19,336	17.2	23,138	83.6
Kitami	28,632	25.5	34,999	81.8
Iburi	540	0.5	2,045	26.4
Hidaka	39	0.0	5,027	0.7
Tokachi	845	0.8	2,363	35.8
Kushiro	3,415	3.0	7,612	44.9
Nemuro	2,929	2.6	7,320	40.0
Chishima	920	0.8	9,276	9.9
Total	112,198[a]	100.0	178,999	62.7

SOURCE: *Shokumin kōhō* 17 (November 1903): 56.
[a]Source gives total as 111,928.

fishery could not support such intense production, and within just five years the number of nets in use had fallen back down to 12,097 sets.[48]

Presented in Tables 10 and 11 are sample budgets for a moderately sized gill-net fishery and a pound-trap fishery in the Shakotan peninsula around 1892. The gill-netter's budget was calculated for an established fisher with forty sets of nets and a crew of three men and one woman (the fisher and his male workers operated the nets, while the woman worked onshore as a cook and fish processor). The annual cost of about 240 yen excludes taxes, interest, and miscellaneous expenses, which together added twenty-five percent or more to the cost of running the fishery. The officials who drew up the budget estimated that in a good year the fishery would generate a gross income of about 433 yen, assuming that most of the catch would be processed into dried herring (*migaki nishin*) and herring roe (*kazunoko*), which commanded higher prices than herring meal. This would mean a net profit of about 100 to 150 yen for the fisher, depending on how much he paid in interest and marketing commissions.

If his fishery generated an income of 100 yen or more annually, the gill-netter and his family could lead a relatively comfortable life, though they would never be able to afford to buy or even lease a pound-trap fishery.

TABLE 10

OPERATING EXPENSES FOR A
GILL-NET FISHERY, C. 1892, IN YEN

Item	Purchase Cost	Annual Cost
Start-up expenses		
Waterfront land (1,160 sq m)	170.	—
Boat and net landings (200 sq m)	90.	—
House	100.	—
Storage building	50.	—
Total	410.	—
Durables		
Boats, gear, and nets		
(40 sets gill nets, 1 boat, etc.)	164.90	50.286
Processing equipment	30.12	10.531
Total	195.02	60.817
Nondurables		
Wages (3 men, 1 woman)	115.	115.
Food	44.05	44.05
Perishables, miscellaneous	19.93	19.93
Total	178.98	178.98
Total	784.	239.797

SOURCE: Hokusui kyōkai, *Hokkaidō gyogyō shikō*, pp. 96–99.

If, however, the scale of the gill-netter's operations fell much below the forty sets of nets used as a standard here, he could find it difficult to support his family. Ishibashi Gen has calculated the income of a hypothetical Hamamasu fisher with twenty to twenty-five sets of gill nets and concludes that his net annual income, after taxes but before interest, would have been only about twenty-nine yen in 1882 and thirty-four yen in 1902.[49] Moreover, a fisher's income varied in response to factors other than scale of operations. First, the annual budget shown in Table 10 assumes that the fisher already owned his own gear and sufficient waterfront land; someone just starting out would need close to 800 yen, not even counting the cost of interest, taxes, and fishing rights. Second, fluctuations in catches could spell disaster, particularly if they came at a time

TABLE 11

OPERATING EXPENSES FOR A
POUND-TRAP FISHERY, C. 1892, IN YEN

Item	Purchase Cost	Annual Cost
Start-up expenses		
Waterfront land (3,300 sq m)	500.	—
Storehouse	200.	—
Net storehouse	50.	—
Fertilizer storehouse	200.	—
Total	950.	—
Durables		
Boats, gear, trap		
(1 pound trap, 6 boats, etc.)	1,131.	214.11
Processing equipment	134.2	25.61
Total	1,265.2	239.72
Nondurables		
Wages (17 workers)	400.	400.
Food	255.	255.
Perishables, miscellaneous	303.8	303.8
Total	958.8	958.8
Total	3,174.	1,198.52

SOURCE: Hokusui kyōkai, *Hokkaidō gyogyō shikō*, pp. 100–103.

in the fisher's life cycle when he required a lot of outside wage labor, as, for instance, when his children were not yet old enough to work.

According to the budget presented in Table 11, for a pound-trap fisher to break even he would have to realize a catch of about 225 tons after bonuses, taxes, and all other expenses. This would generate income of just under 1,300 yen, or enough to pay expenses and still generate a small profit. A pound-trap fisher could have a reasonable expectation of a profit most years, particularly if he owned a square trap, which might produce 450 tons or more of herring in a good season. There is no question, however, that operating a pound-trap fishery was a gamble, particularly for fishers who lacked either the resources or the inclination to ride out the occasional poor catch. However, fishers who did own a substantial amount of gear could be confident of some profit except in the most disastrous of seasons.

As the herring stock came under pressure, fishers found it increasingly difficult to maintain production at profitable levels, although those who could afford to operate fisheries at a number of locations generally fared better than their neighbors. For example, Oguro Kaemon, a fisher based in Gokatte, a village on the outskirts of Esashi, shifted his operations frequently in response to changing conditions in the fishery.[50] In the 1860s and 1870s Oguro owned or leased a series of pound traps in his home village and in nearby communities along the coast between Esashi and Kumaishi. By the beginning of the twentieth century, however, catches in southern Hokkaido had become so poor that he was forced to lend out most of the traps he maintained locally and lease new fishing grounds on Rebun, an island off the extreme north coast of Hokkaido.[51] For a time poor catches at home were compensated for by good ones in Rebun, but by 1906 and 1907 things were so bad at all of his fisheries that Oguro was forced to sublet his two traps on Rebun. Ironically, in 1908 the vicinity of Esashi saw its first substantial run of herring in more than a decade, but most of the fish went unharvested because few people had bothered to retain any fishing gear. Oguro, however, did manage a small catch with twenty sets of rotting gill nets.[52]

Those who could not afford to lease pound traps at productive fisheries had little choice but to move if they wanted to remain independent producers. Predictably, however, relocating often resulted in conflict with vested interests in the areas chosen by migrants. This was certainly the case in Karafuto, as we shall see in Chapter 6. Another example of this sort comes from the Nemuro region, a remote area in northeastern Hokkaido, where small fishers fought against the domination of the former contractor, Fujino Kihei, and a handful of other large operators.[53] Small fishers in Nemuro attempted twice between 1892 and 1905 to gain the right to fish with gill nets, which had been prohibited by the Development Agency shortly after the Restoration.[54] Until the 1890s the prohibition had been of little consequence because there were so few small fishers in the vicinity. However, as fishing grounds on the Japan Sea coast became increasingly congested, gill-netters began to look to Nemuro and other districts in the northeast for new fisheries to exploit. Thus in 1892 a group of about four hundred fishers petitioned for permission to use gill nets in the area. However, they met with defeat because the local fishing association, controlled by Fujino and others with similar interests, opposed them. The pound-trap operators argued that the economic interests of large fishers coincided with the developmental concerns of the state, and the state agreed. That settled the matter until 1903, when 2,400 small fishers presented a new request to the government. Local pound-trap fishers again tried to block the movement, this time with the claim that gill-netting would damage the environment. However, their argument did not survive a study conducted by the prefectural fishery authorities, so beginning in 1906 small fishers were permitted to use gill nets in Nemuro, although only a few hundred ever actually did so.

After World War I the Hokkaido fishery fell into a slump from which it never recovered. As if the steadily shrinking catches of the 1920s and 1930s were not bad enough, fishers had to deal with the fact that the market for herring meal, like just about every other market in Japan, fell into a prolonged depression after the boom years of the war. The price of herring fell from an average 15.84 yen/ton between 1927 and 1929 to 12.22 yen/ton in 1930 and 10.61 yen/ton in 1931.[55]

By the mid-1920s it was evident to prominent fishers and bureaucrats alike that drastic measures would have to be taken to forestall the total collapse of the fishery. In 1925 a group that included prefectural officials, leaders of regional fishing associations, and representatives of Hokkaidō Takushoku Bank (or Takugin, the quasi-official development bank) met to discuss the possibility of amalgamating herring-fishing operations throughout Hokkaido and Karafuto into a single company. Since a single company could allocate its resources far more effectively than a disparate group of thousands of individual fishers, it was felt that it would be possible to relieve some of the pressure on the herring stock while realizing profits through efficient management. Another, unstated, goal was to help Takugin recover some of the loans it had outstanding to pound-trap fishers who had borrowed against their fishing rights.[56]

Nothing came of the 1925 meeting, but talks continued intermittently for the next several years, until an agreement was finally reached in 1931. The organizers of the original discussions had entertained grand hopes of joining all pound-trap and gill-net fishers throughout Hokkaido and Karafuto, but in the end they had to settle for pound-trap fishers in the principal herring-fishing districts of western Hokkaido, from Shiribeshi in the south to Sōya in the north. (A separate company was created in Karafuto.) The company, named Gōdō Gyogyō (Amalgamated Fishing), was formed when fishers contributed fishing rights, land, boats, and gear in exchange for stock in the new firm.[57] Many fishers oversaw production at their old fisheries as employees of the company.

Almost from its inception Gōdō Gyogyō's main line of business seemed to be the supervision of the dismemberment of the fishery. When it began operations in 1932, the company owned 1,245 fisheries, or fifty-two per-cent of the total 2,298 pound-trap rights on the Japan Sea coast of Hok-kaido, but it immediately reduced the number of traps in use to 900 and closed the rest. Riddled with debt and hurt by a succession of poor catches, Gōdō Gyogyō was in serious financial trouble almost as soon as it was founded. It got out of trouble by being acquired by Nippon Shokuryōhin Kōgyō, a company in the Nissan cartel, in December 1934. The two companies merged the following year to form Nippon Suisan, with Gōdō Gyogyō as a subsidiary of the new firm. Thereafter the com-pany distanced itself from direct management of fishing operations in fa-vor of leasing fishing rights. Thus by 1935 the company had cut back to 814 pound-trap fisheries, of which it operated 380 itself, leased another 120 to individuals, and let the remaining 314 sit idle. Gōdō Gyogyō did not survive the enactment of antitrust laws after World War II, and it dis-banded in December 1947.[58]

The creation of Gōdō Gyogyō was possible only because fishing rights had become a commodity before the decline of the fishery in the 1920s. It represented a more rational way of organizing production, but it was so rational that it was completely divorced from the idea of fishing as a way of life. By about 1939 villages like Hamamasu had almost become ghost towns, as even the local petty capitalists had been ousted and their fish-eries literally dismantled in accordance with the demands of efficient management.[59] The story of the rise and fall of Gōdō Gyogyō is a fitting conclusion to this chapter because the company epitomizes the close rela-tionship between the institutional structure of the fishery and the evolu-tion of production within it. The monopolization of fishing rights by a subsidiary of a Honshu cartel in the mid-1930s was perhaps the logical culmination of nearly a century of capitalist development in the fishery.

CHAPTER FIVE

Capitalism and Immiseration

The members of the Kumaishi Village Women's Association certainly had their work cut out for them. After a herring catch of 3,600 tons in 1903, the fishers of Kumaishi, a small community on the western edge of what had once been the Wajinchi, harvested only 98 tons in 1904 and nothing at all for three successive seasons after that. Things were so bad that many people simply lost hope and got rid of their boats and gear. Those who had the wherewithal to do so pulled up stakes and ventured north to Karafuto before they lost everything; they took some of their neighbors along as hired hands.[1]

By the beginning of the twentieth century the herring stock had been so heavily harvested that the shoals of spawning fish rarely made it as far as the old Wajinchi. Those in the south who still sought to make a living at fishing had to leave home to do so. Thus southern Hokkaido, once the domain of small, independent producers, had by the end of the nineteenth century become like an extension of northern Tōhoku—a depressed reservoir of labor for other, more productive regions. The disruption this caused in Kumaishi was typical:

> The extreme hardship brought on by a long succession of poor catches has forced the men here to head to Kamchatka and elsewhere to work every summer. Like fishers everywhere, the men used to love to drink and the women were much taken with fancy clothes; and the lack of cooperation among villagers had made a shambles of local administration.[2]

But thanks to the efforts of the women's association, founded in 1909 with the encouragement of the mayor, local women started wearing cotton instead of silk kimono even on formal occasions, and "public drunkenness was completely eradicated" from the village. The attempts of the village women to restore order in the face of falling catches and a rising cost of living brought neither herring nor prosperity back to Kumaishi, but they did satisfy the urge of government officials to trim imaginary fat and as such were laudable enough to rate mention in *Shokumin kōhō*, the prefectural administration's magazine promoting colonization.[3] In the meantime the economic base of village life in Kumaishi became weaker with every missed herring run.

Hard times came to Kumaishi and other villages in southern Hokkaido at a time when the herring fishery was, on the whole, still a vibrant industry. The average harvest during the ten years beginning in 1901 was about 578,000 tons, well below the peak 738,000-ton average of the previous decade, but still more than double the average catch of 236,000 tons of 1931–40, when the fishery was on the verge of total collapse. If catches had been distributed evenly throughout Hokkaido, the livelihoods of fishers in places like Kumaishi would have remained stable well into the twentieth century. But because production fell first in the family fishers' stronghold in southern Hokkaido, people who had failed to acquire fishing rights at still-productive grounds in the north often had little practical choice but to become wage laborers at pound-trap fisheries.

The residents of Kumaishi, like the mass of ordinary fishers, experienced relative immiseration even as the total output of the fishery remained high because they did not, for the most part, participate as capitalists in the capitalist fishery. Indeed, the phenomenal growth in the output of the fishery during the late nineteenth century actually contributed to their immiseration because it sped the decimation of the herring stock and made the fishery attractive to entrepreneurs looking for a speculative investment opportunity. I use the term "relative immiseration" because the real issue is not how fishers' material standards of living improved or declined; rather, the salient question is how the development of a capitalist fishery undermined the independence of small operators. "Independence" here refers to an individual's (or a household's) control over his or her (or its) own productive activities. After all, fishers' living standards rose and fell with the herring catch, fertilizer prices, and the cost of living, but independence, once lost, was rarely regained.

The social configuration of the fishery changed after the Meiji Restoration. Like the contract fishers of the Tokugawa period, the capitalists came principally from commerce, but the resemblance to the contractors ended there. While the contractors had been privileged merchants, the new capitalists were independent entrepreneurs, competing in a relatively free market. Small producers remained a significant element in the fishery until its final collapse in the middle of the twentieth century, but their position became increasingly precarious. A few managed to join the ranks of the capitalist entrepreneurs, but many others—like the men of Kumaishi—joined workers from the agricultural villages of northern Honshu as part of the seasonal proletariat of the pound-trap fishery.

Social disruption was a natural by-product of the rapid transformation of the fishery, and not surprisingly conflict rather than consensus characterized the relations between pound-trap operators and gill-netters and between capital and labor. Yet despite the dislocation of the late nineteenth and early twentieth centuries, small fishers and wage laborers never mounted a fundamental challenge to the emergence of the capitalist mode of production in the fishery. Conflict instead entailed things like disputes over the specific rights of gill-netters in areas dominated by the pound-trap fishery and frequent instances of flight by wage laborers dissatisfied with the conditions of their employment.

We might speculate that the conflict was not more fundamental because gill-netters, so long as they retained some independence, saw themselves as petty capitalists or at least as having the potential eventually to become petty capitalists by acquiring a pound trap. This attitude is revealed in the behavior of gill-netters in Karafuto after 1905 (the subject of the following chapter) and contrasts with the attitude of the net cutters of 1855, who evidently did not see any common interests between themselves and the people they attacked. Moreover, fishery workers, whose proletarianization was seasonal (at least initially), may have retained an identity as something other than wage laborers—those from Hokkaido as family fishers and those from Honshu as cultivators—even when ostensibly supplementary income from work in the fishery was more important to their livelihoods than income derived from other activities,[4] or perhaps even when they spent the bulk of the year moving from fishery to fishery, returning home for no more than a month or two in the winter.

Capitalists

According to a history of the Rumoi fishery written around 1913, a wealthy fisher was one who could afford to live elsewhere—usually Otaru or Hakodate—most of the year. He stayed at his fishery only as

long as it was necessary to oversee the production of herring meal; the
rest of the time he spent with his family in more comfortable surround-
ings, leaving a caretaker to look after his boats, gear, and buildings.
However, a poor fisher—a gill-netter—could hardly afford to live at all.
He relied heavily on credit to finance his fishing and to see his family
through the winter. He got by as best he could harvesting not only herring, trout, salmon, and other types of fish, but also kelp, sea cucumbers,
shellfish, and anything else the waters of the Sea of Japan would yield. A
middling fisher—a petty capitalist with one or two pound traps—may
not have enjoyed the luxurious life of a more substantial operator, but
neither did he suffer the deprivations of a gill-netter's existence and indeed was usually well enough off to dabble in money lending or some
other sort of mercantile activity. The history of Rumoi noted that since
middling fishers were generally a frugal lot, one might expect their operations to be fairly stable, but in fact they left the fishery quite readily—
much more so than either wealthy operators or gill-netters, particularly
after the unusually poor catches of 1898–99 and 1907–10. Those who
left, however, were easily replaced.[5]

The quintessential wealthy fishers in Hokkaido were two former contractors with extensive holdings on the remote and sparsely populated
coast of the Sea of Okhotsk and adjoining areas to the west and east. In
1888, Suhara Kakubei, who eventually lost his fishing empire to Mitsui
Bussan after years of misfortune and mismanagement, operated 185
pound traps and employed nearly 2,600 workers in Rumoi, Tomamae,
and Teshio on the northwest coast of Hokkaido, and Etorofu in the
southern Kurils. Fujino Kihei, who was based in Ōmi and had branch offices in Hakodate, Fukuyama, Nemuro, Abashiri, and Monbetsu, owned
182 pound traps at fisheries spread over ten districts in northeastern
Hokkaido and the southern Kurils. His fisheries produced 21,750 tons of
herring, trout, and salmon in 1888. Both Suhara and Fujino also operated shipping agencies—Suhara's fleet included a steamship—and marketed fertilizer through subsidiary wholesalers in Osaka.[6]

Obviously, it takes capitalists to run a capitalist fishery, and men like
Suhara and Fujino certainly fit the bill. However, most capitalists in the
capitalist fishery were not wealthy operators with dozens of pound-trap
fisheries scattered along the coast of Hokkaido but rather were more like
the middling entrepreneurs described above, who owned or leased no
more than a pound trap or two. Most capitalists, moreover, had started
out as neither contractors nor gill-netters but as merchants or the employees of pound-trap fishers.

To illustrate this point, I have examined the careers of ninety pound-trap operators from two areas of western and northern Hokkaido. Table 12 gives information on fifty-six pound-trap fishers in Iwanai and Furuu districts on the Shakotan peninsula, an area that developed early into a major center of herring production; Table 13 lists thirty-four operators in Sōya and neighboring districts at the northwest tip of Hokkaido, a region that did not see much development until well into the Meiji period. Neither list gives anything like an exhaustive view of the pound-trap fishery in the 1890s; the data are, however, suggestive, even if not fully representative.[7]

I have divided the fishers in the sample into three groups on the basis of their backgrounds.[8] The first group includes independent fishers like the ones who, with the contractors, pioneered the pound-trap fishery in the Ezochi in the 1840s and 1850s. These people may have had mercantile interests, but their roots were in the gill-net fishery of southern Hokkaido. Araida Yosaburō's father, a gill-netter from Kamiiso on the southern coast of Hokkaido, was an example of this type. He moved to Iwanai in the 1850s, where he continued to fish with gill nets for about a decade. A series of good catches left him with enough cash to buy a pound trap during the Keiō period (1865–68). Yosaburō, born in Iwanai in 1858, eventually took over the family fishery.[9]

Fishers like this represent the best case of economic development in Hokkaido. They began as petty proprietors, but thanks to various combinations of hard work, good luck, and generous lines of credit, they were able to cross over to the pound-trap fishery. If the wealth created by the rapid growth of the fishery during the latter half of the nineteenth century had been distributed evenly, we would expect to see many success stories like this. However, as Tables 12 and 13 reveal, only twenty percent (eleven of fifty-six) of the pound-trap fishers in the sample for Iwanai and Furuu were former gill-netters, while just twenty-seven percent (nine of thirty-four) of those in the Sōya area had begun with gill nets. That is, more than three-fourths of the pound-trap operators listed did not start out as gill-net fishers. Moreover, the movement of gill-netters into the pound-trap fishery was concentrated in the early years of the expansion of the new technology: eight of eleven former gill-netters in Iwanai and Furuu made the switch before 1877, including five who changed over before the Restoration. The late development of the Sōya area blurs the differences among the groups somewhat, but even there former gill-netters generally began using pound traps earlier than the others.

TABLE 12

POUND-TRAP OPERATORS IN
IWANAI AND FURUU, C. 1897

No.	Type[a]	Entry into Pound-Trap Fishery	No.	Type[a]	Entry into Pound-Trap Fishery
1.	G	1847	29.	L	1881
2.	G	1840s–1850s	30.	L	1885
3.	G	1853	31.	L	1885
4.	G	1859	32.	L	1887
5.	G	c. 1865	33.	M	1845
6.	G	early Meiji	34.	M	1847
7.	G	early Meiji	35.	M	1865
8.	G	after 1873	36.	M	early Meiji
9.	G	1880	37.	M	after 1872
10.	G	1881	38.	M	1873
11.	G	1887	39.	M	1873
12.	L	1856	40.	M	1876
13.	L	1859	41.	M	1878
14.	L	c. 1859	42.	M	1880
15.	L	c. 1861	43.	M	c. 1880
16.	L	1862	44.	M	1880s
17.	L	after 1865	45.	M	1882
18.	L	early Meiji	46.	M	1883
19.	L	1869	47.	M	1884
20.	L	1871	48.	M	1886
21.	L	1873	49.	M	1886
22.	L	1873	50.	M	1886
23.	L	1877	51.	M	1886
24.	L	c. 1877	52.	M	1888
25.	L	1878	53.	M	1891
26.	L	1879	54.	M	c. 1891
27.	L	after 1879	55.	M	c. 1892
28.	L	before 1880	56.	M	1893

SOURCE: Takasaki, *Kaokuzuiri Hokkai risshi hen*, vols. 1–3; Katsura, *Iwanai Furuu nigun shi.*

[a]G = former gill-netter; L = former wage laborer; M = merchant

TABLE 13

POUND-TRAP OPERATORS IN SŌYA,

ESASHI, RISHIRI, AND REBUN, C. 1897

No.	Typeᵃ	Entry into Pound-Trap Fishery	No.	Typeᵃ	Entry into Pound-Trap Fishery
1.	G	after 1869	18.	L	1892
2.	G	after 1883	19.	L	1892
3.	G	1884	20.	L	1892
4.	G	c. 1885–1891	21.	L	1895
5.	G	c. 1885–1895	22.	M	c. 1887
6.	G	c. 1889	23.	M	after 1887
7.	G	c. 1889	24.	M	1888
8.	G	1889	25.	M	1889
9.	G	1891	26.	M	1890
10.	L	1877	27.	M	1890
11.	L	after 1879	28.	M	1893
12.	L	c. 1880s	29.	M	1893
13.	L	1885	30.	M	c. 1895
14.	L	1886	31.	M	1895
15.	L	1887	32.	M	1896
16.	L	1888	33.	M	1896
17.	L	1889	34.	M	1897

SOURCE: Takasaki, *Kaokuzuiri Hokkai risshi hen*, vol. 4.
ᵃG = former gill-netter; L = former wage laborer; M = merchant

These figures suggest that through the early 1870s those independent fishers who could afford to make the transition to pound traps did so, while most others remained locked into the petty production of the gill-net fishery because they did not have access to the credit or other financial resources necessary to make the step up. This certainly seems to have been the case in Hamamasu. In 1879, a touring official, Sakai Tadaiku, classified the vast majority (149 of 179, or eighty-three percent) of the households in the district as "poor," with the remainder split between "middle class" (25 households, or fourteen percent) and "wealthy" (5 households, or three percent).[10] A quarter century later, in 1903, about eighty-seven percent (164 of 189) of the gill-netter households in the district maintained no more than the forty sets of gill nets considered necessary for a viable fishing operation, while only a handful operated the hundred or more sets that would have put them in a position to consider conversion to a pound trap.[11]

The second group of pound-trap operators consists of men who became entrepreneurs as a result of their work experience at large fisheries. They followed a traditional route to success in Japanese society, one we might call achieved ascription, in which a capable employee is rewarded for years of loyal service with fictive ties to his employer's household, either through adoption as son-in-law cum heir-apparent or through sponsorship in the establishment of a new enterprise linked to his patron's through a network of formal and informal ties (*noren wake*). The members of this group commonly came from northern Honshu and accordingly had no family ties to fishing, though they did have personal experience in the everyday workings of a pound-trap fishery as laborers and/or supervisors. An example of this sort is Sawaguchi Toyojirō, who, in 1860, left his family in Aomori at the age of seventeen to make his fortune in Iwanai. After Sawaguchi worked for eighteen years in various capacities at a series of fisheries in the area, an employer finally lent him enough money and property to set up his own pound-trap fishery.[12] In the Iwanai-Furuu sample, thirty-eight percent (twenty-one of fifty-six) of the pound-trap operators followed careers similar to Sawaguchi's, and in Sōya, thirty-five percent (twelve of thirty-four) of the pound-trap fishers fell into this category. Although they generally did not become pound-trap fishers as early as the former gill-netters, the members of this group established themselves in and around the 1870s, when the institutional structure of the fishery was still evolving.

The final—and largest—group of pound-trap fishers consisted of merchants who invested capital accumulated in commerce into the fishery. They were capitalist entrepreneurs for whom the bottom line *was* the bottom line, men with neither a background nor experience—nor, perhaps, even a long-term interest—in fishing. Kaneko Kishichirō was such a man. Originally from Sado island, he was twenty when he arrived in Iwanai in 1865 to work as a dry-goods merchant. Business went well, so he expanded, adding a pawnshop and later a sake brewery to his little business empire. He also lent money to fishers on a substantial scale. Finally, in 1893, he acquired a pound-trap fishery (perhaps from a defaulting client) as yet another sideline to his dry-goods business.[13] In Iwanai and Furuu, men like Kaneko accounted for forty-three percent (twenty-four of fifty-six) of the pound-trap operators, while in the Sōya region they made up thirty-eight percent (thirteen of thirty-four) of the pound-trap fishers. This group entered the fishery the latest, with fifteen of twenty-four merchants in Iwanai-Furuu becoming involved only the 1880s and early 1890s, in what was clearly a movement away from a fishery dominated by experienced fishers. Middling fishers in places like Rumoi left the fishery readily when times were bad and were easily replaced when times became good again because so many of them were in fact merchants and not career fishers.

There is nothing in Kaneko's background to suggest that he had any direct, personal experience in fishing—not that he would have needed any: even if he could not tell the difference between *dō nishin* and *sasame nishin* (two varieties of fertilizer made from similar types of herring offal), he would easily have been able to hire someone who could. Indeed, anyone with the money and the inclination could buy or lease a ready-made pound-trap fishery almost on demand. For example, in December 1884, one Sōma Jintarō leased a fishery in Hamamasu, complete with waterfront land, a pound trap, storehouses and other buildings, and over one hundred separate pieces of gear and other goods—even four barrels of pickled herring—for 300 yen per year for three years. Examples of this sort abound.[14]

Although the sample of pound-trap operators presented here is too small and was compiled from sources too subjective to support a sustained analysis, we can draw several tentative conclusions about the pound-trap fishers as a group. First, the trend toward merchant domination of the fishery is attributable in part to the impact of technological innovation, which made the fisheries large, industrial enterprises amenable to control by people with managerial skills, with or without experience in fishing; and in part to the legal and institutional changes outlined in Chapter 4, which attracted commercial interests to the fishery as a speculative investment.[15]

Second, the decline of former gill-netters was a function of the ascendancy of merchants because it was merchants, in their role as suppliers of credit, who regulated the entry of newcomers into the pound-trap fishery. Merchant capital moved from the realm of circulation—money lending—to the realm of production as merchants used their control over credit to acquire fishing rights through foreclosure. This process naturally restricted the options available to small fishers who relied on merchants for funding, and, in the eyes of concerned officials, it "impeded the smooth development of the fishery."[16]

Finally, as merchants without a long-term interest in fishing began investing in the fishery, it may have become more difficult for fishery workers to obtain the necessary patronage to establish themselves as independent entrepreneurs if for no other reason than that the ties between merchant fishers and their workers lasted only as long as the merchants' involvement in the fishery. This final conclusion is necessarily speculative because of the lack of biographical data for fishers in the early twentieth century, when, presumably, enough merchants would have been involved in the fishery long enough to sponsor the independent business activities of their employees. Still, over the long term we can see a qualitative change in the organization of fishing operations, from the quite large but still household-centered enterprises of former contractors like Fujino and Suhara—Suhara's downfall was precipitated in part by his adopted son's embezzlement of large sums of money[17]—to the bureaucratic organization of fishing companies like the ones that eventually dominated the Okhotsk Sea fishery in the 1920s and 1930s. This type of change turned fishery workers into "salarymen" who could aspire to become permanently employed supervisors (*yakubito*)—but not bosses (*oyakata*) in their own right.

Whatever their origins, gill-netters and pound-trap fishers alike relied heavily on credit to finance their operations. The only ones who could get by without credit were those fishers with operations so big they could finance numerous others as well as themselves. The prefectural government estimated that in 1889 the annual credit market was over 3.8 million yen, a figure it calculated on the assumption that it cost about one thousand yen to operate each of the 3,241 pound traps and about three yen to work each of the 197,789 sets of gill nets registered in the fishery. The actual operating costs were often much higher, depending on the location of the fishery.[18] Moreover, since the government's calculations did not take into account either the secondary credit market, in which essentially the same money was lent and re-lent by big fishers to smaller fishers and by all fishers to their workers, or the abundance of renegotiated loans, the 3.8-million-yen figure represents only "new" money pumped into the fishery in 1889; the sum of all credit transactions was actually far higher.

The money for all this lending came ultimately from fertilizer brokers in Osaka and its environs, as well as merchants in Tokyo, Nagoya, and other large cities.[19] Although Osaka capital occasionally came directly into the fishery, it more commonly passed through the hands of Hokuriku-based shippers (who were often fertilizer brokers in their own right) or local merchants in Hokkaido. Once the capital entered the Hokkaido credit market, it usually went to fishers by way of merchants dealing in marine products. Funds sometimes went directly to gill-netters, especially if they lived in or near a large port, but more often they went first to pound-trap operators, who then extended credit to local fishers.[20]

Merchant money lenders in towns like Hakodate, Esashi, and Otaru ran businesses similar to that of the Kishida house described in Chapter 3. The merchant community in each port had its own economic sphere. Accordingly, Hakodate capital flowed into fisheries all along the Pacific coast to Nemuro and beyond, into Karafuto, the Kurils, and Russian/Soviet territory. Merchants in Esashi extended credit to fishers in southwestern Hokkaido, while those in Otaru financed fishing operations on the northwest coast of the island. However, Fukuyama, which had been a center of economic life under the Matsumae domain, fell into a prolonged depression shortly after the Meiji Restoration, despite the fact that a number of merchants and large fishers maintained bases there well into the 1890s.[21]

Credit transactions generally took one of three different forms. The most common, accounting for half or more of all transactions in the herring fishery, was the supply-lending (*shikomi*) method discussed in Chapter 3. As in the Tokugawa period, fishers received advances of cash and commodities in the winter and repaid them, with interest, the following summer. Small fishers benefited in some ways from the economic changes of the late nineteenth century because the abolition of the contracting system and the liberalization of trade between Hokkaido and Honshu increased their options in securing access to both credit and markets. At the same time, however, the bonds of dependency fostered by supply-lending relationships became tighter. Instead of receiving credit throughout the year (*shūnen jikomi*), small fishers were expected to settle their accounts promptly at the end of the fishing season (*gyoki jikomi*); and for those who could not meet their obligations, foreclosure on gear and fishing grounds put up as collateral was as likely a consequence as renegotiation of the debt.[22]

In the Tokugawa period, too, supply lending had involved a mix of informal patronage and formal, contractual relations, but the recipe in the late nineteenth century called for a larger measure of formal and contractual elements. With such contractual relations, creditors readily foreclosed on defaulting clients, a development that compromised the independence of small fishers even if it did not immediately result in their proletarianization. Thus, a fisher who had lost his land and gear to a creditor and had in effect become a tenant enjoyed far less control over the locus, scale, and nature of his production than one who owned his means of production.

Still, ordinary supply lending, even as it was practiced in the late nineteenth century, was considerably less immiserating for small fishers than
a second common form of credit, called green-paddy sales (*aota uri*). Under this method, the creditor fixed a price for the following season's herring catch in advance and forwarded his client that amount, less twenty
to thirty percent in interest and marketing commissions. This system had
the advantage of shifting the risk of a disastrous catch to the creditor, but
it also meant that the fisher would not profit from a catch larger than the
preseason estimate. For that reason, perhaps, only nearly destitute fishers
who owned fishing rights but no gear of their own readily turned to it.
The sources treat this form of credit as a variation on ordinary supply
lending,[23] but in fact green-paddy credit was a highly exploitative arrangement, more akin to wage labor than anything else because the fisher re-
linquished all control over both the production and disposition of his
catch. Indeed, the only difference—albeit an important one—was that
the fisher retained freedom over his daily routine.

An example of green-paddy selling in action comes from Hamamasu
in 1878–79. In November 1878, a small fisher named Katō Jūsaburō received 127 yen from Honma Toyoshichi, the adopted son and successor
of the former contractor of the Hamamashike fishery, Nakagawaya
Yūsuke. Under the terms of the agreement, Katō was to repay the loan by
turning over to Honma all the herring meal he produced during the 1879
season. Whether Katō's catch proved sufficient to cover the amount of
the loan depended, of course, on the price set for the herring meal. But
the contract did not stipulate a price; rather, that was left for Honma to
determine at his own discretion at a later date. The agreement also allowed Honma to tack on an additional three percent sales commission to
Katō's debt. In the event that he did not produce enough fertilizer to ful-
fill his obligation, Katō agreed to provide the labor services of his two
sons for as long as necessary to make up the difference.[24] Honma's
records do not say what became of the 127 yen's worth of herring meal,
but in July 1879—the month that his green-paddy debt came due—Katō
borrowed fifty yen from Honma for a term of one month at thirty-six
percent annual interest, which certainly indicates that his financial problems were not over.[25]

Even with provisions to make up shortfalls written into this type of
credit agreement, it must have been difficult for lenders to get fishers to
meet their obligations because the economic incentive to produce was so
weak. For fishers, too, the arrangement was surely unsatisfactory: they
could circumvent the most exploitative elements of the credit relation-

ship by producing as little as possible but only at the cost of losing favor with their creditors; willfully limiting production, moreover, negated their hopes for attaining higher income and greater independence through hard work. Perhaps because of these problems, green-paddy arrangements fell into decline around the end of the nineteenth century and by 1909 accounted for only about three to four percent of the credit coming out of Hakodate.[26]

A third form of credit, in which the fisher put up as collateral first lien on a predetermined amount of herring (*shūkaku teitō*), was something of a cross between the two methods outlined above. It was similar to ordinary supply lending in that the fisher could repay his debt in either cash or kind, with the main difference being that the amount of fish necessary to meet the obligation was fixed in advance and thus immune to the ups and downs of the fertilizer market. This method, which was found most often in southern Hokkaido, also gave the fisher more control over the disposition of his catch than either of the first two methods because he was ostensibly free to sell it (or at least any surplus) on the open market. In practice, however, most fishers marketed their entire catch through a single creditor.[27]

Honma Toyoshichi engaged in this type of lending as well. In January 1878 he advanced commodities to a local fisher named Abe Kichitarō, in exchange for which Abe agreed to give Honma fifteen tons of herring meal later in the year. Sometime before the end of the fishing season a desperate Abe approached Honma for a further loan of foodstuffs. At first Honma refused, saying that Abe had reached his credit limit, but he later gave in because it appeared that Abe might go hungry otherwise. It cost Abe an additional 37.5 tons of fertilizer not to starve. But it seems that Honma's instincts about his client's credit-worthiness were correct, for Abe skipped town that summer, leaving only about thirty-eight tons of fish meal behind.[28]

Since credit in the fishery was linked to Honshu financial markets, not surprisingly broad economic trends affected the ability of fishers to obtain funds. For example, a March 1887 newspaper report from the Shakotan peninsula noted that the credit market had finally begun to relax after a prolonged period of tight money during the Matsukata deflation. As a practical matter, this relaxation meant that small fishers were able to return to a staple diet of rice after several years of locally grown potatoes, millet, and other grains—and just in time, too, since they had been so hard up the previous year they had not saved any grain for seed.[29] However, the same economic upturn that made it possible for small fishers to

be picky about their carbohydrates carried with it the potential to undermine their independence. Creditors pressured fishers into acquiescing to
green-paddy loans because they wanted to buy cheap before the fishing
season and sell dear after, when they expected fertilizer prices to rise sub-
stantially. Sure enough, the price of herring meal rose from 4.52 yen/ton
in 1886 to 7.52 yen/ton in 1887.[30]

A Seasonal Proletariat

Consider the options open to someone in the village of Otoshibe in
southeastern Hokkaido in late December 1884. The waters off the village—considered one of the best fisheries in southern Hokkaido—had
not seen a decent herring catch since 1880; a poor harvest had left the
community with rapidly dwindling supplies of millet, barley, potatoes,
and other staples of the local diet; and the Matsukata deflation had made
it almost impossible for fishers to secure credit. Villagers knew that when
the food ran out—as it would sometime in February—they would be
forced to dig through the deep mountain snow in search of bracken
(*warabi*) roots to help keep themselves alive.[31] Bracken root is not a particularly versatile ingredient for cooking, though it can be ground into a
paste that will substitute for rice cakes (*mochi*)—standard fare at New
Year's—in a pinch.

Given a choice between living off bracken-root paste and working for
wages in the herring fishery, most villagers in Otoshibe would no doubt
have gladly opted for work. The document describing Otoshibe's plight
makes no mention of labor recruiters in the village, but the opportunities
for wage work were surely well known to residents. Fishers in other communities in southern Hokkaido turned to wage labor when falling
catches and other circumstances made independent fishing difficult, so
we might speculate that the first steps toward proletarianization were
taken in years like 1884, when fishers had no other way to make ends
meet.

Having no fish, no food, and no credit in the winter of 1884 did not
necessarily condemn a small fisher in Otoshibe to a lifetime of wage labor. So long as his family held onto some gear, a fisher could sign onto a
fishing crew for one season and still hope that in the next catches would
improve enough and the credit market relax enough for him to return to
independent production. In any case, his wage labor would be limited to
several months during the spring and summer, away from home and family and thus remote from his identity as a small, independent fisher in a

community of other small, independent fishers. But both identity and community were bound to be jeopardized when the need to work for wages became a regular part of the fisher's life. ·

This section examines the growth of wage labor and the development of labor relations in the fishery in the late nineteenth and early twentieth centuries. It describes the growth of exogenous dependency and the nature of the relative immiseration of the seasonal proletariat of the Hokkaido fishery. Specifically, it addresses two discrete problems: the first concerns the social and economic forces that created a pool of workers available for wage labor in the fishery; and the second, the material conditions of life of those workers.

In the opening chapter I noted that an economic history of the fishery would be simple if I could describe the transformation of a completely self-sufficient community of fisher families into a disparate group of completely dependent fishery laborers. We have already seen, however, from our discussion of credit relations that small fishers were never completely self-sufficient. Nor were most fishery workers completely dependent, in part because they often did something else for a living much of the year: they were at most seasonal proletarians. It is possible, moreover, to distinguish among a number of levels of proletarianization, varying with the degree to which a worker's livelihood depended upon his ability to sell his labor. The truly proletarianized were those who moved from fishery to fishery in Hokkaido, Karafuto, and Kamchatka throughout the year. In Karafuto they were called "musk deer" (*jakō jika*) because they roamed around so much. On the other end of the scale were those—*demen* in the Hokkaido dialect—who worked only as casual day laborers during peak production times; frequently the *demen* were residents of agricultural villages near the coast who received their wages in herring—two to five baskets (*mokko*) a day for a woman, five to ten for a man—which they then processed into food for their families.[32]

Our assessment of the social costs of the development of the capitalist fishery requires us, moreover, to distinguish between workers from Hokkaido fishing villages and those from northern Honshu agricultural districts. In 1889, workers from Hokkaido constituted about thirty percent of the total labor force in the herring fishery (18,112 of 59,989 workers), while those from Honshu accounted for the remaining seventy percent (41,877 workers). Laborers from southern Hokkaido were valued by pound-trap operators for their experience and skill—after all, many were independent fishers in the off-season—but only a small number participated in the pound-trap fishery; instead, most worked for gill-netters based in or around their home villages. Workers from Honshu, however, were employed almost exclusively in the pound-trap fishery.[33]

In addition to workers from Honshu and southern Hokkaido, Ainu laborers, particularly from the inland districts of Ishikari (north of Sapporo) and the coastal sections of Iburi and Hidaka provinces in eastern Hokkaido, participated in the fishery. However, because the Ainu were no longer treated as a special category of labor, it is impossible to say how many of them worked as fishery laborers. Honma Toyoshichi of Hamamasu sent labor recruiters to Ishikari and other areas with large Ainu populations to find workers for the 1881 season. He also expressed interest in having a group of Sakhalin Ainu relocated to Hamamasu, where they might be put to work in the fishery. In fact, with 164 members, the Ainu community at Hamamasu in 1880 was still large enough to support the four-day bear festival (*iyomante*), the most important religious observance of the native people. Moreover, in 1896 Honma hired two workers with Ainu given names from the Saru district of Hidaka under terms similar to those for Wajin workers.[34]

Without question, wage labor in the fishery sustained Ainu communities throughout Hokkaido, even those in the relatively isolated inland districts of Hidaka, Tokachi, and Kushiro provinces that, since the late nineteenth century, have attracted anthropologists, missionaries, and tourists in search of "real" Ainu communities relatively unsullied by Japanese influence. In such areas, the community, acting through the *ukosanio*, or assembly of the headman and local household heads, selected the men and women who would respond to the recruiting efforts of the employment agents who traveled to their villages.[35]

We have already seen that the presence of workers from Tōhoku had at least as much to do with changes in the structure of Tōhoku agriculture as it did with developments within the herring fishery because, of course, the overwhelming majority of fishery workers from Honshu were from farming, not fishing, villages. For example, a study of 564 workers from Sannohe district, Aomori, between 1917 and 1919 revealed that 485 (eighty-six percent) considered themselves farmers, while seventy-two (thirteen percent) were day laborers, and the remaining seven (one percent) were artisans; none, in other words, considered himself a fisher.[36] As in the Tokugawa period, young men from places like the Shimokita peninsula were easily attracted by the prospect of a better life in Hokkaido. In the village of Ōhata, more than a fourth (765 of 2,823) of the residents in 1880 were migrant laborers (*dekasegi*) in Hokkaido; even in less extreme cases up to one-tenth of the people—and surely a much higher percentage of the able-bodied men—from villages on the north coast of the peninsula engaged in migrant labor. Even as recently as the 1950s, anyone not bound to Shimokita by family responsibilities went to Hokkaido to work in the fishing and lumber industries because it was so much better economically than staying at home.[37]

Whatever their perceptions of the physical and psychological burdens of the work, Tōhoku peasants interviewed after World War II agreed that labor in the fishery had been a positive economic opportunity because there were no similar opportunities for them closer to home. For instance, without the fishery the best many younger sons of tenant farmers in the interior of Akita in the early twentieth century could hope for was work in neighboring households for room and board—but no pay—as a way to reduce the number of mouths to feed at home.[38] But the objective economic benefits of the opportunity to work for wages must be viewed separately from the social dislocation that inevitably resulted when a large number of villagers were away from home for much of the year. In 1940, a bureaucrat studying labor problems in the Okhotsk Sea fishery spoke of workers in a village in Akita in the following terms:

> The migrant fishery workers [here] have no desire to improve their lot, but instead are content to spend their days merely eating, drinking, sleeping—and sometimes causing trouble for the people of nearby communities. "Migrant fisher" [*dekasegi gyofu*] is a dirty word in these parts.[39]

The growth of the capitalist fishery had a very different impact on small fishers in southern Hokkaido. Their proletarianization can be directly attributed to the closing of access to fishing grounds, the tightening of credit, and the technological innovation and attendant ecological damage that accompanied the rapid development of the fishery. The advent of a capitalist fishery was a more directly immiserating process for them because of their proximity to the forces shaping the development of the industry. That is, a Tōhoku peasant's decision to seek wage labor in Hokkaido was a response to immiserating forces—tenancy, for instance— that had already taken their toll before he had anything to do with the fishery. But structural change was much more a zero-sum game for a small fisher in Hokkaido, as when, for example, he lost his gear and waterfront land to a creditor who immediately rented the gear and land back to him or, worse, offered him a place in his own fishing crew.

At the same time, however, the process of proletarianization was not necessarily as abrupt for small fishers as it was for Tōhoku peasants. Laborers from Tōhoku were locked into the capitalist fishery because they had never been an integral part of the precapitalist fishery. We have seen that it was occasionally possible for workers to rise through the ranks of the labor hierarchy to become fishery operators, but the fisheries they operated were themselves capitalist enterprises. Whatever other identity Tōhoku workers may have retained as peasant cultivators in Honshu during the off-season had nothing directly to do with their status as proletarians in the fishery. Conversely, every small fisher fit somewhere on a status continuum that ranged from gill-netters who retained complete control over production (but, because of the way credit worked, not over the disposition of their produce), down to people from southern Hokkaido villages who worked for wages year-round with little hope of ever becoming independent. Between these extremes were fishers who pooled their resources and labor with relatives and neighbors in a cooperative-production (kyōdō eigyō) arrangement; fishers who rented their fishing gear but retained control over production ("tenants"); fishers who joined cooperative crews that fished for a share of the catch with borrowed gear and supplies ("sharecroppers") (bukata); fishers involved in green-paddy credit relations; and fishers who repaid debts of supplies of food and commodities received year-round with seasonal labor in the herring fishery.[40]

For small fishers, proletarianization could occur overnight, but it was more likely to be an incremental process, a long, slow slide from having complete, to having little, and finally to having no control over the means or the processes of production. The situation was further complicated by the fact that an individual fisher could occupy a number of different positions on the status continuum during his lifetime. Thus, while the knowledge that 18,112 residents of Hokkaido were working for wages in the fishery in 1889 tells us a lot about the structure of the herring fishery and something about the general direction of the development of southern Hokkaido village society, it does not tell us how many of the 18,112 individuals would be working for wages for the rest of their lives or how many were merely young men waiting to succeed to their fathers' fisheries. Nor, unfortunately, does it tell us anything about how the removal of women from the fishery after the decline of household production affected gender relations or family structure. But there is no doubt that dramatic changes took place within village communities, both in Hokkaido and Honshu, as a result of the growth of wage labor and the concomitant destruction of the material basis of power relations within the household. As Michael Lewis has shown, this was certainly the case in Toyama, where the wives of fishery workers, many of whom were dockworkers themselves, organized the 1918 rice riots.[41]

Traditional labor recruitment involved direct negotiations between a fisher or his agent and prospective workers. Pound-trap operators or their representatives (either full-time employees of the operator or boat pilots working on commission) typically traveled to Tōhoku villages to sign on workers for the coming season; alternatively, they sometimes sent out notices asking those seeking work to gather at some designated spot. Workers hired directly from their villages through personal contacts were considered the most reliable, so any fisher who could afford to recruit labor in this manner did so.[42] Prospective workers could also take the initiative by traveling directly to a fishery to secure work, often as day laborers to augment the regular crew during peak production times. Such laborers were often viewed with suspicion, however, because of the high incidence of flight by workers in mid-season. Accordingly, they were hired mostly by fishers in relatively unproductive areas in the southern and eastern parts of the island.[43]

Another method of labor recruitment was to work through professional employment agencies (*shūsen'ya*), located mostly in Hakodate and Otaru but also in some Tōhoku cities and towns. The larger agencies were organized as joint-stock "migrant-fisher protection" companies (*dekasegi gyofu hogo kaisha*), the avowed purpose of which was to "reduce the vice [*akuhei*] endemic among fishery workers and promote the mutual interest of employer and employee."[44] The novelist Kobayashi Takiji not unreasonably portrayed the shadiest of the employment agencies lined up along the Hakodate wharves as little more than the debt-collection arms of saloons and brothels: when some unfortunate ran up a huge tab, thugs would escort him to an agent who signed him on as a cannery worker in Kamchatka or the Sea of Okhotsk and turned the wage advance over to the brothel in payment of the debt.[45]

Most observers did not think much of the character of fishery workers. Although the home ministry, in a study done in 1899, described laborers who had contracted to work prior to the beginning of the season as generally hard-working and reliable, it said that casual workers were unwilling to work, gambled frequently, demanded large portions of their wages in advance, threatened physical violence against their employers, and absconded in mid-season only to move elsewhere and defraud another operator.[46] This study echoed the sentiments of Hida Ryūdō, an 1882 visitor to Hokkaido, who said that workers "borrow their wages in advance and immediately plot escape." The workers are very well paid, continued Hida, but they "squander their money and fall deeper into depravity with each passing day. No more than two or three out of a thousand ever send money home to their parents. And because they borrow more and more in advance from their employers every year,

the workers [fall so deep in debt that they] eventually find it impossible to
return home."[47] Without a doubt, hardened veterans of the fishery were
tough and could be difficult to handle. Honma Toyoshichi noted in his
journal for 25 December 1880 that three of five workers he had hired just
the day before had done no work but instead had spent all their time
drinking and picking fights with other workers. "They are dissolute beyond all hope," he wrote, obviously exasperated.[48]

Fishery operators were hardly innocent victims however: "Employers
offer sweet-sounding contracts, but after the work is done they make a
hundred excuses for not paying wages or bonuses," complained Hida.[49]
The home ministry called for stern measures to counter the rising incidence of flight but went on to note that workers had to endure terrible
working and living conditions, "often no better than slavery."[50] Yet despite the inhumane conditions, the majority of workers were in fact diligent and obedient, and the number of potential workers showed no signs
of declining.[51]

Absconding workers were indeed a perennial headache for fishery operators. During a large herring run it was possible for laborers to find
temporary work for wages that were as high as one yen per day in 1882.
(In contrast, in the same year, a casual laborer outside the fishery earned
a daily wage of about thirty sen in Iwanai.) Since the seasonal wage for
an average worker at about the same time was around thirty-five yen, it
was not uncommon for an unscrupulous (or enterprising, depending on
one's perspective) worker to sign a contract and accept a large advance
on his wages, only to abscond shortly after arriving at his employer's fishery and spend the rest of the season working as a day laborer. Because no
fishery operator could afford the time or effort needed to chase after
every errant worker, laborers could often flee almost at will.[52] Honma's
journal records a number of attempts at flight by workers (often preceded by a fight with another laborer or some other incident), though
most who absconded were either quickly apprehended or returned on
their own. In one case, however, the absconder was discovered working
at another fishery, which prompted Honma to demand that the other
fisher provide either a replacement or cash as compensation.[53]

Understandably, fishers' organizations tried to combat the problem.[54]
Honma came up with a plan for an elaborate system of passes and registration to prevent unauthorized movement by fishery workers. A Mr. Doi
of the Hokkaido Fisheries Association (Hokusui Kyōkai) developed a
scheme that called for local government authorities to confiscate workers' identification papers as a way to curb mobility.[55] So far as I can ascer-

tain, neither of these plans was ever put into effect on anything more than a local scale,[56] but the state did demonstrate concern, even if it could not effectively curtail the problem. The state was interested in part for the same reasons as fishery operators but also because the relative anonymity of the Hokkaido fishery made it a popular destination for draft dodgers from Honshu. Thus the Development Agency instructed fishers as early as 1875 not to hire any laborers who had not registered as transients (*kiryū*) with local authorities, an order that was repeated by the prefectural government nine years later; Honma wrote compliance with this rule into his proposed regulations.[57]

Workers may have quit their fisheries in mid-season because they feared that in the event of a bad catch they would not receive the wages and bonuses due to them at the end of the season. Flight could therefore serve as a kind of preemptive strike against breaches of contract by fishery operators. An analogous situation prevailed in the cod fishery of Newfoundland, where creditors would sometimes foreclose on a fisher in mid-season if it seemed likely that the catch would be too small for the fisher to meet all of his obligations. In this manner nervous creditors often ruined fishers who might otherwise have turned a profit.[58]

In the absence of unionization, flight or the threat of flight served to protect workers from unusually bad treatment at any given fishery, though it did not assure them of good treatment in the industry as a whole. In any event, abscondence, whether motivated by desperation or by a desire to defraud an employer of advance wages, was a method of last resort. As a breach of contract it was illegal. Moreover, the fleeing worker left his guarantor—usually his father or other close relative—responsible for repaying whatever advance wages he had received. Consequently, even while acknowledging the importance of flight as a form of worker resistance, we should not see it as a significant ameliorative of the immiserating impact of wage labor in the fishery. However well it may have worked for some individual laborers, it was not a realistic long-term answer to the problem of poor working conditions.

Workers dissatisfied with conditions in the fishery could, of course, seek employment elsewhere. But for most workers that was a let-them-eat-cake solution to their problems. In northern Tōhoku and southern Hokkaido, where there were few local opportunities for wage work, people sought employment through well-established networks that sent women to textile mills and brought men to the Hokkaido fishery. For men, no reasonable alternative—industrial labor in a major city, for instance—was likely to be much more attractive than work in the fishery. At the very least, seasonal work in the fishery allowed workers to return home during the off-season. Moreover, whatever its drawbacks, work in the fishery paid better, was less dangerous, and was seen as more honorable than labor in Hokkaido's other major industries, construction and mining, both of which relied heavily on convict labor throughout the Meiji period.[59]

The uncertainty of the catch and the possibility that workers might simply leave gave rise to a profound conflict of interest between workers and employers. Workers sought to protect themselves by getting as much of their wages as possible up front, while retaining a system of bonuses based on total productivity to ensure that they would be duly rewarded in the event of a very good harvest of fish.[60] Fishery operators, however, did not want to invest a lot of money in workers who might never actually show up; and at any rate they probably considered the demands of creditors more compelling than requests for workers' back pay—assuming, of course, that there was any money to distribute in the first place.

Workers' wages varied considerably according to experience, recruitment method, and region. Moreover, because Tōhoku peasants chose to seek work in the fishery in response to economic conditions at home, a good harvest, like that of 1886, could keep peasants at home and push wages up, while a poor one could drive large numbers of workers north and hold wages down, as it did in 1903.[61] In general, the more productive the fishery, the better the wages (and the more intense the labor). The best-paid workers around 1890 were pilots in places like Bikuni and Atsuta, who made a base wage of about eighty yen per season. In contrast, a pilot at a fishery along the depressed Hiyama coast earned a seasonal wage of only about thirty yen. The differential for lower-ranking workers was less (twenty to thirty-five yen in the best areas, fifteen to twenty-five yen in the worst).[62]

Fishers paid their workers in four different ways. The first was to pay the entire base wage in advance, a method that obviously required the employer's complete trust in his workers. It was found almost exclusively in villages in the vicinity of Hakodate, where fishers and their workers had long-standing relationships. A second method was to advance the worker two-thirds or more of his seasonal wage when the contract was signed. This was a popular choice when contracting for laborers in Tōhoku villages, perhaps because it ensured that the laborer's family would get a substantial portion of the money. The third and fourth methods, used most commonly when hiring workers through agents, were to pay either about one-fourth of the wage or only travel expenses in advance. These methods were no doubt motivated by the fear that the la-borer might never show up for work.[63]

In addition to base wages, bonuses tied to productivity were an important source of income for fishery workers, both in Hokkaido and elsewhere.[64] The bonuses (*teate*) were also called "nine-one money" (*kuichikin*) because the fishery operator would commonly keep ninety percent of the season's profits for himself and divide the remaining one-tenth, less taxes and operating expenses, among his workers. Fishers, es-pecially in highly productive regions, frequently tried to reduce or elimi-nate bonus payments. Honma, for example, distributed only five percent of the profits to his workers, a practice followed by a number of other op-erators.[65] The practice never disappeared, however, and it was the corner-stone of the wage structure employed in the factory ships of the 1920s and 1930s.

The bonus system ensured that workers maintained an interest in the productivity of the fishery. In that sense it was superficially similar to the practice of sharecropping (*bukata*), though fishers under the sharecrop-ping system divided seventy (or sometimes sixty) percent of the catch among themselves but received no wages.[66] As a practical matter bonuses provided an incentive for hard work, particularly during herring runs, when the intensity of fishers' labor could make or break a season's prof-its. Workers may therefore have viewed it as just compensation for the extra work of a good season. The downside was that fishery operators could and did manipulate the bonus system, both as a carrot to induce workers to act in ways that were at once self-exploitative and a source of conflict among workers (like working through meal breaks) and as a stick to threaten those who did not seem to be pulling their own weight. The use of the bonus system as a stick seems to have been most prevalent in the factory ships and canneries of the Sea of Okhotsk fishery.[67] In the smaller herring fisheries of Hokkaido, where bonuses appear more com-monly to have been calculated on a fixed scale, the system was a useful way for the fisher to distribute part of the risk of a bad catch among his workers. This desire to distribute risk may explain why the bonuses were higher and wages lower in areas where catches were erratic than in dis-tricts with consistently good returns.[68]

According to a home ministry study, one reason work in the fishery was so popular was the extraordinarily "simple" (*junboku*) nature of the people of Aomori and Akita prefectures, which supplied the overwhelm-ing majority of workers. One suspects, however, that another reason given

TABLE 14

ŌTAKI SANZŌ'S WAGE ACCOUNT, 1899

Item	Amount (yen)
Wages	20.000
Bonus	0.100
Total credits	20.100
Wage advance	7.000
Cash loans	1.000
Purchases	12.619
Docked wages (26 days)	4.081
Total charges	24.700
Balance	(4.600)

SOURCE: "Seisansho" [10 July 1899], "Hamamasu gun Honma-ten gyogyō kankei shorui toji."

by the ministry's study—that wages were far better than anything available at home—was more significant.[69] However, wages were not always as good as they may have seemed to "simple" and inexperienced workers recruited by boat pilots seeking to fill a quota;[70] indeed, workers sometimes wound up owing their employers money at the end of the herring season.[71] For example, Table 14 is the wage account of Ōtaki Sanzō, a worker originally from Yamagata but resident in Hamamasu, who finished the 1899 season 4.60 yen in debt to his employer, Honma Toyoshichi. Most of the purchases Ōtaki made were for petty commodities like cloth, footwear, and foodstuffs that cost only a few sen apiece, but over the course of several months they added up to a substantial amount of money, as did the wages Ōtaki lost when he was off the job. Ōtaki's tiny bonus, just ten sen, did not help him much either. For reasons the surviving documents do not make clear, a boat pilot paid 2.11 yen of Ōtaki's debt for him, but he had to come up with the remaining 2.49 yen out of his own pocket.

Ōtaki's case may not have been typical, but neither was it unique. The Honma papers mention other workers that year who incurred debts larger than their seasonal wages, including one who was hired for twenty yen but ended up 15.262 yen in arrears. In every case for which there are data, docked pay for work missed (for any reason) was an important element in putting the worker into debt. It is easy to see how: in 1897, laborers at Honma's Aikappu fishery were charged for medical care and drugs in addition to having twenty to twenty-five sen deducted for every day they were off the job.[72]

Although most workers did in fact manage to avoid leaving the fishery in debt, they did not necessarily take much home. Records for Honma's fishery in 1900 reveal that the average final balance (including bonuses) for 106 workers was 8.819 yen, though the amounts ranged from 0.83 yen to 35.35 yen, with most hovering around the mean.[73] Of course, the final balance did not represent a laborer's total compensation for a season's work since he would have received a cash advance when he signed a contract (twenty-six workers who signed contracts with Honma between 1895 and 1900 received advances totaling 6.00 yen to 37.514 yen and averaging 14.41 yen)[74] and perhaps some cash during the fishing, as well as commodities with a cash value. Still, it is easy to see how many people fell into the pattern described by Hida:

> After the herring season finishes the workers move on to the kelp fishery and when that's done they move again to the autumn salmon fishery. In the winter they are supposed to return home, but in fact most are so heavily in debt that they cannot, so they cut wood to earn a meager living until the next herring season comes around.[75]

Given the nature of the Hokkaido herring fishery, with production dispersed among hundreds of fishing grounds of unequal and unstable value, it is not surprising to learn that factory industrialization never took place. In the 1920s and 1930s, however, a surrogate for full industrialization did emerge in the factory ships that canned crab and salmon in the Sea of Okhotsk. Unlike the comparatively small capitalist enterprises of Hokkaido, the factory ships were owned and operated by large, modern corporations based in Hakodate or Tokyo.

The factory ships' ties to the herring fishery were twofold: first, many of the entrepreneurs who made fortunes in the crab fishery began their careers in the herring fisheries of Hokkaido and Karafuto, so there was a certain continuity of both purpose and capital; second—and more important—the work force was drawn from the same pool of poor, unskilled peasants from northeastern Honshu, and poor, skilled fishers from southern Hokkaido. These were men (and a few women) for whom the declining Hokkaido fishery was no longer of any use, so they had little choice but to endure the extremely long hours and arduous routine of the six-month voyages into Soviet waters. The pay was good, at least compared with what was available at home, but it was scant compensation for the danger and indignity the workers suffered.

Many elements of the labor relations that prevailed in the Hokkaido herring fishery were later reproduced in the Sea of Okhotsk.[76] However, working conditions in the new fisheries were far worse than in Hokkaido. One former worker, Watanabe Masasuke of Eramachi, a fishing village just outside Fukuyama, was first recruited along with about twenty other men from the same village in 1931 by an acquaintance who had already made the voyage once before. He described his experiences on a factory ship as "Hell on Earth":

> I worked on factory ships for five years, and I can tell you that no one signed on expecting to come home alive, it was so tough. "I won't go next time, I really won't go," everyone would say. "I won't go on the factory ship." [*Kondo goso igane, kondo goso iganette . . . kani kōsen nante igane.*] But then the time would come and there'd be no other way to make any money, so we all had to endure the hardship and go back.[77]

The factory ships usually set sail from Hakodate around the tenth of April and did not return to port until sometime in October. Flight was not a viable option at sea, so workers had little choice but to make the best of appalling working conditions. The typical workday began at around three or four in the morning, though workers got up as early as one o'clock when things were *really* busy. They rarely quit before about nine or ten at night and sometimes toiled considerably later. The grueling work schedule was the product of a conspiracy between the crabs, who had to be harvested wherever and whenever they were found, and the managers of the large fishing companies in Tokyo, who had stockholders to please. The only reprieve came during bad weather, when it was not possible to send boats out to fish. Strict work discipline was enforced by foremen whose brutality was underwritten by a strict quota system, to which their own livelihoods were linked.

Former workers agreed that polished rice, generally unavailable at home, was one of the attractions of the job, but their overall impression of the diet was that it was bad and monotonous. The main dish at breakfast, lunch, and dinner was rice, accompanied by miso soup or perhaps pickles. Sanitary conditions aboard ship were terrible, a situation exacerbated by the fact that few carried doctors, though most had a pharmacist. Neither factory ships nor onshore canneries made provisions for the leisure activities of workers, partly because of a lack of concern for such things on the part of employers and partly because of a lack of leisure time on the part of the workers: sleep was the only sanctioned recreational activity.[78]

Conditions were no better at the onshore canneries in the northern Kurils, according to a secret report prepared by the Hokkaido prefectural government in 1938.[79] The report's description of the appalling working conditions at the canneries is particularly credible considering that, far from a polemic along the lines of Kobayashi's *Factory Ship*, the document was written by bureaucrats for distribution within government circles only. The authors of the report urged reform of conditions that included twenty-one-hour workdays, poor food and sanitary conditions, and a wage structure that, because of its emphasis on performance-related bonuses, encouraged workers to remain on the job even when they were clearly too ill to continue.

The Sea of Okhotsk fishery absorbed much of the labor that was displaced by the decline of the Hokkaido herring fishery in the 1920s and later. Thus in 1938 the largest group of Japanese fishery workers in Soviet waters (7,731, or 41.3 percent, of 18,712) were residents of Hokkaido, with laborers from Akita (4,382, or 23.4 percent), Aomori (3,821, or 20.4 percent), and Iwate (1,151, or 6.2 percent) supplying most of the rest.[80] As can be seen from the data on destinations of fishery workers in 1930, the same situation prevailed in other fisheries, though the proportional representation of each prefecture varied considerably:

Workers from Hokkaido		*Workers from Aomori*	
Kamchatka	8,788	Hokkaido	11,560
Karafuto	5,519	Maritime Prov.	5,281
Toyama	200	Karafuto	1,995
Maritime Prov.	177	Kamchatka	0
Other	35	Other	204
Total	14,719	Total	19,040

Workers from Akita		*Workers from Iwate*	
Hokkaido	5,515	Hokkaido	1,561
Kamchatka	2,351	Kamchatka	1,246
Karafuto	1,365	Shizuoka	151
Maritime Prov.	341	Karafuto	121
Other	67	Other	508
Total	9,639	Total	3,587[81]

TABLE 15

RESIDENCE OF FISHERY WORKERS

ENTERING HOKKAIDO, 1930

Prefecture	Number	(%)
Aomori	11,560	42.2
Akita	5,515	20.1
Ishikawa	3,016	11.0
Toyama	1,979	7.2
Niigata	1,680	6.1
Iwate	1,561	5.7
Other	2,126	7.7
Total	27,437	100.0

SOURCE: Aomori ken chihō shokugyō shōkai jimukyoku, *Tōhoku chihō, Hokkaidō nō-, san-, gyoson shokugyō shōkai no mondai,* part 2, pp. 66–68.

Table 15 reveals that even with competition from new fisheries in the north, the largest group of outside workers in Hokkaido continued to come from the traditional areas of northern Tōhoku, with Hokuriku providing most of the rest.

The point of this brief overview of working conditions aboard the factory ships is to highlight the continuities between the Hokkaido herring fishery and the large-scale, industrial capitalism of the canneries. With the decline of fishing in Hokkaido work aboard the factory ships became the most feasible way for small fishers and peasants in Hokkaido and Tōhoku to make a living. The wages they earned were good, but workers had to endure all manner of hardship and deprivation. The trip from fishing villages in southern Hokkaido to the icy waters of the Sea of Okhotsk was clearly an immiserating one for factory-ship workers—immiserating both in the sense of material deprivation and in the sense of a loss of independence.

This description raises questions about the nature of immiseration. Usually, immiseration is used to refer to a decline in economic standing—a decreasing ability to obtain adequate food, shelter, and clothing. This I term absolute, or material, immiseration. However, here I have treated immiseration as a process whereby individuals lose control over their own lives in a way that is not immediately or necessarily linked to income or other quantitative measures of living standards. Rather, immiseration is a social construct, tied to individuals' perceptions of their relative place in society. Accordingly, I call this relative, or social, immiseration. I have focused on relative immiseration because any measure of well-being, even a superficially objective one like caloric intake, is necessarily subjective. To demonstrate that independence was a genuine concern for small fishers, and therefore a reasonable standard of their perception of their place in society, the following chapter examines their response to assaults on their position as petty proprietors.

The immiseration of fishers in the material sense became historically important only after the process of immiseration in the social sense had been completed—that is, after fishery workers had lost all control over the means and processes of production. Thus, the immiseration of a small fisher in the 1880s entailed a gradual loss of independence, as reflected by a growing need to work for wages part of the year to supplement an otherwise inadequate income from individual fishing operations the rest of the year. The question of whether the fisher's total income was higher or lower as a result of his entry into the labor market is secondary, if not immaterial, in this context. However, an immiserated fishery worker in the 1930s really was miserable: having no independence left to lose, he literally risked his life for six months at a time in Soviet waters, fishing or packing crabmeat sixteen to twenty-two hours a day under strict supervision and in unsanitary conditions.

This semantic shift is more than a rhetorical device. During the development of capitalism, the fewer alternatives people have to selling their labor, the more vulnerable they become to exploitation by the people buying that labor. The sum of alternatives is the degree of their independence. Thus, immiseration refers to two aspects of the same process: first a loss of independence and then, when the alternatives are gone, an attack on material well-being. Eventually, labor organization and state action may bring about a new equilibrium, in which workers are protected from the worst abuses of capitalist production relations. But until then, workers are vulnerable. More simply, the companies operating the factory ships could not have subjected their workers to inhumane treatment if the workers had had a reasonable alternative to labor in the factory ships. But, as Watanabe said, "The time would come and there'd be no other way to make any money, so we all had to endure the hardship and go back [to the factory ships]." [82]

CHAPTER SIX

A Right to Be Rational

Karafuto, 1905–1935

Even by Hokkaido's standards, Karafuto (Sakhalin) is a cold and lonely place. Chekhov likened it to hell (frozen over, no doubt).[1] Yet during the decade after Japan acquired the southern half of the island from Russia in 1905, more than sixty thousand Japanese—perhaps a third of them fishers from Hokkaido, Tōhoku, and Hokuriku—moved there.[2] The fishers were attracted by the abundant herring, trout, and salmon living in the icy northern waters, and they naturally thought that the Japanese government would be happy to have them. After all, just as they and their forebears had settled the Hokkaido coast, their migration north would contribute to the growth and prosperity of Japan's latest territorial acquisition. This combination of patriotic zeal and personal ambition no doubt served to accentuate their frustration and outrage when the authorities made it clear that their dreams of rich catches were to remain unfulfilled.

The government had other plans for the Karafuto fish. The colonial administration needed to secure a steady source of tax revenue to finance development projects. The best way to do this was to confirm the fishing rights of pound-trap operators who had been active in Russian Sakhalin and to grant similar rights to new operators from Hokkaido. Family fishers were free to stay in Karafuto, but they could not fish herring, salmon, or trout. That left cod, flounder, crab, kelp, and miscellaneous other varieties of marine life that offered little hope of a steady income. Despite the hardships, however, the small fishers stubbornly remained in Karafuto.

For nine years they struggled with the government to get the fishing rights they felt were rightfully theirs.

Why did the small fishers bother to fight the government? Contemporary commentators called them gamblers "concerned only with getting rich quick."[3] But the gamble was the same for herring fishers everywhere—if the fish ran, times were good; if not, times were bad. The only way to fix the odds in one's favor was to have a number of nets (preferably pound traps) in different places, so a good catch at one fishery would offset a poor one elsewhere. Catches were more reliably good in Karafuto than in Hokkaido, and there was less competition. But life was essentially the same crapshoot for small fishers in both places. Gamblers, whether by temperament or circumstance, had no need to go to Karafuto to ply their trade.

To understand the small fishers' behavior, we must first consider what Karafuto represented to them when the Japanese took over in 1905. At the time of its acquisition, the territory was a tabula rasa: aside from a few hundred native Ainu, Nivkhi (Gilyak), and Uilta (Oroke), only several dozen destitute Russian subjects, left over from the island's years as a penal colony, remained thinly scattered about the southern half of the island; few, if any, of these people were herring fishers. Karafuto was thus different from Taiwan, Korea, and other colonies acquired through modern Japanese imperialism. Moreover, unlike Hokkaido, which was already part of Japan when it acquired juridical status as a colony in 1868, Karafuto was for all practical purposes new territory. To be sure, Wajin fishers and bakufu officials had established a presence there in the late eighteenth century, and between 1854 and 1875 the entire island was jointly occupied by Japan and Russia, but there was little continuity between the earlier period and the four decades of Japanese colonial administration after 1905. Moreover, although Japanese pound-trap operators had leased fishing rights in Sakhalin before the war, the new administration was under no particular constraint to respect those rights.[4]

In the Hokkaido fishery, as we have seen, social and economic relations were the product of two centuries of development. Whatever aspirations fishers and officials there may have had for the future had to be adapted to the institutional and ecological legacy of that past development. In Karafuto, however, there were no such constraints: the resource remained abundant, the institutional ties to the past were inconsequential, and even the ecosystems of the native peoples functioned independently of the herring fishery.

In short, fishers and officials in Karafuto could create from scratch any sort of fishery they chose. Significantly, the major actors in the fishing economy—pound-trap operators, gill-netters, and the state—all envisioned a capitalist future for Karafuto. Conflict thus centered on the terms of participation in the capitalist economy. Family fishers moved to Karafuto in pursuit of a dream of entrepreneurial success that was no longer possible in the declining Hokkaido fishery. Pound-trap operators and the officials who supported them, conversely, saw the efforts of the small fishers as an impediment to the rational development of the fishery, an attempt to gain entry to what they considered to be the already-closed ranks of capitalist entrepreneurs.

The issues contested in Karafuto were clearly significant well beyond the limited context of the herring fishery. Expressed in the idiom of net types and fishing licenses was a debate over the fundamental nature of subjecthood in the modern imperial state, a debate being carried on throughout Japan during the first two decades of the twentieth century. If, as Carol Gluck argues, a major goal of the Meiji oligarchs had been to create a "sense of nation" among the Japanese people, the period immediately following the Russo-Japanese War saw ordinary citizens define for themselves their role as participants in that newly realized nation.[5] The history of Karafuto after 1905 thus presents us with a unique opportunity to see the debate over the nature of citizenship phrased in terms of immediate and practical policy considerations, with both sides of the conflict presenting their arguments clearly and coherently.

The real attraction of Karafuto for the household fishers, then, was the prospect of independence and full participation in the entrepreneurial fishery. As we have seen, by the beginning of the twentieth century Hokkaido had become a difficult place for small fishers to live and work in. Those in productive areas in the west and north faced intense competition for both fish and the land to process it, while fishers in the south found it hard to make a living at all. With proletarianization a very real prospect if they remained in Hokkaido, small fishers saw the Japanese takeover of Karafuto in 1905 as a way to participate in the capitalist fishery while there was still enough land and fish to go around.

Independence was not, however, simply a question of income or material well-being. Fishers persisted in their efforts to secure fishing rights at the expense of opportunities for immediate income as fishery workers. Those who obeyed the fishing laws often suffered great hardship, while those who broke them ran the risk of fines, imprisonment, and loss of boats and gear. And while family fishers were foundering on flounder or poaching herring, pound-trap operators in Karafuto had to import thousands of laborers every spring to work at their fisheries because they were unable to recruit workers locally.

Poachers and Petitioners

In August 1905, while Karafuto was still under Japanese military occupation, the Department of Civil Affairs (Minseisho), the Army's civilian administrative unit, issued a Provisional Order Governing Karafuto Fisheries that became the basis for later regulations.[6] The Provisional Order served to confirm the rights of Japanese who had operated fisheries between 1875 and 1905, when all of Sakhalin had been under Russian administration. Japanese who had fishing rights (either directly or through a Russian national) during the 1903 season were allowed to retain rights to fishing grounds they operated. Rights to remaining fisheries (mostly those that had been abandoned by Russians leaving Karafuto after the Japanese occupation) were auctioned off. The decision to confirm the rights of Japanese pound-trap operators was economically sound. Whatever immediate value the island had was the product of years of effort by Japanese entrepreneurs, and the payoff was immediate: revenues from leases on pound-trap fisheries totaled 848,274 yen—eighty-one percent of the Karafuto operating budget—in 1907.[7]

The Provisional Order allowed only the use of pound traps for herring, salmon, and trout fishing. A separate order provided for the establishment of a licensing system for harvesting cod, flounder, kelp, and other varieties of marine life that were lumped into a single, "miscellaneous" (*zatsuryō*) category.[8] The government allowed the use of a number of net types for "miscellaneous" fishing, but the gill nets necessary for small-scale herring fishing were not included among them.

The first family fishers to migrate to Karafuto arrived in Maoka, on the west coast, in March 1906. Although they had ostensibly come to fish cod, in fact most new arrivals had neither the experience nor the capital to succeed at anything other than herring fishing. Some tried to make a go at cod or kelp anyway, while others intended from the beginning to fish herring whether the government allowed it or not.[9] For its part, the government knew that the prospects for many fishers were dim, and it did little to encourage immigration. In contrast to agricultural settlers, who received travel allowances, tools, seed, and land from the state, fishers received no aid whatsoever. But because the government needed the revenue generated by fishing licenses (which totaled 198,000 yen, or about nineteen percent of the Karafuto budget, in 1907), it did nothing to prevent immigration.[10] The fishers hardly needed encouragement. The year-round Japanese population of Karafuto increased from 1,990 in 1905 to 10,806 in 1906 and 28,688 in 1910. Through 1910, about 24.9 percent of all household heads were family fishers (followed by farmers, 19.2 percent; industrial workers, 18.8 percent; and merchants, 17.0 percent).[11]

Trouble between the government and the family fishers began immediately. The first clash came in April 1906, when Kumagai Kiichirō, director of the Department of Civil Affairs, prohibited the practice of "herring collecting" (*hiroi nishin*). During a run the spawning fish pushed close to shore, with the result that many were left stranded on the beach. After a storm the number of fish washed up onto the beach in this manner could reach enormous levels. In an extreme case, in May 1911, prolonged bad weather near Nodasan "left more than 2,000 koku [1,500 tons] of herring on local beaches, prompting residents to abandon their work to collect the fish. . . . The local economy improved as a result."[12] Pound-trap operators were not interested in the inefficient business of collecting beached herring, so they customarily ignored the fish or at most demanded a token share. Villagers could therefore see no reason why the herring should not be free for the taking.

The government designed the law prohibiting the collection of beached herring to deny poachers the chance to pass off illegally caught fish as legitimately gathered herring. This attempt at crime deterrence effectively turned the majority of family fishers into petty criminals. It also set the stage for later cooperation between cod specialists and other small fishers because it forced the cod fishers to buy herring for bait (at four times the price of processed fish) instead of collecting it themselves.[13]

The action led to the first organized attempts to change the fishing laws. Two groups formed in Maoka in July 1906. The Licensees' Union (Kansatsu Kumiai) attracted "cod fishers and other steady types from Maoka and the area to the south," who hoped to get fishing licenses for the 1907 season and to secure herring for bait; it was not immediately concerned with getting permission to use gill nets. Standing in opposition to it was the Association for the Recognition of Gill-Net Use (Sashiami Kōkyo Kiseikai), which joined local merchants (whose prosperity depended on small fishers) and poor residents of Kushunnai, Nodasan, and other communities on the northwest coast. True to its name, it sought immediate approval of gill-net use.[14]

The gill-net association promptly selected representatives to petition Kumagai for a revision of the fishing laws. They used arguments remarkably similar to those employed by pound-trap operators in their unsuccessful attempt to prevent gill-netters from operating in Nemuro a few

years earlier.[15] The petitioners complained that the sacrifices they had
made in coming to Karafuto entitled them to long-term fishing rights and
reasonably priced bait. They also argued that "gill nets do not disrupt
herring spawning patterns"—recent events in Hokkaido had proven
that—and "the recognition of gill-net fishing would . . . greatly benefit
the national economy and the development of Karafuto," as it was the
only way to ensure "the rapid influx of immigrants from Honshu and
Hokkaido . . . and the establishment of [permanent] fishing villages."[16]
Kumagai rejected the petition without comment.

The association then took its case to the central government. In February 1907 it presented a petition signed by 186 merchants and fishers to
both houses of the Twenty-third Imperial Diet.[17] The petitioners tried
to take an objective tone in an attempt to play down the element of self-
interest in their request. A section on "the establishment of fishing villages" stressed exploitation of the rich local marine resources as the key
to growth and refuted government assertions that agriculture could succeed in the island, with the conclusion that "one can only pity the dim-
wittedness of those who argue for the primacy of agriculture in the development of Karafuto." As in the petition presented to Kumagai, the
emphasis was on the benefits of gill nets over pound traps in the conser-
vation of marine resources. Finally, in case the ecological angle was not
persuasive enough, the petition noted that if gill-net fishing were permitted, license-fee receipts alone would surpass current revenues from pound-
trap fishery leases.

The pound-trap operators fought the family fishers through their own
organizations. The first organization of Karafuto pound-trap fishery operators, founded in 1880, when the island was still under Russian rule,
was reorganized after the occupation by those who had received preferential leases. Newcomers formed several organizations of their own, but,
in response to changes in government regulations governing fishing associations, the pound-trap operators eventually reorganized themselves into
three regional groups (covering the east, west, and Aniwa Bay coasts), all
under the umbrella of the Federation of Karafuto Pound-Trap Fishery
Associations (Karafuto Tateami Gyogyō Kumiai Rengōkai) in June
1909.[18] The pound-trap operators submitted a counter-petition to the
same Diet session, in which they used essentially the same argument as
the gill-netters: they deserved preferential treatment as a reward for the
sacrifices they had made in developing the fishery during the long years of
Russian rule, and pound traps were technologically more sophisticated
and in fact better for the environment than gill nets.[19]

The family fishers appeared to have won, as their petition was adopted without debate by the House of Representatives.[20] Unfortunately for them, however, mere adoption of the petition could not force government revision of the fishing laws—and neither the cabinet nor the colonial authorities in Karafuto showed any inclination to act on the Diet's recommendation.

Military administration ended in May 1907 with the establishment of the Department of Karafuto (Karafuto *chō*), under the Ministry of Home Affairs. Kusunose Yukihiko replaced Kumagai as governor of Karafuto, but Kumagai remained in the colonial administration under Kusunose. Wada Kenzō was brought in from the Hokkaido prefectural government to head the fisheries department. Wada, a staunch supporter of the one-net policy, believed that the key to the Karafuto fishery's future competitiveness was to use the best technology available to maximize quality and minimize costs.[21]

In the meantime, the family fishers continued to organize and petition for change, despite the failure of their "victory" in Tokyo to bring about any concrete results. Interest in a second meeting of family fishers, held in Maoka in August 1907, was strongest among residents of Maoka and Kushunnai—where enforcement of antipoaching laws was strictest—and less so to the south and along Aniwa Bay. The meeting resulted in a memorial presented to Governor Kusunose the same month, in which the fishers tried to sway the governor with a tug at the heartstrings:

> The number of small fishers has doubled during the past year. We have . . . poured all our families' resources into coming to Karafuto. We have depleted our savings to buy gear, make nets, import boats, and find and hire able workers. The majority of us have brought our families in the intention of staying in Karafuto permanently.[22]

Unlike the February petition, the new document did not stress the notion that what was good for family fishers was good for Karafuto; ensuring the fishers' livelihoods was reason enough for change. For example, the Karafuto Fishery Law permitted pound-trap operators to add a second net per fishery; the pound-trap operators used that provision, according to the petition, as an excuse to enlarge their waterfront landholdings at the expense of family fishers. The document went on to note that the 1907 cod catch had been poor; although fishing is a volatile occupation anywhere, it said, at least "in Honshu there are ways of diverting capital away from fishing" in a bad year, while in Karafuto "fishers must expend a large amount of capital and labor" regardless of the result. A bad cod catch therefore has immediate and disastrous effects on the fishers (and the local economy because the pound-trap operators take their profits back to the mainland with them), so the small fishers should have access to herring to minimize their risk.

The petitioners' claims of dire hardship must be considered in light of evidence they themselves presented on the scale of their operations. They said that they had poured their entire savings into securing boats, gear, and labor, and were paying 300 yen per boat for bait alone.[23] The Kara-futo government estimated the start-up cost for cod fishers to be approximately 187 yen per boat, more than four times the basic, seasonal wage of about 43 yen for a herring-fishery laborer.[24] This estimate implies resources (or at least access to credit) greater than a marginal fisher in search of the promised land could muster. That, combined with the fishers' obvious lack of skill at cod fishing and eagerness to use gill nets, suggests that they had been middling gill-netters before moving to Kara-futo.[25] If so, they were not in danger of starvation so much as of losing their dreams of becoming upwardly mobile entrepreneurial fishers in the new territory. The plaintive tone of the petition instead reflects their lack of aptitude for cod fishing, which was described in a government report:

> The [cod] catch was extremely large in 1906, but the following year the fish moved to deeper waters, forcing fishers to follow them far out to sea. Moreover, the weather in 1907 was worse than in the preceding year, causing fishers much damage. Inexperienced operators who had set themselves up hastily did not get the catches they had expected and suffered great losses. As a result, the number of fishers declined steeply in 1908. . . . But the stock of fish has not decreased, and fishers coming seasonally from [Rishiri, Rebun, and elsewhere] have maintained their operations undisrupted. . . . They harvest an average of 1,200 soku [112.5 tons] per boat, with little annual fluctuation in catches.[26]

Kusunose did not accept the petition, but he seemed sympathetic to the fishers' cause and told a group of representatives that he would be willing to consider any proposal that respected the rights of pound-trap operators and guaranteed protection of marine resources. The petition writers accordingly went back to the drawing board and came back a month later with a practical plan that was both constructive and accommodating—and, ironically, much less beneficial to gill-netters than the settlement eventually reached in 1915.[27] It proposed the establishment of fishing associations like those in Hokkaido, except they would be organized on a smaller scale (about a hundred households each, rather than an entire district). Members of the associations would be able to fish herring with gill nets but only on a scale determined by the government (the petition suggested a modest five sets of nets and a maximum catch of 22.5 tons per household; a single haul of a pound trap yielded up to 150 tons).[28] The gill-net fisheries thus established would be spaced so as not to interfere with existing pound-trap fisheries. The petition said that the fishers would be willing to submit to close government supervision of the organization and activities of the associations, and it even proposed a system of communal responsibility whereby any group that failed to punish a member guilty of poaching would have its license revoked.

The willingness of the gill-net activists to compromise contrasted with the attitude of the pound-trap operators. In February 1908 they approached the Twenty-fourth Imperial Diet with a request for a reversal of the adoption of the family fishers' petition of the previous year.[29] The document covered three major issues: the relative benefits of pound traps versus gill nets; the proposed fishing associations; and the best way to establish a stable community in Karafuto.

The pound-trap operators used two lines of reasoning to support their position on the net issue. First, the future development of Karafuto demanded that the most sophisticated technology available be used in the herring fisheries. Gill nets not only harmed herring spawning patterns, the petition said, they also interfered with pound-trap use and therefore should be banned. In fact, the only reason gill-net fishing existed at all in Hokkaido was that gill-net use predated pound-trap fishing by years and was thus tolerated out of government respect for local custom. Such sentimentality had no place in Karafuto. Second, because gill-net fishing required so little capital and labor, the petitioners predicted that the moment the laws changed, Karafuto would be overrun by hordes of irresponsible small fishers, who would promptly destroy the island's economic base forever.

Moreover, the petition continued, the local fishing associations proposed by the gill-netters would be powerless to control the behavior of thousands of individual fishers during a herring run. After all, "associations are organizations of individuals. Given that the individuals who would form the gill-net associations are ignorant fishers, there is little hope of forming disciplined organizations." The leaders of the associations, if not actually "fools," would at best be "uneducated and unreliable." Competition for leadership posts would breed all sorts of evil, and in the end "the ambitious leaders would agitate the fishers for their own purposes."[30]

The petition ended with a refutation of the small fishers' claim that gill-net fishing would spur the growth of stable, permanent communities. The pound-trap operators argued that the stability of such communities would disappear within a few years, along with the herring. If the family fishers were really interested in making a life in Karafuto, they should join their diligent brethren in cod fishing. They did not because all their talk of setting up villages was simply whitewash to camouflage their intent to poach herring. Rather than the shiftless and ambitious family fishers, the real backbone of Karafuto society should be the workers in the seasonal pound-trap fishery, who would, under the sponsorship of their employers, gradually move permanently to the island, where they would take up farming and commerce to supplement their fishery wages.

Stupid, unreliable, greedy—the petition epitomizes the attitude of the pound-trap operators toward small fishers. "Vagrants" (*furōnin*) was a common description of family fishers because of their unwillingness to settle down to a respectable life of agriculture. A commentator associated with the pro-government newspaper, the *Karafuto nichinichi shinbun*, complained of the luxurious lives led by small fishers:

> Anyone accustomed to seeing the miserable way fishers in Honshu live would doubt his eyes if he took one look at the small fishers of Karafuto. They deck themselves out in fancy clothes, with an expensive obi, a watch, fashionable hat and the latest footwear; they frequent the geisha houses in town and quaff beer when they stay at home.[31]

All they want, the commentator continued, is to be petty capitalists (*shō-shihonka*), in charge of four or five employees. Their problems with the large operators are the product of "their desire to use labor rather than to work themselves."[32]

At the heart of this dislike of fishers was a profound suspicion of fishing as a way of life. Agriculture was never economically viable in Karafuto, despite the government's concerted efforts to make it so. Nevertheless, officials applauded any sign of fishers turning toward the land. A 1913 newspaper editorial, echoing remarks made by a high colonial official, saw the movement of once "rootless and derelict" west-coast fishers, at last "diligent" and "willing to settle down" into a life of farming, as ample cause for optimism for Karafuto's future.[33]

Government officials in Karafuto never openly questioned the validity of the claim that pound traps were better for the environment, despite the counter-assertions of the family fishers. The pound-trap operators' position was that the low start-up cost of gill-net fishing would encourage a mass migration to Karafuto if the laws were ever changed (this did not in fact occur) and that those people would overwhelm the fishery through sheer numbers. But the state-of-the-art pound traps used in Karafuto could bring in a half-million or more herring in a single haul—five to seven times the *seasonal* catch of a small gill-net fisher.[34] At an estimated

22.5 tons per household, it would take eighty gill-net families to match the typical annual production of a single pound-trap fishery with two nets and a catch of 900 tons each. On the basis of this arithmetic there was no clear basis to reject the request for fishing associations.

Nevertheless, the petition committee of the lower house of the Imperial Diet recommended approval of the pound-trap operators' petition, after Kumagai, acting as government representative, made a statement supporting the document. Discussion in committee centered on the need for long-term stability in Karafuto fishing, in part to ensure a steady flow of tax revenues. Both houses adopted the petition without debate.[35]

In May 1908, just months after the pound-trap operators won the second round in the Diet, Hiraoka Sadatarō, governor of Fukushima prefecture, replaced Kusunose as head of the Karafuto government. The "down-to-earth and not at all bureaucratic" Hiraoka was seen as a future star of the Seiyūkai.[36] (Incidentally, he was also the grandfather of the writer Mishima Yukio.) Both groups bombarded the new governor with memorials even before he took his post, but upon his arrival in Karafuto, Hiraoka made it quite clear that he had no intention of altering the one-net principle. However, he did show sympathy for the economic plight of the family fishers and seemed determined to reach some kind of settlement. Hiraoka apparently thought he had hit upon an amicable solution when he ordered the organization of thirty-nine fisheries under twenty regional cooperatives.[37] Local fishers did not get permission to use gill nets at the fisheries; rather, the cooperatives leased the grounds to pound-trap operators and distributed the income to members as dividends. That way, the one-net principle remained intact while local residents benefited indirectly from herring, salmon, and trout fishing.

The system was not perfect. Although fishers near Maoka were initially happy with the settlement because the best grounds were in that area, the majority of fisheries were of poor quality or were in particularly remote areas, leaving little hope of significant dividends for most members. Moreover, the herring catch the first year under the cooperatives, 1909, was bad (about 127,500 tons, compared with 149,844 tons in 1908 and 175,737 tons in 1907),[38] and policing of poaching was strict (a corollary of the implementation of the cooperative system), making for hard times for many fisher families. Furthermore, because newcomers were not allowed to join, whatever benefits the system did offer were limited to residents of the immediate vicinity at the time of the organization of the cooperatives. If Hiraoka had hoped to derail the gill-net movement by setting up the fishing cooperatives, he was in for a disappointment. The cooperatives failed to generate much revenue—most paid no dividends at all—and fishers were bitter over the intensified enforcement of antipoaching laws.[39]

The fishers' bitterness crystallized in the formation of the Alliance to Reform Karafuto Fisheries Administration (Karafuto Gyosei Kaikaku Kisei Dōmeikai) in 1909. This group, and its later incarnation, the Karafuto People's Association (Karafuto Minkai), presented a generally united front to the government and pound-trap operators in the struggle that followed.

The conflict over the fishing system came to a boil on 9 June 1909, with the Ōdomari Incident. Ichiki Kitokurō, then vice-minister of home affairs, arrived on that day in Ōdomari, a port on Aniwa Bay and Karafuto's second largest town, to begin a tour of inspection. Governor Hiraoka met Ichiki and accompanied him to the Ōdomari District Office. Between four hundred and a thousand townspeople and fishers, "banners flying,"[40] followed them to the office in the hope of presenting their case to Ichiki. A few representatives of the fishers met with the vice-minister and governor, but the crowd outside, fueled by an abundant supply of sake, grew impatient and tried to force its way into the building. People started breaking furniture and throwing rocks, and eventually someone poured kerosene over a pile of firewood and lit it, nearly setting the building on fire. In the words of Miyajima Matsuji, one of the representatives meeting with the officials:

> We were meeting with the governor when, through the window, we could see that a horrible disturbance—a riot—was taking place. The situation grew difficult, and what with people yelling "Kill the governor!" and such, Governor Hiraoka must have thought that the lives of Vice-Minister Ichiki and himself were in danger because the normally composed governor became flustered and called the army . . . and ordered them to send troops to Ōdomari. . . [As we left the building] both sides of the road were filled with the still extremely excited crowd. Vice-Minister Ichiki, Governor Hiraoka, Bureau Chief Maeda, and the rest were as pale as corpses. Only [Ōdomari] District Vice-Governor Ikegami was calm and smiling.[41]

The army, with the help of the police, eventually quelled the riot, with one death and a number of injuries resulting from shots fired into the crowd by soldiers. The family fishers' group and the pound-trap operators agreed that the riot was not a premeditated event, and it was the only significant instance of physical violence on the part of the fishers.[42] Afterward, Hiraoka made sure that no small fishers got near Ichiki.[43] The vice-minister became a bitter enemy of the fishers and used his considerable influence in the central government to hinder the progress of their movement.

After the incident twenty people were arrested, nineteen charged with

rioting and three newspaper reporters charged also with violating the
newspaper law (two of whom also participated in the disturbance). Thirteen of the twenty were fishers, and two each were merchants and artisans, in addition to the three reporters. Ten of the nineteen were eventually acquitted of the rioting charges, while the others were given jail terms
ranging from twenty-five days to one year.[44]

The reporters were all connected with a pro-gill-net newspaper in
Ōdomari, the *Karafuto jiji*. The paper ran a series of articles in the period
just before and after the riot (15 May to 18 June 1909) appealing to the
people of Karafuto to work to change the system. The articles compared
the Karafuto fishing system to the English corn laws. Where English
peasants had cried, "Give us bread or give us death!" the Karafuto fishers should say, in effect, "Give us herring or give us death!" The articles
also accused Karafuto officials of corruption and a willingness to sell out
to the pound-trap operators. The reporters paid fines ranging from 50 to
100 yen.[45]

Relations between the government and the family fishers worsened after the Ōdomari Incident. The following year, 1910, the government once
again stepped up its antipoaching campaign, this time revoking land leases
issued to fishers caught poaching. Since all land in Karafuto belonged to
the government, the effect was to force those caught to leave their villages or even to leave Karafuto entirely. Poachers' nets and boats were
confiscated and allowed to rot (wet nets were stacked in warehouses),
while whatever fish they had caught was auctioned on the spot.[46] A newspaper report described the situation in one village:

> Nayashi is famous for the arrogance of its officials, and the petty bureaucrats
> there are especially fearsome. . . . The local residents, after many years of
> holding back their grievances, are now united and have recently started to as-
> sert their will. The officials have consequently tried to squelch the movement
> by . . . confiscating all nets set out to dry, on the grounds they belong to poach-
> ers. . . . Not to be outdone, the fishers have responded by filing theft com-
> plaints on the nets.[47]

On the northwest coast half or more of the residents of some villages had
arrest records. Kushunnai, a settlement of about two hundred households
(one-fifth of whom were fishers), had a police force of thirty-nine men to
control poaching.[48]

Meanwhile, the fishers continued to organize and petition for change.
They formed the Karafuto People's Association on 12 December 1912
for the express purpose of changing the fishery laws. On the twenty-
fourth of that month the new group presented yet another petition to

Governor Hiraoka.[49] This time the tone of the document was desperate, defiant—and hyperbolic. It said that the impracticality of living off "miscellaneous" fishing was apparent and that "seventy percent of the small fishers would starve to death" if the government enforced the fishery law to the letter, and even if it did not, surviving the winter would be a challenge:

> The authorities have an obligation to protect [family fishers]. . . . The government cannot sacrifice 30,000 residents to support 300-odd pound-trap [fisheries]. . . . The authorities protect the strong instead of the weak, who need protection . . . and deny permanent residents . . . the opportunity of sharing in the benefits of . . . herring, trout, and salmon fishing, [all of which are] suited to family management.[50]

The governor refused to accept the petition, but he did attempt to placate the People's Association by extending the period during which flounder fishing with dragnets was allowed into April and May. This extension promised to increase the efficiency of fishing, but the government placed so many restrictions on the use of dragnets and such harsh penalties for poaching (a three-year suspension of the violator's license, plus loss of land for the poacher and three guarantors) that the benefits of the change were limited.[51]

In March 1913 the People's Association stepped up efforts to have the law revised in anticipation of the expiration of the pound-trap operators' fishing licenses in September. A group of representatives went to Tokyo and, despite being tailed by Special Higher Police wary of radicals in the wake of the Great Treason Incident of 1911, presented petitions to both houses of the Imperial Diet, Premier Yamamoto Gonnohyōe, and Home Minister Hara Takashi.[52] In an attempt to play on government concern with declining public morals, they freely admitted that coastal villagers poached herring on a large scale: "Schoolchildren stand in the streets, looking out for police as their parents engage in activity tantamount to stealing."[53]

The pound-trap operators were not quiet during all of this activity of course. They presented their own petition to the Diet.[54] They urged rejection of any effort to change the law:

> Clearly the best way to improve [the small fishers'] situation is for them to enter into relations of employment with pound-trap operators. Because of the difficulty of obtaining labor in Karafuto, pound-trap operators are forced to expend great sums to bring laborers from distant areas. If the small fishers already in Karafuto took the place of the outside laborers, there is no doubt that

their incomes would increase greatly. Moreover, it would be to their advantage if they weaned themselves of their distaste for labor. . . . They are reluctant to devote themselves to their ostensible occupation—harvesting miscellaneous varieties of fish—because they want to live without having to work.[55]

Once again, the family fishers' efforts to win the support of the Diet failed, though by now the government saw that the problem was not going to solve itself. After the People's Association petition was rejected, a group of legislators submitted a memorial requesting reconsideration. The memorial was referred to a committee that included an officer of the pound-trap operators' association, Uchiyama Kichita, and it was voted down.[56]

Despite the repeated setbacks in the Diet, the tide was beginning to turn in favor of the family fishers. The People's Association got an important boost when groups from each house of the Diet accepted its invitation to come to Karafuto on a tour of inspection in the summer of 1913. The delegation included a number of opposition politicians, who may have been eager for an opportunity to embarrass the pro-Seiyūkai Hiraoka. The fishers visited by the delegation from the House of Peers had various opinions, but all agreed that the present system was intolerable, especially because it was impossible to combine fishing and farming, a common strategy of Honshu fishers. The fishing and planting seasons overlapped, and, in any case, the necessarily large scale of Karafuto agriculture made part-time farming extremely difficult. Poaching was an unfortunate, but inevitable, result of the people's total dependence on fishing.[57]

The Peers met with Hiraoka on 29 June. They composed an eight-point statement based on the results of their fact-finding trip: (1) The condition of the family fishers in the areas visited by the group was desperate; (2) herring poaching was an open secret; (3) poaching was detrimental to education and public morals; (4) little good had come of government programs enacted for the benefit of small fishers; (5) police power had proven ineffectual in controlling poaching; (6) family fishers should be allowed to fish herring with gill nets; (7) even barring immediate abolition of the ban on gill nets, at the very least controls on the scale and timing of dragnet fishing should be reconsidered; and (8) the family fishers deserved compassion and assistance in bettering their situation, and those who were able should be encouraged to take up farming.[58] Governor Hiraoka acknowledged the validity of the first five points but refused to consider opening the fishing grounds to gill nets. He said that if the family fishers would simply stop worrying about herring there was no reason why they should not be able to make a decent living.

The delegation from the lower house of the Diet included members of every political party except the Seiyūkai, which had declined an invitation to send a representative. This group also met with Hiraoka. The governor explained that if he permitted unrestricted herring fishing, Karafuto would be overrun by "tens of thousands" of people, with the result that within a few years all marine life of any value would be wiped out. He added that family fishers' complaints that they could not get by without herring were not valid. While poor farmers in Honshu ate white rice only at New Year's, he said, "the people of Karafuto eat rice all the time, drink beer, and even occasionally go to a restaurant to be entertained by geisha."[59]

Like the Peers, the lower-house members had a question-and-answer session with Hiraoka, which I paraphrase here:[60]

> Isn't poaching an open secret?—Yes, it is, and that is why we are cracking down.
>
> Isn't the current state of affairs extremely injurious to the moral education of children?—Yes, it is, and we feel that this is lamentable.
>
> Haven't the authorities done very little to help the poor fishers? The thirty-nine fisheries allotted to the cooperatives have not been effective in raising the standard of living of the fishers.—That depends on your point of view. We are pleased with the results thus far.
>
> Isn't it impossible to control fishing with police power?—Yes, it is difficult, but we have no choice.
>
> Is there no way to allow herring, trout, and salmon fishing by some other means than pound traps?—That is your opinion, and I respect it as such, but there is no way I am going to relax my position on this matter.
>
> We are not necessarily suggesting that you allow unrestricted fishing but merely that the laws be revised to make some allowance for gill nets and dragnets, as well as pound traps.—I am sorry, but that is quite impossible.

After that frank and constructive exchange of ideas, the delegation returned to Tokyo.

In an interview sponsored by the Karafuto Association (Karafuto Kyōkai), the political arm of the pound-trap operators' association, Hiraoka elaborated on his view of the fishing problem.[61] He maintained that the sole reason for his staunch support of pound-trap fishing was concern for the future of marine resources—and the steady source of revenue the fishery provided the state. The Karafuto government required an annual herring catch of 150,000 tons for tax-revenue purposes, he said, but had no need for production beyond that level. With pound traps, catches could be controlled, so there was less chance of overfishing. He recognized the need to help the family fishers and promised to open additional pound-trap fisheries to the cooperatives by gradually buying out existing operators and transferring any fishing grounds surrendered by lessors. Hiraoka said that he hoped the cooperatives would eventually be able to manage actual operations at their fisheries. He said, moreover, that he was eager to see the fishers' standard of living improve but only to "the level of the better-off farmers." The governor added that unless the family fishers were willing to go through lean times they could never hope to attain independence. Therefore, he concluded, he was holding back on the expansion of fishing grounds for cooperatives until some future time when the fishers were "ready."

Soon it did not matter what Hiraoka thought. The Yamamoto cabinet fell on 16 April 1914 in the aftermath of the Siemens Incident, and Ōkuma Shigenobu, the old liberal, took over as premier. Hiraoka's support in Tokyo quickly waned as evidence of widespread corruption and political bad sportsmanship came to light. He was accused of misusing the income from ten fisheries that had been set aside for the benefit of the Ainu population, funneling 100,000 yen from Karafuto Bussan (a cartel that had been accorded special treatment in the disposition of fishery leases) to Hara Takashi, and various other indiscretions. He was eventually tried for corruption but was acquitted for lack of evidence.[62] He resigned on 5 June 1914 and retired to obscurity at his home in Hyōgo.[63]

Not long before Hiraoka was forced out of office, the Karafuto People's Association presented one last petition to the Diet. In a brief memorial, presented in March 1914 to the House of Peers, the fishers complained of their inability to survive without herring fishing.[64] At the same time, the Otaru Chamber of Commerce submitted a petition asking that gill-net fishing be permitted "on a scale that does not intrude upon the rights of pound-trap operators."[65] The Hokkaido merchants were sympathetic because Otaru was the main port for commerce with Karafuto, yet the pound-trap operators were based mostly in Hakodate and thus took their business there.

The Peers' petition committee, thanks in part to the efforts of the members who had toured Karafuto, passed the fishers' petition readily, and it looked as though the fishers might at last get the results they were hoping for. However, on the floor of the Diet, Ichiki Kitokurō, the fishers' nemesis since the Ōdomari riot, argued strongly against passage, his main point being that if the Diet let the petition through this time its rejection of past petitions would look foolish. Fickle, vain, or simply deferring to Ichiki's feelings, the Peers killed the request on the floor of the Diet instead of simply rubber-stamping the petition committee's recommendations.[66]

That was the darkness before the dawn, however, because the change of cabinet brought with it new personnel sympathetic to the plight of the

Karafuto fishers. Prime Minister Ōkuma appointed Tochigi governor Okada Bunji to head the Karafuto government. Okada was sympathetic to the family fishers, and on 3 July 1915 the Karafuto Fishery Law was amended to permit gill-net fishing by cooperative members in fishing grounds held by the cooperatives.[67] Okada maintained that he had not abandoned the basic, one-net policy; the change, he said, was an extraordinary measure designed to foster the healthy development of fishing communities in Karafuto.[68] Newspaper editorials in Karafuto welcomed the decision as a prudent compromise that would at once preserve the island's marine resources, alleviate the economic difficulties of family fishers, and encourage respect for the law and a responsible attitude toward fishing, but they warned that if the family fishers thought they were getting a license to decimate Karafuto's herring, they were in for an unpleasant surprise.[69]

The change was not exactly the full liberalization of herring fishing that the fishers had dreamed of, but it appeared to be enough. On 6 July, "ecstatic" fishers in Maoka held a lantern parade, while two weeks later the residents of Ōdomari prefaced their costume party, lantern parade, and drinking contest with a memorial service for Makino Nenomatsu, killed by soldiers in the Ōdomari riot, and Ishiguro Tokujirō, who had died in prison afterward.[70] The Karafuto People's Association disbanded within weeks. But the family fishers did not live happily ever after.

After Victory

Okada was right when he said that the basic philosophy of the fishing system remained unchanged despite the granting of limited gill-net fishing rights. The governor of Karafuto fixed the number of gill nets available to each local fishing cooperative, and these groups—not their individual members—held the fishing rights. The government did, however, work to spread the benefits of the cooperative system, allowing new residents to join after August 1913 and increasing both the number of cooperatives and the fisheries they controlled (as Hiraoka had promised) after 1915. At the time of the revision of the fisheries law, the twenty cooperatives were reorganized into twenty-eight, though the number of fisheries remained the same at thirty-nine. In 1920 the government cleared the way for the cooperatives to operate up to sixty-seven fishing grounds; however, because private individuals retained contractual rights to most grounds adjacent to fishing villages, and few cooperatives could afford to buy them out, the change had little practical meaning for family fishers.

The Karafuto government responded by creating sixty-four new fisheries (valued at approximately 700,000 yen), which it parceled out to the co-operatives. The fishers' groups then arranged to exchange these fisheries with pound-trap operators for others closer to their settlements, with the result that by the spring of 1921 their holdings totaled sixty-one fishing grounds. In 1929 the government allowed the cooperatives up to eighty-two fisheries and in 1933, eighty-six. Finally, in March 1934 all restrictions on fishery holdings were abolished.[71] However, because the fisheries given to the cooperatives were either surrendered by pound-trap operators or newly opened, they tended to be of indifferent quality, and as a result the better fisheries became seriously overcrowded.[72]

The cooperative system was plagued by all manner of difficulty from its establishment in 1908. Before 1915, the cooperatives sometimes found it difficult to find pound-trap operators to lease their fisheries, or to collect rents in bad years.[73] Occasionally, the leaders of the cooperatives set up joint-stock companies and leased the grounds to themselves. Ideally, this action showed that the members were pursuing self-sufficient operation of their fisheries, but all too often it meant simply that a handful of leaders had co-opted their cooperatives' rights. Even if the leaders were not actually corrupt, the practice led to serious conflicts of interest.[74]

The problems did not go away after the revision of the law. The leases on cooperative fisheries did not expire until after the 1916 season at the earliest, and some ran through 1920, so the family fishers had to choose between trying to buy out their tenants' leases or waiting until they expired. They usually made that decision after considering the size of recent catches and the dividends they had earned.[75] Leaving actual fishing operations in outside hands was often financially prudent, but it negated the spirit of the struggle that had led to the change in law and therefore must have caused would-be small proprietors much frustration.

For example, in March 1917, the Honto cooperative on the southwest coast leased three of its seven fisheries to a local company for an annual total of 2,725 yen plus licensing fees due the Karafuto government.[76] The fisheries were erratic producers (one yielded a respectable 969 tons in 1914, but only 176 tons in 1912 and 355 tons the following year),[77] so taking the stable income promised by the contract may have been a good idea, even if it yielded only about ten to sixteen yen per member (the cooperative was growing during this period, going from 170 members in 1914 to 268 in 1919). Since member dividends were dropping annually (in the peak year, 1911, members received 42.50 yen each; in 1913 this figure fell to 34.50 yen and in 1915 to a mere 17.70 yen), they may have been especially anxious to take the sure thing.[78]

While the members of the Honto cooperative were busy being rational with their fisheries, many small fishers (perhaps even including some from Honto) continued to poach herring at productive fisheries, victims either of the quirks of the cooperative system or of the now violently fluctuating—but generally declining—herring catches.[79] Whether poachers or not, around 1923 one writer warned that "virtually resourceless fishers are in danger of falling into laborer status, and it is difficult to encourage fishers with capital to immigrate."[80]

In 1926 the government once again revised the fishing law, this time to allow fishers to use small pound traps (*kotateami*) at fishing grounds managed by the cooperatives.[81] The operators of small pound traps worked in much the same way as owners of larger nets. The nets were almost always controlled by individuals, not by net unions (*amikumi*), despite Karafuto government regulations that small pound traps should be owned by groups of cooperative members. (The operators got around the rules by creating fictitious unions.)[82] Small-pound-trap operators, like their big-league counterparts, employed large numbers of laborers, usually from outside Karafuto. In 1932, for example, a total of 46,611 people were engaged in herring, trout, and salmon fishing. Of these, about 15,000 were gill-netters and 2,000 their employees; 9,000 worked for large-pound-trap operators; and the remaining 20,000 worked small pound traps.[83] Cutthroat competition among small-pound-trap operators led to serious overcrowding of prime fisheries. In some areas along the coast of Aniwa Bay small pound traps were stacked two or three deep offshore.[84]

By 1935 a definite regional variation in the use of small pound traps could be seen.[85] On the east coast, the 719 members of the fifteen (of a total seventeen) cooperatives for which data are available operated some 407 small pound traps, with no more than one net per operator apparently the norm. Only nine cooperatives reported having any gill nets at all, and of those only four had a total of 100 or more sets. The heavy use of pound traps seems to be related to the depression of herring fishing on the east coast, where the small size of the cooperatives (an average of 47 members each, compared with 142 on Aniwa Bay and 112 on the west coast) suggests that marginal gill-netters either went elsewhere or left fishing altogether.

On Aniwa Bay, the 1,845 members of the twelve (of a total fourteen) fishers' groups for which data are available operated a total 1,361 small pound traps. Gill-netters were active at eleven of the cooperatives, but the scale of their operations was small, except at Notoro, on the south-west tip of the bay, where 266 members operated 4,810 sets in addition to 141 small pound traps.

In contrast to the east and Aniwa Bay coasts, gill-netters clearly domi-nated the herring fishing industry on the west coast. Only 107 small pound traps, but at least 15,721 sets of gill nets, were in use at the eleven of nineteen fishing cooperatives for which data are available. At only one cooperative did fishers use as many as twenty-seven small pound traps; at most cooperatives they used fewer than ten, and at one, none at all.

The strength of gill-net fishing here at this late date was a result of the heavy concentration of family fishers on the west coast from the first years after the Russo-Japanese war. The gill-net movement was always strongest in the area around Maoka and to the north, so it is easy to sup-pose that the local residents' commitment to fishing as a way of life, de-spite erratic catches, was stronger than that of the casual fishers of the east coast. For example, the Higashi Rebun cooperative on the east coast was established by "lumberjacks and charcoal makers who moved to the area and found that they could not resist the herring and trout runs nearby." But because "most of the members were never genuine fishers, many have turned to other [lines of work] in the aftermath of a series of poor catches."[86] In contrast, at the Kaiba-mura cooperative on the west coast, "the once plentiful herring have not run at all since 1929 [i.e., for six years]; a few members have left [fishing], but most continue to eke out a meager living collecting sea urchins and seaweed." Membership in the cooperative had fallen by only one person, to 124, between 1923 and 1935.[87] The flip side of this commitment to fishing as a way of life was an inability to make a living at anything else, barring work as a wage la-borer at a pound-trap fishery. Before 1915, examples of the poverty of family fishers usually came from the west coast; after 1915, small fishers in this region remained poor (if better off than before) and therefore were unable to make the step up to small pound traps after the law change of 1926.

The move to permit small-pound-trap use thus effectively sorted the Karafuto fishers into a number of upscale operators, whose methods dif-fered only in scale from the entrepreneurs running the older pound-trap fisheries, and a larger group that continued to rely mostly on family la-bor. Within little more than a decade, what had been a broad class of small operators underwent the very process of differentiation that had brought its members from Hokkaido to Karafuto.

This development would be ironic if there were any reason to believe

the family fishers ever intended to remain a broad class of small operators. Whatever the majority of small fishers thought, a number of them,
whether enterprising or merely "ambitious,"[88] clearly had big plans for
themselves. They acted on those plans and gradually came to dominate
herring fishing in Karafuto. By 1926, 122 of 427 (twenty-nine percent)
pound-trap fisheries were in the hands of Karafuto residents. Between
1927 and 1932, pound-trap operators (including local residents) harvested between 65,000 and 95,000 tons of herring annually, while fishing
cooperatives had catches ranging from 229,000 to 439,000 tons.[89]

While the small-pound-trap operators were clawing their way up the
social ladder, their predecessors in pound-trap fishing had already begun
to look beyond individual management toward consolidated fishery operations. Karafuto Bussan, a cartel of twenty-two operators, was the first
major example of this type. Pound-trap operators with rights after 1914
included seven companies, including Karafuto Bussan (four fisheries),
Nakatsuka Gyogyō (five fisheries), and Karafuto Gyogyō (seven fisheries).

Only one other operator in 1914 could match Nichiro Gyogyō's twelve
fisheries, yet by the late 1910s Karafuto was basically a sideline for the
company, which had moved most of its operations to Kamchatka and
other Russian/Soviet territory. By the outbreak of World War II, Nichiro
Gyogyō monopolized Japanese salmon and trout canning facilities in Soviet territory.[90] Its flamboyant president, Tsutsumi Seiroku, was a pioneer
developer of the factory ships (*kani kōsen*), whose inhuman working conditions Kobayashi Takiji made famous. The other operator with twelve
fisheries in 1914, Oguma Kōichirō, built his empire by buying up fishing
rights during the Russo-Japanese War. Like Nichiro Gyogyō, he later
moved the bulk of his operations to Soviet territory.[91]

At the end of 1919, in a move that anticipated similar action in Hokkaido by six years, the pound-trap operators' association sponsored a conference of its members to explore the benefits of joint management. Early
the following year a select committee put forward a list of fourteen "Advantages of Consolidation,"[92] including "it will facilitate a cut in the labor
force and alleviate the lamentable practice of competing for laborers"
(item 1). Also, since "it will permit operation of profitable fisheries only"
(item 2), the operators could "turn unprofitable fisheries over to local
fishers, a mutually beneficial measure that will at once discourage poaching and promote good relations with local residents" (item 3). In addition, the committee noted that fishery mergers could cut costs and raise
efficiency through joint processing, marketing, and purchasing, as well
as put the operators in a better position to deal with the government and
local fishing cooperatives.

Although the large operators clearly recognized the advantages of joint management, the difficulties of working out a specific plan that would satisfy the fishery owners, the government, and the fishing cooperatives prevented any concrete action until 1932, when catches in Karafuto, like Hokkaido, had fallen to unprofitably low levels. In that year Karafuto Kyōdō Gyogyō (Karafuto United Fisheries) was founded. Original plans had called for it to be part of Gōdō Gyogyō and, like the Hokkaido firm, to operate fisheries directly, but it ended up serving mostly to help secure credit for its members, who retained control over their operations.[93] Even if Karafuto Kyōdō Gyogyō was not the massive fishing conglomerate some had hoped for, it—like its Hokkaido counterpart, Gōdō Gyogyō—did represent one logical conclusion to the development of the Karafuto fishery. Forty-three of the forty-seven fishing cooperatives and 2,743 of 4,670 member fishers participated in the company, signaling the small fishers' "arrival" as capitalists.[94] It was too bad they arrived after all the fish were gone.

Subjecthood and Entrepreneurship

If they wanted to, small fishers "could make forty to fifty yen in just a month or two working at the pound-trap fisheries. They make no attempt to secure this attractive income, and instead spend their time scheming up ways to poach fish because of their unspeakably bad feelings toward the pound-trap operators and their contempt for working for others."[95] In a world of market rationality, the fishers would have worked for the pound-trap operators. They would have been assured of steady employment and a reasonably stable—if not especially high—income. They would have been relieved of the need to set fire to the Ōdomari District Office building or to train their children to look out for police. And they would have remained wage laborers for the rest of their lives.

The family fishers of Karafuto were rational, but their rationality was not confined to the marketplace. They wanted steady employment and a stable income, and would have preferred to avoid poaching and arson, but not at the cost of remaining wage laborers for the rest of their lives. They valued independence over material security, especially because they understood that the material security of wage labor could be ephemeral without control over the processes of production.

Independence ultimately represented freedom, not from risk but from the business decisions of employers who had no long-term interest in their workers' ability to earn a livelihood. Like the family fishers, the Ainu of southern Karafuto (who had preserved their traditional economy) understood what was at stake and tried to remain aloof from the exogenous dependency of the labor market. A 1910 newspaper article reported that only two Ainu fisheries actually employed Ainu because "the natives [*dojin*] dislike working as fishing laborers." The problem was that the summer trout season interfered with their farming schedule, and the September salmon runs overlapped with the fall hunting season. Those who traded their self-sufficiency for cash incomes found themselves completely dependent on their employers for their livelihood, but the wages paid to Ainu—about thirty yen for a six-month period—were not enough to support a family through the winter.[96]

Laborers from Honshu did not have the luxury of opting for self-sufficiency: "A poor harvest throughout the Tōhoku region this year is expected to force an unusually large number of small farmers to seek work at fisheries [in Hokkaido and Karafuto] next season," reported a newspaper in 1913.[97] They consequently had to accept whatever was offered in Karafuto. Typically, laborers received (and used) a large portion of their seasonal wage in advance, before New Year's, so that all they got after fishing was payment representing a share of the catch. If there was no catch, they received nothing. In 1915, a disastrous season on the east coast forced fishers to release their employees in June. Empty-handed and "empty-bellied laborers fill the road to Toyohara," where, "because they do not have money to get home, they have to find some kind of work. . . . This is by no means the first time, as this kind of thing is seen to a greater or lesser extent every year."[98]

Still, getting paid to starve in Karafuto was better than starving for free in Aomori. Anyone willing to suffer abuse on top of that could do even better. "People say that the Satō fishery [in Kushunnai] differs from others in that it hires only exceptionally strong workers, and for wages thirty percent higher than elsewhere, but in return works them rather hard." In 1912, more than thirty laborers simultaneously got diarrhea from the poor water and tried to take time off. "The foreman thought it was their usual trick of feigning sickness to avoid work, so, using brute force, got the sick laborers out of bed and put them to work at an especially arduous task. Seeing this, their healthy coworkers became furious," declared a strike, and began wrecking the buildings at the fishery. Thirty-one workers were eventually arrested, and four were tried and sentenced to terms ranging from three months to a year.[99]

Of course, most laborers made it through the fishing season without being laid off or put into jail, and former gill-netters, as skilled workers, would have been in a better position than unskilled hands from Tōhoku. Nevertheless, lacking control over their work conditions and daily routine, they would have suffered the same fundamental vulnerability as other wage laborers.

Gill-netters, dependent on credit and markets, were in a precarious position themselves, but the measure of control they retained over their day-to-day affairs gave them an air of respectability that fishery workers lacked. In contrast, wage laborers, whether at fisheries, construction sites, mines, or lumberyards, occupied the lowest rung of the Karafuto social ladder. Their "betters" despised them: "Fishery workers from Aomori are, as a rule, lazy . . . but those from Nanbu [i.e., the Shimokita peninsula] and [the] Tsugaru [peninsula] are especially bad."[100] Manual laborers from Tōhoku were soft and prone to drink too much, said one newspaper editorial, and were therefore practically useless. Local labor was even worse. What Karafuto's construction sites and coal mines needed was cheap and sturdy Koreans.[101] (The authorities eventually acted on the idea, with the result that thousands of Koreans were left stranded after World War II in Sakhalin, where they remain.)[102]

A gill-netter who turned to wage labor was unlikely ever to become a gill-netter again. But a fisher who made the step down surrendered more than his means of production in the transition. He gave up his social status and his chance for material success. His peers, instead of being small fishers like himself, were now the younger sons of tenant farmers from the depressed hill country of northern Honshu, at best semiskilled workers with no special affinity for fishing. What for a Tōhoku peasant was an attractive opportunity to supplement agricultural income with much-needed cash was for a former gill-net fisher the end of the road.

That was reason enough to cling to gill-net fishing, but independence offered something more—the chance to move up to pound-trap fishing and the world of the petty entrepreneur. As we have seen, by the turn of the twentieth century it was nearly impossible for gill-netters in Hokkaido to convert to pound-trap fishing. It was very expensive (it cost about 13,500 yen, exclusive of land, labor, and fees, to start a pound-trap fishery in 1913),[103] and it was difficult to obtain good waterfront land at a reasonable price. But even in Hokkaido small fishers, if they were very lucky and well connected, could occasionally make the transition. The odds did not have to be good—so long as they were not nil—to keep hope alive. And the odds for small fishers were bound to be better in Karafuto than in Hokkaido.

The family fishers' decision to move to Karafuto was thus based on a rational assessment of the best way to realize their dreams of success. But more than just dreams, they also had a right to success or at least a right to a chance for success. When the Karafuto government tried to undercut the independence that was a prerequisite to social advancement, they resisted. Significantly, their resistance took the form of a movement to change the law—that is, to gain social affirmation of their right to independence. In this they differed from the small fishers who sailed up the west coast of Hokkaido in 1855 cutting pound traps in a violent denial of the new technology and all that it implied.

The differences between the net slashers of 1855 and the petitioners of a half-century later were not simply fortuitous. Rather, they reflect a shift in political discourse that was itself a by-product of the economic changes Japan had seen during that period. As Andrew Gordon puts it, "The rise of Japan as a nation-state and a capitalist society led to important changes in popular thought and behaviour."[104] Gordon characterizes the period between 1905 and 1918 as a transitional one in the history of urban disturbances, in which city dwellers, often influenced by organized interest groups—politicians, lawyers, journalists, small businessmen, and the like—demonstrated a new national political awareness. The years framed by the Hibiya riots of 1905 and the rice riots of 1918 are the starting point for Gordon's inquiry into the nature of "imperial democracy" during the first three decades of the twentieth century.[105] By extension, the period marks the end of traditional political discourse characterized by a concern with moral economy.

The petit-bourgeois consciousness of the Karafuto fishers, combined with the presence of journalists and shopkeepers in the movement, gave their actions a tone very similar to that of crowds in Tokyo during the same period. The contrast with the traditional style of protest employed by participants in the rice riots on the Toyama coast in 1918 is striking.[106] At first glance this contrast seems paradoxical since the Toyama protests not only occurred in fishing villages but in an area with strong ties to Hokkaido and Karafuto.[107] However, the gill-net movement was an expression of the Karafuto fishers' desire for economic independence, while the rice riots of Toyama were motivated by the subsistence concerns of villagers still tied largely (but not wholly) to a household economy. In other words, the Toyama protests were about eating, while the Karafuto conflict was about the terms of participation in the new economic order.

The Toyama villagers' use of traditional forms of protest recalled a time when the relative social standing of peasant protesters was not the focus of debate. During the Tokugawa period peasants could appeal to the benevolence of the lord only because all concerned parties understood the social and political distance between lord and peasant. Tokugawa peasants in effect manipulated their subordinate position to pressure the authorities into accommodating their demands.[108] In Toyama the same strategy worked because the issue was the rectification of specific moral wrongs attributable to state policy and the rapacity of individual merchants.

In Karafuto, however, the ultimate issue—though the principals did not always realize it—was where people fit in the newly redefined social and economic hierarchy. A sort of moral economy was still operative, but instead of appealing for benevolence, protesters demanded fair treatment as imperial subjects. The protesters in Karafuto had in effect already posited for themselves a place in the new order—a place the state did not accept. As a result, the two groups worked at cross purposes: the small fishers considered themselves as entitled as anyone to reap the benefits of entrepreneurship, while officials were eager to see them resign themselves to a life of wage labor because that position better fit government plans for the economic development of Karafuto. Unlike Tokugawa peasant protests, or even the 1918 Toyama rice riots, critical mutual assumptions of social and economic roles and responsibilities were not operative in Karafuto.

This perspective sheds light on earlier conflicts, such as the Chichibu rebellion of 1884, as well. Scholars generally portray the Chichibu conflict as an important transitional event, but they differ on whether it was primarily the last gasp of the old moral economy or the first articulation of a new political consciousness. Herbert Bix and Irwin Scheiner arrive at the first view, albeit via very different routes, while Irokawa Daikichi and Roger Bowen both see Chichibu as an expression of grass-roots democracy—indigenous for Irokawa, imported from the West for Bowen—consistent with Japan's broader modern transformation.[109] Perhaps Chichibu is so difficult to interpret because it combined elements of both old and new styles of protest: the rebels were fighting *both* for their right to subsistence in accordance with old notions of moral economy *and* for a new position as citizens in the Meiji state. It is suggestive that proto-industrial silk-thread production was the backbone of the Chichibu economy: on the eve of the rebellion up to eighty percent of the local people were involved in some way in sericulture.[110] We might speculate that the Chichibu rebels' experience in rural manufacturing under the Tokugawa regime gave rise to a moral economy for rational peasants like that of the Karafuto fishers.

Ironically, once the family fishers of Karafuto had attained their hard-earned independence, they had to learn that, with the gradual collapse of the fishing industry, that kind of independence was becoming obsolete. Pound-trap operators all relied on the outside to keep themselves in business. Even those who financed their own fishing operations depended on fertilizer brokers in Hakodate and Osaka to market their produce, while the others had to throw themselves at the mercy of supply merchants every autumn.

Yonebayashi Isaburō, a former laborer who later rose to become a fishing tycoon in Karafuto, went bankrupt in a spectacular example of what could happen if the supply merchants' mercy was not forthcoming. In 1910 bad fishing and bad management forced him to run up a three or four hundred thousand yen tab with Hakodate merchants. He needed at least another quarter-million yen to finance his 1911 operations. Extending a total of a half-million yen or more of credit to a single fisher was out of Hakodate's league, so Yonebayashi was forced to approach the really big suppliers in Kōbe. A Tamura Ichirō lent him 500,000 yen, but he had to put all his fisheries up as collateral (they normally would have been worth 800,000 yen). The 1911 season did not work out, and Yonebayashi lost everything. The last anyone heard, he had moved to Korea to make a new start, but the word in Hakodate was that no one would lend him as much as five hundred yen.[111] At least no one suggested that he become a fishery laborer again.

CHAPTER SEVEN

Conclusion

Traditional Industry and Indigenous
Capitalism in Nineteenth-Century Japan

"Herring . . . are my life," explained Saga Kichijirō, a seventy-nine-year-old fisher from Rumoi, when asked by a reporter in January 1988 why he persisted in setting his gill nets every spring, despite the fact that there had not been a substantial herring run in the area since 1954.[1] Saga's patience apparently paid off, as he harvested small but growing catches of herring in 1985, 1986, and 1987. Nevertheless, there is no doubt that his dreams of seeing the good old days of the fishery return will never be fulfilled. For one thing, ecological damage, once done, is hard to repair.[2] The herring catch in Rumoi in 1987 was an "excellent" seven hundred tons, but that is minuscule when compared with even the worst years of the late nineteenth and early twentieth centuries.[3] Nor would there be much point in processing hundreds of thousands of tons of herring meal anyway, now that chemical fertilizers are so readily available. Even in the unlikely event the herring did return *and* there was a market for them, the labor-intensive production of the old days would no longer be practical, necessary, or desirable.

Still, Saga is not the only one nostalgic for the heyday of the fishery. Every spring, newspapers in Hokkaido receive letters from old-timers misty-eyed about the vibrant and prosperous past. A favorite image is the tantalizing aroma of fresh-caught herring cooking on an open fire—a far cry from the putrid stench that hit Thomas Blakiston's nostrils when he arrived in Hakodate in 1861.[4] (In fact, most fishers had more exotic tastes: the robust flavor of *makuri*—herring that had been held in a storage shed until it had begun to ferment—was always a crowd pleaser.)[5] The demise of the herring fishery was a tragedy for fishers, environmentalists, and seafood lovers alike. Analyzing its demise does, however, allow us to draw conclusions about what occurred in the past without having to risk speculation on the future.

My goal in this study has been to clarify the origins and nature of the capitalist transformation of the Hokkaido fishery. I have been concerned in particular with the indigenous roots of capitalism in the fishery and with the immiserating impact of capitalist social and economic relations on small fishers. In both cases the connection between social relations within the fishery and the state structure surrounding it has been critical to my argument. I will conclude by briefly placing the Hokkaido fishery within the broader context of early modern and modern Japanese history, with particular reference to these issues.

Between about 1830 and 1860 the herring fishery underwent the beginnings of a transformation to capitalism. The impetus for structural change came from within the fishery itself, but all developments were shaped by the political and institutional environment of the state. Matsumae, while hardly a typical domain, was nonetheless integrated both politically and ideologically into the Tokugawa state. Its institutions, having originated in the Ainu trade, had built into them a tolerance—even a need—for economic growth. Indeed, the unique features of Matsumae's origins and later development make it an extreme example of a domain dependent upon commerce for its prosperity and stability. In this respect it was rivaled only by Tsushima, which functioned as an intermediary in trade and diplomatic relations between Japan and Korea.[6]

Matsumae was an integral part of the Tokugawa economy. Its development is best seen within the broader context of Tokugawa economic history, for without the growth of commercial agriculture to feed demand for fertilizer, the Hokkaido fishery would never have been a viable enterprise in the first place. Commercial agriculture was itself a product of the integrating forces of the bakuhan state, for it was in response to state needs that the transportation routes and markets necessary for cash cropping developed. The same was true for the fishery: the shipping routes that carried herring meal and other commodities between Hokkaido and Osaka (and many other ports) were charted in the 1670s by Kawamura Zuiken (1618–99), who had been ordered by the bakufu to find a way to transport tax grain from Sakata to Edo.[7]

Matsumae's dependence on commerce differed only in degree—not substance—from that of the bakufu and other domains. The Tokugawa state, despite its ostensible relegation of merchants to a lowly position, relied on them to get goods to market in order to generate cash for samurai stipends, expenses arising from alternate attendance duties, and other feudal obligations. The bakufu and all domains thus had to reach some sort of accommodation with the commercial class. The adaptation of domain institutions in Matsumae to commercial growth—the way, for example, trading posts evolved into contract fisheries—was consistent with practice elsewhere. Indeed, domains throughout the country made extensive use of merchant contractors (*ukeoinin*) to regulate the production and distribution of essential commodities.[8] In the bakufu, Tanuma Okitsugu was aggressive in his attempts to tailor policies to economic realities rather than simply to force the economy to conform to preconceived ideal forms.[9] Unlike commerce in other domains, commerce in Matsumae was not linked to an agricultural economy, so the effects of commercialization on domain institutions were not obscured by the fiction that subsistence agriculture was the only legitimate economic activity. This difference made Matsumae an ideal environment for proto-industrial development. The distinctiveness of Matsumae, then, lay not in the simple fact of commercialization or the presence of merchant capital but rather in the way commercial and political institutions interacted.

The emphasis on rice cultivation in other jurisdictions inhibited the sort of broad regional specialization found in Europe and thus precluded the demographic transformation necessary to fuel full factory industrialization. Under the *kokudaka* system a daimyo's place in the institutional hierarchy of the Tokugawa state was measured in terms of the putative agricultural productivity of his domain. Although it very quickly ceased to reflect actual economic conditions, the *kokudaka* system retained its institutional importance throughout the Tokugawa period. Even as many domains came to tolerate and even actively foster a wide variety of economic activities, peasants were expected to grow grain—preferably rice—unless there was some compelling reason for them not to do so. When officials pressed peasants to produce as much rice as possible— even where climatic or technological conditions made rice cultivation impractical—they were responding to the position of rice as a measure not only of wealth but also of status in the feudal polity.

The *kokudaka* system thus was an institutional hurdle to economic development, although not an insurmountable one. For daimyo and their officials the critical distinction was not between subsistence and commercial agriculture, or even between agriculture and industry, but rather between rice and nonrice production.[10] Whether proto-industrialization occurred—or, more precisely, whether other commodities could supplement or even replace rice in the domain economy—became largely a question of a domain's attitude toward nonrice production.[11]

In Hokkaido, rice cultivation was impossible, so the herring fishery became a proxy for agriculture. In a sense, herring was "rice" in Matsumae: its economy revolved around the fishery in a way that satisfied the requirements of the feudal polity, while opening the door for considerable proto-industrial and eventually even capitalist development. In places where rice cultivation was more feasible, the authorities could adopt a narrower definition of "rice," with the result that support for industry—and even commercial agriculture—was not readily forthcoming. For instance, the southern Kantō was the locus of a number of industries, most notably soy-sauce brewing and sardine-fertilizer processing, that drew labor from the peasant population. However, local authorities were either unwilling or unable to appreciate the value of these industries. Instead of seeing their potential benefits, all they saw was the decline of agriculture. Rather than profiting from industrial growth, they vainly tried to get villagers to go back to the fields.[12]

The inability of the Tokugawa state to take full advantage of proto-industrial development reflects the rigidity of a feudal polity. Economic institutions may come under pressure and begin to change, but they cannot complete the process of transformation so long as political impediments remain.[13] In Japan proto-industrialization had its ultimate origins in the political integration of the early Tokugawa period and the subsequent development of transportation routes and markets to deliver tax grain and other commodities to a burgeoning urban population. Later, however, the sort of structural change prompted—indeed, required—by proto-industrialization was impeded by the institutional structure of the Tokugawa polity. Once the feudal polity was eliminated by the reforms following the Meiji Restoration, economic change proceeded at a rapid pace, so that Japan was a genuinely capitalist economy by the beginning of the twentieth century. One casualty of this transformation was rice, which lost its ideological and institutional place of honor in the Japanese political economy with the enactment of the land-tax reform of 1873.

In Matsumae the accommodation of the polity to commerce opened the door to proto-industrial development and eventually to capitalism. In contrast, the Nanbu domain—the archetypical "backward" region[14]— offers an example of proto-industrialization without capitalism. Nanbu can be seen as a microcosm of the entire country, with the central Kitakami river valley representing the "advanced" agricultural regions and the mountains and coast the "backward" centers of proto-industrial development. Agricultural, but not industrial, production in the domain was centered on the Kitakami valley, which included the castle town of Morioka. Proto-industry—most notably large-scale commercial fishing and fish processing (not herring, alas!) and ironworking—was found along the Pacific coast and in the mountains separating the coast from the Kitakami valley.

Interestingly, the most highly industrialized parts of the domain saw the most serious occurrences of unrest among Nanbu's notoriously contentious peasants; the best known instances of conflict (the Sanhei rebellions of 1847 and 1853) involved disputes over domain commercial and industrial policies, and were directed in large part against merchants who had purchased samurai status from the domain. The disorder in Nanbu may be attributed to the fact that the impetus for economic growth came from the proto-industrial hinterland, but the feudal institutional structure—located as it was both physically and ideologically in the agricultural core—could not adapt.[15]

In Nanbu the regional diversity of economic activity encouraged the development of proto-industry, but manufacturing remained under the domination of merchant capital, backed by the sanction of domain monopolies and monopsonies. Incidents like the Sanhei rebellions, in which peasants reacted against tight domain (and hence merchant-capital) control over the economy, may have represented failed attempts to open the door to future capitalist development.

The Nanbu example is presented as a counterpoint to the Hokkaido fishery to accentuate the fact that institutional structure, rather than the activities of merchant capital, is ultimately the key to understanding the causes and outcomes of economic change. It was not the prominence or quiescence of merchant capital that determined the course of proto-industrial or capitalist development in Hokkaido because merchant capital is inherently conservative, choosing domination at the point of exchange rather than at the point of production whenever possible.[16] This is not to say that the state alone caused capitalism in Hokkaido, merely that the state is a key variable in understanding how changes in social and economic relations evolved. Given the fact that Matsumae did not develop in political or economic isolation from the rest of Tokugawa Japan, nor did it deviate in function from the basic institutional norms of the bakuhan state, we can conclude that the potential for capitalist development was present in the Tokugawa economy as a whole.

Recognizing the potential for capitalism in the Tokugawa economy is not the same, however, as positing a single, inevitable course of development. Paradoxically, the same innovations that spurred growth often inhibited more profound change. Edward Pratt argues that the institutional adaptation of the Tokugawa polity to commercial growth after the middle of the eighteenth century fostered the rise of a class of rural elites, the *gōnō* (usually rendered "wealthy peasants"). These rural elites built commercial and proto-industrial ventures around marketing networks that had been established under official auspices to serve urban consumer demand.[17] The actual course of proto-industrialization in a given area was always subject to a variety of constraints, both political and environmental. *Gōnō* in areas with high agricultural productivity retained a presence in farming longer than others, for the simple reason that they lacked a strong incentive to gamble on industry or commerce. Although a commitment to agriculture on the part of rural elites did not prevent proto-industrialization, it may have softened the disruptive impact of economic change on social relations within the village community. Conversely, in localities with low levels of food-crop production—typically mountainous regions involved in sericulture—poor peasants often lost their land and became wholly dependent upon industrial employment. Whether productivity was high or low, a farmer's initial decision to enter industry or to remain solely in farming was subject to other factors, such as tax levels (and whether taxes were paid in cash or in kind, and whether they were calculated as a percentage of each year's crop or set at a fixed rate). These same conditions continued to affect the *gōnō*'s behavior once he had become involved in proto-industrial endeavors.[18]

A Tokugawa peasant's decision to participate in a proto-industrial enterprise, whether as entrepreneur or as worker, can be understood only in the context of the institutional structure of the bakuhan state. But every time a peasant switched from growing rice to spinning thread, and every time a well-to-do villager invested money made in sericulture in new land, a nail was hammered into the coffin of the system that had given rise to these activities in the first place. By the time all the nails had been hammered in, the participants in the economic system found that their positions had been altered irrevocably.

Still, not every instance of proto-industrialization developed into factory industrialization. Indeed, at times the very vigor of proto-industrial enterprise hindered further development. For instance, Pratt finds that after the Meiji Restoration silk-reeling regions with a history of proto-industrialization were often slow to adopt modern technology, while other areas "enjoyed far greater maneuverability." This difference occurred partly because "the shift to mechanized production did not simply entail the application of modern technology to traditional crafts." Native technology "maintained a powerful hold over production not only because of its profitability, but because it meshed well with the social structure and needs of the populace at the time."[19] Merchants in established proto-industrial regions had little immediate motivation to abandon tried-and-true methods, while competitors new to the silk business had every incentive to start at as advanced a level of technology as possible.

Modern technology may have prevailed in the long run, but, as Kären Wigen points out, early-twentieth-century Japanese silk production essentially retained its labor-intensive, handicraft character.[20] The persistence of proto-industrial production in textile manufacturing, which nevertheless was Japan's first highly mechanized industry, indicates that the economics of structural transformation was not simply a matter of applying the most advanced technology available to a chosen sector. Studies of the Meiji economy often assume that because Western technology was inherently superior, traditional industries were doomed to disappear quickly. In fact, as Pratt and Wigen demonstrate, traditional methods were often the more "rational" choice in the silk-thread industry. Even after the opening in 1872 of the Tomioka filature—big, modern, expensive, and not at all profitable—native manufacturing techniques endured and were in fact the driving force behind economic development in the area for decades.[21] The parallel to this development in Hokkaido was the continued expansion of gill-net fishing throughout the nineteenth century, despite the appearance of the pound trap.

Henry Rosovsky once asked, "Is it really necessary to move back farther and farther in time in order to appreciate the significant dimensions of a recent and entirely different past?"[22] He said no; but now we know that the Tokugawa past was not nearly so "entirely different" and unconnected as it once seemed. Japan was not magically transformed within just a few decades by the introduction of Western technology and institutions after 1868; but neither did every instance of proto-industrialization develop smoothly into full-blown industrial capitalism. Whether there was a direct causal link between given instances of proto-industrial development and capitalism, however, the evolution of capitalist social and economic relations was profoundly affected by earlier conditions.

The connection between proto-industrialization and capitalism is particularly clear in places like Hokkaido, where both the "before" and "after" pictures depict a changing fertilizer-processing industry. A more discerning eye is needed in other regions, where the pressures of proto-industrial development at the local level and institutional change at the national level sometimes combined to alter regional economies beyond recognition. Wigen's careful study of the Shimoina region of southern Shinano reveals the subtle process of long-term change. During the Tokugawa period Shimoina's paper and transport industries were the center of a thriving proto-industrial complex; Wigen presents evidence that suggests the evolution of capitalist production in at least some sectors of the paper industry. After the Meiji Restoration silk and forestry took over, and Shimoina was integrated into not only the national economy but the world economy as well. The cost, however, was that the region's geopolitical position—even its integrity as a geographical unit—was compromised in the process, and a once vibrant area was reduced to a backwater.[23] An analysis that had begun or ended in 1868 would have missed the important connections between Shimoina's proto-industrial development and the impact of capitalist development directed by the Meiji state.

After the Meiji Restoration the state implemented policies that affirmed the predominance of the capitalist fishery in Hokkaido. Indeed, the transformation was not really complete until state institutions had fully adjusted to the advent of capitalist production through the formalization of property and fishing rights at the beginning of the twentieth century. It was during this second stage of the emergence of capitalism that small fishers experienced relative immiseration.

Relative immiseration in the context of the fishery meant that small fishers gradually lost their ability to function as independent proprietors. Some experienced a decline in their material living standards as a result of this process, and others did not. But, as I have emphasized throughout this study, the question is not of primary importance here because aggregate measures of economic growth tell us little about fishers' perceptions of their relative position in society and nothing about the way production was organized.

The same is true when we look beyond the fishery to the way the changes of the Meiji period affected ordinary people throughout Japan. The flip side of the systematic recognition of property rights by the state was the dispossession of those whose rights were *not* recognized. After the land-tax reform such people became tenants whose independence was curtailed by the demands of landlords. Thus, just as the proletarianization of small fishers was a construct of the state's policies toward the fishery, the differentiation of the Honshu peasantry into landlords and tenants was a function of the formalization of property rights in land. In both cases the impetus for structural change came from within the economy, but the change was not completed until the state had provided an institutional context for the new relations among producers.

When faced with the reality of the capitalist mode of production, people had to either accommodate themselves to it or succumb to proletarianization. Most people who became wage laborers did not, of course, have any real choice at all: they were proletarianized because they no longer had the resources to maintain independent production. Many Japanese, particularly in urban areas, compensated for this loss of independence by embracing the ideology of "imperial democracy," which affirmed the right of citizens to participate in the emergent new order.[24] Of course, those who had the wherewithal to do so protected themselves in other ways too. Thus fishers moved to places like Karafuto in an attempt to establish themselves as petty capitalists before it was too late.

The irony is that the state preferred to see the Japanese people resign themselves to capitalism rather than accommodate themselves to it. Thus conflicts like the one over fishing rights in Karafuto were really about the fishers' right to participate in a capitalist economy that did not need any new capitalists. The desire of small fishers in Karafuto to preserve their independence contrasts with the attitude of officials in Toyama prefecture, who in 1891 studied ways to send "surplus" residents of several coastal districts to Hokkaido, where they could be put to work as wage laborers in the herring fishery.[25]

Today, the functional equivalents of the Hokkaido fishery workers are the rural men who spend each winter far from their homes in northern Japan loading the barrels of pork that ballast postwar Japan's ship of state—working, that is, on dams, bridges, and other big-ticket public works projects. Whatever the discomforts of their lives, they are without question better off than their forbears on the herring-fishing crews. But their prosperity—if indeed they see themselves as prosperous—is an incidental by-product of state-driven economic development rather than a central goal of government policy. In that sense their situation is not at all different from that of the Hokkaido fishers whose entrepreneurial successes and immiserated failures alike were of little immediate consequence to a Meiji state eager for rapid growth whatever the proximate costs.

Notes

Abbreviations

ECS   Esashi chō shi henshūshitsu, ed. *Esashi chō shi.* 6 volumes. Esashi: Esashi chō, 1978–81.

MCS   Matsumae chō shi henshūshitsu, ed. *Matsumae chō shi.* 6 volumes. Matsumae: Matsumae chō shi henshūshitsu, 1974–88.

RCNS   Resource Collection for Northern Studies, Hokkaidō University Library.

SHS   Hokkaidō chō, ed. *Shinsen Hokkaidō shi.* 7 volumes. Sapporo: Hokkaidō chō, 1936–37.

YCS   Yoichi chō shi hensanshitsu, ed. *Yoichi chō shi: Shiryōhen.* 1 volume to date. Yoichi: Yoichi chō, 1986.

1. Commercialization, Proto-Industrialization, and Capitalism

1. Thomas Wright Blakiston, *Japan in Yezo* (Yokohama: Japan Gazette, 1883), p. 5.

2. William W. Kelly, *Deference and Defiance in Nineteenth-Century Japan* (Princeton: Princeton University Press, 1985), p. 24.

3. Richard Smethurst, *Agricultural Development and Tenancy Disputes in Japan, 1870–1940* (Princeton: Princeton University Press, 1986), stresses the benefits of commercialization and capitalism for the peasantry. Taking a much dimmer view is Mikiso Hane, *Peasants, Outcastes, and Rebels: The Underside of*

Modern Japan (New York: Pantheon, 1982). See the discussion in Kelly, *Deference and Defiance in Nineteenth-Century Japan*, pp. 14–25.

4. See Marius B. Jansen and Gilbert Rozman, eds., *Japan in Transition: From Tokugawa to Meiji* (Princeton: Princeton University Press, 1986); Thomas C. Smith, *Native Sources of Japanese Industrialization, 1750–1920* (Berkeley: University of California Press, 1988); and the introductory chapter to Andrew Gordon's study of labor relations, *The Evolution of Labor Relations in Japan: Heavy Industry, 1853–1955* (Cambridge: Council on East Asian Studies, Harvard University, 1985). Business histories, such as W. Mark Fruin, *Kikkoman: Company, Clan, and Community* (Cambridge: Council on East Asian Studies, Harvard University, 1983), try to bridge the gap, though their concern is not with the transformation of social relations.

5. Maurice Dobb, *Studies in the Development of Capitalism* (New York: International Publishers, 1947), pp. 1–11.

6. James C. Scott, *The Moral Economy of the Peasant: Rebellion and Subsistence in Southeast Asia* (New Haven, Conn.: Yale University Press, 1976).

7. This definition of capitalism is adapted from Dobb, *Studies in the Development of Capitalism*, p. 7. The feudal mode of production is characterized, according to Rodney Hilton, "Introduction," in *The Transition from Feudalism to Capitalism*, ed. Rodney Hilton (London: Verso Editions, 1978), p. 30, by an "exploitative relationship between landowners and subordinated peasants, in which the surplus beyond subsistence of the latter, whether in direct labour or in rent in kind or in money, is transferred under coercive sanction to the former."

8. Susan B. Hanley and Kozo Yamamura, *Economic and Demographic Change in Preindustrial Japan, 1600–1868* (Princeton: Princeton University Press, 1977), p. 12.

9. Kazushi Ohkawa and Henry Rosovsky, "A Century of Economic Growth," in *The State and Economic Enterprise in Japan: Essays in the Political Economy of Growth*, ed. William W. Lockwood (Princeton: Princeton University Press, 1965), p. 58; Eric L. Jones, *Growth Recurring: Economic Change in World History* (Oxford: Clarendon Press, 1988).

10. In addition to Hanley and Yamamura, *Economic and Demographic Change in Preindustrial Japan*, see Kozo Yamamura, "Toward a Reexamination of the Economic History of Tokugawa Japan, 1600–1867," *Journal of Economic History* 33 (1973): 509–41, and Susan B. Hanley, "A High Standard of Living in Nineteenth-Century Japan: Fact or Fantasy?" *Journal of Economic History* 43 (1983): 183–92.

11. Thomas C. Smith, "Peasant Time and Factory Time in Japan," *Past and Present* 111 (1986): 165–97.

12. Hayami Akira, "Kinsei Nihon no keizai hatten to 'Industrious Revolution,'" in *Tokugawa shakai kara no tenbō: Hatten, kōzō, kokusai kankei*, ed. Hayami Akira, Saitō Osamu, and Sugiyama Shin'ya (Tokyo: Dōbunkan, 1989).

13. For an excellent discussion of this type of problem, see Philip C. C. Huang, *The Peasant Economy and Social Change in North China* (Stanford: Stanford University Press, 1985).

14. Thomas C. Smith, *The Agrarian Origins of Modern Japan* (Stanford: Stanford University Press, 1959).

15. On Chichibu, see Irokawa Daikichi, *The Culture of the Meiji Period,*

translation ed. Marius B. Jansen (Princeton: Princeton University Press, 1985), and Irwin Scheiner, "The Mindful Peasant: Sketches for a Study of Rebellion," *Journal of Asian Studies* 32 (1973): 579–91; for a different interpretation, see Roger Bowen, *Rebellion and Democracy in Meiji Japan* (Berkeley: University of California Press, 1980). On the Hibiya riots, see Andrew Gordon, "The Crowd and Politics in Imperial Japan: Tokyo, 1905–1918," *Past and Present* 121 (1988): 141–70. On the rice riots, see Michael Lewis, *Rioters and Citizens: Mass Protest in Imperial Japan* (Berkeley: University of California Press, 1990).

16. Peter Kriedte, Hans Medick, and Jürgen Schlumbohm, *Industrialization before Industrialization* (Cambridge: Cambridge University Press; Paris: Editions de la Maison des Sciences de l'Homme, 1981), p. 6. The proto-industrialization model has run into criticism from various quarters, some of it prompted by the confusion concerning the precise role rural industry is supposed to have played in the process of structural transformation. For a critique of the proto-industrialization model in general, and particularly its claims for universal applicability, see D. C. Coleman, "Proto-Industrialization: A Concept Too Many," *Economic History Review*, 2d series, 36 (1983): 435–48. See also the debate surrounding the value of Kriedte, Medick, and Schlumbohm, *Industrialization before Industrialization*, particularly Geoff Eley's defense of that work—"The Social History of Industrialization: 'Proto-Industry' and the Origins of Capitalism," *Economy and Society* 13 (1984): 519–39—the response by Frank Perlin—"Scrutinizing Which Moment?" *Economy and Society* 14 (1985): 374–98—and the numerous works cited in those articles, especially Maxine Berg, Pat Hudson, and Michael Sonenscher, eds., *Manufacture in Town and Country before the Factory* (Cambridge: Cambridge University Press, 1983). For a response to their German critics, see Peter Kriedte, Hans Medick, and Jürgen Schlumbohm, "Proto-Industrialization on Test with the Guild of Historians: Response to Some Critics," *Economy and Society* 15 (1986): 254–72. See also the discussions in Kären Wigen, *The Making of a Japanese Periphery, 1750–1920* (Berkeley: University of California Press, 1994), pp. 8–9, and William D. Wray, "Afterword," in *Managing Industrial Enterprise: Cases from Japan's Prewar Experience*, ed. William D. Wray (Cambridge: Council on East Asian Studies, Harvard University, 1989), pp. 365–71.

17. See the discussion in Kriedte, Medick, and Schlumbohm, *Industrialization before Industrialization*, pp. 1–11.

18. Franklin Mendels, "Proto-Industrialization: The First Phase of the Industrialization Process," *Journal of Economic History* 32 (1972): 246.

19. Kriedte, Medick, and Schlumbohm, *Industrialization before Industrialization*, pp. 147–48.

20. Myron Gutmann, *Toward the Modern Economy: Early Industry in Europe* (Philadelphia: Temple University Press, 1988).

21. Mendels, "Proto-Industrialization," p. 252.

22. Saitō Osamu's discussion of Japanese proto-industrialization—*Puroto-kōgyōka no jidai* (Tokyo: Hyōronsha, 1985)—which is summarized below, is framed largely in terms of the different courses taken by silk-reeling areas of the northern Kantō and Shinano and cotton-spinning regions in the Kinai after foreign trade was reopened.

23. Perlin, "Scrutinizing Which Moment?" pp. 386–87.

188 Notes to Pages 10–12

24. See E. Patricia Tsurumi, *Factory Girls: Women in the Thread Mills of Meiji Japan* (Princeton: Princeton University Press, 1990), and Takizawa Hideki, *Mayu to seishi no kindaishi* (Tokyo: Kyōikusha, 1979).

25. See Gary P. Leupp, "'One Drink from a Gourd': Servants, Shophands, and Laborers in the Cities of Tokugawa Japan" (Ph.D. diss., University of Michigan, 1989), pp. 500–545, for an overview of rural industries in Tokugawa Japan. See also a number of case studies: William B. Hauser, *Economic Institutional Change in Tokugawa Japan: Ōsaka and the Kinai Cotton Trade* (Cambridge: Cambridge University Press, 1974); David L. Howell, "Hard Times in the Kantō: Economic Change and Village Life in Late Tokugawa Japan," *Modern Asian Studies* 23 (1989): 349–71; Arne Kalland, "Pre-modern Whaling in Northern Kyūshū," in *Silkworms, Oil, and Chips . . .* (Proceedings of the Economics and Economic History Section of the Fourth International Conference on Japanese Studies, Paris, September 1985), ed. Erich Pauer (Bonn, 1986); Shunsaku Nishikawa, "Grain Consumption: The Case of Chōshū," in *Japan in Transition: From Tokugawa to Meiji*, ed. Marius B. Jansen and Gilbert Rozman (Princeton: Princeton University Press, 1986); Edward E. Pratt, "Village Elites in Tokugawa Japan: The Economic Foundations of the Gōnō" (Ph.D. diss., University of Virginia, 1991); Saitō Osamu, "The Rural Economy: Commercial Agriculture, By-Employment, and Wage Work," in *Japan in Transition: From Tokugawa to Meiji*, ed. Marius B. Jansen and Gilbert Rozman (Princeton: Princeton University Press, 1986); Thomas C. Smith, "Farm Family By-Employments in Preindustrial Japan," *Journal of Economic History* 29 (1969): 687–715; and Wigen, *The Making of a Japanese Periphery*.

26. Saitō, *Puroto-kōgyōka no jidai*, pp. 168–69. See also Saitō Osamu, "Population and the Peasant Family Economy in Proto-Industrial Japan," *Journal of Family History* 8 (1983): 30–54.

27. Saitō, *Puroto-kōgyōka no jidai*, pp. 197–205.

28. Ibid., p. 173.

29. Contrary to the general pattern discerned by Saitō, communities of outcaste leather workers in the Kansai region did develop higher population densities as a result of their proto-industrial activities. Although the Japanese population as a whole leveled off after the mid-eighteenth century, the outcaste population grew steadily throughout the Tokugawa period, apparently as the result of natural increase rather than the recruitment of new outcastes from the commoner population. Hatanaka Toshiyuki, "Kinsei 'senmin' mibunron no kadai," in *Sōten: Nihon no rekishi*, ed. Aoki Michio and Hosaka Satoru (Tokyo: Shinjinbutsu ōraisha, 1991), 5: 179–80.

30. Saitō, *Puroto-kōgyōka no jidai*, p. 168.

31. Smith, *The Agrarian Origins of Modern Japan*.

32. According to Mendels, "Proto-Industrialization," p. 245, "Those [in continental Europe] who had remained isolated from market forces and those who had become fully specialized in commercial agriculture did not feel the necessity of turning to modern industry as much as those who had been depending on handicrafts." However, Gay L. Gullickson, *Spinners and Weavers of Auffay: Rural Industry and the Sexual Division of Labor in a French Village, 1750–1850* (Cambridge: Cambridge University Press, 1986), p. 65, while conceding that "proto-industrialization may have occurred more often in subsistence farming or

pastoral regions," argues that "seasonal unemployment and landlessness, not poor land, were the distinguishing features of proto-industrial regions."
33. Kriedte, Medick, and Schlumbohm, *Industrialization before Industrialization*, p. 108.
34. Hanley and Yamamura, *Economic and Demographic Change in Preindustrial Japan*, organize their whole book in terms of this dichotomy but in doing so follow common practice. For a discussion of the innovative aspects of their treatment of regional differences, see Kären Wigen, "The Geographic Imagination in Early Modern Japanese History: Retrospect and Prospect," *Journal of Asian Studies* 51:1 (February 1992): 11–13.
35. Saitō, *Puroto-kōgyōka no jidai*, p. 176.
36. For a general overview, see Arai Eiji, *Kinsei no gyoson* (Tokyo: Yoshikawa kōbunkan, 1970).
37. Sasahara Masao, "Kinsei Kishū ni okeru takoku gyogyō no henshitsu," *Chihōshi kenkyū* 168 (December 1980): 31–54; Tajima Yoshiya, "Kinsei Kishū gyohō no tenkai," in *Seisan no gijutsu* (*Nihon no kinsei*, vol. 4), ed. Hayama Teisaku (Tokyo: Chūō kōronsha, 1992); Arne Kalland, "In Search of the Abalone: The History of the *Ama* in Northern Kyūshū," in *Seinan chiiki no shiteki tenkai*, ed. Seinan chiikishi kenkyūkai (Tokyo: Shibunkaku, 1988), 1: 588–617.
38. Kawaoka Takeharu, *Umi no tami: Gyoson no rekishi to minzoku* (Tokyo: Heibonsha, 1987).
39. Kawamura Suguru and Miura Shigekazu, "Kujūkurihama jibikiami gyogyō no hatten to kōzō," in *Zairai gijutsu no hatten to kinsei shakai* (*Gijutsu no shakai shi*, vol. 2), ed. Sasaki Junnosuke (Tokyo: Yūhikaku, 1983); Yamaguchi Tōru, "Kinseiteki koyō no ichi danmen: Jibikiami gyogyō o chūshin ni," *Rekishi to minzoku: Kanagawa daigaku Nihon jōmin bunka kenkyūjo ronshū* 5 (1990): 7–66.
40. Hayami, "Kinsei Nihon no keizai hatten to 'Industrious Revolution,'" p. 22.
41. In Europe, too, "proto-industrialization was most likely to occur where urban and rural needs complemented each other." Gullickson, *Spinners and Weavers of Auffay*, p. 67.
42. Wigen, *The Making of a Japanese Periphery*, p. 119.
43. Thomas C. Smith, "Pre-modern Economic Growth: Japan and the West," *Past and Present* 60 (1973): 127–60.
44. Shinbo Hiroshi and Hasegawa Akira, "Shōhin seisan, ryūtsū no dainamikkusu," in *Keizai shakai no seiritsu* (*Nihon keizai shi*, vol. 1), ed. Hayami Akira and Miyamoto Matao (Tokyo: Iwanami shoten, 1988), and Howell, "Hard Times in the Kantō."
45. C. Pemberton Hodgson, *A Residence at Nagasaki and Hakodate in 1859–1860, with an Account of Japan Generally* (London: Richard Bentley, 1861), p. 48.
46. A. H. Savage Landor, *Alone with the Hairy Ainu: Or, 3,800 Miles on a Pack Saddle in Yezo and a Cruise to the Kurile Islands* (London: John Murray, 1893; reprint New York: Johnson Reprint Company, 1970).
47. I examine the issues outlined here in depth in David L. Howell, "Ainu Ethnicity and the Boundaries of the Early Modern Japanese State," *Past and Present* 142 (1994): 69–93.

48. Ōishi Naomasa, "Kita no bushidan: Andō shi," in *Nihonkai to hokkoku bunka* (*Umi to rettō bunka*, vol. 1), ed. Amino Yoshihiko (Tokyo: Shōgakukan, 1990), pp. 318–42; Kaiho Mineo, "Hoppō kōeki to chūsei Ezo shakai," in *Nihonkai to hokkoku bunka* (*Umi to rettō bunka*, vol. 1), ed. Amino Yoshihiko (Tokyo: Shōgakukan, 1990), pp. 255–86; Murai Shōsuke, *Ajia no naka no chūsei Nihon* (Tokyo: Azekura shobō, 1988), pp. 339–43.

49. See Murai Shōsuke, "Kenmu, Muromachi seiken to higashi Ajia," in *Kōza Nihon rekishi*, ed. Rekishigaku kenkyūkai and Nihonshi kenkyūkai (Tokyo: Tōkyō daigaku shuppankai, 1985), 4: 1–42, and the discussion of a "pan-Japan Sea" region in medieval Japan in Murai, *Ajia no naka no chūsei Nihon*, pp. 126–28.

50. For a discussion of the way the Tokugawa bakufu asserted its legitimacy through its ordering of international relations, see Ronald P. Toby, *State and Diplomacy in Early Modern Japan* (Princeton: Princeton University Press, 1984). See also Arano Yasunori, *Kinsei Nihon to higashi Ajia* (Tokyo: Tōkyō daigaku shuppankai, 1988); Asao Naohiro, ed., *Sekaishi no naka no kinsei* (*Nihon no kinsei*, vol. 1) (Tokyo: Chūō kōronsha, 1991); and Fukaya Katsumi, Kitajima Manji, and Katō Eiichi, eds., *Bakuhansei kokka to iiki, ikoku* (Tokyo: Azekura shobō, 1989).

51. As Kamiya Nobuyuki, "Nihon kinsei no tōitsu to Dattan," in *Nihon zenkindai no kokka to taigai kankei*, ed. Tanaka Takeo (Tokyo: Yoshikawa kōbunkan, 1987), pp. 166–72, points out, the initial object of the buffer was not Russia but rather the Jurchens, whose Qing dynasty later controlled China.

52. Donald Keene, *The Japanese Discovery of Europe, 1720–1830*, rev. ed. (Stanford: Stanford University Press, 1969); Bob Tadashi Wakabayashi, *Antiforeignism and Western Learning in Early-Modern Japan: The New Theses of 1825* (Cambridge: Council on East Asian Studies, Harvard University, 1986), pp. 73–86; John A. Harrison, *Japan's Northern Frontier* (Gainesville: University of Florida Press, 1953).

53. See Kelly, *Deference and Defiance in Nineteenth-Century Japan*, pp. 14–25, for a discussion of the continuity/disjunction issue. In addition, the articles in Jansen and Rozman, *Japan in Transition*, stress the continuities in every major facet of society, save the intellectual, while Tetsuo Najita and J. Victor Koschmann, eds., *Conflict in Modern Japanese History: The Neglected Tradition* (Princeton: Princeton University Press, 1982), part 1, contains several articles examining discontinuities in the Restoration period. Anne Walthall, *Social Protest and Popular Culture in Eighteenth-Century Japan* (Tucson: University of Arizona Press, 1986), deals with the 1780s, but with an eye on the 1860s.

54. Harry Harootunian, "Ideology as Conflict," in *Conflict in Modern Japanese History: The Neglected Tradition*, ed. Tetsuo Najita and J. Victor Koschmann (Princeton: Princeton University Press, 1982), p. 60. People were, however, quite aware of the political and military events of the Restoration period. See the discussion of the diary of Hirasawa Toyosaku, a resident of Oshamanbe on the southeast coast of Hokkaido, in Kaiho Mineo, *Bakuhansei kokka to Hokkaidō* (Tokyo: San'ichi shobō, 1978), pp. 268–82.

55. "Ichinen no yume Ezo miyage" [n.d.], Hokkaidō Prefectural Archives.

56. Dobb, *Studies in the Development of Capitalism*, p. 7.

2. Not Quite Capitalism

1. Doc. I-10-55 [1828/11], Hayashi-ke monjo, *Yoichi chō shi: Shiryōhen*, ed. Yoichi chō shi hensanshitsu (Yoichi: Yoichi chō, 1986), 1: 182–83 (hereafter cited as Hayashi-ke monjo, YCS).

2. When referring to the Tokugawa period, I will use "Hokkaido" to refer to the islands included in the present Hokkaido prefecture, including Hokkaido, nearby islands, and the so-called Northern Territories of Kunashiri, Etorofu, Shikotan, and the Habomai Islands; "Wajinchi" to refer to that part of southern Hokkaido open to non-Ainu Japanese (Wajin) settlement; and "Ezochi" to refer to the remainder of Hokkaido, which was, in principle, not open to permanent Japanese settlement until 1855. I prefer "Ezochi" to "Ezo" ("Yezo"), which is frequently used in Western accounts of Hokkaido before 1869, because "Ezo" was usually used in Matsumae to refer to the Ainu people, not their homeland, and in any case "Ezo" as a geographical term implies all of Hokkaido, whereas "Ezochi" refers to a specific portion of it. A fuller discussion of the Wajinchi/Ezochi dichotomy will follow. I will use "Matsumae" to designate the domain. The Matsumae domain's castle town, Fukuyama, is now (and was sometimes during the Tokugawa period) called Matsumae, but, for the sake of simplicity, I will use only Fukuyama.

3. Although it was generally treated as a 10,000-koku domain, Matsumae never participated directly in the *kokudaka* system, in which the productivity of a domain's landholdings was expressed in terms of fictive rice yields. Because the land surveys (*kenchi*) that formed the basis for official yield assessments were never conducted in Matsumae, neither peasant tax obligations nor retainer stipends were expressed in terms of koku of rice (one koku equals approximately 180 liters). See the discussion in Kaiho, *Bakuhansei kokka to Hokkaidō*, pp. 14–16, 135–46, 151–80. In this Matsumae differed even from the Tsushima domain, whose economy was based almost entirely on trade with Korea. A common misperception is that Tsushima's landholdings outside of mainland Kyushu were never surveyed and were thus without *kokudaka*; in fact, a survey conducted in 1627 yielded an assessment of about 17,560 koku. See Moriyama Tsuneo, "Tsushima han," in *Nagasaki ken shi: Hansei hen*, ed. Nagasaki ken shi henshū iinkai (Tokyo: Yoshikawa kōbunkan, 1973), pp. 813–19, 856–59, 884–87. Another misperception is that the bakufu, in recognition of Tsushima's economic and diplomatic importance, officially accorded it status as a 100,000-koku domain. In fact, the domain in effect treated *itself* that way, even after the bakufu expressly denied its request for 100,000-koku status. See Shin Tsushima-tō shi henshū iinkai, ed., *Shin Tsushima-tō shi* (Izuhara: Shin Tsushima-tō shi henshū iinkai, 1964), pp. 354–55. I am indebted to Professor Tashiro Kazui for guiding me to these sources.

4. Kaiho, *Bakuhansei kokka to Hokkaidō*, pp. 23–24. Financial problems led to infighting among domain elders so severe that the bakufu issued a stern warning to the domain in 1681.

5. For general overviews of Meiji development policies, see Harrison, *Japan's Northern Frontier*, and Augustin Berque, *La riziére et la banquise: Colonisation et changement culturel à Hokkaidô* (Paris: Publications Orientalistes de France, 1980).

6. Kaiho Mineo, "Hokkaidō ni okeru hōkensei shodankai settei e no ichi shi-ron," *Chihōshi kenkyū* 119 (October 1972): 46–47.

7. My characterization of these newcomers from Honshu as Wajin follows conventional practice, but according to Kaiho Mineo, *Rettō hoppōshi kenkyū nōto* (Sapporo: Hokkaidō shuppan kikaku sentā, 1986), pp. 76–78, it is not clear that the groups that later formed the Matsumae house and its retainer band consid-ered themselves to be ethnically distinct from the Ainu at this time, though they certainly did by the end of the sixteenth century. Takeda Nobuhiro himself, how-ever, was originally from the province of Wakasa and therefore clearly a Wajin. Kaiho has written extensively on the formative period of Hokkaido history; the discussion here largely follows his work in both substance and interpretation. Readily accessible treatments can be found in *Kinsei no Hokkaidō* (Tokyo: Kyōikusha, 1979), and especially *Chūsei no Ezochi* (Tokyo: Yoshikawa kō-bunkan, 1987); more specialized studies are contained in *Nihon hoppōshi no ronri* (Tokyo: Yūzankaku, 1974); *Bakuhansei kokka to Hokkaidō*; and, particu-larly, *Kinsei Ezochi seiritsu shi no kenkyū* (Tokyo: San'ichi shobō, 1984). In ad-dition, he has edited a collection of pertinent documents, *Chūsei Ezo shiryō* (Tokyo: San'ichi shobō, 1983). See also the summary of this period in Richard Louis Edmonds, *Northern Frontiers of Qing China and Tokugawa Japan: A Comparative Study of Frontier Policy* (Chicago: Department of Geography, Uni-versity of Chicago, 1985), pp. 41–49.

8. For the documents, see the domain's official history, "Fukuyama hifu" [1776], comp. Matsumae Hironaga, book 8, in *Shinsen Hokkaidō shi*, ed. Hok-kaidō chō (Sapporo: Hokkaidō chō, 1936), 5: 80, 83 (hereafter cited as SHS). For a general discussion of Hideyoshi's so-called red-seal letters (*shuinjō*), which provided the model for the black-seal letters (*kokuinjō*) of Ieyasu, see Mary Eliza-beth Berry, *Hideyoshi* (Cambridge: Council on East Asian Studies, Harvard Uni-versity, 1982), pp. 101–2.

9. Matsumae, "Fukuyama hifu," book 8, SHS, 5: 82. See the discussion of the significance of these documents in Kaiho, *Chūsei no Ezochi*, pp. 254–69, 282–300.

10. On Ainu in Tōhoku and their contacts with Hokkaido Ainu, see Namikawa Kenji, *Kinsei Nihon to hoppō shakai* (Tokyo: Sanseidō, 1992), and Namikawa Kenji, "Kinsei zenki ni okeru Matsumae, Ezochi to kita Tōhoku," *Matsumae han to Matsumae* 24 (March 1985): 1–16. On the Tsugaru domain's attitude toward the rebellious Ainu, see Kikuchi Isao, *Bakuhan taisei to Ezochi* (Tokyo: Yūzankaku, 1984), pp. 59–61. For the 1833 episode, see "Zassho" [1833/12/3], book 16, Kikuchi-ke monjo, box 31, Aomori Prefectural Library. On Matsumae efforts to restrict Ainu trade before 1672, see Kaiho, *Bakuhansei kokka to Hokkaidō*, pp. 20–24. One crude but effective technique used to keep the Ainu in the Ezochi was to threaten their lives when they tried to leave; see the discussion of Chikurage, chieftain of the Yoichi Ainu, in Emori Susumu, *Hokkaidō kinseishi no kenkyū: Bakuhan taisei to Ezochi* (Sapporo: Hokkaidō shuppan kikaku sentā, 1982), p. 176.

11. The basic sources on Shakushain's War are: "Ezo hōki" [n.d.], in *Nihon shomin seikatsu shiryō shūsei*, ed. Takakura Shin'ichirō (Tokyo: San'ichi shobō, 1969), 4: 639–50; Matsumiya Kanzan, "Ezo dan hikki" [1710], in ibid., 4: 387–400; and "Tsugaru ittōshi" [1731], book 10, in *Shinpen Aomori ken sōsho*,

ed. Shinpen Aomori ken sōsho kankōkai (Tokyo: Rekishi toshosha, 1974), 1: 263–407. See the analyses of the rebellion's significance in Kaiho, *Nihon hoppōshi no ronri*, pp. 61–98; Kaiho, *Kinsei Ezochi seiritsu shi no kenkyū*, pp. 284–318; Kikuchi, *Bakuhan taisei to Ezochi*, pp. 50–69; and Emori, *Hokkaidō kinseishi no kenkyū*, pp. 183–89. See also two separatist histories of the Ainu (written, significantly, by non-Ainu): Ōta Ryū, *Ainu kakumei ron: Yūkara sekai e no "taikyaku"* (Tokyo: Ainu moshiri jōhōbu, 1973), and Shin'ya Gyō, *Ainu minzoku teikō shi*, rev. ed. (Tokyo: San'ichi shobō, 1977).

12. Kaiho, *Bakuhansei kokka to Hokkaidō*, pp. 21–23.

13. "Ezo hōki," p. 643.

14. On Ainu troops, see ibid., p. 647; on Ainu spies in the employ of the Tsugaru domain, see Asakura Yūko, "Ezo ninshiki no keisei: Toku ni keiki to shite no jōhō o megutte," in *Kita kara no Nihonshi*, ed. Hokkaidō, Tōhoku shi kenkyūkai (Tokyo: Sanseidō, 1990), 2: 126–51; on Shōdayū (who was burned at the stake for his role in the conflict), see Matsumiya, "Ezo dan hikki," p. 398.

15. Kaiho, *Bakuhansei kokka to Hokkaidō*, pp. 21–23. For an analysis critical of Kaiho, see Ōi Haruo, "'Shakushain no ran (Kanbun 9-nen Ezo no ran)' no saikentō," *Hoppō bunka kenkyū* 21 (1992): 1–66.

16. See Kaiho, *Bakuhansei kokka to Hokkaidō*, pp. 20–24, and Emori, *Hokkaidō kinseishi no kenkyū*, pp. 186–87.

17. The use of the term "Wajinchi" here is anachronistic, as it was rarely if ever used before the nineteenth century. Emori, *Hokkaidō kinseishi no kenkyū*, pp. 75–81, notes that domain documents usually refer to the area simply as the *zaigō*, a generic term for domain territories outside a castle town. Visitors used terms like "Shamochi" (*shamo* is a Japanese corruption of the Ainu term for Wajin), "Nipponchi," or simply "Matsumaechi" or "Matsumaeryō." My use of "Wajinchi" follows contemporary scholarly practice.

18. Kaiho, *Kinsei no Hokkaidō*, pp. 72–73, 75; Suzue Eiichi, *Hokkaidō chōson seidoshi no kenkyū* (Sapporo: Hokkaidō daigaku tosho kankōkai, 1985), pp. 76–77. On the Ainu in the Wajinchi, see Emori, *Hokkaidō kinseishi no kenkyū*, pp. 74–139. See also Edmonds, *Northern Frontiers of Qing China and Tokugawa Japan*, pp. 85–112, 122–33.

19. Emori Susumu, *Shinpen monogatari hanshi: Matsumae*, as cited by Suzue, *Hokkaidō chōson seidoshi no kenkyū*, p. 13. Kamiya, "Nihon kinsei no tōitsu to Dattan," p. 170, takes a view similar to Emori's.

20. See Emori Susumu, *Ainu no rekishi* (Tokyo: Sanseidō, 1987), pp. 66–105, and Howell, "Ainu Ethnicity and the Boundaries of the Early Modern Japanese State." For a similar instance of outside manufactures taking on an increasingly important cultural role, see Richard White, *The Roots of Dependency: Subsistence, Environment, and Social Change among the Choctaws, Pawnees, and Navajos* (Lincoln: University of Nebraska Press, 1983).

21. A list of posts and the retainers who held them as of the late eighteenth century can be found in Shirayama Tomomasa, *Matsumae Ezochi basho ukeoi seido no kenkyū*, rev. ed. (Tokyo: Gannandō shoten, 1971), pp. 35–40.

22. Kaiho, *Rettō hoppōshi kenkyū nōto*, p. 82.

23. See Kaiho, *Chūsei no Ezochi*, chaps. 3 and 4, for a discussion of medieval Tōhoku society.

24. Kanno Watarō, *Ōmi shōnin no kenkyū* (Tokyo: Yūhikaku, 1941), chap. 8.

25. Western studies have tended to focus on large *tozama* domains, which enjoyed an unusual degree of political and economic autonomy. For instance, Albert Craig, *Chōshū in the Meiji Restoration* (Cambridge: Harvard University Press, 1961), writes of domain "nationalism" in Chōshū, and Luke S. Roberts, "The Merchant Origins of National Prosperity Thought in Eighteenth Century Tosa" (Ph.D. diss., Princeton University, 1991), very deliberately refers to "national" prosperity thought and "international" (i.e., interdomainal) trade in Tosa. The cumulative effect of such studies has been to make large, unitary domains seem more typical than they really were. For a case study that focuses on an area outside of a major domain, see Wigen, *The Making of a Japanese Periphery*. On the relationship between the bakufu and domains in general, see Conrad Totman, *Politics in the Tokugawa Bakufu* (Cambridge: Harvard University Press, 1967), which emphasizes the power of the bakufu, and Harold Bolitho, *Treasures among Men* (New Haven, Conn.: Yale University Press, 1974), which stresses the daimyo's loyalty to their own domains.

26. Asao Naohiro, *Sakoku* (*Nihon no rekishi*, vol. 17) (Tokyo: Shōgakukan, 1975).

27. Kaiho, *Bakuhansei kokka to Hokkaidō*, pp. 14–16.

28. Toby, *State and Diplomacy in Early Modern Japan*; Arano, *Kinsei Nihon to higashi Ajia*.

29. Arano, *Kinsei Nihon to higashi Ajia*, pp. i–xvi, 3–28. For a discussion of the concepts of the "civilized" and the "barbarian" as they relate to Tokugawa Japan, see Wakabayashi, *Anti-foreignism and Western Learning in Early-Modern Japan*, pp. 17–57.

30. Arano, *Kinsei Nihon to higashi Ajia*, pp. 43–44. See also the discussion in Kamiya, "Nihon kinsei no tōitsu to Dattan," pp. 166–71.

31. See Wakita Osamu, "The *Kokudaka* System: A Device for Unification," *Journal of Japanese Studies* 1:2 (Summer 1975): 297–320, for an overview of the origins of the *kokudaka* system.

32. Kaiho, *Bakuhansei kokka to Hokkaidō*, pp. 14, 151–80, discusses Matsumae's *kokudaka*. During the seventeenth century Matsumae was treated inconsistently: at Edo castle the daimyo was at times relegated to sit with bannermen (*hatamoto*) with 7,000-koku fiefs, while at the same time the domain's military obligations were equivalent to those of a 45,000-koku domain. In 1716 its status was finally set as equivalent to 10,000 koku.

33. Kitajima Masamoto, "Kan'ei-ki no rekishiteki ichi," in *Bakuhansei kokka seiritsu katei no kenkyū*, ed. Kitajima Masamoto (Tokyo: Yoshikawa kōbunkan, 1978), pp. 3–9.

34. Kaiho, *Bakuhansei kokka to Hokkaidō*, p. 14.

35. Matsumae, "Fukuyama hifu," book 24, SHS, 5: 202–3.

36. See the sample contracts in Shirayama, *Matsumae Ezochi basho ukeoi seido no kenkyū*, pp. 87–96.

37. The Ishikari fishery in the west was actually a conglomerate of thirteen small parcels on the Ishikari River, but it is counted as one fishery here because the entire group usually went to one contractor. It produced salmon, not herring, almost exclusively.

38. Shirayama, *Matsumae Ezochi basho ukeoi seido no kenkyū*, fig. 3, following p. 264, and pp. 98–109.

39. See Hauser, *Economic Institutional Change in Tokugawa Japan*, pp. 126–32, and Walthall, *Social Protest and Popular Culture in Eighteenth-Century Japan*, pp. 88–89, 93, for accounts of the impact of rising fertilizer prices on cotton cultivation in the Kinai region.

40. Arai, *Kinsei no gyoson*, pp. 495–501; Arai Eiji, *Kinsei Nihon gyosonshi no kenkyū* (Tokyo: Shinseisha, 1965), pp. 539–59; "Ōsaka koemonoshō kumiai enkakushi" [1901], in *Ōsaka keizai shiryō shūsei*, ed. Ōsaka keizai shiryō shūsei kankō iinkai (Osaka: Ōsaka shōkō kaigisho, 1974), 5: 115, 163. The word for dried sardines (*hoshika*) was also used as a generic term for any commercial fertilizer made from processed fish or fish by-products. Thus references to dried sardines in discussions of fertilizer use, such as Smethurst, *Agricultural Development and Tenancy Disputes in Japan*, p. 199, or Smith, *Native Sources of Japanese Industrialization*, p. 177, should probably be interpreted to include herring meal.

41. Arai, *Kinsei Nihon gyosonshi no kenkyū*, p. 543; Hasegawa Shinzō, "Kinsei kōki ni okeru Ezochi-san gyohi no Kantō nōson e no dōnyū," *Matsumae han to Matsumae* 12 (July 1978): 14–26. For data on specific ports, see Kaitakushi, ed., "Tōhoku shokō hōkokusho" [1880], in *Meiji zenki sangyō hattatsu shi shiryō*, ed. Meiji bunken shiryō kankōkai (Tokyo: Meiji bunken shiryō kankōkai, 1959), vol. 2. In 1888 distribution patterns resembled those described here for the late Tokugawa period. See Hokusui kyōkai, ed., *Hokkaidō gyogyō shikō*, 1890, reprint of 1935 ed. (Tokyo: Kokusho kankōkai, 1977), pp. 73–74. See also Katada Seishi, *Hokkaidō naikoku bōeki shi no kenkyū* (*Hokkaidō chihōshi kenkyū* special supplement 11) (Sapporo: Hokkaidō chihōshi kenkyūkai, 1965); Takase Tamotsu, "Kaga han ni okeru gyohi no fukyū," *Nihon rekishi* 354 (November 1977): 58–79.

42. Arai, *Kinsei Nihon gyosonshi no kenkyū*, pp. 540–41. See also Maeno Ryūshin, *Kitamaebune no jidai: Kinsei igo no Nihonkai kaiunshi* (Tokyo: Kyōikusha, 1979); Miyamoto Matao and Uemura Masahiro, "Tokugawa keizai no junkan kōzō," in *Keizai shakai no seiritsu* (*Nihon keizai shi*, vol. 1), ed. Hayami Akira and Miyamoto Matao (Tokyo: Iwanami shoten, 1988), pp. 271–324; Robert G. Flershem, "Some Aspects of Japan Sea Trade in the Tokugawa Period," *Journal of Asian Studies* 23:3 (May 1964): 405–16.

43. Shirayama, *Matsumae Ezochi basho ukeoi seido no kenkyū*, pp. 133–47. For an account of a visit to his fishery in 1859 by Hayashi Chōzaemon, see Yoichi chō shi hensanshitsu, ed., *Yoichi onbasho mimawari nikki* [1859] (*Yoichi chō shi shiryō sōsho*, vol. 3) (Yoichi: Yoichi chō shi hensanshitsu, 1973).

44. Hokkaidō chō, ed. *Hokkaidō shi* (Sapporo: Hokkaidō chō, 1918), app. 3 (statistics), pp. 43–44; see also E. A. Hammel, "A Glimpse into the Demography of the Ainu," *American Anthropologist* 90:1 (March 1988): 25–41. On the effects of smallpox on the Ainu, see, for example, two descriptions of late-eighteenth-century epidemics: Matsuda Denjūrō, "Hokuidan" [n.d.], and Kushihara Shōhō, "Igen zokuwa" [1793], in *Nihon shomin seikatsu shiryō shūsei*, ed. Takakura Shin'ichirō (Tokyo: San'ichi shobō, 1969), 4: 98–99 and 4: 490–91, respectively. The bakufu sent doctors to the Ezochi to inoculate some 6,400 Ainu against the disease in 1858; see the account by one of them, Kuwata Ryūsai, "Ezo no kyōkai" [1859], Resource Collection for Northern Studies, Hokkaidō University Library (hereafter RCNS). Smallpox also figures in the traditional Ainu oral liter-

ature, the *yukar*; see, for example, "Lullaby," in Donald L. Philippi, trans. and ed., *Songs of Gods, Songs of Humans: The Epic Tradition of the Ainu* (Princeton: Princeton University Press; Tokyo: University of Tokyo Press, 1979), pp. 240–42.

45. For an early example of "lending" Ainu workers, see docs. I-2-3 [1814/12], I-2-4 [1815/1], I-2-6 [1815/12], Hayashi-ke monjo, YCS, 1: 20–23.

46. This discussion of Ainu labor is based largely on Takakura Shin'ichirō, *Ainu seisakushi*, rev. ed. (Tokyo: San'ichi shobō, 1972), pp. 287–314. See also Emori, *Ainu no rekishi*.

47. "Ezochi kinban kokoroekata" [1832], Okudaira-ke monjo, cited in Takakura, *Ainu seisakushi*, p. 292.

48. See, for example, the case of the Sakhalin Ainu Tokonbe, described by Kikuchi Isao, *Hoppōshi no naka no kinsei Nihon* (Tokyo: Azekura shobō, 1991), pp. 279–301.

49. The following description of the Kunashiri-Menashi rebellion is based on ibid., pp. 302–37; Takakura, *Ainu seisakushi*, pp. 102–9; and Narumi Kentarō, "Ezochi, Hokkaidō to Shimokita hantō no kōryūshi kō," in *Ezochi, Hokkaidō: Rekishi to seikatsu*, ed. Chihōshi kenkyū kyōgikai (Tokyo: Yūzankaku, 1981), pp. 146–64.

50. John J. Stephan, "Ezo under the Tokugawa *Bakufu*, 1799–1821: An Aspect of Japan's Frontier History" (Ph.D. diss., University of London, 1969), is the most complete account of the first bakufu takeover of Hokkaido.

51. Satō Yūshō, "Shimokita nōgyomin no Ezochi dekasegi ni tsuite," in *Hokkaidō no kenkyū*, ed. Kaiho Mineo (Osaka: Seibundō, 1982), 3: 260–64. On Ainu assimilation, see John J. Stephan, *The Kuril Islands* (Oxford: Clarendon Press, 1974), pp. 104–10, and Kikuchi Isao, "Gaiatsu to dōkashugi," in *Hokkaidō no kenkyū*, ed. Kaiho Mineo (Osaka: Seibundō, 1983), 4: 1–30. For a survey of Russo-Japanese relations in this period, see George Alexander Lensen, *The Russian Push toward Japan* (Princeton: Princeton University Press, 1959); Harrison, *Japan's Northern Frontier*; and Keene, *The Japanese Discovery of Europe*, chaps. 3 and 6.

52. Stephan, "Ezo under the Tokugawa *Bakufu*," pp. 70–72; Satō Yūshō, "Ezochi bakuryōka seisaku no igi," in *Hokkaidō no kenkyū*, ed. Kaiho Mineo (Osaka: Seibundō, 1983), 4: 31–54.

53. Stephan, "Ezo under the Tokugawa *Bakufu*," pp. 101–4.

54. For the Golovnin Incident, see Vasalii Golovnin, *Memoirs of a Captivity in Japan during the Years 1811, 1812, and 1813; with Observations on the Country and the People*, 2d ed., 3 vols. (London: Henry Colburn & Co., 1824). On the profitability of direct administration, see Stephan, "Ezo under the Tokugawa *Bakufu*," p. 238. For Matsumae's samurai outplacement policy, see Kikuchi Isao, "Bakuhanseika Hokkaidō dekasegi, ijū no tenkai shojōken to dōtai," in *Bakuhansei kara kindai e*, ed. Hayashi Hideo and Yamada Shōji (Tokyo: Kashiwa shobō, 1979), pp. 125–29.

55. Tabata Hiroshi, "Bakufu chokkatsu jidai," in *Hokkaidō daihyakka jiten*, ed. Hokkaidō shinbunsha (Sapporo: Hokkaidō shinbunsha, 1981), 2: 372, and Kaiho Mineo, "Hakodate bugyō," in *Hokkaidō daihyakka jiten*, ed. Hokkaidō shinbunsha (Sapporo: Hokkaidō shinbunsha, 1981), 2: 391–92. On the prostitutes, see "Hakodate omote inbaijo no ken" [1856/5/3], in *Dai-Nippon komonjo: Bakumatsu gaikoku kankei monjo*, ed. Tōkyō teikoku daigaku bun-

gakubu shiryō hensan gakari (Tokyo: Tōkyō teikoku daigaku, 1922), 14: 99–101. On bakufu attempts to force the assimilation of the Ainu, see Kikuchi, *Bakuhansei kokka to Ezochi*, pp. 153–76; Kikuchi, *Hoppōshi no naka no kinsei Nihon*, pp. 252–78; and Howell, "Ainu Ethnicity and the Boundaries of the Early Modern Japanese State," pp. 89–91.

56. Suzuki Takahiro, "Bunkatsu shihaika no nishi Ezochi," in *Hokkaidō no kenkyū*, ed. Kaiho Mineo (Osaka: Seibundō, 1983), 4: 201–35.

57. Ibid., p. 204.

58. Moriya Yoshimi, "Bakufu no Ezochi seisaku to zaichi no dōkō," *Tōhoku gakuin daigaku Tōhoku bunka kenkyūjo kiyō* 16 (November 1984): 131–58; Moriya Yoshimi, "Hakodate sanbutsu kaisho to 'moto shiire shihō,'" in *Hokkaidō no kenkyū*, ed. Kaiho Mineo (Osaka: Seibundō, 1983), 4: 161–200.

59. Tajima Yoshiya, "Bakumatsuki 'basho' ukeoiseika ni okeru gyomin no sonzai keitai: Nishi Ezochi Utasutsu Isoya ryōbasho no baai." *Shakai keizai shigaku* 46:3 (1980): 69.

60. Seki Hideshi, "Bakumatsu ni okeru Shōnai han no Rumoi chihō keiei o meguru shomondai (1)," *Hokkaidō chihōshi kenkyū* 90 (February 1973): 94–99.

61. "Hamamashike yōyōgaki tojikomi" [1865], Satō-ke monjo B10, RCNS.

62. Tabata Hiroshi, "Meiji shoki no gyogyō seido ni tsuite: Gyobamochi seido no kōsatsu," *Atarashii dōshi* 41 (25 August 1970): 1–15.

63. Uemura Hideaki, *Kita no umi no kōekishatachi: Ainu minzoku no shakai keizaishi* (Tokyo: Dōbunkan, 1990), pp. 117–204.

64. See the discussion of treasures and indemnities in Kikuchi, *Hoppōshi no naka no kinsei Nihon*, pp. 122–48.

65. Doc. I-14-12 [1833/10], Hayashi-ke monjo, YCS, 1: 337–39.

66. Blakiston, *Japan in Yezo*, pp. 29–30.

67. Hayami Uichirō, "Kita Ezochi yō oboegaki" [1863], and Yoshida Setsuzō, "Hokuchi kaitaku shimatsu tairyaku" [c. 1881], RCNS.

68. Tabata Hiroshi, "Basho ukeoi seido hōkaiki ni okeru ukeoinin shihon no katsudō: Nishikawa-ke monjo no bunseki," in *Hokkaidō no kenkyū*, ed. Kaiho Mineo (Osaka: Seibundō, 1982), 3: 287–325.

69. "Hamamashike yōyōgaki tojikomi" [1865], Satō-ke monjo.

70. See, for example, Seki Hideshi, "Imin to chiiki shakai no seiritsu: Tomamae chihō ni okeru gyogyō imin, dekasegi no dōkō to gyoson no seiritsu katei," in *Hokkaidō no kenkyū*, ed. Seki Hideshi (Osaka: Seibundō, 1983), 5: 225–78; Seki Hideshi, "Ritō shakai no keisei katei ni tsuite (1): Bunka nenkan–Meiji shoki ni okeru Rishiri-tō no gyogyō to gyomin no dōkō," *Hokkaidō kaitaku kinenkan chōsa hōkoku* 23 (1984): 7–16; Emori Susumu, "Meiji kaitakuki Nemuro chihō gyogyō kōzō no shiteki tenkai," *Hokkaidō keizai shi kenkyū* 19 (1965): 23–47.

71. By the 1880s agents were appearing in remote Ainu villages in eastern Hokkaido to recruit fishery workers in the same way they hired workers in Tōhoku villages. See Watanabe Hitoshi, *The Ainu Ecosystem: Environment and Group Structure* (Tokyo: University of Tokyo Press, 1972), p. 88.

72. As Elizabeth Fox-Genovese and Eugene D. Genovese, *Fruits of Merchant Capital: Slavery and Bourgeois Property in the Rise and Expansion of Capitalism* (New York: Oxford University Press, 1983), pp. 6–7, put it: "Although [merchant capital] provided a powerful solvent to feudal and seigneurial relations and

contributed mightily to the emergence of a world market, it could not create capitalist social relations or a new system of production. To the extent that it remained commercial and money-dealing capital—to the extent that it escaped becoming an agent of industrial capital—it eventually became an impediment to the emergence of the capitalist mode of production. This paradox had in fact appeared as early as antiquity and had marked every age of European, as well as non-European, history." As Fox-Genovese and Genovese note, however, this is a point of long-standing contention among scholars.

73. Leupp, " 'One Drink from a Gourd,' " pp. 500–508.

74. It is worthwhile to note, however, that the merchant overseeing a putting-out operation was just as interested as the proto-factory operator in getting the surplus value of peasant labor—rather than the use value of the commodities being produced—and thus equally fulfilled a key criterion of capitalist production. In other words, Leupp's distinction between putting-out and manufactures is more valuable when looking at labor than when considering the purposes of production. See the discussion of the so-called manufactures debate among pre-World War II Japanese Marxist historians and particularly the analysis of the work of Hattori Shisō, in Germaine A. Hoston, *Marxism and the Crisis of Development in Prewar Japan* (Princeton: Princeton University Press, 1986), pp. 95–126.

3. The Capitalist Transformation

1. "Ezokoku shiki" [c. 1780–1800], cited in Hokkaidō suisanbu gyogyō chōseika and Hokkaidō gyogyō seido kaikaku kinen jigyō kyōkai, eds., *Hokkaidō gyogyō shi* (Nagano: Hokkaidō suisanbu gyogyō chōseika and Hokkaidō gyogyō seido kaikaku kinen jigyō kyōkai, 1957), p. 103 (hereafter cited as *Hokkaidō gyogyō shi*).

2. The huts, called *hamagoya*, survived as late as 1882. Hashimoto Takanao, "Esashi hamagoya no mukashi banashi," *Ezo ōrai* 4 (August 1931): 124–25.

3. Mutō Kanzō, "Ezo nikki" [1798], in *Nihon shomin seikatsu shiryō shūsei*, ed. Takakura Shin'ichirō (Tokyo: San'ichi shobō, 1969), 4: 15.

4. Hanley and Yamamura, *Economic and Demographic Change in Preindustrial Japan*, p. 12.

5. See E. Sydney Crawcour, "Economic Change in the Nineteenth Century," in *The Cambridge History of Japan*, ed. Marius B. Jansen (Cambridge: Cambridge University Press, 1989), 5: 612–14.

6. Sakakura Genjirō, "Hokkai zuihitsu" [1739], in *Hokumon sōsho*, ed. Ōtomo Kisaku (Tokyo: Hokkō shobō, 1943–44), 2: 43.

7. "Ezo Matsumae kikigaki (Tsugaru kenbunki tsuki)" [1758], RCNS, leaf 43.

8. Hezutsu Tōsaku, "Tōyūki" [1784], in *Hokumon sōsho*, ed. Ōtomo Kisaku (Tokyo: Hokkō shobō, 1943–44), 2: 325.

9. Ibid., p. 325.

10. Furukawa Koshōken, "Tōyū zakki" [1789], in *Kinsei shakai keizai sōsho*, ed. Honjō Eijirō (Tokyo: Kaizōsha, 1927), 12: 108, 113. For an account of Furukawa's tour of Tōhoku and Hokkaido, see Harold Bolitho, "Travelers' Tales: Three Eighteenth-Century Travel Journals," *Harvard Journal of Asiatic Studies* 50 (1990): 485–504.

11. Furukawa, "Tōyū zakki," p. 129.

12. Mino Norio, "Nishin gyogyō to shinrin hakai: Furubira chō ni okeru rei," *Hokkaidō kaitaku kinenkan chōsa hōkoku* 26 (1987): 9–12.

13. "Mashike unjōya mondōgaki" [1865/8], "Hamamashike yōyōgaki tojikomi," Satō-ke monjo.

14. Mogami Tokunai, "Ezokoku fūzoku ninjō no sata" [1791], in *Nihon shomin seikatsu shiryō shūsei*, ed. Takakura Shin'ichirō (Tokyo: San'ichi Shobō, 1969), 4: 447; Yajima Satoshi, "Kinsei kōki Matsumaechi ni okeru nenjū gyōji shūzoku," in *Hokkaidō no kenkyū*, ed. Kaiho Mineo (Osaka: Seibundō, 1982), 3: 327–64.

15. Yajima Satoshi, "Nishin gyoba no minzoku," in *Hokkaidō no kenkyū*, ed. Yajima Satoshi (Osaka: Seibundō, 1985), 7: 218–21. In the early twentieth century "nearly all local customs" of Nebuta village, near Fukuyama, were taken from Tsugaru. Oshima kyōikukai, ed., "Hakodate shichō kannai chōson shi" [c. 1918], comp. and ed. Suzue Eiichi, *Matsumae han to Matsumae* 24 (March 1985): 43. Taboos involving women were not unusual in fishing communities elsewhere in Japan. See Arne Kalland, *Shingū: A Study of a Japanese Fishing Community* (London and Malmö: Curzon Press, 1981), p. 57.

16. Suzue, *Hokkaidō chōson seidoshi no kenkyū*, p. 57.

17. Ibid., pp. 63–65.

18. Ibid., pp. 76–77.

19. Hokkaidō chō, *Hokkaidō shi*, appendix 3, p. 42.

20. The following account of the Tenpō years in Matsumae is taken from Hakodate ken, comp., "Matsumae Tenpō kyōkōroku" [1929], Hokkaidō shi hensan shiryō 415, RCNS; it is an abridged version of "Bikō chochiku ikken" [1886], which was based on interviews with elderly residents conducted by officials of Hakodate prefecture in villages under its jurisdiction. For a general description of the Tenpō period, including the famine, see Harold Bolitho, "The Tempō Crisis," in *The Cambridge History of Japan*, ed. Marius B. Jansen (Cambridge: Cambridge University Press, 1989), 5: 116–67.

21. Hirao Rosen, "Matsumae kikō" [1855], in *Hakodate shi shi: Shiryōhen*, ed. Hakodate shi (Hakodate: Hakodate shi, 1974), 1: 278–79. See Rosen's sketch of the customs office in SHS, 2: following p. 158.

22. Hirao, "Matsumae kikō," p. 279.

23. "Mashike unjōya mondōgaki" [1865/8], "Hamamashike yōyōgaki tojikomi," Satō-ke monjo.

24. "Tabibito aratamekata" [n.d.], in *Nihon zaisei keizai shiryō*, ed. Ōkurashō (Tokyo: Ōkurashō, 1925), 10: 223–24.

25. Ibid., pp. 223–24. A total of 109 new residents were naturalized in Fukuyama between 1860 and 1866. Of these, eighty (seventy-three percent) were men, and all but four came from Tōhoku, Hokuriku, or Ōmi. "Hayashi-ke monjo: Ban nikki" [1860–66], in Matsumae chō shi henshūshitsu, ed., *Matsumae chō shi* (Matsumae: Matsumae chō shi henshūshitsu, 1974–88), 2: 655–1040 (hereafter cited as MCS).

26. "Mashike unjōya mondōgaki" [1865/8], "Hamamashike yōyōgaki tojikomi," Satō-ke monjo.

27. See loose docs. 1–6, Sasanami-ke monjo, RCNS.

28. *Hokkaidō gyogyō shi*, p. 113.

29. Independent fishers appear not to have been prominent at the small con-

tract fisheries close to the Wajinchi border until the end of the Tokugawa period. See, for example, Futoro murayakuba, ed., "Futoro gun Futoro mura gaikyō" [1908], and Kudō murayakuba, ed., "Kudō gun Kudō mura enkaku" [c. 1920], RCNS.

30. Matsuura Takeshirō, *Takeshirō kaiho nikki* [1856–57], 2 vols., ed. Takakura Shin'ichirō (Sapporo: Hokkaidō shuppan kikaku sentā, 1978), 1: 388.

31. The register is reproduced in Saitō Jōsaku, *Isoya son shi* (Sapporo: Saitō Jōsaku, 1981), pp. 29–212.

32. "Mashike unjōya mondōgaki" [1865/8], "Hamamashike yōyōgaki tojikomi," Satō-ke monjo.

33. Saitō, *Isoya son shi*, pp. 213–56. The independent producers are listed in the register as "herring fishery holders" (*nishinba mochi*), which indicates they held rights to waterfront land to process their catch. In contrast to almost all the entries for independent producers, those for hired laborers (*temadori*) rarely indicate ownership of nets or boats. The remaining households in the village included five "migrant workers" (*dekasegi*), whose place in production relations is unclear, and a number of agricultural settlers.

34. See, for example, docs. I-9-29 [1829], I-11-13 [1830/8], I-11-14 [1830/8], I-14-13 [1833/10], I-26-8 [1840], Hayashi-ke monjo, YCS, 1: 155, 295–96, 296–97, 339, 648–49; Tajima, "Bakumatsuki 'basho' ukeoiseika ni okeru gyomin no sonzai keitai," pp. 65–66.

35. Tajima, "Bakumatsuki 'basho' ukeoiseika ni okeru gyomin no sonzai keitai," pp. 63–64.

36. Innkeepers performed a number of services for contractors. For example, Satō Eiemon, contractor of the Isoya and Utasutsu fisheries, relied on two innkeepers to look after his laborers wintering in the Ezochi. See "Tabibitotōri Takedatsuke" [1859–71] and "Tabibitotōri Yagi-tsuke" [1859–71], Hokkaidō shi hensan shiryō 197, 198, RCNS. These inns functioned like the urban employment agencies examined by Gary P. Leupp, *Servants, Shophands, and Laborers in the Cities of Tokugawa Japan* (Princeton: Princeton University Press, 1992), pp. 69–72.

37. "Zassho tojikomi" [1866], Nakagawaya monjo, Baba Collection, Hakodate Municipal Library; "Hamamashike yōyōgaki tojikomi" [1865–66], Satō-ke monjo.

38. An adult man needed an annual income equivalent to at least 1.8 koku of rice to support himself; this would have cost just under 3 ryō at Osaka prices at that time. Even allowing for higher commodity prices in Hokkaido fishery wages were not bad. On income needs, see Leupp, *Servants, Shophands, and Laborers in the Cities of Tokugawa Japan*, p. 104; on prices, see Miyamoto Mataji, ed., *Kinsei Ōsaka no bukka to rishi* (Osaka: Ōsaka daigaku kinsei bukka shi kenkyūkai, 1963), pp. 117, 124.

39. Tajima, "Bakumatsuki 'basho' ukeoiseika ni okeru gyomin no sonzai keitai," pp. 66–67.

40. Saitō, *Isoya son shi*, pp. 29–212.

41. Ibid., pp. 213–56.

42. "Gyoba ninbetsu narabi ni amikazu kakiage" [1868/3], in *Atsuta mura shiryō kōhon: Sasaki-ke monjo*, ed. Atsuta mura shiryōshitsu (Atsuta: Atsuta mura shiryōshitsu, 1967), pp. 24–42.

43. "Oboe" [1866/1], "Hamamashike yōyōgaki tojikomi," Satō-ke monjo.

44. "Onshakkindaka narabi ni namen kakiage" [1866/7], Nakagawaya monjo, Baba Collection, Hakodate Municipal Library.

45. "Shiokoshi mura," in *Akita ken no chimei* (*Nihon rekishi chimei taikei*, vol. 5), ed. Imamura Yoshitaka (Tokyo: Heibonsha, 1980), p. 61. The article does not draw an explicit connection between the earthquake and the prevalence of people from Shiokoshi in the fishery. An alternative explanation is that people in the Yuri district of Dewa province, which included Shiokoshi, began seeking work in the Ezochi after salt production fell in the face of imports of inexpensive salt from the Inland Sea region. Igawa Kazuyoshi, "Kinsei no seien gijutsu to engyō keiei," *Kōryū no Nihonshi*, as cited by Kikuchi, *Hoppōshi no naka no kinsei Nihon*, p. 342.

46. For a description of the depressed state of the peninsular economy, see the 1873 document cited by Sasazawa Royō, *Shimokita hantō shi*, 3rd rev. ed. (Ōhata: Shimokita kyōdokai, 1962), pp. 5–6.

47. Hasegawa Toshiyuki, "Bakuhan taiseika ni okeru Ezochi dekasegi o meguru shomondai: Shimokita hantō nōmin no dekasegi o chūshin to shite," *Usori* 15 (1978): 20–47. See also Takeuchi Toshiyoshi, *Shimokita no sonraku shakai: Sangyō kōzō to sonraku taisei* (Tokyo: Miraisha, 1968), pp. 51–80, and Narumi Kentarō, "Shimokita dekasegi shi kō," *Usori* 13 (1976): 51–59.

48. Takeuchi, *Shimokita no sonraku shakai*, p. 56.

49. Murabayashi Gensuke, "Genshi manpitsu fudo nenpyō" [1804–18], in *Michinoku sōsho*, ed. Aomori ken bunkazai hogo kyōkai, 1960 (reprint, Tokyo: Kokusho kankōkai, 1982), 6: 131–32.

50. Hasegawa, "Bakuhan taiseika ni okeru Ezochi dekasegi o meguru shomondai," pp. 26–33. When Shimokita peasants went to Hokkaido they apparently brought Ainu customs back with them. In 1809, 1810, and 1813 local officials banned the use of *attush*, an Ainu outer garment made from bark cloth, and prohibited the shaving of women's eyebrows in the Ainu manner. Murabayashi, "Genshi manpitsu fudo nenpyō," 6: 138, 150, 246, reported also that during the Tenmei period (1780–88) domain officials had forbidden the use of the Ainu language. On *attush*, see Kodama Mari, "Ainu minzoku no ifuku to fukushokuhin," in *Hokkaidō no kenkyū*, ed. Yajima Satoshi (Osaka: Seibundō, 1985), 7: 294–97. Although it is possible that these injunctions were directed in part toward residual Ainu communities in Shimokita, it is likely that Wajin fishers sought out *attush* and other Ainu garments because they were so much more practical for cold, wet weather than anything the Wajin could make for themselves. Kikuchi Isao, "Kinsei Ōu shakai no'Ezo' mondai," in *Hokkaidō no kenkyū*, ed. Kaiho Mineo (Osaka: Seibundō, 1983), 4: 91–118, and Namikawa, "Kinsei zenki ni okeru Matsumae, Ezochi to kita Tōhoku," pp. 11–15; Emori Susumu, personal communication, 1987.

51. Kakizaki Hirotsune, "Kuchigaki todome" [1837], Hakodate Municipal Library.

52. Hasegawa, "Bakuhan taiseika ni okeru Ezochi dekasegi o meguru shomondai," pp. 26–33.

53. Esashi chō shi henshūshitsu, ed., *Esashi chō shi* (Esashi: Esashi chō, 1978–81), 5: 419 (hereafter cited as ECS).

54. Nihon gakushiin, ed., *Meijizen Nihon gyogyō gijutsushi* (Tokyo: Nihon gakujutsu shinkōkai, 1959), pp. 410–13.

55. Takasaki Ryūtarō, *Kaokuzuiri Hokkai risshi hen* (Hakodate: Hokutōsha, 1897), 4: leaf 33.
56. Hokkaidō chō naimubu suisanka, ed., *Hokkaidō suisan yosatsu chōsa hōkoku* (Tokyo: Hokkaidō chō naimubu suisanka, 1892), p. 106.
57. For data on herring-meal prices, see Shinbo Hiroshi, *Kinsei no bukka to keizai hatten* (Tokyo: Tōyō keizai shinpōsha, 1978), pp. 250–51; Miyamoto, *Kinsei Ōsaka no bukka to rishi*, pp. 316–21.
58. SHS, 2: 262–63.
59. Shirayama Tomomasa, "Ezochi amikiri sōdō shimatsu: Kinsei nishin ami hattatsu shi sobyō," *Nihon rekishi* 257 (October 1969): 105.
60. For Yoichi, docs. I-23-4 [1846], I-25-6 [n.d.], Hayashi-ke monjo, YCS, 1: 554–55, 596–97; for Hamamashike, Hamamasu suisan kumiai, ed., "Gyogyō enkakushi" [1911], Hokkaidō Prefectural Library, leaf 5.
61. Shirayama, "Ezochi amikiri sōdō shimatsu," pp. 105–6. See also "Ansei nenkan zaruami sōjō tanmatsu" [n.d.], ECS, 2: 1363–80, and "Nishi Ezochi amikiri sōdō narabi ni tateami myōga no oboe" [n.d.], MCS, 2: 1055–69, upon which all secondary accounts are based.
62. SHS, 2: 600–609.
63. Hakodate magistrates to senior council, doc. 143 [1860/1/21], Tōkyō daigaku shiryō hensanjo, ed., *Dai-Nippon komonjo: Bakumatsu gaikoku kankei monjo* (Tokyo: Tōkyō daigaku shuppankai, 1969), 34: 286–88; SHS, 2: 746–48.
64. See, for example, "Tateami sōdan torikiwame hikae" [1866], Sasanami-ke monjo, ECS, 2: 1283–94.
65. Ōsaka Heizō, "Oshima no kuni Nishi gun Kumaishi mura gyogyō enkakushi" [1910], Hokkaidō Prefectural Library, pp. 6–9; for 1869 figures, "Esashi-zai hachikason nishintori ninzū hikae" [1870/1], in "Taneda-ke monjo," Hokkaidō shi hensan shiryō 200, RCNS.
66. Takahata Sen'ichi, *Otaru-kō shi* (Takikawa: Takahata Sen'ichi, 1899), p. 69.
67. "Satō-ke shōyō shorui (2)" [1868], Hokkaidō shi hensan shiryō 135–10, RCNS.
68. "Gyoba ninbetsu narabi ni amikazu kakiage," pp. 24–42.
69. For discussions of the place of moral economy in peasant-domain relations, see Irwin Scheiner, "Benevolent Lords and Honorable Peasants: Rebellion and Peasant Consciousness in Tokugawa Japan," in *Japanese Thought in the Tokugawa Period, 1600–1868*, ed. Tetsuo Najita and Irwin Scheiner (Chicago: University of Chicago Press, 1978), pp. 39–62; Stephen Vlastos, *Peasant Protests and Uprisings in Tokugawa Japan* (Berkeley: University of California Press, 1986); and Walthall, *Social Protest and Popular Culture in Eighteenth-Century Japan*.

70. *Ezochi no tateami yameba shimajū*
     tairyō wa me no mae ni, mae ni.
     Shamochi no nishin no aru yue ni
     funebune kudari wa takusan ni, okami no
     goshūnō mo tanto tanto.
     Kotoshi ya tairyō mansaku da.

"Shinban negoto monku tairyō mansaku bushi" [1862], cited in Shirayama, "Ezochi amikiri sōdō shimatsu," pp. 106–7.

71. Doc. I-33 [1843], Hayashi-ke monjo, YCS, 1: 810.

72. Kikuchi, "Gaiatsu to dōkashugi"; Kaiho, *Nihon hoppōshi no ronri*, pp. 266–68.

73. See the discussion in David L. Howell, "Hokkaidō ni okeru gyogyō gijutsu to gyoson no keisei katei: Bakumatsuki-Meiji chūki o chūshin ni," *Hokudai shigaku* 28 (1988): 30–32.

74. Docs. I-23-25 [1858/2] and I-23-25-2 [1858/2], Hayashi-ke monjo, YCS, 1: 592–93.

75. Tajima Yoshiya, "Kinsei kōki gyokaku nishin no shūka katei: Nishi Ezochi Yoichi basho o rei to shite," *Rekishi to minzoku: Kanagawa daigaku Nihon jōmin bunka kenkyūjo ronshū* 1 (1986): 167.

76. Doc. I-46-6-3 [1856], Hayashi-ke monjo, YCS, 1: 1266.

77. Takeya [Hayashi] Chōzaemon to Nabeya Kichiemon, doc. I-39-20 [1857/3/2], doc. I-23-25-3 [1858/2], Hayashi-ke monjo, YCS, 1: 593–94.

78. Satō Eiemon to Nakagawaya Yūsuke [1866/5/12], "Hamamashike yōyōgaki tojikomi," Satō-ke monjo.

79. Takahata, *Otaru-kō shi*, p. 73.

80. Two village officials from Kaminokuni, Sasanami Kyūemon and Hisasue Heizō, appear to have been among the fourteen signers of the 1858 agreement in Yoichi. See doc. I-23-25 [1858/2], Hayashi-ke monjo, YCS, 1: 592–93.

81. See "Kishida San'emon monjo: Ryōke shikomi" [1688–1911], ECS, 2: 1162–63, for two examples of destitute fishers offering the services of their sons as collateral for a debt.

82. Hezutsu, "Tōyūki," p. 326.

83. Tabata Hiroshi, "Basho ukeoi seido hōkaiki ni okeru ukeoinin shihon no katsudō," pp. 320–25.

84. See, for example, Kalland, *Shingū*, pp. 36–41, 137–40.

85. ECS, 2: 43–44.

86. William D. Wray, "Shipping: From Sail to Steam," in *Japan in Transition: From Tokugawa to Meiji*, ed. Marius B. Jansen and Gilbert Rozman (Princeton: Princeton University Press, 1986), pp. 250–54; Mori Shōgo, *Bezaisen ōkanki: Hokkaidō, Iwanai o hiraita hitobito* (Tokyo: Nihon keizai hyōronsha, 1983), p. 125.

87. "Kishida San'emon monjo: Ryōke shikomi," pp. 1070–1233.

88. On interest rates, see Ronald P. Toby, "Both a Borrower and a Lender Be: From Village Moneylender to Rural Banker in the Tempō Period," *Monumenta Nipponica* 46:4 (Winter 1991), pp. 499–503; Dan Fenno Henderson, *Village "Contracts" in Tokugawa Japan* (Seattle: University of Washington Press, 1975), pp. 106–18; John Henry Wigmore, *Law and Justice in Tokugawa Japan, Part III-A: Contract: Legal Precedents* (Tokyo: Kokusai bunka shinkōkai, 1970), pp. 256–86; and Miyamoto, *Kinsei Ōsaka no bukka to rishi*, pp. 45–49. On the price paid by Kishida for herring, see, for example, the loan taken out by one Nagakawa Riemon in 1840, "Kishida San'emon monjo: Ryōke shikomi," pp. 1198–1200; on prices charged by supply merchants, see Hokusui kyōkai, *Hokkaidō gyogyō shikō*, pp. 713–14.

89. "Kishida San'emon monjo: Ryōke shikomi," pp. 1182–83.

90. Ibid., p. 1211.

91. See the petition of 1854/8 presented to the domain by a group of west-coast contractors, SHS, 2: 608.

92. See the series of documents in "Shoyō tojikomi" [1861], Date-ke monjo, MCS, 3: 832–39, and the discussion in Moriya, "Bakufu no Ezochi seisaku to zaichi no dōkō," pp. 153–56.

93. Moriya, "Bakufu no Ezochi seisaku to zaichi no dōkō," p. 156.

94. "Otasshigaki no utsushi" [1865/12], "Hamamashike yōyōgaki to-jikomi," Satō-ke monjo; "Zassho tojikomi" [1866], Nakagawaya monjo.

95. Satō Eiemon to Fukuyama town elders [1866/3/29]; Satō Eiemon to Nakagawaya Yūsuke [1866/2/3]; Satō Eiemon to Ike Yūsuke (a Shōnai official) [1866/2/3], "Hamamashike yōyōgaki tojikomi," Satō-ke monjo.

96. Nakagawaya Yūsuke to Hamamashike intendant [1866/1]; Nakaga-waya Yūsuke to Satō Eiemon [1866/2/29], "Hamamashike yōyōgaki tojikomi," Satō-ke monjo. See also the documents relating to this matter in "Zassho toji-komi" [1866, 1867], Nakagawaya monjo.

97. Moriya, "Bakufu no Ezochi seisaku to zaichi no dōkō," pp. 131–48.

98. Kudō Mutsuo, "Tsugaru Fukaura-kō to bakumatsu ni okeru kaisen no nyūshin jōkyō," *Kaijishi kenkyū* 28 (April 1977): 26–42. See also Takase, "Kaga han ni okeru gyohi no fukyū."

99. See the account of the incident involving Shōnai in Kelly, *Deference and Defiance in Nineteenth-Century Japan*, pp. 66–104.

100. Matsuzaki Iwaho, *Kaminokuni son shi* (Kaminokuni: Kaminokuni murayakuba, 1956), pp. 100–121; MCS, vol. 1, part 2, pp. 1160–83.

101. Suzuki Takahiro, "Matsumae ryōmin no fukuryō undō," *Matsumae han to Matsumae* 7 (March 1975): 15–34.

102. Ibid., p. 32.

103. Moriya, "Bakufu no Ezochi seisaku to zaichi no dōkō," pp. 148–50.

104. Ibid., pp. 148–50; Suzuki, "Matsumae ryōmin no fukuryō undō," pp. 24–30.

105. Toby, "Both a Borrower and a Lender Be."

106. See the discussion of the centrality of interpretations of the Meiji Restoration in modern Japanese historiography in Hoston, *Marxism and the Crisis of Development in Prewar Japan*. For a reflection of this scholarship in English, see E. H. Norman, *Origins of the Modern Japanese State: Selected Writings of E. H. Norman*, ed. John W. Dower (New York: Pantheon, 1975).

107. Pratt, "Village Elites in Tokugawa Japan," and Roberts, "The Mer-chant Origins of National Prosperity Thought in Eighteenth Century Tosa."

108. Pratt, "Village Elites in Tokugawa Japan," pp. 7–8.

109. Roberts, "The Merchant Origins of National Prosperity Thought in Eighteenth Century Tosa," pp. 209–24.

110. Kalland, *Shingū*; Arne Kalland, "A Credit Institution in Tokugawa Japan: The Ura-tamegin Fund of Chikuzen Province," in *Europe Interprets Japan*, ed. Gordon Daniels (Tenterden, Kent, England: Paul Norbury Publica-tions, 1984), pp. 3–12.

111. Although he eschews terms like *feudalism* and *capitalism*, Jones, *Growth Recurring*, structures his argument around this point.

112. Kriedte, Medick, and Schlumbohm, *Industrialization before Industrialization*, p. 10.

113. See ibid., pp. 9–10, and Eley, "The Social History of Industrialization," pp. 523–26, on the differences among the authors' conceptions of proto-industrialization. Franklin Mendels subtitled the article in which he coined the term *proto-industrialization* "the first phase of the industrialization process," which certainly suggests a teleology.

4. The Institutions of a Capitalist Fishery

1. For a partisan account of the Ofuyu Incident, with extensive reprints of contemporary newspaper coverage, see Ishibashi Gen, *Hamamasu son shi* (Hamamasu: Hamamasu mura, 1980), pp. 503–7, 1187–1227; see also Koshizaki Sōichi, "Ofuyu jiken ni tsuite," *Hokkaidō chihōshi kenkyū* 79 (November 1970): 6–11.

2. Ishibashi, *Hamamasu son shi*, pp. 501–3; Rumoi chō, ed., *Rumoi chō shi* (Rumoi: Rumoi chō, 1945), pp. 138–39.

3. On border disputes between Matsumae villages, see Suzue, *Hokkaidō chōson seidoshi no kenkyū*, pp. 77, 100; on conflict between contract fisheries, see Kaiho, *Kinsei Ezochi seiritsu shi no kenkyū*, pp. 319–56; on fishing rights outside of Hokkaido, see Ninohei Tokuo, *Gyogyō kōzō no shiteki tenkai* (Tokyo: Ochanomizu shobō, 1962), chap. 1; Arne Kalland, "Sea Tenure in Tokugawa Japan: The Case of the Fukuoka Domain," in *Maritime Institutions in the Western Pacific* (*Senri Ethnological Studies*, vol. 17), ed. Kenneth Ruddle and Tomoya Akimichi (Osaka: National Museum of Ethnology, 1984).

4. The fishery accounted for about seventy-five percent of the gross product of Hokkaido in 1881 and over forty percent in 1897. It was superseded by agriculture as the largest industry in 1900 and by manufacturing as the second largest in 1907. In 1891, about forty-one percent (by value) of all manufactured marine products in Japan originated in Hokkaido; herring, the most important catch in the country, accounted for 68.4 percent of the Hokkaido harvest. *Hokkaidō gyogyō shi*, pp. 225–27, 234. On development policies in general, see Takakura Shin'ichirō, *Hokkaidō takushoku shi* (Sapporo: Hakuba shoin, 1947).

5. Blakiston, *Japan in Yezo*, p. 60.

6. Nakai Akira, "Hokkaidō ni okeru gyogyō seido no hensen: Kindaiteki gyogyōken no seiritsu to tenkai," *Atarashii dōshi* 3:1 (January 1965): 4; Tabata Hiroshi, " 'Fukuyama, Esashi sōdō' no kenkyū," in *Hokkaidō no kenkyū*, ed. Seki Hideshi (Osaka: Seibundō, 1983), 5: 143–223.

7. I examine these issues in detail in Howell, "Ainu Ethnicity and the Boundaries of the Early Modern Japanese State." For a discussion of the late Tokugawa precedent for the Meiji state's policy of Ainu assimilation, see Kikuchi, *Bakuhan taisei to Ezochi*, pp. 153–76, and Kikuchi, *Hoppōshi no naka no kinsei Nihon*, pp. 34–54. On specific Meiji policies toward the Ainu, see Kaiho Yōko, *Kindai hoppōshi: Ainu minzoku to josei to* (Tokyo: San'ichi shobō, 1992), part 1. On policy toward the Ainu in general, see Takakura, *Ainu seisakushi*, and Emori, *Ainu no rekishi*.

8. Discrimination has forced many people of Ainu ancestry to hide their roots, though some have recently started to "come out." See, for example, the case of a seventy-five-year-old half-Ainu who revealed her background to her family after fifty years of secrecy: "Ainu minzoku to san'insen (1)," *Hokkaidō shinbun*, 18 June 1992.

9. Of course, Wajin continued to prey upon the Ainu even after the Meiji Restoration. See the complaints of a local official concerning Wajin con artists who cheated Ainu in isolated communities out of land and money, forcing them to seek labor in the fishery: "Bunai Kamikawa, Akan, Ashoro sangun kakuson ni atsukaisho setchi no gi jōshin" [26 January 1885] (request from Kushiro district secretary Miyamoto Chimaki to Nemuro prefecture), in "Nemuro ken kyūdojin" [1882–86], RCNS.

10. Watanabe, *The Ainu Ecosystem*; Uemura, *Kita no umi no kōekishatachi*.

11. On Ainu dissatisfaction with their position in the fishery, see Yamada Shin'ichi, "Iboshi Hokuto den e no kokoromi," paper presented at the Erumu Shidankai, Sapporo, 1992; on self- or communally employed Ainu kelp fishers, see the report dated 13 October 1884 by Officer Ensai Katsuzō to Yabe Kyōhei, chief of the Akkeshi police department, in "Nemuro ken kyūdojin."

12. Nakai, "Hokkaidō ni okeru gyogyō seido no hensen," pp. 1–6.

13. The Ezochi-Wajinchi distinction was lost after Hokkaidō ("Northern Sea Circuit") became the official name of the island in the eighth month of 1869.

14. Ōkurashō, ed., *Kaitakushi jigyō hōkoku furoku: Furei ruiju* (Tokyo: Ōkurashō, 1875), 1: 841.

15. *Hokkaidō gyogyō shi*, pp. 349–51.

16. Tabata, "Meiji shoki no gyogyō seido ni tsuite," is the most detailed account of the dismantling of the contract-fishery system.

17. Ibid., pp. 3–5; *Hokkaidō gyogyō shi*, pp. 351–53.

18. Imada Mitsuo, *Nishin bunka shi: Maboroshi no nishin kamuicheppu* (Sapporo: Kyōdō bunkasha, 1987), p. 256.

19. Nakai, "Hokkaidō ni okeru gyogyō seido no hensen," pp. 3–4. On the application of the land-tax reform elsewhere in Japan, see Kozo Yamamura, "The Meiji Land Tax Reform and Its Effects," in *Japan in Transition: From Tokugawa to Meiji*, ed. Marius B. Jansen and Gilbert Rozman (Princeton: Princeton University Press, 1986), pp. 382–99.

20. Suzue Eiichi, "Kaisan kanba chiso sōtei kankei monjo: Kaidai," MCS, 4: 1–19.

21. The diversity of local treatments of fishing rights does, however, make it difficult to generalize about the impact of this and other Meiji policy shifts. For example, Hōri Miyashizu, *Zushū Uchiura gyomin shiryō no kenkyū: Meiji shonen ni okeru "kyūhei torinaoshi" undō to sono rekishiteki igi* (Tokyo: Rinjinsha, 1966), has documented the variation in customary fishing rights in a homogeneous group of six villages on a small bay in western Izu.

22. Nakai, "Hokkaidō ni okeru gyogyō seido no hensen," p. 3.

23. Ibid., pp. 4–5.

24. Ishibashi, *Hamamasu son shi*, pp. 709–10.

25. On the Meiji fishery law, see Ninohei Tokuo, *Meiji gyogyō kaitaku shi* (Tokyo: Heibonsha, 1981), chap. 4.

26. Nakai, "Hokkaidō ni okeru gyogyō seido no hensen," pp. 5–6. For de-

tailed analyses of transfers of fishing rights in two districts, see Yamada Takeshi, "Rishiri-tō ni okeru nishin teichi gyogyōken no sonzai keitai: 'Menkyo gyogyō genbo' no naiyō to kōsatsu," *Hokkaidō kaitaku kinenkan chōsa hōkoku* 24 (1985): 39–88, and Yamada Takeshi, "Furubira chihō ni okeru nishin teichi gyogyōken no hensen (1): 'Menkyo gyogyō genbo' no naiyō to kōsatsu," *Hokkaidō kaitaku kinenkan chōsa hōkoku* 26 (1987): 27–36.

27. Only a reference to the survey ("Dekasegi no mono namen sono hoka haishaku kasho kensūgaki") in a letter to a Shōnai official survives. Nakagawaya Yūsuke to Hamamashike intendant [1865/10/26], "Hamamashike yōyōgaki tojikomi," Satō-ke monjo.

28. Suzue, *Hokkaidō chōson seidoshi no kenkyū*, pp. 103–18. The oldest extant reference to a transfer of waterfront land dates to 1688, just as the herring fishery was assuming commercial importance. For the transfer document, see "Kishida San'emon monjo: Ryōke shikomi," pp. 1070–71.

29. "Kaminokuni mura nayaba aratame" [1747] and "Hama kenchiwari chō" [1748], both in ECS, 2: 1275–79, 1257–74. See the discussion in Suzue, *Hokkaidō chōson seidoshi no kenkyū*, pp. 103–6, 109–17.

30. Suzue, *Hokkaidō chōson seidoshi no kenkyū*, pp. 115–21.

31. Ishikawa Hiroshi, "Wajinchi (Matsumaechi) ni okeru 'basho' to gyogyōken: Esashi chō shozai shiryō o chūshin to shite," *Atarashii dōshi* 44–45 (15 March–31 March 1971): 1–12, 1–8. Although Ishikawa does not cite it, his work is obviously indebted to Habara Yūkichi, *Nihon gyogyō keizai shi*, 4 vols. (Tokyo: Iwanami shoten, 1952–55).

32. *Hokkaidō gyogyō shi*, p. 38.

33. Doc. 4 [4 January 1877], "Chiso sōtei kankei shorui," MCS, 4: 132.

34. Doc. 73 [1876], "Chiso sōtei kisoku todome," MCS, 4: 86.

35. Ibid., pp. 86–87.

36. Docs. 4 [4 January 1877] and 5 [4 January 1877], "Chiso sōtei kankei shorui," MCS, 4: 132–35.

37. Doc. 73 [1876], "Chiso sōtei kisoku todome," MCS, 4: 86.

38. Figures for Eramachi were calculated from data in docs. 3 and 3-1 [1879], "Kaisan kanba chikenjō uketorishō tojikomi," MCS, 4: 589–99; those for Kumausu were calculated from data in "Kumausu mura kaisan kanba chiken daichō" [1883], Hokkaidō shi hensan shiryō 9, RCNS. Standard landholdings are cited in *Hokkaidō gyogyō shi*, pp. 255–56.

39. In 1886 only thirty-nine pound traps were in use in the district of Matsumae, as compared with 26,984 sets of gill nets. Hokkaidō chō, ed., *Hokkaidō chō tōkeisho*, 1886 ed. (Sapporo: Hokkaidō chō, 1888), pp. 267–70.

40. Yamamura, "The Meiji Land Tax Reform and Its Effects," takes a generally positive view of the impact of the reform on agricultural districts.

41. Katsura Gengo, *Iwanai Furuu nigun shi* (Iwanai: Katsura Gengo, 1894), p. 26.

42. Arthur F. McEvoy, *The Fisherman's Problem: Ecology and Law in the California Fisheries, 1850–1980* (Cambridge: Cambridge University Press, 1986), p. 6.

43. Ibid., p. 10.

44. See Howell, "Hokkaidō ni okeru gyogyō gijutsu to gyoson no keisei katei."

45. On the effects of the Matsukata deflation, see Takahata, *Otaru-kō shi*, p. 139. The price of herring meal fell from 10.68 yen/ton in 1880 to 7.85 yen/ton in 1881, and continued to drop throughout the deflationary period, reaching a low of 4.28 yen/ton in 1885. Murao Motonaga, *Hokkaidō gyogyō shiyō* (Tokyo: Murao Motonaga, 1897), table following p. 710.

46. *Hokkaidō gyogyō shi*, pp. 322, 325, 243–44, 229–30.

47. Hokkaidō chō, "Shiribeshi no kuni Yoichi gun nishin sashiami chōsa" [1899], RCNS.

48. Rumoi suisan kumiai, ed., "Rumoi gyogyō enkakushi" [c. 1913], RCNS.

49. Ishibashi, *Hamamasu son shi*, pp. 481–82.

50. [Oguro Kaemon], "Mansai kiroku" [c. 1908], Hokkaidō Prefectural Library.

51. Rebun and nearby Rishiri both had large numbers of absentee fishery operators, particularly from the Shakotan peninsula. See Seki Hideshi, "Ritō shakai no keisei katei ni tsuite (2): Meiji shoki-Taishō chūki ni okeru Rishiri-tō Oniwaki mura o chūshin ni," *Hokkaidō kaitaku kinenkan chōsa hōkoku* 24 (1985): 3–20; Yamada Takeshi, "Rishiri-, Rebun-tō ni okeru nishin gyoba no gyorō shūzoku," in *Nihonkai to hokkoku bunka*, ed. Amino Yoshihiko (Tokyo: Shōgakukan, 1990), pp. 513–53; and Yamada, "Rishiri-tō ni okeru nishin teichi gyogyōken no sonzai keitai," pp. 39–47.

52. The fishery in Hiyama subprefecture, which includes the area around Esashi, went into a precipitous decline after the 113,000-ton harvest of 1897, with hauls of only 525 tons in 1906 and 459 tons in 1907. The 21,237 tons caught in 1908 must have seemed fabulous by comparison. The last substantial herring run in the area was in 1916. Imada, *Nishin bunka shi*, pp. 257, 274.

53. The following discussion is based on Emori Susumu, "Nemuro chihō ni okeru nishin sashiami seigan undō," *Atarashii dōshi* 27 (31 March 1968): 1–9. For more on the development of the Nemuro fishery, see Emori, "Meiji kaitakuki Nemuro chihō gyogyō kōzō no shiteki tenkai."

54. The agency did lift restrictions on gill-net use in some parts of the district in 1875. Development Agency Ordinance no. 40 [18 September 1875], in Ōkurashō, *Kaitakushi jigyō hōkoku furoku*, 1: 870.

55. Calculated from data in *Hokkaidō gyogyō shi*, p. 621.

56. Ibid., pp. 681, 691.

57. The president of Gōdō Gyogyō was Mitsui Yonematsu, former administrative vice-minister of commerce and industry. Chalmers Johnson, *MITI and the Japanese Miracle: The Growth of Industrial Policy, 1925–1975* (Stanford: Stanford University Press, 1982), p. 107.

58. *Hokkaidō gyogyō shi*, pp. 685–87; Ishibashi, *Hamamasu son shi*, pp. 634–39.

59. Ishibashi, *Hamamasu son shi*, pp. 612–14.

5. Capitalism and Immiseration

1. Ōsaka, "Oshima no kuni Nishi gun Kumaishi mura gyogyō enkakushi," pp. 10, 27–28.

2. "Kumaishi mura fujinkai no bifū," *Shokumin kōhō* 73 (July 1913): 103–4.

3. Ibid.

4. See the sample family budgets in Aomori ken chihō shokugyō shōkai jimukyoku, ed., *Tōhoku chihō, Hokkaidō nō-, san-, gyoson shokugyō shōkai no mondai* (Aomori: Aomori ken chihō shokugyō shōkai jimukyoku, 1935), pp. 24, 37–38.

5. Rumoi suisan kumiai, "Rumoi gyogyō enkakushi," leaves 29–30.

6. *Hokkaidō gyogyō shi*, p. 238. On Suhara see also Tanaka Osamu, *Nihon shihonshugi to Hokkaidō* (Sapporo: Hokkaidō daigaku tosho kankōkai, 1986), chap. 6, and Tajima Yoshiya, "Kita ni mukatta Kishū shōnin: Suhara Kakubei-ke no jiseki," in *Nihonkai to hokkoku bunka (Umi to rettō bunka*, vol. 1), ed. Amino Yoshihiko (Tokyo: Shōgakukan, 1990), pp. 374–426.

7. The data are taken from Takasaki, *Kaokuzuiri Hokkai risshi hen*, and Katsura, *Iwanai Furuu nigun shi*. See the background discussion on these works and the nature of the data in Howell, "Hokkaidō ni okeru gyogyō gijutsu to gyoson no keisei katei," pp. 32–35.

8. These categories are not, of course, mutually exclusive. Gill-netters' sons often worked for wages before establishing themselves as independent producers, and the son of a merchant might end up a wage laborer. However, the relevant criterion in classifying pound-trap operators is not family origin so much as the experience that led most directly to the individual's entry into the pound-trap fishery. Thus the fisher's son who worked for wages for a few years before succeeding to the family gill-net fishery, which he then converted to pound traps, would be counted as a former gill-netter, while his brother, adopted into his employer's household after years of service, would be classified a former wage laborer.

9. Katsura, *Iwanai Furuu nigun shi*, pp. 85–86.

10. Sakai Tadaiku, "Hokkaidō junkōki" [1879], 3 books, RCNS, book 2, leaves 79–80. Unfortunately, Sakai does not say what the basis for his classification of fishers was.

11. Ishibashi, *Hamamasu son shi*, pp. 474–78; Hokusui kyōkai, *Hokkaidō gyogyō shikō*, pp. 100–103.

12. Katsura, *Iwanai Furuu nigun shi*, pp. 150–51.

13. Ibid., pp. 94–95.

14. "Kaisan kanbachi, tatemono, gyogu, shobuppin shakuyō shō" [23 December 1884] and "Shakuyōbutsu meisaisho" [23 December 1884]; see also, for instance, "Gyogu shobuppin shakuyō shō" [24 March 1887], "Shakuyō shōsho" [23 July 1889], and Honma Toyoshichi to Sawaya Shinzaburō [25 November 1885], "Hamamasu gun Honma-ten gyogyō kankei shorui toji," RCNS.

15. See the discussion in Howell, "Hokkaidō ni okeru gyogyō gijutsu to gyoson no keisei katei," pp. 36–37.

16. Hokkaidō chō naimubu suisanka, *Hokkaidō suisan yosatsu chōsa hōkoku*, p. 96.

17. Tanaka, *Nihon shihonshugi to Hokkaidō*, p. 293.

18. Hokkaidō chō naimubu suisanka, *Hokkaidō suisan yosatsu chōsa hōkoku*, pp. 93–94; compare pp. 148–49, 151–52.

19. See Miyamoto Mataji, "'Ōsaka Hokkai-san niuke ton'ya kumiai enkakushi' no kaisetsu," in *Ōsaka keizai shiryō shūsei*, ed. Ōsaka keizai shiryō

shūsei kankō iinkai (Osaka: Ōsaka shōkō kaigisho, 1977), 10: 573–617, and "Hokkaidō niuke ton'ya kumiai kisoku" [1902], in *Ōsaka shōgyō shi shiryō*, ed. Ōsaka shōkō kaigisho (Osaka: Ōsaka shōkō kaigisho, 1964), vol. 28, especially leaves 96–97. On fertilizer brokers in Ōmi, see Mizuhara Masamichi, "Meiji zenki ni okeru ryūtsū kikō no saihen: Ōmi Hachiman no hiryōshō kumiai no baai," *Shiga daigaku keizaigakubu fuzoku shiryōkan kenkyū kiyō* 13 (March 1980): 29–84, and Mizuhara, "Meiji zenki ryūtsū kikō no saihen katei ni okeru ichirei: Shiga ken Ōmi Hachiman no Nakaichi Shōkai ni tsuite," *Shiga daigaku keizaigakubu fuzoku shiryōkan kenkyū kiyō* 15 (March 1982): 45–94.

20. For example, Honma Toyoshichi, a pound-trap fisher in Hamamasu, noted in his journal for 10 November 1880 that he had begun lending to gill-netters on that day. Honma-ten, "Ishikari no kuni Hamamasu gun Moi mura Honma-ten gyogyō nikki" [1881], Hakodate Municipal Library.

21. Hokkaidō chō naimubu suisanka, *Hokkaidō suisan yosatsu chōsa hōkoku*, pp. 154–55. On Hakodate, "Hakodate yori kyōkyū suru gyogyō shihon," *Shokumin kōhō* 47 (March 1909): 46; on Fukuyama, see Kobayashi Masato, "Meiji nijūnendai ni okeru Matsumae shōnin no dōkō," *Matsumae han to Matsumae* 13 (March 1979): 22–34, and Kuwabara Masato, ed., "*Hakodate shinbun* keisai no Matsumae chō kankei kiji," *Matsumae han to Matsumae* 26, 28 (March 1986, March 1987): 44–87, 68–123.

22. Hokkaidō chō naimubu suisanka, *Hokkaidō suisan yosatsu chōsa hōkoku*, pp. 95–97, 154.

23. Ibid., p. 97; see also Takao Michinori, *Hokkai suisan jikkan* (Tokyo: Yūrindō, 1896), pp. 26–29.

24. Katō to Honma [26 November 1878], "Hamamasu gun Honma-ten gyogyō kankei shorui toji."

25. Katō to Honma [12 July 1879], ibid.

26. "Hakodate yori kyōkyū suru gyogyō shihon," *Shokumin kōhō* 47 (March 1909): 46.

27. Hokkaidō chō naimubu suisanka, *Hokkaidō suisan yosatsu chōsa hōkoku*, p. 97.

28. Draft letter from Honma to district officials [13 August 1875], "Hamamasu gun Honma-ten gyogyō kankei shorui toji."

29. "Furubira teiki tsūshin," *Hokkai shinbun*, 8 March 1887.

30. "Otaru tokubetsu tsūshin," ibid., 15 March 1887; Murao, *Hokkaidō gyogyō shiyō*, table following p. 710.

31. "Kayabe gun Otoshibe mura jikkyō no gi ni tsuki jōshin" [24 December 1884], in "Otoshibe murayakuba shorui (2)," Hokkaidō shi hensan shiryō 48-2, RCNS. On Otoshibe's worth as a fishery, Hokkaidō chō naimubu suisanka, *Hokkaidō suisan yosatsu chōsa hōkoku*, p. 103.

32. Hokkaidō chō naimubu suisanka, *Hokkaidō suisan yosatsu chōsa hōkoku*, p. 140. Casual laborers were commonly assigned to carry wooden baskets of fish from boat landings to processing stages, which gave rise to the nickname "basket carrier" (*mokko seoi*).

33. Ibid., pp. 140–44.

34. Honma-ten, "Honma-ten gyoba nikki," entries for 19 December 1880 (labor recruiters to Ishikari) and 14 December 1880 (bear festival). Short ex-

cerpts of this journal have been published in Taniuchi Kō, "Hokkaidō nishi kaigan ni okeru nishin gyoba: Atsuta mura o chūshin to shite (2)," *Atsuta mura shiryōshitsu kiyō* 5 (October 1966): 1–10. The Ainu population of 164 in Hamamasu in 1880 was down from 311 in 1810 but still somewhat above the 145–50 of the 1890s. See Hamamasu mura [Masuda Ryō], "Hamamasu enkakushi" [1900], Hokkaidō Prefectural Library, pp. 317–20. For the 1896 contracts, see "Hamamasu gun Honma-ten gyogyō kankei shorui toji."

35. Watanabe, *The Ainu Ecosystem*, p. 88, describing conditions in Tokachi in the 1880s.

36. Tōkyō chihō shokugyō shōkai jimukyoku, ed., "Hokkaidō nishin gyogyō rōdō jijō" [1928], in *Gyomin* (*Kindai minshū no kiroku*, vol. 7), ed. Okamoto Tatsuaki (Tokyo: Shinjinbutsu ōraisha, 1978), p. 531.

37. Kaitakushi, "Tōhoku shokō hōkokusho," p. 379 (see also pp. 319, 353, 369); Takeuchi, *Shimokita no sonraku shakai*, pp. 120–26. Similar conditions prevailed in villages in Toyama prefecture, which also supplied large numbers of workers to the Hokkaido fishery. Lewis, *Rioters and Citizens*, pp. 38–39.

38. See the oral-history accounts in Satō Kin'yū, *Hokuyō no dekasegi: Hokuhen gyoba ni ikita kosaku nōmin no kindaishi* (Akita: Akita bunka shuppansha, 1985), and Matsumura Chōta, *Akita no dekasegi: Gyominhen*, 3rd ed. (Akita: Akita bunka shuppansha, 1978).

39. Anakura Moriya, "Dekasegi gyofu hogo kumiai no kaiso ni tsuite," *Hokuyō gyogyō* 1:4 (August 1940): 30.

40. Hokkaidō chō naimubu suisanka, *Hokkaidō suisan yosatsu chōsa hōkoku*, pp. 99–100, 140, 147–48.

41. Lewis, *Rioters and Citizens*, chap. 2.

42. Hokkaidō chō naimubu suisanka, *Hokkaidō suisan yosatsu chōsa hōkoku*, pp. 144–45. For an example of this type of labor recruitment, see the letter dated 13 November from Nakayama Matsuzō of Ōsawada village, Aomori, to Furuu fisher Tatsuke Shinjūrō, reporting that he had recruited about seventy workers at wages ranging from twenty-two to thirty-five yen each and that all the workers would proceed to Hokkaido together on the fifth day of the lunar new year (doc. B41 [c. 1901], Tatsuke-ke monjo, RCNS). In 1896 Honma Toyoshichi paid a commission of 4.50 yen to one Iwata Sadakichi of Horobetsu for recruiting five workers (Honma to Iwata [10 July 1896], "Hamamasu gun Honma-ten gyogyō kankei shorui toji").

43. Hokkaidō chō naimubu suisanka, *Hokkaidō suisan yosatsu chōsa hōkoku*, pp. 144–45.

44. Takahata, *Otaru-kō shi*, p. 142. Three of the earliest companies were Hokushinsha (capitalized at 2,000 yen), established in 1881 to supply labor to both the fishery and agriculture; Hokkaidō Yatoinin Hogo Kaisha (capitalized at 50,000 yen), founded in 1883; and Kyōekisha (capitalized at 60,000 yen), also set up in 1883. See the charter of another such company, Hokkaidō Dekasegi Gyofu Hogo Kaisha: [Okazaki Shuzō], "Hokkaidō dekasegi gyofu hogo kabushiki gaisha kari teigi narabi ni sōritsu shui" [1904] (Kuroishi: Hokkaidō dekasegi gyofu hogo kabushiki gaisha), Hakodate Municipal Library.

45. Kobayashi Takiji, *Kani kōsen*, 1929 (Tokyo: Iwanami shoten, 1967); see also the translation by Frank Motofuji, *"The Factory Ship" and "The Absentee*

Notes to Pages 137–140

Landlord" (Tokyo: University of Tokyo Press; Seattle: University of Washington Press, 1973), pp. 1–83. Compare Satō, *Hokuyō no dekasegi,* passim.

46. Naimushō sōmukyoku, "Hokkaidō gyogyō torishirabesho" [1899], cited in Taniuchi, "Hokkaidō nishi kaigan ni okeru nishin gyoba," pp. 16–17. For similar characterizations of Meiji industrial workers, see Gordon, *The Evolution of Labor Relations in Japan,* pp. 25–38.

47. Hida Ryūdō, "Hokkaidō kikō shōshutsu" [1882], RCNS. Very similar comments can also be found in Kaitakushi, ed., *Hokkaidō shi* (Tokyo: Ōkurashō, 1884), pp. 14–15.

48. Honma-ten, "Ishikari no kuni Hamamasu gun Moi mura Honma-ten gyogyō nikki."

49. Hida, "Hokkaidō kikō shōshutsu."

50. Officials demonstrated similar concerns about the textile industry in the 1880s and 1890s. See Sheldon Garon, *The State and Labor in Modern Japan* (Berkeley: University of California Press, 1987), pp. 20–21.

51. Naimushō sōmukyoku, "Hokkaidō gyogyō torishirabesho," cited in Taniuchi, "Hokkaidō nishi kaigan ni okeru nishin gyoba," pp. 19–20. Again, a very similar assessment was made in 1884 by Kaitakushi, *Hokkaidō shi,* pp. 14–15.

52. Hida, "Hokkaidō kikō shōshutsu." On day laborers' wages in Iwanai, see Katsura, *Iwanai Furuu nigun shi,* pp. 37–38. See also the newspaper account from 1881 cited in Kuwabara, *"Hakodate shinbun* keisai no Matsumae chō kankei kiji," *Matsumae han to Matsumae* 28 (March 1987): 94, and "Otaru tsūshin," *Hokkai shinbun,* 15 March 1887.

53. Honma-ten, "Ishikari no kuni Hamamasu gun Moi mura Honma-ten gyogyō nikki," entries for 9 April and 12 April 1881; see also entries for 12 March and 23 March 1881.

54. At about the same time, employers' organizations in the textile industry came up with plans similar to those outlined here to combat mobility among their workers. See Koji Taira, *Economic Development and the Labor Market in Japan* (New York: Columbia University Press, 1970), pp. 110–16.

55. Honma Toyoshichi, "Hokkaidō gyogyō yatoifu tōbō bōgyoan kisō" [c. 1889], RCNS; Takao, *Hokkai suisan jikkan,* pp. 88–89. See also Honma's notes on organizing a conference, sponsored by the Hokkaido Fisheries Association, on the problem in "Hamamasu gun Honma-ten gyogyō kankei shorui toji."

56. In the late 1880s, Momoishi village, Aomori, issued passes (*dekasegi shōmeisho*) to migrant workers from the village. Taniuchi, "Hokkaidō nishi kaigan ni okeru nishin gyoba," p. 33.

57. See Departmental Ordinance 530 [9 December 1875] and Civil Affairs Bureau Regulation otsu-80 [December 1875], in Kaitakushi, ed., *Kaitakushi fureiroku,* 1875 ed. (n.p., 1881), pp. 684, 866; Prefectural Regulation otsu-82 [25 March 1884] in "Iwanai Furuu gun'yakusho sankō shorui" [c. 1883], RCNS; and Honma, "Hokkaidō gyogyō yatoifu tōbō bōgyoan kisō," article 23.

58. Gerald M. Sider, *Culture and Class in Anthropology and History: A Newfoundland Illustration* (Cambridge: Cambridge University Press; Paris: Editions de la Maison des Sciences de l'Homme, 1986), p. 17.

59. The same sorts of recruitment networks that led Tōhoku peasants into the Hokkaido fishery took western Japanese farmers to Hawaii. See Alan Takeo

Moriyama, *Imingaisha: Japanese Emigration Companies and Hawaii, 1894–1908* (Honolulu: University of Hawaii Press, 1985). On convict labor, see Nagai Hideo, "Iwayuru 'kangoku beya' rōdō no shakaiteki haikei," *Hokkaidō musashi joshi tanki daigaku kiyō* 24 (1992): 1–20; Sapporo kyōdo o horu kai, ed., *Sengo mo tsuzuita takobeya rōdō: Makomanai Beigun kichi kensetsu kōji* (Sapporo: Sapporo kyōdo o horu kai, 1987).

60. Takayama Itarō, "Karafuto gyogyō rōmu jijō: Hokuyō rōmu to no kankei o shu to shite," *Hokuyō gyogyō* 2:9 (September 1941): 26–31.

61. "Otaru gyogyōsha no kinkyō," *Hokkai shinbun*, 1 March 1887; "Gyofu no irikasegi oyobi sono funachin," *Shokumin kōhō* 13 (March 1903): 66.

62. Hokkaidō chō naimubu suisanka, *Hokkaidō suisan yosatsu chōsa hōkoku*, pp. 145–46.

63. Ibid., pp. 147–48.

64. See, for example, Yamaguchi, "Kinseiteki koyō no ichi danmen," for a discussion of bonuses (called *atari*) in the Chiba sardine fishery.

65. See his calculations of bonus money for 207 workers in 1900 (6.6264 yen per worker), "Teatekin shirabe hyō" [9 July 1900], "Hamamasu gun Honma-ten gyogyō kankei shorui toji." See also Hokkaidō chō naimubu suisanka, *Hokkaidō suisan yosatsu chōsa hōkoku*, pp. 146–47, and "Kuichi haishite gobu to naru," *Hokkai shinbun*, 18 March 1887.

66. Hokkaidō chō naimubu suisanka, *Hokkaidō suisan yosatsu chōsa hōkoku*, pp. 99–100.

67. This is a frequent theme in the accounts of former workers given in Satō, *Hokuyō no dekasegi*, and Matsumura, *Akita no dekasegi*.

68. Hokkaidō chō naimubu suisanka, *Hokkaidō suisan yosatsu chōsa hōkoku*, pp. 140–47.

69. Naimushō sōmukyoku, "Hokkaidō gyogyō torishirabesho," cited in Taniuchi, "Hokkaidō nishi kaigan ni okeru nishin gyoba," pp. 19–20.

70. See Takayama, "Karafuto gyogyō rōmu jijō," pp. 26–31.

71. Lewis, *Rioters and Citizens*, pp. 39–40, gives examples of wage deductions levied against fishery workers from Toyama, many of whom were active in the Hokkaido fishery.

72. "Gyofu seisan zankin shishutsu chōsahyō" [10 July 1897], "Hamamasu gun Honma-ten gyogyō kankei shorui toji."

73. "Meiji sanjūsannendo bun seisan zankin uketori shō" [9 July 1900] and "Shō" [1900], ibid.

74. Calculated from eighteen contracts in ibid.

75. Hida, "Hokkaidō kikō shōshutsu."

76. This account of labor conditions is based mostly on Asari Masatoshi, "Hokuyō gyogyō to dekasegi rōdō," in *Hokkaidō no kenkyū*, ed. Kuwabara Masato (Osaka: Seibundō, 1983), 6: 210–59. See also Asari Masatoshi, "Hokuyō gyogyō ni okeru kōsen kani gyorō," *Matsumae han to Matsumae* 13–14 (March-September 1979): 81–108, 61–90; Satō, *Hokuyō no dekasegi*; Matsumura, *Akita no dekasegi*; Kuwabara Masato, ed., "Kyōdo ni ikiru" (oral-history project), *Matsumae han to Matsumae* 27 (February 1987): entire issue; and Anakura Moriya, "Kita Chishima gyogyō rōdō ni kansuru ichi kōsatsu," *Hokuyō gyogyō* 1:7 (November 1940): 15–34.

77. Kuwabara, "Kyōdo ni ikiru," pp. 23–26.
78. Ikeda Yoshinaga, "Hokuyō gyogyō rōmu to eisei jōkyō ni tsuite: Shu to shite kita Chishima ni okeru," *Hokuyō gyogyō* 1:2 (June 1940): 18–20.
79. Hokkaidō chō gakumubu shokugyōka, ed., *Kita Chishima gyogyō narabi ni sono rōdō jijō ron* [marked "secret"] (n.p., 1938).
80. Ibid., p. 16.
81. Aomori ken chihō shokugyō shōkai jimukyoku, *Tōhoku chihō, Hokkaidō nō-, san-, gyoson shokugyō shōkai no mondai*, part 2, pp. 40–42. Figures are numbers of workers.
82. Kuwabara, "Kyōdo ni ikiru," pp. 23–26.

6. A Right to Be Rational

1. Anton Chekhov, *The Island: A Journey to Sakhalin*, trans. Luba and Michael Terpak (Westport, Conn.: Greenwood Press, 1977), p. xxxiv. Throughout this chapter I will use Karafuto to refer to the portion of the island under Japanese rule and Sakhalin otherwise. Likewise, I will use only the Japanese versions of place names.
2. Karafuto chō, ed., *Karafuto chōji ippan*, 1915 ed. (Toyohara: Karafuto chō, 1916); Karafuto chō, ed., *Daiikkai kokusei chōsa hōkoku* (Toyohara: Karafuto chō, 1923), pp. 179–81. Takakura, *Hokkaidō takushoku shi*, p. 281, states that in 1909 fishers constituted forty-three percent of the households and seventy-two percent of the Karafuto Wajin population of about 24,000. This proportion dropped as farmers and other immigrants came in.
3. Taniguchi Hidesaburō, *Karafuto shokumin seisaku* (Tokyo: Takushoku shinpōsha, 1914), p. 337.
4. For a general history of Sakhalin in English, see John J. Stephan, *Sakhalin: A History* (Oxford: Clarendon Press, 1971). For a short account of Japanese rule in Karafuto, see Takakura, *Hokkaidō takushoku shi*, chap. 7. On the native peoples of Sakhalin and their ties to the Hokkaido Ainu, see Uemura, *Kita no umi no kōekishatachi*, pp. 21–38. On Japanese fishing activities in Sakhalin before 1905, see Tanba Heitarō, *Roryō Sagaren-tō gyogyō chōsa hōkoku* (Tokyo: Nōshōmushō suisankyoku, 1900).
5. Carol Gluck, *Japan's Modern Myths* (Princeton: Princeton University Press, 1985); Andrew Gordon, *Labor and Imperial Democracy in Prewar Japan* (Berkeley: University of California Press, 1991); Lewis, *Rioters and Citizens*.
6. The Provisional Order (*Karafuto gyogyō karikisoku*) is reprinted in Okada Yoshitane, ed., *Karafuto-tō shokisoku ruijū* (Wakkanai: Karafuto shinbunsha, 1906), pp. 1–5. It formed the basis for the Karafuto Fishery Law (*Karafuto gyogyō rei*) (Imperial Ordinance 96, 31 March 1907; amended through Imperial Ordinances 252, October 1908, and 318, December 1908), which is reprinted in Karafuto chō chōkan kanbō, ed., *Karafuto hōrei ruiju* (Toyohara: Karafuto chō, 1909), pp. 479–81.
7. This income declined gradually as tax revenues from other industries increased but still accounted for twenty-five percent (550,419 yen) in 1916. Karafuto teichi gyogyō suisan kumiai, ed., *Karafuto to gyogyō* (Toyohara: Karafuto teichi gyogyō suisan kumiai, 1931), pp. 283–84.
8. The Fishing License Regulations (*Gyogyō kansatsu kisoku*) (Dept. of Civil

Affairs Notification 4, 3 October 1905) and amendments (Dept. of Civil Affairs Notifications 5, 9 October 1905, and 6, 14 October 1905), are reprinted in Okada, *Karafuto-tō shokisoku ruijū*, pp. 55–61.

9. Sugimoto Zennosuke, *Karafuto gyosei kaikaku enkakushi* (Maoka: Karafuto gyosei kaikaku enkakushi kankōkai, 1935), p. 11. The number of licensed cod boats doubled between 1906 and 1907 (836 to 1,705), but catches did not rise accordingly—the result, according to the official view of the Karafuto government, of an influx of inexperienced newcomers. Karafuto chō, ed., *Karafuto yōran*, 1907 ed. (Tokyo: Ryūbunkan, 1908), pp. 176–78.

10. Sugimoto, *Karafuto gyosei kaikaku enkakushi*, p. 46.

11. Karafuto chō, ed., *Karafuto chōji ippan*, 1910 ed. (Toyohara: Karafuto chō, 1911), p. 20; Karafuto chō, *Daiikkai kokusei chōsa hōkoku*, pp. 179–81.

12. "Nodasan gyokyō," *Karafuto nichinichi shinbun*, 25 May 1911.

13. Sugimoto, *Karafuto gyosei kaikaku enkakushi*, p. 21. The government noted with approval in 1908 that "a market, albeit a small one, has emerged for fresh herring for cod bait," to supplement the less profitable production of herring meal. Karafuto chō, *Karafuto yōran* (1907 ed.), p. 173.

14. Sugimoto, *Karafuto gyosei kaikaku enkakushi*, pp. 25–26.

15. Emori, "Nemuro chihō ni okeru nishin sashiami seigan undō."

16. Sugimoto, *Karafuto gyosei kaikaku enkakushi*, pp. 27, 28.

17. Tsuji Seitarō, *Karafuto-tō kaihatsu ni kansuru seigan* [1907], RCNS. Sugimoto, *Karafuto gyosei kaikaku enkakushi*, pp. 30–42, reprints the petition and gives a sympathetic summary of the events surrounding its presentation.

18. Karafuto teichi gyogyō suisan kumiai, *Karafuto to gyogyō*, pp. 169–202.

19. Ibid., pp. 152–53.

20. The petition was adopted by the House of Representatives on the recommendation of the Petition Committee on 27 March 1907. Dai-Nippon teikoku gikai shi kankōkai, ed., *Dai-Nippon teikoku gikai shi* (Tokyo: Dai-Nippon teikoku gikai shi kankōkai, 1930), vol. 6 [23rd Imperial Diet], p. 1671.

21. See Wada's report on the prospects of the Karafuto fishery, presented to the governor of Hokkaido in December 1905: "Karafuto-tō gyogyō chōsa hōkoku" [1905], RCNS.

22. "Karafuto-tō jūmin kyūzai ni tsuki seigan," reprinted in Sugimoto, *Karafuto gyosei kaikaku enkakushi*, p. 58.

23. Ibid., p. 60.

24. Karafuto chō, *Karafuto yōran* (1907 ed.), pp. 173, 180–81.

25. In 1906 the cod fishery was still dominated by experienced fishers, who harvested 112.5 tons or more of fish each, while in 1907 the average catch dropped by half or more. Ibid., pp. 178–79.

26. Karafuto chō, ed., *Karafuto yōran*, 1913 ed. (Toyohara: Karafuto chō, 1914), p. 124.

27. Sugimoto, *Karafuto gyosei kaikaku enkakushi*, pp. 75–76. The petition, "Sashiami kumiai tokkyo no gi ni tsuki seigan," is reprinted on pp. 76–90.

28. Karafuto tateami gyogyō suisan kumiai rengōkai, ed., *Hoppō gyogyō no shiori* (Tokyo: Karafuto tateami gyogyō suisan kumiai rengōkai, 1912), p. 10.

29. The petition, "Karafuto-tō nishin sashiami gyogyō hinin no seigansho," is reprinted in Sugimoto, *Karafuto gyosei kaikaku enkakushi*, pp. 93–101.

30. Item 10 of the petition, ibid., pp. 98–99.

31. Taniguchi, *Karafuto shokumin seisaku*, pp. 337–38.
32. Ibid.
33. "Gyoson no shinfūchō," *Karafuto nichinichi shinbun*, 28 October 1913.
34. Karafuto tateami gyogyō suisan kumiai rengōkai, *Hoppō gyogyō no shiori*, p. 10.
35. On the committee discussion, see Sugimoto, *Karafuto gyosei kaikaku enkakushi*, pp. 101–6; for the floor of the Diet, see Dai-Nippon teikoku gikai shi kankōkai, *Dai-Nippon teikoku gikai shi*, vol. 7 [24th Imperial Diet], pp. 123 (House of Peers), 552 (House of Representatives).
36. Sugimoto, *Karafuto gyosei kaikaku enkakushi*, p. 163. On Hiraoka, see also Sugimoto Ken, *Karafuto: Kaerazaru shima* (Tokyo: TBS-Buritanika, 1979), pp. 196–203, and Saga Rentarō [Nagai Kenzō], *"Kanritsu" Karafuto chūgakkō to Natsume Sōseki* (Sapporo: Minami Karafuto mondai kenkyūjo, 1987), pp. 22–30.
37. The application of the revised national Fishery Law (Law 58, 1910) to Karafuto in 1911 provided for the establishment of cooperatives at the discretion of the governor. Karafuto chō, ed., *Karafuto chō shisei sanjūnen shi* (Toyohara: Karafuto chō, 1936), p. 327.
38. Karafuto chō, *Karafuto yōran* (1913 ed.), pp. 116–17.
39. "Kaizen no daiippo (futatabi kumiai gyoba ron)," *Karafuto nichinichi shinbun*, 22 October 1910; "Kumiai gyoba kakushinkai," ibid., 3 July 1913.
40. "Karafuto gyomin no bōkō," *Yomiuri shinbun*, 11 June 1909.
41. Cited in Sugimoto, *Karafuto gyosei kaikaku enkakushi*, pp. 185–86.
42. Taniguchi, *Karafuto shokumin seisaku*, p. 317; Tazawa Mihō [Rishichi], *Karafuto kigyōka no shishin* (Toyohara: Karafuto kigyōka no shishinsha, 1924), pp. 187–88.
43. Ichiki canceled a planned tour of inspection of the west coast because of "unrest among small fishers" in the area. "Karafuto no fuon," *Yomiuri shinbun*, 16 June 1909.
44. Sugimoto, *Karafuto gyosei kaikaku enkakushi*, pp. 172–81, reprints a large part of the Karafuto District Court decision on the case.
45. The court decision includes extended quotations (ibid., pp. 174–77) of the *Karafuto jiji* articles.
46. See, for example, "Mitsuryō nishin no bosshū," *Karafuto nichinichi shinbun*, 23 May 1911.
47. "Nayashi tayori," *Karafuto nichinichi shinbun*, 17 July 1910.
48. Kyōgoku Takayoshi, Nomura Masuzō, and Tōdō Terumaru, *Karafuto no kenkyū* (Tokyo: Yamada Saburō, 1914), 1: 12–14.
49. "Chinjōsho," reprinted in Sugimoto, *Karafuto gyosei kaikaku enkakushi*, pp. 236–42.
50. Items 5 and 7, ibid., pp. 238–39.
51. See the discussion in ibid., pp. 244–50.
52. The petitions are reprinted or summarized in ibid., pp. 261–87.
53. The petition to Hara, in ibid., p. 282.
54. "Karafuto gyosei kaisei hantai no riyū," reprinted in part in ibid., pp. 290–98.
55. Item 5, Section 3, ibid., p. 296.

56. See ibid., pp. 307–12, for a blow-by-blow account.

57. Kyōgoku, Nomura, and Tōdō, *Karafuto no kenkyū* 1: 10–14. Hiraoka himself admitted that problems of timing and scale made it difficult to balance fishing and farming—as did the indisposition of the family fishers toward agriculture. "Chōkan no shisei hōshin: Nijūkunichi Karafuto chō ni oite shisatsudan ni taisuru setsumei," *Karafuto nichinichi shinbun*, 4 July 1913.

58. Kyōgoku, Nomura, and Tōdō, *Karafuto no kenkyū* 1: 17–21. The delegation read but did not formally present the seventh and eighth points to Hiraoka and later cut them from their statement. In the formal petition presented to Hiraoka they amended the sixth point to read, "some appropriate means other than pound traps" in place of "gill nets."

59. Yamamiya Tōkichi, *Karafuto no kenkyū* (Tokyo: Yamada Saburō, 1914), 2: 20–21.

60. Ibid., pp. 22–25.

61. Taniguchi Hidesaburō, ed., *Hiraoka Karafuto chō chōkan danwa: Karafuto no gyogyō seido* (n.p.: Karafuto kyōkai, [1913]), pp. 8–17.

62. Sugimoto Ken, *Karafuto: Kaerazaru shima*, pp. 196–97, 203; Saga, *"Kanritsu" Karafuto chūgakkō to Natsume Sōseki*, pp. 22–30.

63. "Hiraoka chōkan jinin," *Karafuto nichinichi shinbun*, 6 June 1914. The article makes no mention of the scandals, nor, indeed, does it give any reason at all for Hiraoka's resignation.

64. "Karafuto gyogyō seido ni kansuru seigan," reprinted in Sugimoto, *Karafuto gyosei kaikaku enkakushi*, pp. 352–54.

65. "Karafuto gyosei kaisei ni kanshi seigan," reprinted in ibid., pp. 354–57.

66. *Teikoku gikai kizokuin giji sokkiroku* (Tokyo: Tōkyō daigaku shuppankai, 1981), vol. 30 [29th–35th Imperial Diets, part 2], pp. 298–300.

67. Article 5, Karafuto Fishery Law, amended through Imperial Ordinance 106, 3 July 1915. Karafuto tateami gyogyō suisan kumiai rengōkai, ed., *Kaisei Karafuto gyogyō hōki* (Hakodate: Karafuto tateami gyogyō suisan kumiai rengōkai, 1917), pp. 31–33.

68. "Gyogyōrei kaisei ni tsuki Okada chōkan dan," *Karafuto nichinichi shinbun*, 4 July 1915.

69. "Chūmoku subeki yūdan," *Karafuto nichinichi shinbun*, 4 July 1915; "Jūken sonpō," ibid., 6 July 1915; "Nokoru mondai," ibid., 7 July 1915; "Kore mo itten," ibid., 8 July 1915; "Gokai o saru toki," ibid., 9 July 1915.

70. "Maoka no chōchin gyōretsu," *Karafuto nichinichi shinbun*, 7 July 1915 (lantern parade); "Ōdomari sashiami shukugikai," ibid., 23 July 1915 (memorial service).

71. Karafuto chō, *Karafuto chō shisei sanjūnen shi*, p. 326. On the trading of fisheries from the pound-trap operators' point of view, see Karafuto teichi gyogyō suisan kumiai, *Karafuto to gyogyō*, pp. 307–8.

72. Tazawa, *Karafuto kigyōka no shishin*, pp. 191–92.

73. "Kaizen no daiippo (futatabi kumiai gyoba ron)," *Karafuto nichinichi shinbun*, 22 October 1910.

74. An apparent example of an ideal cooperatively held company (notwithstanding the fact that it tottered on the brink of bankruptcy in 1911) is one set up by the "comparatively industrious small fishers" of the Seventh West Coast Co-

operative. ("Nishi kaigan no shokaisha," *Karafuto nichinichi shinbun*, 7 January 1911.) All sorts of financial monkey business surrounded the management of the Fifth West Coast and Third Aniwa Bay cooperatives. ("Nayoro kumiai tai dantai funjō jiken no shinsō," ibid., 7 January 1911; "Ōdomari no daigigoku," ibid., 18 January 1911.)

75. "Kumiai gyoba no kongo: Keiyaku kaijo ikan," ibid., 9 July 1915; "Kumiai gyoba chinshakusha shitsumon: Wannai keieisha no shuchō," ibid., 10 July 1915.

76. "Gyogyōken taishaku keiyakusho" [1917], Hokkaidō Prefectural Library.

77. Karafuto tateami gyogyō suisan kumiai rengōkai, ed., *Taishō sannen kaisei gyogyōryō narabi ni saikin sankanen shūkakudaka* (n.p., 1915), pp. 35–36.

78. Suzuki Tayoji, *Karafuto suisan dantai taikan* (Ōdomari: Karafuto suisansha, 1935), p. 209.

79. Karafuto chō, *Karafuto chō shisei sanjūnen shi*, p. 325. Between 1905 and 1913 the northwest coast of Karafuto had the most desirable fisheries, but they declined sharply after that; the coast of Aniwa Bay and the central and southern parts of the east coast were productive between 1913 and 1918 but faded later. See *Karafuto gyosei no enkaku*, c. 1921, Hokkaidō Prefectural Library.

80. Tōyama Shin'ichirō, *Karafuto no jijō to shōrai* (n.p., c. 1923), pp. 7–8.

81. Regulations Concerning the Application of the Fishery Law in Karafuto (*Karafuto ni okeru gyogyōhō shikō kisoku*), Departmental Ordinance 12, 1926. Reprinted in Karafuto chō, *Karafuto chō shisei sanjūnen shi*, pp. 326–27.

82. Ōtaka Kentarō and Nishikawa Yoshihiro, "Karafuto no gyogyō chōsa: Karafuto no suisan," in "Oshoro-maru Shōwa hachinendo renshū kōkai gyogyō chōsa hōkokusho," ed. Hokkaidō teikoku daigaku suisan senmonbu gyorōka (1933), RCNS.

83. Ibid.

84. Ibid.

85. The statistics used in the following discussion are from the descriptions of fishing cooperatives in Suzuki, *Karafuto suisan dantai taikan*, pp. 78–252.

86. Ibid., p. 95.

87. Ibid., pp. 214–15.

88. Taniguchi, *Karafuto shokumin seisaku*, p. 314.

89. Ōtaka and Nishikawa, "Karafuto no gyogyō chōsa"; Suzuki, *Karafuto suisan dantai taikan*, p. 295.

90. Karafuto tateami gyogyō suisan kumiai rengōkai, *Taishō sannen kaisei gyogyōryō narabi ni saikin sankanen shūkakudaka*, pp. 1–59; on Nichiro Gyogyō, see the company history: Okamoto Nobuo, *Nichiro Gyogyō keiei shi* (Tokyo: Suisansha, 1971).

91. Satō Suguru, *Oguma Kōichirō den* (Hakodate: Hakodate shōkō kaigisho, 1958), pp. 122–46.

92. Karafuto teichi gyogyō suisan kumiai, *Karafuto to gyogyō*, pp. 315–16.

93. Suzuki, *Karafuto suisan dantai taikan*, pp. 293–341.

94. Ibid., p. 297.

95. Taniguchi, *Karafuto shokumin seisaku*, pp. 345–46.

96. "Dojin gyoba to dojin," *Karafuto nichinichi shinbun*, 3 September 1910.
97. "Gyofu yatoiire chūi," ibid., 30 November 1913.
98. "Furyō no sanjō," ibid., 22 June 1915; "Hibi kenbun," ibid., 19 June 1915.
99. "Kushunnai no gyofu bōkō jiken," ibid., 9 May 1912; also, "Kushunnai no gyofu dōmei bōkō jiken senpō," ibid., 15 May 1912; "Sōdō jiken kōhan," ibid., 29 June 1912; "Sōdō jiken no hanketsu," ibid., 30 June 1912; "Sōdō jiken no hanketsu," ibid., 5 July 1912.
100. "Yatoi gyofu no shingenshō," ibid., 11 April 1911.
101. "Karafuto to rōryoku mondai," ibid., 21–22 September 1911. For a proposal that the indigenous peoples of Karafuto be put to work as industrial laborers, see Nakame Satoru, *Dojin kyōka ron* (Tokyo: Iwanami shoten, 1918), pp. 94–108.
102. "Saharin zanryū Kankoku-, Chōsen-jin ni Soren no hairyo," *Hokkaidō shinbun*, 27 November 1987. Between sixty and eighty thousand Koreans were taken to Karafuto during World War II; about thirty-six thousand persons of Korean descent (including second- and third-generation Koreans) remain in Sakhalin today: "Zai-Saharin Kankokujin issei: Miyori nai 150-nin, 9-gatsu ni eijū kikoku," *Hokkaidō shinbun*, 21 June 1992.
103. Karafuto chō, *Karafuto yōran* (1913 ed.), pp. 117–20.
104. Gordon, "The Crowd and Politics in Imperial Japan," p. 147.
105. Gordon, *Labor and Imperial Democracy in Prewar Japan*, pp. 13–25. Gordon's "imperial democracy" is more commonly known as "Taishō democracy." See his discussion of the terms, pp. 5–10.
106. Lewis, *Rioters and Citizens*, chap. 2.
107. Ibid., pp. 38–42. Not only did many men from the Toyama coast work in fisheries in Hokkaido, Karafuto, and Soviet territory, but women in Toyama labored as dockworkers, unloading herring meal from the north and loading grain destined for Hokkaido and Karafuto.
108. See Vlastos, *Peasant Protests and Uprisings in Tokugawa Japan*, pp. 16–18.
109. Herbert P. Bix, *Peasant Protest in Japan, 1590–1884* (New Haven, Conn.: Yale University Press, 1986), pp. 209–14; Scheiner, "The Mindful Peasant"; Irokawa, *The Culture of the Meiji Period*, pp. 151–95, and Bowen, *Rebellion and Democracy in Meiji Japan*, pp. 49–69 and passim.
110. Bowen, *Rebellion and Democracy in Meiji Japan*, p. 103.
111. Tenkai-sei, "Karafuto tai Hakodate," *Karafuto nichinichi shinbun*, 3 April 1912.

7. Conclusion

1. Kawashima Hiroyuki, "Yanshū no yume," *Hokkaidō shinbun*, 10 January 1988.
2. McEvoy, *The Fisherman's Problem*, pp. 149–55, discusses the ecological damage done by the decimation of the California sardine fishery.
3. Kawashima, "Yanshū no yume."

4. See, for example, the letters to the editor from Arisaka Yoshinori, 77, and Shigematsu Sumi, 63, *Hokkaidō shinbun*, 20 March 1987 and 16 June 1987; compare Blakiston, *Japan in Yezo*, p. 5.

5. Kon Zensaku, "Nishinryō oboegaki," *Hokkaidō no bunka* 4 (September 1963): 28.

6. Tashiro Kazui, "Foreign Relations during the Edo Period: *Sakoku* Reexamined," *Journal of Japanese Studies* 8:2 (Summer 1982): 283–306.

7. Furuta Ryōichi, *Kawamura Zuiken* (Tokyo: Yoshikawa kōbunkan, 1988), pp. 17–44; E. Sydney Crawcour, "Kawamura Zuiken: A Seventeenth Century Entrepreneur," *Transactions of the Asiatic Society of Japan* 3rd ser., 9 (1966): 1–23. See also Miyamoto and Uemura, "Tokugawa keizai no junkan kōzō." Kawana Noboru, *Kashi ni ikiru hitobito: Tonegawa suiun no shakai shi* (Tokyo: Heibonsha, 1982), has an informative discussion of river transportation networks in the Kantō.

8. The Nanbu and Matsumoto domains controlled forestry in this manner. Hasegawa, "Bakuhan taiseika ni okeru Ezochi dekasegi o meguru shomondai," pp. 26–33; Conrad Totman, *The Green Archipelago: Forestry in Preindustrial Japan* (Berkeley: University of California Press, 1989), pp. 70–71.

9. John W. Hall, *Tanuma Okitsugu, 1719–1788: The Forerunner of Modern Japan* (Cambridge: Harvard University Press, 1955).

10. As Sidney W. Mintz, *Sweetness and Power: The Place of Sugar in Modern History* (New York: Viking Press, 1985), demonstrates so well, the preoccupation of the Japanese with rice as a staple food is consistent with practice in most cultures. See also Fernand Braudel, *The Structures of Everyday Life: The Limits of the Possible* (*Civilization and Capitalism, 15th-18th Century*, vol. 1) (New York: Harper & Row, 1979), for a discussion of staple grains throughout the world.

11. Much of the economic thought of the Tokugawa period can be seen as an attempt to rationalize commerce and industry as legitimate alternatives to a rice-based economy. See, for example, Tetsuo Najita, *Visions of Virtue: The Kaitokudō Merchant Academy in Tokugawa Japan* (Chicago: University of Chicago Press, 1987), and Roberts, "The Merchant Origins of National Prosperity Thought in Eighteenth Century Tosa."

12. Howell, "Hard Times in the Kantō," pp. 357–64.

13. Kriedte, Medick, and Schlumbohm, *Industrialization before Industrialization*, pp. 95–96.

14. Hanley and Yamamura, *Economic and Demographic Change in Preindustrial Japan*, chap 6.

15. For treatments of economic development and peasant rebellion in Nanbu see, in addition to ibid.: Herbert P. Bix, "Miura Meisuke, or Peasant Rebellion under the Banner of 'Distress,'" *Bulletin of Concerned Asian Scholars* 10:2 (1978): 18–26; Herbert P. Bix, "Leader of Peasant Rebellions: Miura Meisuke," in *Great Historical Figures of Japan*, ed. Murakami Hyoe and Thomas J. Harper (Tokyo: Japan Culture Institute, 1978); Mori Kahei, *Nanbu han hyakushō ikki no kenkyū* (*Mori Kahei chosakushū*, vol. 7) (Tokyo: Hōsei daigaku shuppan kyoku, 1974 [1935]), pp. 345–570; Moriya Yoshimi, "Bakuhan kōshin han no keizai jōkyō: Morioka han bakumatsu hyakushō ikki no yobiteki kōsatsu no

tame ni," *Nihonshi kenkyū* 150–51 (1975): 184–202; Iwamoto Yoshiteru, *Kinsei gyoson kyōdōtai no hensen katei: Shōhin keizai no shinten to sonraku kyōdōtai* (Tokyo: Ochanomizu shobō, 1977); and Yokoyama Toshio, *Hyakushō ikki to gimin denshō* (Tokyo: Kyōikusha, 1977), pp. 173–96.

16. Sider, *Culture and Class in Anthropology and History*, pp. 34–35. Sider, p. 189, it should be noted, argues that merchant capital was in fact dynamic: "To claim . . . that merchant capital . . . remains within the sphere of circulation, and in no significant way alters prior or more autonomous modes of production, is to miss the whole dynamic of social and cultural differentiation . . . in the formation of the modern world."

17. Pratt, "Village Elites in Tokugawa Japan," chap. 1.

18. See the case studies of three cotton and three silk regions, ibid., chaps. 4–5.

19. Edward E. Pratt, "Proto-Industry and Mechanized Production in Three Raw Silk Regions" (paper delivered at the 43rd annual meeting of the Association for Asian Studies, New Orleans, 1991), pp. 17–18.

20. Wigen, *The Making of a Japanese Periphery*, p. 291.

21. Ibid., pp. 173–74, 289–91; Pratt, "Proto-Industry and Mechanized Production in Three Raw Silk Regions."

22. Henry Rosovsky, "Japan's Transition to Modern Economic Growth, 1868–1885," in *Industrialization in Two Systems: Essays in Honor of Alexander Gerschenkron*, ed. Henry Rosovsky, as cited by Sydney Crawcour, "The Tokugawa Period and Japan's Preparation for Modern Economic Growth," *Journal of Japanese Studies* 1:1 (Autumn 1974), p. 115.

23. See Wigen, *The Making of a Japanese Periphery*, especially chap. 8, and Kären Wigen, "Social and Spatial Divisions of Labor in Nineteenth Century Shinano: Mapping the Contested Terrain of Paper Craft Production" (paper delivered at the 43rd annual meeting of the Association for Asian Studies, New Orleans, 1991).

24. Gordon, *Labor and Imperial Democracy in Prewar Japan*.

25. Doc. 235 [18 February 1891], Toyama ken, ed., *Toyama ken shi: Shiryōhen* (Toyama: Toyama ken, 1978), 6: 692–93.

Works Cited

Manuscript Sources

"Ezo Matsumae kikigaki (Tsugaru kenbunki tsuki)" [1758]. Resource Collection for Northern Studies, Hokkaidō University Library.

"Gyogyōken taishaku keiyakusho" [1917]. Hokkaidō Prefectural Library.

Hakodate ken, comp. "Matsumae Tenpō kyōkōroku" [1929]. Hokkaidō shi hensan shiryō 415, Resource Collection for Northern Studies, Hokkaidō University Library. (Copy of part of "Bikō chochiku ikken" [1886], compiled by Hakodate ken.)

"Hamamashike yōyōgaki tojikomi" [1865–66]. Satō-ke monjo B10, Resource Collection for Northern Studies, Hokkaidō University Library.

"Hamamasu gun Honma-ten gyogyō kankei shorui toji" [c. 1878–1909]. Resource Collection for Northern Studies, Hokkaidō University Library.

Hamamasu suisan kumiai, ed. "Gyogyō enkakushi" [1911]. Hokkaidō Prefectural Library.

Hayami Uichirō. "Kita Ezochi yō oboegaki" [1863]. Resource Collection for Northern Studies, Hokkaidō University Library.

Hida Ryūdō. "Hokkaidō kikō shōshutsu" [1882]. Resource Collection for Northern Studies, Hokkaidō University Library.

Hokkaidō chō. "Shiribeshi no kuni Yoichi gun nishin sashiami chōsa" [1899]. Resource Collection for Northern Studies, Hokkaidō University Library.

Honma-ten. "Ishikari no kuni Hamamasu gun Moi mura Honma-ten gyogyō nikki" [1881]. Hakodate Municipal Library.

Honma Toyoshichi. "Hokkaidō gyogyō yatoifu tōbō bōgyoan kisō" [c. 1889]. Resource Collection for Northern Studies, Hokkaidō University Library.

"Ichinen no yume Ezo miyage" [n.d.]. Hokkaidō Prefectural Archives.

"Iwanai Furuu gun'yakusho sankō shorui" [c. 1883]. Resource Collection for Northern Studies, Hokkaidō University Library.

Kakizaki Hirotsune. "Kuchigaki todome" [1837]. Hakodate Municipal Library.

"Kumausu mura kaisan kanba chiken daichō" [1883]. Hokkaidō shi hensan shiryō 9, Resource Collection for Northern Studies, Hokkaidō University Library.
Kuwata Ryūsai. "Ezo no kyōkai" [1859]. Resource Collection for Northern Studies, Hokkaidō University Library.
"Nemuro ken kyūdojin" [1882–86]. Resource Collection for Northern Studies, Hokkaidō University Library.
[Oguro Kaemon]. "Mansai kiroku" [c. 1908]. Hokkaidō Prefectural Library.
"Onshakkindaka narabi ni namen kakiage" [1866]. Nakagawaya monjo, Baba Collection, Hakodate Municipal Library.
Ōsaka Heizō. "Oshima no kuni Nishi gun Kumaishi mura gyogyō enkakushi" [1910]. Hokkaidō Prefectural Library.
"Otoshibe murayakuba shorui (2)" [c. 1884]. Hokkaidō shi hensan shiryō 48-2, Resource Collection for Northern Studies, Hokkaidō University Library.
Sakai Tadaiku. "Hokkaidō junkōki" [1879]. 3 books, Resource Collection for Northern Studies, Hokkaidō University Library.
Satō Eiemon. "Shokakitodome" [c. 1860]. Hokkaidō shi hensan shiryō 198. Resource Collection for Northern Studies, Hokkaidō University Library.
"Satō-ke shōyō shorui (2)" [1868–72]. Hokkaidō shi hensan shiryō 135-10, Resource Collection for Northern Studies, Hokkaidō University Library.
"Tabibitotōri Takeda-tsuke" [1859–71]. Hokkaidō shi hensan shiryō 197, Resource Collection for Northern Studies, Hokkaidō University Library.
"Tabibitotōri Yagi-tsuke" [1859–71]. Hokkaidō shi hensan shiryō 198, Resource Collection for Northern Studies, Hokkaidō University Library.
"Taneda-ke monjo" [c. 1870]. Hokkaidō shi hensan shiryō 200, Resource Collection for Northern Studies, Hokkaidō University Library.
Tatsuke-ke monjo. Resource Collection for Northern Studies, Hokkaidō University Library.
Wada Kenzō. "Karafuto-tō gyogyō chōsa hōkoku" [1905]. Resource Collection for Northern Studies, Hokkaidō University Library.
Yoshida Setsuzō. "Hokuchi kaitaku shimatsu tairyaku" [c. 1881]. Resource Collection for Northern Studies, Hokkaidō University Library.
"Zassho" [1833]. Kikuchi-ke monjo, Aomori Prefectural Library.
"Zassho tojikomi" [1866–67]. Nakagawaya monjo, Baba Collection, Hakodate Municipal Library.

Published Documentary Sources

"Ansei nenkan zaruami sōjō tanmatsu" [n.d.]. In Esashi chō shi: Shiryōhen, volume 2, edited by Esashi chō shi henshūshitsu. Esashi: Esashi chō, 1978.
"Chiso sōtei kankei shorui" [1876–77]. In Matsumae chō shi: Shiryōhen, volume 4, edited by Matsumae chō shi henshūshitsu. Matsumae: Matsumae chō shi henshūshitsu, 1980.
"Chiso sōtei kisoku todome" [1876]. In Matsumae chō shi: Shiryōhen, volume 4, edited by Matsumae chō shi henshūshitsu. Matsumae: Matsumae chō shi henshūshitsu, 1980.
Dai-Nippon teikoku gikai shi kankōkai, ed. Dai-Nippon teikoku gikai shi. 18 volumes. Tokyo: Dai-Nippon teikoku gikai shi kankōkai, 1926–30.

"Ezo hōki" [n.d.]. In *Nihon shomin seikatsu shiryō shūsei*, volume 4, edited by Takakura Shin'ichirō. Tokyo: San'ichi shobō, 1969.

Furukawa Koshōken. "Tōyū zakki" [1789]. In *Kinsei shakai keizai sōsho*, volume 12, edited by Honjō Eijirō. Tokyo: Kaizōsha, 1927.

Futoro murayakuba, ed. "Futoro gun Futoro mura gaikyō" [1908]. Resource Collection for Northern Studies, Hokkaidō University.

"Gyoba ninbetsu narabi ni amikazu kakiage" [1868]. In *Atsuta mura shiryō kōhon: Sasaki-ke monjo*, edited by Atsuta mura shiryōshitsu. Atsuta: Atsuta mura shiryōshitsu, 1967.

"Hakodate omote inbaijo no ken" [1856]. In *Dai-Nippon komonjo: Bakumatsu gaikoku kankei monjo*, volume 14, edited by Tōkyō teikoku daigaku bungakubu shiryō hensan gakari. Tokyo: Tōkyō teikoku daigaku, 1922.

"Hama kenchiwari chō" [1748]. In *Esashi chō shi: Shiryōhen*, volume 2, edited by Esashi chō shi henshūshitsu. Esashi: Esashi chō, 1978.

Hayashi-ke monjo. In *Yoichi chō shi: Shiryōhen*, volume 1, edited by Yoichi chō shi hensanshitsu. Yoichi: Yoichi chō, 1986.

"Hayashi-ke monjo: Ban nikki" [1860–66]. In *Matsumae chō shi: Shiryōhen*, volume 2, edited by Matsumae chō shi henshūshitsu. Matsumae: Matsumae chō shi henshūshitsu, 1977.

Hezutsu Tōsaku. "Tōyūki" [1784]. In *Hokumon sōsho*, volume 2, edited by Ōtomo Kisaku. Tokyo: Hokkō shobō, 1943–44.

Hirao Rosen. "Matsumae kikō" [1855]. In *Hakodate shi shi: Shiryōhen*, volume 1, edited by Hakodate shi. Hakodate: Hakodate shi, 1974.

Hokkaidō chō, ed. *Hokkaidō chō tōkeisho*. 1886 edition. Sapporo: Hokkaidō chō, 1888.

"Hokkaidō niuke ton'ya kumiai kisoku" [1902]. In *Ōsaka shōgyō shi shiryō*, volume 28, edited by Ōsaka shōkō kaigisho. Osaka: Ōsaka shōkō kaigisho, 1964.

"Kaisan kanba chikenjō uketorishō tojikomi" [1879]. In *Matsumae chō shi: Shiryōhen*, volume 4, edited by Matsumae chō shi henshūshitsu. Matsumae: Matsumae chō shi henshūshitsu, 1980.

"Kaminokuni mura nayaba aratame" [1747]. In *Esashi chō shi: Shiryōhen*, volume 2, edited by Esashi chō shi henshūshitsu. Esashi: Esashi chō, 1978.

"Kishida San'emon monjo: Ryōke shikomi" [1688–1911]. In *Esashi chō shi: Shiryōhen*, volume 2, edited by Esashi chō shi henshūshitsu. Esashi: Esashi chō, 1978.

Kudō murayakuba, ed. "Kudō gun Kudō mura enkaku" [c. 1920]. Resource Collection for Northern Studies, Hokkaidō University Library.

Kushihara Shōhō. "Igen zokuwa" [1793]. In *Nihon shomin seikatsu shiryō shūsei*, volume 4, edited by Takakura Shin'ichirō. Tokyo: San'ichi shobō, 1969.

Matsuda Denjūrō. "Hokuidan" [n.d.]. In *Nihon shomin seikatsu shiryō shūsei*, volume 4, edited by Takakura Shin'ichirō. Tokyo: San'ichi shobō, 1969.

Matsumae Hironanga, comp. "Fukuyama hifu" [1776]. In *Shinsen Hokkaidō shi*, volume 5, edited by Hokkaidō chō. Sapporo: Hokkaidō chō, 1936.

Matsumiya Kanzan. "Ezo dan hikki" [1710]. In *Nihon shomin seikatsu shiryō shūsei*, volume 4, edited by Takakura Shin'ichirō. Tokyo: San'ichi shobō, 1969.

Matsuura Takeshirō. *Takeshirō kaiho nikki* [1856–57]. 2 volumes, edited by Takakura Shin'ichirō. Sapporo: Hokkaidō shuppan kikaku sentā, 1978.

Mogami Tokunai. "Ezokoku fūzoku ninjō no sata" [1791]. In *Nihon shomin
    seikatsu shiryō shūsei*, volume 4, edited by Takakura Shin'ichirō. Tokyo:
    San'ichi shobō, 1969.
Murabayashi Gensuke. "Genshi manpitsu fudo nenpyō" [1804–18]. In *Michi-
    noku sōsho*, volumes 6–7, edited by Aomori ken bunkazai hogo kyōkai,
    1960. Reprint, Tokyo: Kokusho kankōkai, 1982.
Mutō Kanzō. "Ezo nikki" [1798]. In *Nihon shomin seikatsu shiryō shūsei*, vol-
    ume 4, edited by Takakura Shin'ichirō. Tokyo: San'ichi shobō, 1969.
"Nishi Ezochi amikiri sōdō narabi ni tateami myōga no oboe" [n.d.]. In *Matsu-
    mae chō shi: Shiryōhen*, volume 2, edited by Matsumae chō shi henshūshitsu.
    Matsumae: Matsumae chō shi henshūshitsu, 1977.
[Okazaki Shuzō]. "Hokkaidō dekasegi gyofu hogo kabushiki gaisha kari teigi
    narabi ni sōritsu shui" [1904]. Kuroishi: Hokkaidō dekasegi gyofu hogo
    kabushiki gaisha. Hakodate Municipal Library.
"Ōsaka koemonoshō kumiai enkakushi" [1901]. In *Ōsaka keizai shiryō shūsei*,
    volume 5, edited by Ōsaka keizai shiryō shūsei kankō iinkai. Osaka: Ōsaka
    shōkō kaigisho, 1974.
Oshima kyōikukai, ed. "Hakodate shichō kannai chōson shi" [c. 1918], compiled
    and edited by Suzue Eiichi. *Matsumae han to Matsumae* 23–24 (February-
    March 1985): 68–84, 33–73.
Sakakura Genjirō. "Hokkai zuihitsu" [1739]. In *Hokumon sōsho*, volume 2,
    edited by Ōtomo Kisaku. Tokyo: Hokkō shobō, 1943–44.
"Shoyō tojikomi" [1861], Date-ke monjo. In *Matsumae chō shi: Shiryōhen*, vol-
    ume 3, edited by Matsumae chō shi henshūshitsu. Matsumae: Matsumae chō
    shi henshūshitsu, 1977.
"Tabibito aratamekata" [n.d.]. In *Nihon zaisei keizai shiryō*, volume 10, edited
    by Ōkurashō. Tokyo: Ōkurashō, 1925.
"Tateami sōdan torikiwame hikae" [1866], Sasanami-ke monjo. In *Esashi chō shi:
    Shiryōhen*, volume 2, edited by Esashi chō shi henshūshitsu. Esashi: Esashi
    chō, 1978.
Teikoku gikai kizokuin giji sokkiroku. 74 volumes. Tokyo: Tōkyō daigaku shup-
    pankai, 1979–85.
Tōkyō chihō shokugyō shōkai jimukyoku, ed. "Hokkaidō nishin gyogyō rōdō
    jijō" [1928]. In *Gyomin* (*Kindai minshū no kiroku*, volume 7), edited by
    Okamoto Tatsuaki. Tokyo: Shinjinbutsu ōraisha, 1978.
"Tsugaru ittō shi" [1731]. In *Shinpen Aomori ken sōsho*, volume 1, edited by
    Shinpen Aomori ken sōsho kankōkai. Tokyo: Rekishi toshosha, 1974.
Tsuji Seitarō. *Karafuto-tō kaihatsu ni kansuru seigan* [1907]. Resource Collec-
    tion for Northern Studies, Hokkaidō University Library.
Yoichi chō shi hensanshitsu, ed. *Yoichi onbasho mimawari nikki* [1859]. (*Yoichi
    chō shi shiryō sōsho*, volume 3.) Yoichi: Yoichi chō shi hensanshitsu, 1973.

Newspapers and Periodicals

Hokkai shinbun, Sapporo.
Hokkaidō shinbun, Sapporo.
Karafuto nichinichi shinbun, Toyohara.

Shokumin kōhō, Sapporo.

Yomiuri shinbun, Tokyo.

Other Sources

Anakura Moriya. "Dekasegi gyofu hogo kumiai no kaiso ni tsuite." *Hokuyō gyogyō* 1:4 (August 1940): 27–31.

———. "Kita Chishima gyogyō rōdō ni kansuru ichi kōsatsu." *Hokuyō gyogyō* 1:7 (November 1940): 15–34.

Aomori ken chihō shokugyō shōkai jimukyoku, ed. *Tōhoku chihō, Hokkaidō nō-, san-, gyoson shokugyō shōkai no mondai.* Aomori: Aomori ken chihō shokugyō shōkai jimukyoku, 1935.

Arai Eiji. *Kinsei Nihon gyosonshi no kenkyū.* Tokyo: Shinseisha, 1965.

———. *Kinsei no gyoson.* Tokyo: Yoshikawa kōbunkan, 1970.

Arano Yasunori. *Kinsei Nihon to higashi Ajia.* Tokyo: Tōkyō daigaku shuppankai, 1988.

Asakura Yūko. "Ezo ninshiki no keisei: Toku ni keiki to shite no jōhō o megutte." In *Kita kara no Nihonshi*, volume 2, edited by Hokkaidō, Tōhoku shi kenkyūkai. Tokyo: Sanseidō, 1990.

Asao Naohiro. *Sakoku.* (*Nihon no rekishi*, volume 17.) Tokyo: Shōgakukan, 1975.

———, ed. *Sekaishi no naka no kinsei.* (*Nihon no kinsei*, volume 1.) Tokyo: Chūō kōronsha, 1991.

Asari Masatoshi. "Hokuyō gyogyō ni okeru kōsen kani gyorō." *Matsumae han to Matsumae* 13–14 (March-September 1979): 81–108, 61–90.

———. "Hokuyō gyogyō to dekasegi rōdō." In *Hokkaidō no kenkyū*, volume 6, edited by Kuwabara Masato. Osaka: Seibundō, 1983.

Berg, Maxine, Pat Hudson, and Michael Sonenscher, eds. *Manufacture in Town and Country before the Factory.* Cambridge: Cambridge University Press, 1983.

Berque, Augustin. *La riziére et la banquise: Colonisation et changement culturel à Hokkaidô.* Paris: Publications Orientalistes de France, 1980.

Berry, Mary Elizabeth. *Hideyoshi.* Cambridge: Council on East Asian Studies, Harvard University, 1982.

Bix, Herbert P. "Leader of Peasant Rebellions: Miura Meisuke." In *Great Historical Figures of Japan*, edited by Murakami Hyoe and Thomas J. Harper. Tokyo: Japan Culture Institute, 1978.

———. "Miura Meisuke, or Peasant Rebellion under the Banner of 'Distress.'" *Bulletin of Concerned Asian Scholars* 10:2 (1978): 18–26.

———. *Peasant Protest in Japan, 1590–1884.* New Haven, Conn.: Yale University Press, 1986.

Blakiston, Thomas Wright. *Japan in Yezo.* Yokohama: Japan Gazette, 1883.

Bolitho, Harold. *Treasures among Men.* New Haven, Conn.: Yale University Press, 1974.

———. "The Tempō Crisis." In *The Cambridge History of Japan*, volume 5, edited by Marius B. Jansen. Cambridge: Cambridge University Press, 1989.

———. "Travelers' Tales: Three Eighteenth-Century Travel Journals." *Harvard Journal of Asiatic Studies* 50 (1990): 485–504.

Bowen, Roger. *Rebellion and Democracy in Meiji Japan.* Berkeley: University of California Press, 1980.

Braudel, Fernand. *The Structures of Everyday Life: The Limits of the Possible.* (*Civilization and Capitalism, 15th–18th Century,* volume 1.) New York: Harper & Row, 1979.

Chekhov, Anton. *The Island: A Journey to Sakhalin.* Translated by Luba and Michael Terpak. Westport, Conn.: Greenwood Press, 1977.

Coleman, D. C. "Proto-Industrialization: A Concept Too Many." *Economic History Review,* 2d series, 36 (1983): 435–48.

Craig, Albert. *Chōshū in the Meiji Restoration.* Cambridge: Harvard University Press, 1961.

Crawcour, E. Sydney. "Kawamura Zuiken: A Seventeenth Century Entrepreneur." *Transactions of the Asiatic Society of Japan,* 3rd series, 9 (1966): 1–23.

———. "The Tokugawa Period and Japan's Preparation for Modern Economic Growth." *Journal of Japanese Studies* 1:1 (Autumn 1974): 113–25.

———. "Economic Change in the Nineteenth Century." In *The Cambridge History of Japan,* volume 5, edited by Marius B. Jansen. Cambridge: Cambridge University Press, 1989.

Dobb, Maurice. *Studies in the Development of Capitalism.* New York: International Publishers, 1947.

Edmonds, Richard Louis. *Northern Frontiers of Qing China and Tokugawa Japan: A Comparative Study of Frontier Policy.* Chicago: Department of Geography, University of Chicago, 1985.

Eley, Geoff. "The Social History of Industrialization: 'Proto-Industry' and the Origins of Capitalism." *Economy and Society* 13 (1984): 519–39.

Emori Susumu. "Meiji kaitakuki Nemuro chihō gyogyō kōzō no shiteki tenkai." *Hokkaidō keizai shi kenkyū* 19 (1965): 23–47.

———. "Nemuro chihō ni okeru nishin sashiami seigan undō." *Atarashii dōshi* 27 (31 March 1968): 1–9.

———. *Hokkaidō kinseishi no kenkyū: Bakuhan taisei to Ezochi.* Sapporo: Hokkaidō shuppan kikaku sentā, 1982.

———. *Ainu no rekishi.* Tokyo: Sanseidō, 1987.

Esashi chō shi henshūshitsu, ed. *Esashi chō shi.* 6 volumes. Esashi: Esashi chō, 1978–81.

Flershem, Robert G. "Some Aspects of Japan Sea Trade in the Tokugawa Period." *Journal of Asian Studies* 23:3 (May 1964): 405–16.

Fox-Genovese, Elizabeth, and Eugene D. Genovese. *Fruits of Merchant Capital: Slavery and Bourgeois Property in the Rise and Expansion of Capitalism.* New York: Oxford University Press, 1983.

Fruin, W. Mark. *Kikkoman: Company, Clan, and Community.* Cambridge: Council on East Asian Studies, Harvard University, 1983.

Fukaya Katsumi, Kitajima Manji, and Katō Eiichi, eds. *Bakuhansei kokka to iiki, ikoku.* Tokyo: Azekura shobō, 1989.

Furuta Ryōichi. *Kawamura Zuiken.* Tokyo: Yoshikawa kōbunkan, 1988.

Garon, Sheldon. *The State and Labor in Modern Japan.* Berkeley: University of California Press, 1987.

Gluck, Carol. *Japan's Modern Myths.* Princeton: Princeton University Press, 1985.

Golovnin, Vasalii. *Memoirs of a Captivity in Japan during the Years 1811, 1812, and 1813; with Observations on the Country and the People.* 2d edition. 3 volumes. London: Henry Colburn & Co., 1824.

Gordon, Andrew. *The Evolution of Labor Relations in Japan: Heavy Industry, 1853–1955.* Cambridge: Council on East Asian Studies, Harvard University, 1985.

———. "The Crowd and Politics in Imperial Japan: Tokyo, 1905–1918." *Past and Present* 121 (1988): 141–70.

———. *Labor and Imperial Democracy in Prewar Japan.* Berkeley: University of California Press, 1991.

Gullickson, Gay L. *Spinners and Weavers of Auffay: Rural Industry and the Sexual Division of Labor in a French Village, 1750–1850.* Cambridge: Cambridge University Press, 1986.

Gutmann, Myron. *Toward the Modern Economy: Early Industry in Europe.* Philadelphia: Temple University Press, 1988.

Habara Yūkichi. *Nihon gyogyō keizai shi.* 4 volumes. Tokyo: Iwanami shoten, 1952–55.

Hall, John W. *Tanuma Okitsugu, 1719–1788: The Forerunner of Modern Japan.* Cambridge: Harvard University Press, 1955.

Hamamasu mura [Masuda Ryō]. "Hamamasu enkakushi" [1900]. Mimeograph, Hokkaidō Prefectural Library.

Hammel, E. A. "A Glimpse into the Demography of the Ainu." *American Anthropologist* 90:1 (March 1988): 25–41.

Hane, Mikiso. *Peasants, Outcastes, and Rebels: The Underside of Modern Japan.* New York: Pantheon, 1982.

Hanley, Susan B. "A High Standard of Living in Nineteenth-Century Japan: Fact or Fantasy?" *Journal of Economic History* 43 (1983): 183–92.

———, and Kozo Yamamura. *Economic and Demographic Change in Preindustrial Japan, 1600–1868.* Princeton: Princeton University Press, 1977.

Harootunian, Harry. "Ideology as Conflict." In *Conflict in Modern Japanese History: The Neglected Tradition,* edited by Tetsuo Najita and J. Victor Koschmann. Princeton: Princeton University Press, 1982.

Harrison, John A. *Japan's Northern Frontier.* Gainesville: University of Florida Press, 1953.

Hasegawa Shinzō. "Kinsei kōki ni okeru Ezochi-san gyohi no Kantō nōson e no dōnyū." *Matsumae han to Matsumae* 12 (July 1978): 14–26.

Hasegawa Toshiyuki. "Bakuhan taiseika ni okeru Ezochi dekasegi o meguru shomondai: Shimokita hantō nōmin no dekasegi o chūshin to shite." *Usori* 15 (1978): 20–47.

Hashimoto Takanao. "Esashi hamagoya no mukashi banashi." *Ezo ōrai* 4 (August 1931): 124–25.

Hatanaka Toshiyuki. "Kinsei 'senmin' mibunron no kadai." In *Sōten: Nihon no rekishi,* volume 5, edited by Aoki Michio and Hosaka Satoru. Tokyo: Shinjinbutsu ōraisha, 1991.

Hauser, William B. *Economic Institutional Change in Tokugawa Japan: Ōsaka and the Kinai Cotton Trade.* Cambridge: Cambridge University Press, 1974.

Hayami Akira. "Kinsei Nihon no keizai hatten to 'Industrious Revolution.'" In *Tokugawa shakai kara no tenbō: Hatten, kōzō, kokusai kankei,* edited by

Hayami Akira, Saitō Osamu, and Sugiyama Shin'ya. Tokyo: Dōbunkan, 1989.

Henderson, Dan Fenno. *Village "Contracts" in Tokugawa Japan.* Seattle: University of Washington Press, 1975.

Hilton, Rodney. "Introduction." In *The Transition from Feudalism to Capitalism,* edited by Rodney Hilton. London: Verso Editions, 1978.

Hodgson, C. Pemberton. *A Residence at Nagasaki and Hakodate in 1859–1860, with an Account of Japan Generally.* London: Richard Bentley, 1861.

Hokkaidō chō, ed. *Hokkaidō shi.* Sapporo: Hokkaidō chō, 1918.

———, ed. *Shinsen Hokkaidō shi.* 7 volumes. Sapporo: Hokkaidō chō, 1936–37.

Hokkaidō chō gakumubu shokugyōka, ed. *Kita Chishima gyogyō narabi ni sono rōdō jijō ron.* N.p.: 1938.

Hokkaidō chō naimubu suisanka, ed. *Hokkaidō suisan yosatsu chōsa hōkoku.* Tokyo: Hokkaidō chō naimubu suisanka, 1892.

Hokkaidō suisanbu gyogyō chōseika and Hokkaidō gyogyō seido kaikaku kinen jigyō kyōkai, eds. *Hokkaidō gyogyō shi.* Nagano: Hokkaidō suisanbu gyogyō chōseika and Hokkaidō gyogyō seido kaikaku kinen jigyō kyōkai, 1957.

Hokusui kyōkai, ed. *Hokkaidō gyogyō shikō.* 1890. Reprint of 1935 edition, Tokyo: Kokusho kankōkai, 1977.

Hōri Miyashizu. *Zushū Uchiura gyomin shiryō no kenkyū: Meiji shonen ni okeru "kyūhei torinaoshi" undō to sono rekishiteki igi.* Tokyo: Rinjinsha, 1966.

Hoston, Germaine A. *Marxism and the Crisis of Development in Prewar Japan.* Princeton: Princeton University Press, 1986.

Howell, David L. "Hokkaidō ni okeru gyogyō gijutsu to gyoson no keisei katei: Bakumatsuki-Meiji chūki o chūshin ni." *Hokudai shigaku* 28 (1988): 30–40.

———. "Hard Times in the Kantō: Economic Change and Village Life in Late Tokugawa Japan." *Modern Asian Studies* 23 (1989): 349–71.

———. "Ainu Ethnicity and the Boundaries of the Early Modern Japanese State." *Past and Present,* 142 (1994): 69–93.

Huang, Philip C. C. *The Peasant Economy and Social Change in North China.* Stanford: Stanford University Press, 1985.

Ikeda Yoshinaga. "Hokuyō gyogyō rōmu to eisei jōkyō ni tsuite: Shu to shite kita Chishima ni okeru." *Hokuyō gyogyō* 1:2 (June 1940): 14–27.

Imada Mitsuo. *Nishin bunka shi: Maboroshi no nishin kamuicheppu.* Sapporo: Kyōdō bunkasha, 1987.

Irokawa Daikichi. *The Culture of the Meiji Period.* Translation edited by Marius B. Jansen. Princeton: Princeton University Press, 1985.

Ishibashi Gen. *Hamamasu son shi.* Hamamasu: Hamamasu mura, 1980.

Ishikawa Hiroshi. "Wajinchi (Matsumaechi) ni okeru 'basho' to gyogyōken: Esashi chō shozai shiryō o chūshin to shite." *Atarashii dōshi* 44–45 (15 March–31 March 1971): 1–12, 1–8.

Iwamoto Yoshiteru. *Kinsei gyoson kyōdōtai no hensen katei: Shōhin keizai no shinten to sonraku kyōdōtai.* Tokyo: Ochanomizu shobō, 1977.

Jansen, Marius B., and Gilbert Rozman, eds. *Japan in Transition: From Tokugawa to Meiji.* Princeton: Princeton University Press, 1986.

Johnson, Chalmers. *MITI and the Japanese Miracle: The Growth of Industrial Policy, 1925–1975.* Stanford: Stanford University Press, 1982.

Jones, Eric L. *Growth Recurring: Economic Change in World History.* Oxford: Clarendon Press, 1988.

Kaiho Mineo. "Hokkaidō ni okeru hōkensei shodankai settei e no ichi shiron." *Chihōshi kenkyū* 119 (October 1972): 45–59.

———. *Nihon hoppōshi no ronri.* Tokyo: Yūzankaku, 1974.

———. *Bakuhansei kokka to Hokkaidō.* Tokyo: San'ichi shobō, 1978.

———. *Kinsei no Hokkaidō.* Tokyo: Kyōikusha, 1979.

———. "Hakodate bugyō." In *Hokkaidō daihyakka jiten*, volume 2, edited by Hokkaidō shinbunsha. Sapporo: Hokkaidō shinbunsha, 1981.

———, ed. *Chūsei Ezo shiryō.* Tokyo: San'ichi shobō, 1983.

———. *Kinsei Ezochi seiritsu shi no kenkyū.* Tokyo: San'ichi shobō, 1984.

———. *Rettō hoppōshi kenkyū nōto.* Sapporo: Hokkaidō shuppan kikaku sentā, 1986.

———. *Chūsei no Ezochi.* Tokyo: Yoshikawa kōbunkan, 1987.

———. "Hoppō kōeki to chūsei Ezo shakai." In *Nihonkai to hokkoku bunka* (*Umi to rettō bunka*, volume 1), edited by Amino Yoshihiko. Tokyo: Shōgakukan, 1990.

Kaiho Yōko. *Kindai hoppōshi: Ainu minzoku to josei to.* Tokyo: San'ichi shobō, 1992.

Kaitakushi, ed. *Kaitakushi fureiroku.* 5 volumes. N.p., 1880–83.

———, ed. *Hokkaidō shi.* Tokyo: Ōkurashō, 1884.

———, ed. "Tōhoku shokō hōkokusho," 1880. In *Meiji zenki sangyō hattatsu shi shiryō*, volume 2, edited by Meiji bunken shiryō kankōkai. Tokyo: Meiji bunken shiryō kankōkai, 1959.

Kalland, Arne. *Shingū: A Study of a Japanese Fishing Community.* London and Malmö: Curzon Press, 1981.

———. "A Credit Institution in Tokugawa Japan: The Ura-tamegin Fund of Chikuzen Province." In *Europe Interprets Japan*, edited by Gordon Daniels. Tenterden, Kent, England: Paul Norbury Publications, 1984.

———. "Sea Tenure in Tokugawa Japan: The Case of the Fukuoka Domain." In *Maritime Institutions in the Western Pacific* (*Senri Ethnological Studies*, volume 17), edited by Kenneth Ruddle and Tomoya Akimichi. Osaka: National Museum of Ethnology, 1984.

———. "Pre-modern Whaling in Northern Kyūshū." In *Silkworms, Oil, and Chips . . .* (Proceedings of the Economics and Economic History Section of the Fourth International Conference on Japanese Studies, Paris, September 1985), edited by Erich Pauer. Bonn, 1986.

———. "In Search of the Abalone: The History of the *Ama* in Northern Kyūshū." In *Seinan chiiki no shiteki tenkai*, volume 1, edited by Seinan chiikishi kenkyūkai. Tokyo: Shibunkaku, 1988.

Kamiya Nobuyuki. "Nihon kinsei no tōitsu to Dattan." In *Nihon zenkindai no kokka to taigai kankei*, edited by Tanaka Takeo. Tokyo: Yoshikawa kōbunkan, 1987.

Kanno Watarō. *Ōmi shōnin no kenkyū.* Tokyo: Yūhikaku, 1941.

Karafuto chō, ed. *Karafuto yōran.* 1907 edition. Tokyo: Ryūbunkan, 1908.

———, ed. *Karafuto chōji ippan.* 1910 edition. Toyohara: Karafuto chō, 1911.

————, ed. *Karafuto yōran*. 1913 edition. Toyohara: Karafuto chō, 1914.

————, ed. *Karafuto chōji ippan*. 1915 edition. Toyohara: Karafuto chō, 1916.

————, ed. *Daiikkai kokusei chōsa hōkoku*. Toyohara: Karafuto chō, 1923.

————, ed. *Karafuto chō shisei sanjūnen shi*. Toyohara: Karafuto chō, 1936.

Karafuto chō chōkan kanbō, ed. *Karafuto hōrei ruiju*. Toyohara: Karafuto chō, 1909.

Karafuto gyosei no enkaku. c. 1921. Mimeograph, Hokkaidō Prefectural Library.

Karafuto tateami gyogyō suisan kumiai rengōkai, ed. *Hoppō gyogyō no shiori*. Tokyo: Karafuto tateami gyogyō suisan kumiai rengōkai, 1912.

————, ed. *Taishō sannen kaisei gyogyōryō narabi ni saikin sankanen shūkaku-daka*. N.p., 1915.

————, ed. *Kaisei Karafuto gyogyō hōki*. Hakodate: Karafuto tateami gyogyō suisan kumiai rengōkai, 1917.

Karafuto teichi gyogyō suisan kumiai, ed. *Karafuto to gyogyō*. Toyohara: Karafuto teichi gyogyō suisan kumiai, 1931.

Katada Seishi. *Hokkaidō naikoku bōeki shi no kenkyū*. (*Hokkaidō chihōshi kenkyū*, special supplement 11.) Sapporo: Hokkaidō chihōshi kenkyūkai, 1965.

Katsura Gengo. *Iwanai Furuu nigun shi*. Iwanai: Katsura Gengo, 1894.

Kawamura Suguru and Miura Shigekazu. "Kujūkurihama jibikiami gyogyō no hatten to kōzō." In *Zairai gijutsu no hatten to kinsei shakai* (*Gijutsu no shakai shi*, volume 2), edited by Sasaki Junnosuke. Tokyo: Yūhikaku, 1983.

Kawana Noboru. *Kashi ni ikiru hitobito: Tonegawa suiun no shakai shi*. Tokyo: Heibonsha, 1982.

Kawaoka Takeharu. *Umi no tami: Gyoson no rekishi to minzoku*. Tokyo: Heibonsha, 1987.

Keene, Donald. *The Japanese Discovery of Europe, 1720–1830*. Revised edition. Stanford: Stanford University Press, 1969.

Kelly, William W. *Deference and Defiance in Nineteenth-Century Japan*. Princeton: Princeton University Press, 1985.

Kikuchi Isao. "Bakuhanseika Hokkaidō dekasegi, ijū no tenkai shojōken to dōtai." In *Bakuhansei kara kindai e*, edited by Hayashi Hideo and Yamada Shōji. Tokyo: Kashiwa shobō, 1979.

————. "Gaiatsu to dōkashugi." In *Hokkaidō no kenkyū*, volume 4, edited by Kaiho Mineo. Osaka: Seibundō, 1983.

————. "Kinsei Ōu shakai no 'Ezo' mondai." In *Hokkaidō no kenkyū*, volume 4, edited by Kaiho Mineo. Osaka: Seibundō, 1983.

————. *Bakuhan taisei to Ezochi*. Tokyo: Yūzankaku, 1984.

————. *Hoppōshi no naka no kinsei Nihon*. Tokyo: Azekura shobō, 1991.

Kitajima Masamoto. "Kan'ei-ki no rekishiteki ichi." In *Bakuhansei kokka seiritsu katei no kenkyū*, edited by Kitajima Masamoto. Tokyo: Yoshikawa kōbunkan, 1978.

Kobayashi Masato. "Meiji nijūnendai ni okeru Matsumae shōnin no dōkō." *Matsumae han to Matsumae* 13 (March 1979): 22–34.

Kobayashi Takiji. *Kani kōsen*. 1929. Tokyo: Iwanami shoten, 1967.

————. *"The Factory Ship" and "The Absentee Landlord."* Translated by Frank

Motofuji. Tokyo: University of Tokyo Press; Seattle: University of Washington Press, 1973.

Kodama Mari. "Ainu minzoku no ifuku to fukushokuhin." In *Hokkaidō no kenkyū*, volume 7, edited by Yajima Satoshi. Osaka: Seibundō, 1985.

Kon Zensaku. "Nishinryō oboegaki." *Hokkaidō no bunka* 4 (September 1963): 24–42.

Koshizaki Sōichi. "Ofuyu jiken ni tsuite." *Hokkaidō chihōshi kenkyū* 79 (November 1970): 6–11.

Kriedte, Peter, Hans Medick, and Jürgen Schlumbohm. *Industrialization before Industrialization*. Cambridge: Cambridge University Press; Paris: Editions de la Maison des Sciences de l'Homme, 1981.

———. "Proto-Industrialization on Test with the Guild of Historians: Response to Some Critics." Translated by Leena Turner. *Economy and Society* 15 (1986): 254–72.

Kudō Mutsuo. "Tsugaru Fukaura-kō to bakumatsu ni okeru kaisen no nyūshin jōkyō." *Kaijishi kenkyū* 28 (April 1977): 26–42.

Kuwabara Masato, ed. "*Hakodate shinbun* keisai no Matsumae chō kankei kiji." *Matsumae han to Matsumae* 26, 28 (March 1986, March 1987): 44–87, 68–123.

———, ed. "Kyōdo ni ikiru." *Matsumae han to Matsumae* 27 (February 1987): entire issue.

Kyōgoku Takayoshi, Nomura Masuzō, and Tōdō Terumaru. *Karafuto no kenkyū*. Volume 1. Tokyo: Yamada Saburō, 1914.

Landor, A. H. Savage. *Alone with the Hairy Ainu: Or, 3,800 Miles on a Pack Saddle in Yezo and a Cruise to the Kurile Islands*. London: John Murray, 1893. Reprint, New York: Johnson Reprint Company, 1970.

Lensen, George Alexander. *The Russian Push toward Japan*. Princeton: Princeton University Press, 1959.

Leupp, Gary P. "'One Drink from a Gourd': Servants, Shophands, and Laborers in the Cities of Tokugawa Japan." Ph.D. dissertation, University of Michigan, 1989.

———. *Servants, Shophands, and Laborers in the Cities of Tokugawa Japan*. Princeton: Princeton University Press, 1992.

Lewis, Michael. *Rioters and Citizens: Mass Protest in Imperial Japan*. Berkeley: University of California Press, 1990.

McEvoy, Arthur F. *The Fisherman's Problem: Ecology and Law in the California Fisheries, 1850–1980*. Cambridge: Cambridge University Press, 1986.

Maeno Ryūshin. *Kitamaebune no jidai: Kinsei igo no Nihonkai kaiunshi*. Tokyo: Kyōikusha, 1979.

Matsumae chō shi henshūshitsu, ed. *Matsumae chō shi*. 6 volumes. Matsumae: Matsumae chō shi henshūshitsu, 1974–88.

Matsumura Chōta. *Akita no dekasegi: Gyominhen*. 3rd edition. Akita: Akita bunka shuppansha, 1978.

Matsuzaki Iwaho. *Kaminokuni son shi*. Kaminokuni: Kaminokuni murayakuba, 1956.

Mendels, Franklin. "Proto-Industrialization: The First Phase of the Industrialization Process." *Journal of Economic History* 32 (1972): 241–61.

Mino Norio. "Nishin gyogyō to shinrin hakai: Furubira chō ni okeru rei." *Hokkaidō kaitaku kinenkan chōsa hōkoku* 26 (1987): 9–12.

Mintz, Sidney W. *Sweetness and Power: The Place of Sugar in Modern History.* New York: Viking Press, 1985.

Miyamoto Mataji, ed. *Kinsei Ōsaka no bukka to rishi.* Osaka: Ōsaka daigaku kinsei bukka shi kenkyūkai, 1963.

———. "'Ōsaka Hokkai-san niuke ton'ya kumiai enkakushi' no kaisetsu." In *Ōsaka keizai shiryō shūsei*, volume 10, edited by Ōsaka keizai shiryō shūsei kankō iinkai. Osaka: Ōsaka shōkō kaigisho, 1977.

Miyamoto Matao and Uemura Masahiro. "Tokugawa keizai no junkan kōzō." In *Keizai shakai no seiritsu (Nihon keizai shi*, volume 1), edited by Hayami Akira and Miyamoto Matao. Tokyo: Iwanami shoten, 1988.

Mizuhara Masamichi. "Meiji zenki ni okeru ryūtsū kikō no saihen: Ōmi Hachiman no hiryōshō kumiai no baai." *Shiga daigaku keizaigakubu fuzoku shiryōkan kenkyū kiyō* 13 (March 1980): 29–84.

———. "Meiji zenki ryūtsū kikō no saihen katei ni okeru ichirei: Shiga ken Ōmi Hachiman no Nakaichi Shōkai ni tsuite." *Shiga daigaku keizaigakubu fuzoku shiryōkan kenkyū kiyō* 15 (March 1982): 45–94.

Mori Kahei. *Nanbu han hyakushō ikki no kenkyū. (Mori Kahei chosakushū*, volume 7.) 1935. Tokyo: Hōsei daigaku shuppan kyoku, 1974.

Mori Shōgo. *Bezaisen ōkanki: Hokkaidō, Iwanai o hiraita hitobito.* Tokyo: Nihon keizai hyōronsha, 1983.

Moriya Yoshimi. "Bakuhan kōshin han no keizai jōkyō: Morioka han bakumatsu hyakushō ikki no yobiteki kōsatsu no tame ni." *Nihonshi kenkyū* 150–51 (1975): 184–202.

———. "Hakodate sanbutsu kaisho to 'moto shiire shihō.'" In *Hokkaidō no kenkyū*, volume 4, edited by Kaiho Mineo. Osaka: Seibundō, 1983.

———. "Bakufu no Ezochi seisaku to zaichi no dōkō." *Tōhoku gakuin daigaku Tōhoku bunka kenkyūjo kiyō* 16 (November 1984): 131–58.

Moriyama, Alan Takeo. *Imingaisha: Japanese Emigration Companies and Hawaii, 1894–1908.* Honolulu: University of Hawaii Press, 1985.

Moriyama Tsuneo. "Tsushima han." In *Nagasaki ken shi: Hansei hen*, edited by Nagasaki ken shi henshū iinkai. Tokyo: Yoshikawa kōbunkan, 1973.

Murai Shōsuke. "Kenmu, Muromachi seiken to higashi Ajia." In *Kōza Nihon rekishi*, volume 4, edited by Rekishigaku kenkyūkai and Nihonshi kenkyūkai. Tokyo: Tōkyō daigaku shuppankai, 1985.

———. *Ajia no naka no chūsei Nihon.* Tokyo: Azekura shobō, 1988.

Murao Motonaga. *Hokkaidō gyogyō shiyō.* Tokyo: Murao Motonaga, 1897.

Nagai Hideo. "Iwayuru 'kangoku beya' rōdō no shakaiteki haikei." *Hokkaidō musashi joshi tanki daigaku kiyō* 24 (1992): 1–20.

Najita, Tetsuo. *Visions of Virtue: The Kaitokudō Merchant Academy in Tokugawa Japan.* Chicago: University of Chicago Press, 1987.

———, and J. Victor Koschmann, eds. *Conflict in Modern Japanese History: The Neglected Tradition.* Princeton: Princeton University Press, 1982.

Nakai Akira. "Hokkaidō ni okeru gyogyō seido no hensen: Kindaiteki gyogyōken no seiritsu to tenkai." *Atarashii dōshi* 3:1 (January 1965): 1–6.

Nakame Satoru. *Dojin kyōka ron.* Tokyo: Iwanami shoten, 1918.

Namikawa Kenji. "Kinsei zenki ni okeru Matsumae, Ezochi to kita Tōhoku." *Matsumae han to Matsumae* 24 (March 1985): 1–16.

———. *Kinsei Nihon to hoppō shakai.* Tokyo: Sanseidō, 1992.

Narumi Kentarō. "Shimokita dekasegi shi kō." *Usori* 13 (1976): 51–59.

———. "Ezochi, Hokkaidō to Shimokita hantō no kōryūshi kō." In *Ezochi, Hokkaidō: Rekishi to seikatsu,* edited by Chihōshi kenkyū kyōgikai. Tokyo: Yūzankaku, 1981.

Nihon gakushiin, ed. *Meijizen Nihon gyogyō gijutsushi.* Tokyo: Nihon gakujutsu shinkōkai, 1959.

Ninohei Tokuo. *Gyogyō kōzō no shiteki tenkai.* Tokyo: Ochanomizu shobō, 1962.

———. *Meiji gyogyō kaitaku shi.* Tokyo: Heibonsha, 1981.

Nishikawa, Shunsaku. "Grain Consumption: The Case of Chōshū." In *Japan in Transition: From Tokugawa to Meiji,* edited by Marius B. Jansen and Gilbert Rozman. Princeton: Princeton University Press, 1986.

Norman, E. H. *Origins of the Modern Japanese State: Selected Writings of E. H. Norman,* edited by John W. Dower. New York: Pantheon, 1975.

Ohkawa, Kazushi, and Henry Rosovsky. "A Century of Economic Growth." In *The State and Economic Enterprise in Japan: Essays in the Political Economy of Growth,* edited by William W. Lockwood. Princeton: Princeton University Press, 1965.

Ōi Haruo. "'Shakushain no ran (Kanbun 9-nen Ezo no ran)' no saikentō." *Hoppō bunka kenkyū* 21 (1992): 1–66.

Ōishi Naomasa. "Kita no bushidan: Andō shi." In *Nihonkai to hokkoku bunka (Umi to rettō bunka,* volume 1), edited by Amino Yoshihiko. Tokyo: Shōgakukan, 1990.

Okada Yoshitane, ed. *Karafuto-tō shokisoku ruijū.* Wakkanai: Karafuto shinbunsha, 1906.

Okamoto Nobuo. *Nichiro Gyogyō keiei shi.* Tokyo: Suisansha, 1971.

Ōkurashō, ed. *Kaitakushi jigyō hōkoku furoku: Furei ruiju.* 2 volumes. Tokyo: Ōkurashō, 1875.

Ōta Ryū. *Ainu kakumei ron: Yūkara sekai e no "taikyaku."* Tokyo: Ainu moshiri jōhōbu, 1973.

Ōtaka Kentarō and Nishikawa Yoshihiro. "Karafuto no gyogyō chōsa: Karafuto no suisan." In *Oshoro-maru Shōwa hachinendo renshū kōkai gyogyō chōsa hōkokusho,* edited by Hokkaidō teikoku daigaku suisan senmonbu gyorōka. 1933. Mimeograph, Resource Collection for Northern Studies, Hokkaidō University Library.

Perlin, Frank. "Scrutinizing Which Moment?" *Economy and Society* 14 (1985): 374–98.

Philippi, Donald L., trans. and ed. *Songs of Gods, Songs of Humans: The Epic Tradition of the Ainu.* Princeton: Princeton University Press; Tokyo: University of Tokyo Press, 1979.

Pratt, Edward E. "Proto-Industry and Mechanized Production in Three Raw Silk Regions." Paper delivered at the 43rd annual meeting of the Association for Asian Studies, New Orleans, 1991.

———. "Village Elites in Tokugawa Japan: The Economic Foundations of the *Gōnō.*" Ph.D. dissertation, University of Virginia, 1991.

Roberts, Luke S. "The Merchant Origins of National Prosperity Thought in Eighteenth Century Tosa." Ph.D. dissertation, Princeton University, 1991.

Rumoi chō, ed. *Rumoi chō shi.* Rumoi: Rumoi chō, 1945.

Rumoi suisan kumiai, ed. "Rumoi gyogyō enkakushi." c. 1913. Mimeograph, Resource Collection for Northern Studies, Hokkaidō University Library.

Saga Rentarō [Nagai Kenzō]. *"Kanritsu" Karafuto chūgakkō to Natsume Sōseki.* Sapporo: Minami Karafuto mondai kenkyūjo, 1987.

Saitō Jōsaku. *Isoya son shi.* Sapporo: Saitō Jōsaku, 1981.

Saitō Osamu. "Population and the Peasant Family Economy in Proto-Industrial Japan." *Journal of Family History* 8 (1983): 30–54.

———. *Puroto-kōgyōka no jidai.* Tokyo: Hyōronsha. 1985.

———. "The Rural Economy: Commercial Agriculture, By-Employment, and Wage Work." In *Japan in Transition: From Tokugawa to Meiji,* edited by Marius B. Jansen and Gilbert Rozman. Princeton: Princeton University Press, 1986.

Sapporo kyōdo o horu kai, ed. *Sengo mo tsuzuita takobeya rōdō: Makomanai Beigun kichi kensetsu kōji.* Sapporo: Sapporo kyōdo o horu kai, 1987.

Sasahara Masao. "Kinsei Kishū ni okeru takoku gyogyō no henshitsu." *Chihōshi kenkyū* 168 (December 1980): 31–54.

Sasazawa Royō. *Shimokita hantō shi.* 3rd revised edition. Ōhata: Shimokita kyōdokai, 1962.

Satō Kin'yū. *Hokuyō no dekasegi: Hokuhen gyoba ni ikita kosaku nōmin no kindaishi.* Akita: Akita bunka shuppansha, 1985.

Satō Suguru. *Oguma Kōichirō den.* Hakodate: Hakodate shōkō kaigisho, 1958.

Satō Yūshō. "Shimokita nōgyomin no Ezochi dekasegi ni tsuite." In *Hokkaidō no kenkyū,* volume 3, edited by Kaiho Mineo. Osaka: Seibundō, 1982.

———. "Ezochi bakuryōka seisaku no igi." In *Hokkaidō no kenkyū,* volume 4, edited by Kaiho Mineo. Osaka: Seibundō, 1983.

Scheiner, Irwin. "The Mindful Peasant: Sketches for a Study of Rebellion." *Journal of Asian Studies* 32 (1973): 579–91.

———. "Benevolent Lords and Honorable Peasants: Rebellion and Peasant Consciousness in Tokugawa Japan." In *Japanese Thought in the Tokugawa Period, 1600–1868,* edited by Tetsuo Najita and Irwin Scheiner. Chicago: University of Chicago Press, 1978.

Scott, James C. *The Moral Economy of the Peasant: Rebellion and Subsistence in Southeast Asia.* New Haven, Conn.: Yale University Press, 1976.

Seki Hideshi. "Bakumatsu ni okeru Shōnai han no Rumoi chihō keiei o meguru shomondai (1)." *Hokkaidō chihōshi kenkyū* 90 (February 1973): 87–101.

———. "Imin to chiiki shakai no seiritsu: Tomamae chihō ni okeru gyogyō imin, dekasegi no dōkō to gyoson no seiritsu katei." In *Hokkaidō no kenkyū,* volume 5, edited by Seki Hideshi. Osaka: Seibundō, 1983.

———. "Ritō shakai no keisei katei ni tsuite (1): Bunka nenkan-Meiji shoki ni okeru Rishiri-tō no gyogyō to gyomin no dōkō." *Hokkaidō kaitaku kinenkan chōsa hōkoku* 23 (1984): 7–16.

———. "Ritō shakai no keisei katei ni tsuite (2): Meiji shoki-Taishō chūki ni okeru Rishiri-tō Oniwaki mura o chūshin ni." *Hokkaidō kaitaku kinenkan chōsa hōkoku* 24 (1985): 3–20.

Shinbo Hiroshi. *Kinsei no bukka to keizai hatten*. Tokyo: Tōyō keizai shinpōsha, 1978.

——— and Hasegawa Akira. "Shōhin seisan, ryūtsū no dainamikkusu." In *Keizai shakai no seiritsu* (*Nihon keizai shi*, volume 1), edited by Hayami Akira and Miyamoto Matao. Tokyo: Iwanami shoten, 1988.

Shin Tsushima-tō shi henshū iinkai, ed. *Shin Tsushima-tō shi*. Izuhara: Shin Tsushima-tō shi henshū iinkai, 1964.

Shin'ya Gyō. *Ainu minzoku teikō shi*. Revised edition. Tokyo: San'ichi shobō, 1977.

"Shiokoshi mura." In *Akita ken no chimei* (*Nihon rekishi chimei taikei*, volume 5), edited by Imamura Yoshitaka. Tokyo: Heibonsha, 1980.

Shirayama Tomomasa. "Ezochi amikiri sōdō shimatsu: Kinsei nishin ami hattatsu shi sobyō." *Nihon rekishi* 257 (October 1969): 104–8.

———. *Matsumae Ezochi basho ukeoi seido no kenkyū*. Revised edition. Tokyo: Gannandō shoten, 1971.

Sider, Gerald M. *Culture and Class in Anthropology and History: A Newfoundland Illustration*. Cambridge: Cambridge University Press; Paris: Editions de la Maison des Sciences de l'Homme, 1986.

Smethurst, Richard. *Agricultural Development and Tenancy Disputes in Japan, 1870–1940*. Princeton: Princeton University Press, 1986.

Smith, Thomas C. *The Agrarian Origins of Modern Japan*. Stanford: Stanford University Press, 1959.

———. "Farm Family By-Employments in Preindustrial Japan." *Journal of Economic History* 29 (1969): 687–715.

———. "Pre-modern Economic Growth: Japan and the West." *Past and Present* 60 (1973): 127–60.

———. "Peasant Time and Factory Time in Japan." *Past and Present* 111 (1986): 165–97.

———. *Native Sources of Japanese Industrialization, 1750–1920*. Berkeley: University of California Press, 1988.

Stephan, John J. "Ezo under the Tokugawa *Bakufu*, 1799–1821: An Aspect of Japan's Frontier History." Ph.D. dissertation, University of London, 1969.

———. *Sakhalin: A History*. Oxford: Clarendon Press, 1971.

———. *The Kuril Islands*. Oxford: Clarendon Press, 1974.

Sugimoto Ken. *Karafuto: Kaerazaru shima*. Tokyo: TBS-Buritanika, 1979.

Sugimoto Zennosuke. *Karafuto gyosei kaikaku enkakushi*. Maoka: Karafuto gyosei kaikaku enkakushi kankōkai, 1935.

Suzue Eiichi. "Kaisan kanba chiso sōtei kankei monjo: Kaidai." In *Matsumae chō shi: Shiryōhen*, volume 4, edited by Matsumae chō shi henshūshitsu. Matsumae: Matsumae chō shi henshūshitsu, 1980.

———. *Hokkaidō chōson seidoshi no kenkyū*. Sapporo: Hokkaidō daigaku tosho kankōkai, 1985.

Suzuki Takahiro. "Matsumae ryōmin no fukuryō undō." *Matsumae han to Matsumae* 7 (March 1975): 15–34.

———. "Bunkatsu shihaika no nishi Ezochi." In *Hokkaidō no kenkyū*, volume 4, edited by Kaiho Mineo. Osaka: Seibundō, 1983.

Suzuki Tayoji. *Karafuto suisan dantai taikan*. Ōdomari: Karafuto suisansha, 1935.

Tabata Hiroshi. "Meiji shoki no gyogyō seido ni tsuite: Gyobamochi seido no kōsatsu." *Atarashii dōshi* 41 (25 August 1970): 1–15.

———. "Bakufu chokkatsu jidai." In *Hokkaidō daihyakka jiten*, volume 2, edited by Hokkaidō shinbunsha. Sapporo: Hokkaidō shinbunsha, 1981.

———. "Basho ukeoi seido hōkaiki ni okeru ukeoinin shihon no katsudō: Nishikawa-ke monjo no bunseki." In *Hokkaidō no kenkyū*, volume 3, edited by Kaiho Mineo. Osaka: Seibundō, 1982.

———. "'Fukuyama, Esashi sōdō' no kenkyū." In *Hokkaidō no kenkyū*, volume 5, edited by Seki Hideshi. Osaka: Seibundō, 1983.

Taira, Koji. *Economic Development and the Labor Market in Japan*. New York: Columbia University Press, 1970.

Tajima Yoshiya. "Bakumatsuki 'basho' ukeoiseika ni okeru gyomin no sonzai keitai: Nishi Ezochi Utasutsu Isoya ryōbasho no baai." *Shakai keizai shigaku* 46:3 (1980): 51–79.

———. "Kinsei kōki gyokaku nishin no shūka katei: Nishi Ezochi Yoichi basho o rei to shite." *Rekishi to minzoku: Kanagawa daigaku Nihon jōmin bunka kenkyūjo ronshū* 1 (1986): 161–203.

———. "Kita ni mukatta Kishū shōnin: Suhara Kakubei-ke no jiseki." In *Nihonkai to hokkoku bunka* (*Umi to rettō bunka*, volume 1), edited by Amino Yoshihiko. Tokyo: Shōgakukan, 1990.

———. "Kinsei Kishū gyohō no tenkai." In *Seisan no gijutsu* (*Nihon no kinsei*, volume 4), edited by Hayama Teisaku. Tokyo: Chūō kōronsha, 1992.

Takahata Sen'ichi. *Otaru-kō shi*. Takikawa: Takahata Sen'ichi, 1899.

Takakura Shin'ichirō. *Hokkaidō takushoku shi*. Sapporo: Hakuba shoin, 1947.

———. *Ainu seisakushi*. Revised edition. Tokyo: San'ichi shobō, 1972.

Takao Michinori. *Hokkai suisan jikkan*. Tokyo: Yūrindō, 1896.

Takasaki Ryūtarō. *Kaokuzuiri Hokkai risshi hen*. 4 volumes. Hakodate: Hokutōsha, 1893–97.

Takase Tamotsu. "Kaga han ni okeru gyohi no fukyū." *Nihon rekishi* 354 (November 1977): 58–79.

Takayama Itarō. "Karafuto gyogyō rōmu jijō: Hokuyō rōmu to no kankei o shu to shite." *Hokuyō gyogyō* 2:9 (September 1941): 26–31.

Takeuchi Toshiyoshi. *Shimokita no sonraku shakai: Sangyō kōzō to sonraku taisei*. Tokyo: Miraisha, 1968.

Takizawa Hideki. *Mayu to seishi no kindaishi*. Tokyo: Kyōikusha, 1979.

Tanaka Osamu. *Nihon shihonshugi to Hokkaidō*. Sapporo: Hokkaidō daigaku tosho kankōkai, 1986.

Tanba Heitarō. *Roryō Sagaren-tō gyogyō chōsa hōkoku*. Tokyo: Nōshōmushō suisankyoku, 1900.

Taniguchi Hidesaburō, ed. *Hiraoka Karafuto chō chōkan danwa: Karafuto no gyogyō seido*. N.p.: Karafuto kyōkai, [1913].

———. *Karafuto shokumin seisaku*. Tokyo: Takushoku shinpōsha, 1914.

Taniuchi Kō. "Hokkaidō nishi kaigan ni okeru nishin gyoba: Atsuta mura o chūshin to shite (2)." *Atsuta mura shiryōshitsu kiyō* 5 (October 1966): entire issue.

Tashiro, Kazui. "Foreign Relations during the Edo Period: *Sakoku* Reexamined." *Journal of Japanese Studies* 8:2 (Summer 1982): 283–306.

Tazawa Mihō [Rishichi]. *Karafuto kigyōka no shishin.* Toyohara: Karafuto kigyōka no shishinsha, 1924.

Toby, Ronald P. *State and Diplomacy in Early Modern Japan.* Princeton: Princeton University Press, 1984.

———. "Both a Borrower and a Lender Be: From Village Moneylender to Rural Banker in the Tempō Period." *Monumenta Nipponica* 46:4 (Winter 1991): 483–512.

Tōkyō daigaku shiryō hensanjo, ed. *Dai-Nippon komonjo: Bakumatsu gaikoku kankei monjo.* 43 volumes to date. Tokyo: Tōkyō daigaku shuppankai, 1910–91.

Totman, Conrad. *Politics in the Tokugawa Bakufu.* Cambridge: Harvard University Press, 1967.

———. *The Green Archipelago: Forestry in Preindustrial Japan.* Berkeley: University of California Press, 1989.

Toyama ken, ed. *Toyama ken shi: Shiryōhen.* 10 volumes. Toyama: Toyama ken, 1970–83.

Tōyama Shin'ichirō. *Karafuto no jijō to shōrai.* N.p., c. 1923.

Tsurumi, E. Patricia. *Factory Girls: Women in the Thread Mills of Meiji Japan.* Princeton: Princeton University Press, 1990.

Uemura Hideaki. *Kita no umi no kōekishatachi: Ainu minzoku no shakai keizai shi.* Tokyo: Dōbunkan, 1990.

Vlastos, Stephen. *Peasant Protests and Uprisings in Tokugawa Japan.* Berkeley: University of California Press, 1986.

Wakabayashi, Bob Tadashi. *Anti-foreignism and Western Learning in Early-Modern Japan: The New Theses of 1825.* Cambridge: Council on East Asian Studies, Harvard University, 1986.

Wakita Osamu. "The *Kokudaka* System: A Device for Unification." *Journal of Japanese Studies* 1:2 (Summer 1975): 297–320.

Walthall, Anne. *Social Protest and Popular Culture in Eighteenth-Century Japan.* Tucson: University of Arizona Press, 1986.

Watanabe Hitoshi. *The Ainu Ecosystem: Environment and Group Structure.* Tokyo: University of Tokyo Press, 1972.

Watanabe Shigeru, ed. *Hokkaidō rekishi jiten.* Sapporo: Hokkaidō shuppan kikaku sentā, 1982.

White, Richard. *The Roots of Dependency: Subsistence, Environment, and Social Change among the Choctaws, Pawnees, and Navajos.* Lincoln: University of Nebraska Press, 1983.

Wigen, Kären. "Social and Spatial Divisions of Labor in Nineteenth Century Shinano: Mapping the Contested Terrain of Paper Craft Production." Paper delivered at the 43rd annual meeting of the Association for Asian Studies, New Orleans, 1991.

———. "The Geographic Imagination in Early Modern Japanese History: Retrospect and Prospect." *Journal of Asian Studies* 51:1 (February 1992): 3–29.

———. *The Making of a Japanese Periphery, 1750–1920.* Berkeley: University of California Press, 1994.

Wigmore, John Henry. *Law and Justice in Tokugawa Japan, Part III-A: Contract: Legal Precedents.* Tokyo: Kokusai bunka shinkōkai, 1970.

Wray, William D. "Shipping: From Sail to Steam." In *Japan in Transition: From Tokugawa to Meiji*, edited by Marius B. Jansen and Gilbert Rozman. Princeton: Princeton University Press, 1986.

———. "Afterword." In *Managing Industrial Enterprise: Cases from Japan's Prewar Experience*, edited by William D. Wray. Cambridge: Council on East Asian Studies, Harvard University, 1989.

Yajima Satoshi. "Kinsei kōki Matsumaechi ni okeru nenjū gyōji shūzoku." In *Hokkaidō no kenkyū*, volume 3, edited by Kaiho Mineo. Osaka: Seibundō, 1982.

———. "Nishin gyoba no minzoku." In *Hokkaidō no kenkyū*, volume 7, edited by Yajima Satoshi. Osaka: Seibundō, 1985.

Yamada Shin'ichi. "Iboshi Hokuto den e no kokoromi." Paper delivered at the Erumu Shidankai, Sapporo, 1992.

Yamada Takeshi. "Rishiri-tō ni okeru nishin teichi gyogyōken no sonzai keitai: 'Menkyo gyogyō genbo' no naiyō to kōsatsu." *Hokkaidō kaitaku kinenkan chōsa hōkoku* 24 (1985): 39–88.

———. "Furubira chihō ni okeru nishin teichi gyogyōken no hensen (1): 'Menkyo gyogyō genbo' no naiyō to kōsatsu." *Hokkaidō kaitaku kinenkan chōsa hōkoku* 26 (1987): 27–36.

———. "Rishiri-, Rebun-tō ni okeru nishin gyoba no gyorō shūzoku." In *Nihonkai to hokkoku bunka (Umi to rettō bunka*, volume 1), edited by Amino Yoshihiko. Tokyo: Shōgakukan, 1990.

Yamaguchi Tōru. "Kinseiteki koyō no ichi danmen: Jibikiami gyogyō o chūshin ni." *Rekishi to minzoku: Kanagawa daigaku Nihon jōmin bunka kenkyūjo ronshū* 5 (1990): 7–66.

Yamamiya Tōkichi. *Karafuto no kenkyū*. Volume 2. Tokyo: Yamada Saburō, 1914.

Yamamura, Kozo. "Toward a Reexamination of the Economic History of Tokugawa Japan, 1600–1867." *Journal of Economic History* 33 (1973): 509–41.

———. "The Meiji Land Tax Reform and Its Effects." In *Japan in Transition: From Tokugawa to Meiji*, edited by Marius B. Jansen and Gilbert Rozman. Princeton: Princeton University Press, 1986.

Yoichi chō shi hensanshitsu, ed. *Yoichi chō shi: Shiryōhen*. 1 volume to date. Yoichi: Yoichi chō, 1986.

Yokoyama Toshio. *Hyakushō ikki to gimin denshō*. Tokyo: Kyōikusha, 1977.

Index

Abe Kichitarō, 131
Agriculture: commercial, 12; in Hokkaido, 7, 27, 42; in Karafuto, 157
Ainu: cultural diversity among, 30; customs, adoption of by Wajin, 201n50; discrimination against, 206n8; economy, 18, 25–26, 29, 31–32, 45–47, 96, 206n9; ethnicity of, 17–18, 30, 42, 46, 74, 95–96; in Karafuto fishery, 134, 164, 171; labor, at contract fisheries, 24–25, 39, 44, 48, 51, 74; labor, and state institutions, 44–47, 48, 57, 96; legal status of, 17–18, 44, 95–96; population decline of, 29, 31, 39, 66, 97, 195n44; resistance by, 28, 40 (*see also* Shakushain's War); status of in Tokugawa state, 27–28, 29, 34, 35; in Tōhoku region, 32
Aizu domain, 42, 66
Akinaiba, 25–26, 31, 32
Akita: domain, 42, 61; prefecture, 145
Andō house, 18
Aomori prefecture, 145
Araida Yosaburō, 123
Arano Yasunori, 34
Asao Naohiro, 34
Ascription, achieved, 126
Ashikaga bakufu, 18
Atsuta fishery, 64, 73, 140
Attush, 201n50

Bakufu. *See* Ashikaga bakufu; Kamakura bakufu; State, Tokugawa

Bakuhan state. *See* State, Tokugawa
Bikuni fishery, 140
Bix, Herbert, 174
Blakiston, Thomas Wright, 1, 46, 94–95, 176
Boshin War, 20, 43
Bowen, Roger, 174

Capital. *See* Credit
Capitalism: definitions, 3–5, 44; emergence in Hokkaido fishery, 88, 90, 121–27, 177; and immiseration, 6, 8, 83, 147, 183–84; and proto-industrialization, 9, 13, 48, 182–83; and state institutions, 44–47, 49, 53, 88, 89, 94; and subjecthood, 170–75; Tokugawa origins of, 2, 88–92, 180–82
Capitalists, 121–28, 170–75
Chichibu rebellion, 9, 174
Chikurage, 192n10
Commercialization, 2–3, 4, 12, 13, 15, 89
Conflict, social, 20–21, 121; over credit, 80–82, 84–86; over fishing rights, 93–94, 112, 116–17, 150, 151–65, 171; and proto-industrialization, 180; over taxation, 95; over technological innovation, 70–72. *See also* Net-cutting incident; Ōdomari Incident; Ofuyu Incident
Contract fisheries, 2, 35–44; abolition of, 27, 43–44, 96, 97–98; credit relations at, 77–78, 79–82; fishing operations at,

Compositor: Star Type
Text: 10/13 Sabon
Display: Sabon
Printer: Thomson-Shore, Inc.
Binder: Thomson-Shore, Inc.